PROJECT TEXT FOR PUBLIC SPEAKING

SIXTH EDITION

Clark S. Carlile

Idaho State University, Professor Emeritus

Arlie V. Daniel

East Central University

 **LONGMAN**

An imprint of Addison Wesley Longman, Inc.

New York • Reading, Massachusetts • Menlo Park, California • Harlow, England
Don Mills, Ontario • Sydney • Mexico City • Madrid • Amsterdam

The authors and publisher gratefully acknowledge the following sources for granting permission to quote from their works:

Project 2: Lisa Griffitts/ *Project 4:* Herbert S. Richey, reprinted with permission from *Vital Speeches of the Day*, April 15, 1977, pp. 386–398/ *Project 4:* Donald N. Dedmon, reprinted with permission from *Vital Speeches of the Day*, October 15, 1983, pp. 14–20/ *Project 5:* Steve Keiffer/ *Project 5:* Janet Rutland/ *Project 6:* Jenkin Lloyd Jones, reprinted with permission from *Vital Speeches of the Day*, May 15, 1973, pp. 473–476/ *Project 6:* Adlai E. Stevenson, Sir Winston Churchill, printed by permission from the *Washington Post*, January 29, 1965, p. A5/ *Project 6:* Jill Roady/ *Project 10:* From *A Time to Speak* by Will A. Linkugel and David M. Berg, © 1970 by Wadsworth Publishing Company, Inc. Reprinted by permission of publisher/ *Project 12:* Martin Luther King, Jr., "I Have a Dream." Reprinted by permission from *Rhetoric of Racial Revolt*, ed. Roy L. Hill (Denver: Golden Bell Press, 1964) pp. 371–375/ *Project 13:* Michele Scott/ *Project 14:* Clint McGaha/ *Project 15:* James Paschall/ *Project 16:* Susan K. Pearson/ *Project 17:* Steven Jones/ *Project 18:* Lynn McNeill/ *Project 19:* Elizabeth Wookey/ *Project 20:* Karen R. Nick/ *Project 21:* Dani Duncan/ *Project 22:* Reprinted with permission of Macmillan Publishing Company from *Basic Public Speaking* by Eugene E. White, © 1988/ *Project 23:* Dina L. Kemper/ *Project 24:* Gerald Vinson/ *Project 26:* Janna Storey/ *Project 27:* Susan Jacobs/ *Project 28:* Shirley Windsor/ *Project 29:* Hardy Patton/ *Project 30:* Thanks to Robert Greenstreet for preparing The Interview/ *Unit VII:* Lee Iacocca/ *Project 31:* Tracy Frederick/ *Project 32:* Kelli Pizzino/ *Project 33:* Arlie Daniel/ *Project 34:* Donna L. Gough/ *Project 35:* Keith Ward/ *Project 35:* Karen Piercy/ *Project 35:* Veronica McCabe Deschambault/ *Project 35:* Jim Miller/ *Project 36:* Krista Williams/ *Project 37:* Robbin Gilbreath/ *Project 37:* Jill Reynolds/ *Project 38:* Dina Louise Kemper/ *Project 38:* Eddie Paul Hunter/ *Unit VIII:* S. I. Hayakawa/ *Project 40:* Dr. Ralph Nichols, reprinted by permission of the author/ *Project 40: The Elements of Public Speaking* by Joseph A. DeVito. Reprinted by permission of Harper & Row, Publishers, Inc./ *Appendix E:* Successful Schools: Good Teachers and Community Support. Reprinted by permission of the author, Jack MacAllister/ *Appendix E:* The Enemies of Responsible Communication: The Voices, the Silences. Reprinted by permission of the author, W. Charles Redding.

Sponsoring Editor: Melissa A. Rosati
Project Editor: B. Pelner
Design Coordinator: Mary Archondes
Text Design Adaptation: North 7 Atelier Ltd., Barbara Bert
Cover Design: Brand X Studio, Robin Hoffmann
Production: Willie Lane/Sunaina Sehwani
Compositor: ComCom Division of Haddon Craftsmen, Inc.
Printer and Binder: Courier Companies, Inc.
Cover Printer: New England Book Components, Inc.

Project Text for Public Speaking, Sixth Edition

Copyright © 1991 by Addison-Wesley Educational Publishers Inc.

All rights reserved. Printed in the United States of America. No part of this book may be used or reproduced in any manner whatsoever without written permission, except in the case of brief quotations embodied in critical articles and reviews. For information address Longman Publishers, 1185 Avenue of the Americas, New York, NY 10036.

Library of Congress Cataloging-in-Publication Data

Carlile, Clark Stites, 1912–
    Project text for public speaking. — 6th ed. / Clark S. Carlile,
Arlie V. Daniel.
        p.   cm.
    Includes bibliographical references.
    ISBN 0-06-041156-2
    1. Public speaking.   I. Daniel, Arlie V.   II. Title.
PN4121.C24   1991   90-49792
808.5′1—dc20   CIP

99 00 CK 12 11 10

Dedicated to our first speech teachers:

Mom and Dad

Contents

Preface

Introduction

You learn best that which you learn by experience. Although it is desirable that a person possess some knowledge of what lies behind the act of public speaking, the ability to stand on your own two feet and demonstrate the power of speech is most important. It is the speech that counts. This project text emphasizes actual speaking experiences. This book is for the person who must give a speech and who wants to know how to prepare and deliver it without a lot of fanfare and in simple, easy-to-understand language.

With emphasis on the three basic purposes for public speaking—to inform, to persuade, and to entertain—the book also discusses speaking under special conditions or on special occasions. It stresses that speakers must know not only the general purpose for their speeches but also the specific purpose for every speech presented.

The book's flexibility permits the selection of speaking experiences in any order and number. Every project consists of definite, complete, and specific information regarding that particular speech, from selecting the topic for a speech to preparing a complete outline to delivering the speech so that it conforms to delivery standards and time limits.

This sixth edition of *Project Text for Public Speaking* offers some revision of past projects and rearranges some other projects. Changes in the text's six editions have always been implemented to update materials and to incorporate new concepts and developments. Changes are also adjusted to the needs of the book's users. Some readers might find a favorite project missing or changed in this edition. Let us assure you that the changes we have made have been prompted by people who use the book on a daily basis and who want practical projects, or by changes in the speech field, which suggest a different direction than the book had taken previously.

New Edition Features

There are also a couple of new projects in this edition. For example, in adding the unit on Speaking in Business and Professional Settings, we added some other projects to the Report and Sales Talk. The two additional projects are Briefings and Proposals—two very important business speeches that are not given much space in other textbooks. In addition, we have added a section on Speech Anxiety and a set of articulation drills in the Appendix. We deleted only one project from the fifth edition—the Pet Peeve Speech, which seemed to be in limited use.

Most of the changes in this edition have been simple and subtle. We want the text to be familiar to past users, as well as useful and helpful for new users. Since we "unitized" the book in the fifth edition, we have kept that basic format, with the addition of one more unit. We hope that the units have helped organize materials for both students and teachers. The book is not intended to be a sequential text that you would start at Project 1 and progress through to Project 41. The first unit is to prepare students to create speeches. The second unit provides background on the modes of delivery, which can be studied at any time. The remaining units provide different opportunities to put into practice the skills taught in the first unit.

We offer several projects in each of the units on informing, persuading, and entertaining so that teachers have options from which to select. No class will be able to present every type of speech in this text; however, the opportunity does exist for students to give most of these speeches over a lifetime. Since this is a "reference book" of speeches, we urge students to keep the book for those times when they need to present speeches in the future. Experience suggests that most students will give additional speeches once they finish their education. If they have this handy reference, they should be able to succeed with any type of speaking situation.

The sixth edition of *Project Text for Public Speaking* retains the friendly, personal style of the five previous editions. As a first book in public speaking, this book provides students with information about the basic concepts and terms of public speaking as well as suggestions on how to perform in the public speaking situation. Any readers, students as well as teachers, who have suggestions for future revisions of this text are encouraged to forward them to the second author.

Acknowledgments

Many people besides the authors have directly contributed to the revisions in the sixth edition of *Project Text for Public Speaking*. Because of their assistance and dedication to the task, this edition is much improved. First, we thank the students at East Central University who provided sample speeches as well as feedback on specific projects. In fact, there were many more students who submitted sample speeches than could be used in the text. But because of the large number of students who generously provided sample speeches, there were many good examples from which to select. Second, we thank the faculty at East Central University who supported the second author during the revision process by reading and reacting to projects and by using projects in their classes so that the authors would have some good sample speeches from which to select. A special thanks to Delma Hall, Donna Gough, Robert Greenstreet, Mary Bishop, and Shirley Windsor for their efforts and contributions.

A special thanks also to the secretaries who worked diligently to make sense of handwritten copies of the manuscript, and who helped put much of this manuscript onto computer disks. The typing of a book manuscript is an awesome task. Thanks for your work and support: Cheryl Melhouse Pflaum, Patricia Melhouse, and Rhonda Hester.

We also greatly appreciate the kind words and helpful suggestions of all of the reviewers who provided input during all of the phases of production from the prospectus through the final draft. We have a better textbook now because of their insight and guidance on the manuscript: Roberta Albrecht, Concordia College; Bill Slagle, Samford University; M.L. Sandoz, Mississippi State University; Randall Capps, Western Kentucky University.

To the Instructor

Teaching from this text should give you great latitude and flexibility. We do not profess to have one best way to teach or use the book, but here are some suggestions that may help you organize your classes for the maximum benefit to your students.

1. Appoint a different student to serve as class leader for each class meeting. While you take roll, the class leader can gather all outlines, copy names and topics of all the speakers, arrange the outlines for you, and then introduce each of the speakers in order. When you have outlines to return with comments and grades written on them, the class leader can also help by returning papers, if the grades are not visible. This not only helps you save time, but it also provides students with additional speaking practice.

2. All outlines should be ready when class convenes, or several days in advance if you prefer early preparation. Reading outlines and commenting on them several days before students are to speak helps prepare students to speak. You may also catch some "inappropriate" topics for the specific assignment.

3. Appointing a student as timekeeper to give prearranged time signals and/or announce the time spoken is helpful. This helps students gauge their speaking rates, and it frees you from the timekeeping task.

4. The projects in this text may be altered by (a) assigning specific topics; (b) requiring a specific number of visual aids or quotations in the speech; (c) requiring a certain number of references to be cited in the speech; (d) requiring the use of a specific type of introduction and/or conclusion; (e) changing speaking notes and time-limit requirements; (f) using different modes of delivery; and (g) combining specific projects.

5. Students may be required to memorize the criticism chart and thus be prepared to give immediate and detailed oral criticism in an organized manner. You can also select certain students to critique orally and others to write critiques of speeches each day. All students should be involved in the critiquing of student oral presentations. Beginning with "What did you like?" usually gives students a good method of beginning to listen and help others see that all speeches have good points. Finishing with "What can *(name)* improve the most?" will help them see that all speeches, no matter how good, can still be improved.

6. Sources by interview, special observation, or specific written materials (or some combination) may be assigned.

7. You may assign certain types of speeches to pairs of students: for example, nomination and acceptance speeches; presenting and accepting a gift or award; or a welcome and a response.

8. Some assignments may be combined: for example, introducing a speaker with any other speaking assignment; master/mistress of ceremonies with a class period; and the forum with any speaking assignment.

9. If you want students to prepare and present an informative speech, you may allow them to select any type of informative speaking, so long as it conforms to the specific requirements of that type of speech. On other occasions, you will want all students to prepare the same type of speech—an announcement, for example.

Clark S. Carlile
Arlie V. Daniel

UNIT I

SPEECH PREPARATION

If I went back to college again, I'd concentrate on two areas: learning to write and to speak before an audience. Nothing in life is more important than the ability to communicate effectively.

Gerald R. Ford

Unit I consists of six projects that help you put a speech together. The first project helps you get started by explaining the process of selecting a speech topic and creating a specific purpose for your speech. Project 2 presents the principles for outlining so you can better organize your ideas before speaking. Projects 3 and 4 deal with developing the body of the speech. More specifically, Project 3 deals with organization and organizational patterns for the body of the speech; Project 4 presents several forms of supporting materials that you can use to develop the body of the speech. Project 5 explains the importance of the introduction in the speech and presents several methods of getting a speech started. Project 6 explains the importance of the conclusion to your speech and presents several methods for effectively and gracefully closing your speech.

PROJECT 1

Getting Started:
Purposes/Audiences/Topics

If you don't know the areas in which you are most successful, you won't make the right choices in your life. Once you know your strongest "success areas," you can make self-fulfilling, rather than self-defeating choices.

—Lila Swell

Students sometimes have the notion that there are certain topics that are inherently good speech topics, whereas all others are to be avoided. These are the same people who want a teacher to provide the special topic that will, by some sort of voodoo magic, provide them with a speech that will astound the world, or at least earn them an "A" in their speech class.

The problem with this type of thinking is that the speech topic you get from someone else does not belong to you. The possibilities and promise that one person sees in a topic will not necessarily be there for someone else. Find your own topics; or better yet, take an idea and incite a speech topic with it.

This project will help you to find speech topics through a process of analyzing your general purpose, yourself (the speaker), your audience, and the occasion. Finally, we will look at turning your topic into a specific purpose.

The General Purpose

Before you can select the proper topic for any speech, you must determine the general purpose of your speech. Some topics will lend themselves better to one of the three generally agreed upon basic purposes for speaking—categories into which all speeches must fall. You may inform, persuade, or entertain your audiences. All speeches can be classified according to the purpose of the speaker.

As a classroom speaker, you may be assigned a general purpose by your instructor. As a speaker in public situations, you may be asked to present a specific type of speech or need to decide for yourself which general purpose you wish to fulfill. Let us look briefly at each of the three general purposes.

To Inform   When you inform an audience, your purpose is to add to the knowledge of the audience. This means that you must present new information to your audience. While the information presented may change someone's mind or entertain someone, your purpose is to present new information to your audience. If you do not present new information, you are not informing. Thus, topics like "How to tie your shoes" would be unsuitable for any group except small children who do not yet know how to tie their shoes. Look for a topic that you know is new to your audience or will extend what they already know on that topic.

To Persuade   When you persuade an audience, your purpose is to change the members of the audience in some way. You may change their opinions on a topic, their attitudes, or ultimately, their behaviors. In short, you want the audience to think, feel, or act in a particular manner. As in the speech to inform, you may add to the knowledge of some audience members, or entertain them, but your purpose is to evoke change. Whatever else happens is incidental to that purpose. In most instances a topic that merely presents new information to the audience will not work—you must have a goal of changing the audience in some way.

To Entertain   When you entertain your audience, your purpose is to provide a pleasurable experience for your audience. A speech to entertain is not a comedy routine or a collection of jokes, but rather a speech that entertains or amuses the listeners. As in the other two speech forms, any persuasion or new information is incidental to your purpose. Most topics can be made entertaining by examining the topic from a new perspective or by looking at the least viewed side.

After your general purpose has been determined, you must next consider three aspects of your speech topic—(1) yourself, the speaker; (2) your audience, the listeners; and (3) the occasion, the reason your audience members have gathered at this time and place.

The Speaker

Begin your search for a topic by looking at yourself and your interests. It doesn't make any difference which general purpose you are fulfilling, you need to have an interest in the topic and some knowledge of the topic before you can make a credible presentation. When you have a natural interest in a topic, it affects you in some way. You have personal experience with the topic and want others to know how you feel.

A good method for determining the topics that interest you and the ones you might talk about is to formulate a list of interests and concerns. Make this an "open" list to which you can continuously add. Typical areas that you might include are: hobbies, personal experiences, vocations, travel, social problems, special interests, and so on. The object here is to list as many possible topics as you can. Do not attempt to evaluate and decide (or) select specific speeches at this point. All you want to do is prepare a list of possibilities that you can look at any time you have an assignment to present a speech. You don't want to start from scratch every time you have an assignment.

The Audience

A second area of concern in deciding on a speech topic is the audience. It is important that you consider your audience while selecting a speech topic because the most interesting topic for you may be dull and boring for your audience members, who (1) have no interest in the topic, (2) know all about the topic, or (3) know very little about the subject area. In the first two instances you would probably want to select an alternate topic; however, in the third instance you may be able to create enough interest to keep the audience's attention.

A good method for determining audience interest and knowledge is to perform an **audience analysis**. Your analysis should consider the various factors that might affect how your audience will react and respond to your topic. To help you analyze your audience, you might start with an analysis of **audience demographics**.

Ages   You might begin by asking, what are the ages of the audience members? The reason you might want to know the ages of various group members is to determine if that age group is interested in the topic you are considering. Teenagers and senior citizens sometimes have the same interests, but you must decide their interests partly based on the range of age levels in your audience.

Sex   Another factor that should be considered is the sex of audience members. You do not want to offend anyone, so your consideration here is an important one. Because most of your audiences will be mixed audiences, you must prepare to speak to both males and females. In those instances where you may have an all female or all male audience, prepare to speak to the needs and interests of that group.

Educational Level   What is the educational level of the audience members? If they are all college graduates, you will prepare to speak differently to them from how you would to a class of grade school children. Likewise, if your audience members are well educated on your topic, your language and level of presentation will be different from a speech presented to an audience of individuals relatively uneducated on your topic.

Political Philosophies   What do audience members think about the way government ought to be run? This analysis does not concern whether audience members are Republicans, Democrats, or independents, because their party affiliation does not always tell us what they think about government spending or their position on other significant government issues. Knowing that audience members tend to be conservative or liberal or moderate in their views toward the operation of our government may suggest topics to speak about or to avoid with this specific audience.

Place of Residence   Where do your audience members live? You wouldn't prepare to talk to a group of Oklahomans the same as you would to a group of New Yorkers or Californians. Because people who live in different regions of the country have different interests, you might need to adapt your topic to that aspect of your audience.

Ethnicity   What ethnic groups does the audience include? Because of the ethnic composition of an audience, you may want to consider some special interests based on this ethnicity. Remember, race is sometimes a part of ethnic background, but it doesn't have to be. A good way to look at this area is to think in terms of "heritage." We all have some customs and habits that we have carried on from our ancestors, even though we may not be aware of where they come from.

Religion   What religions comprise the group? Sometimes you may want to know what religious groups will be represented in your audience so you can avoid topics that may run counter to the teachings of those religions. For example, most speakers will avoid persuading a fundamentalist group that abortion is an appropriate alternative. Other audiences may be drawn together because of common religious interests. You can use this commonality to select a topic that will appeal to your audience.

Group Interests   What are some common interests of the group? If there is some common interest that draws the audience members together, that may be the thread to weave a common thread for a topic. Such groups are sororities and fraternities or school clubs. If this common interest is what brings the group together, use it to create a topic that will speak to their common interest. Sometimes the cultural interests of a group may unite its members so that a topic of importance or interest will be easy to identify.

Occupations   This is an issue of basically blue-collar versus white-collar workers. Issues that affect and interest management-type personnel may not interest people at the worker level. People who work for a salary or a commission are not always interested in the same topics as those who work on an hourly basis. There is also a difference in motivation for each of these groups. Use this knowledge to help you find a topic that well relate best to the individuals in your audience.

Socioeconomic Status   Knowing that one class is more representative than others may suggest a topic of interest for you. For instance, you would not want to talk about welfare payments to a group of millionaires; likewise, you wouldn't talk about investing in the stock market to a group whose members are all receiving welfare. Sometimes a person's economic status also affects other attitudes relating to such areas as political philosophy, occupation, and group interests.

Once you have completed the demographic analysis, you will want to apply the information you have gathered to a specific topic. For example, what should the audience know about my topic, given their backgrounds? What interests do they have in the topic area? Will the audience members want to hear about this topic? How can I create interest for the audience? Can I relate the topic to the audience?

The Occasion

The third area of concern is the occasion. Unless you know why your audience members have gathered and the conditions of the gathering, you may select a topic that is totally irrelevant or inappropriate for your audience. Some occasions are self-evident and need little consideration, for example, the Fourth of July, commencement, or a funeral. On these occasions the topic is most evident and your choices are considerably limited.

On other occasions you may need to make careful consideration of the reason for the group to gather and what would be appropriate to that occasion. Examples might include club meetings, a school or church group meeting, a civic group concerned about some local issue, and so on. In finding out about the occasion, you will need to determine exactly what the group expects from you. For example, what are their special interests? What is the mood of the occasion?·What are the time limits placed on you? Are you expected to talk on a specific topic or may you select one? A careful approach to analyzing the occasion will help you select a topic that is appropriate not only to yourself, but also to your audience and the occasion on which the speech is to be given.

The Specific Purpose

After you have considered the general purpose, yourself as the speaker, the audience, and the occasion, you are ready to select the one topic that you think you can make interesting and is appropriate under the set of circumstances you encounter. Then you must narrow that broad topic so that it is manageable within the time limits established earlier.

One of the most effective methods for narrowing a topic is called the "inverted pyramid." In this method you put a pyramid on its peak and place the broad topic at the base, like this:

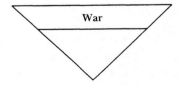

It is obvious that you can't talk about war in a ten-minute speech. The topic has entire volumes of materials written about it. So, you begin by limiting the topic in time—the 1900s, for example. There are several wars that could be of interest to any specific audience. To Irish descendants, the continuing war between Ireland and England could be of interest. To an audience of Middle East immigrants, the wars in the Middle East could be of interest. Of course, the wars in which the United States has been involved would be of particular interest to most American audiences. Thus, narrow your topic to a specific war. Now your pyramid looks like this:

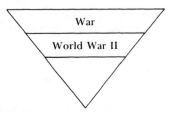

Next, you may have to select a specific area of that war to look at. Depending on the factors you analyzed earlier, you may select such topics as troop movements, the European war, the Pacific war, a specific battle, and so on. As you can see, this topic is still too extensive to be covered in a ten-minute speech. So, you put this topic in the pyramid and limit it. Continue working your topic down by limiting it in time, geographical area, and scope until you have a topic that can be talked about in ten minutes.

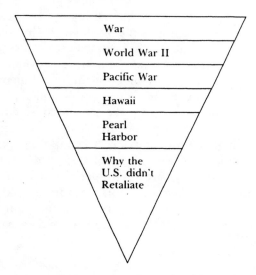

Now that you have the specific topic to talk about, you must prepare your specific purpose. The specific purpose is a statement of the expected response by the audience to a specific topic, for example, to explain to the audience why the United States did not immediately retaliate against Japan for bombing Pearl Harbor. Once you have completed the specific purpose, you can write your thesis, which becomes the controlling purpose or central idea of the speech. The thesis will be discussed in more detail in Project 2. The specific purpose indicates what you intend and aids you in preparing your speech. The thesis guides your research and also guides the audience through your speech. Remember, the thesis you formulate at this point should be considered temporary. You may need to change it later, depending on the information you find in your research.

Let's look at another method of going from the general purpose to the specific purpose with a topic. Suppose your assignment is to inform your audience such as in Project 12. Begin by reminding yourself that your general purpose is to inform; then look at your topic list and find a general topic that interests you and that you think would be appropriate to both your classmates and classroom situation. An example might be the "The Stock Market."

Since you know that you can't speak about all aspects of the stock market, begin to think in terms of what your classmates already know and might be interested in learning more about. You must also consider the time limits set by your instructor so you can consider the amount of material to include. For instance, let's say you will be allowed ten minutes for your speech. So, you decide that you can develop three areas fairly well, and the areas which would probably be new and of interest to your classmates are: how to invest in stocks, what kinds of stocks to invest in, and what to do after you invest. Notice that each of these subjects could be developed into separate speeches—they are too general yet. You now need to select one of these areas to provide you with a more specific topic that you can handle in the time limits and maintain the interest of your audience. Let's say you have decided that your audience would be most interested in "How to invest in a stock." Now you have a specific purpose—to inform your audience how to invest in a stock.

This project has presented the essential elements for selecting a topic and narrowing that topic to a point that it is usable. Remember, always relate your topic to yourself as the speaker, your audience as listeners, and to the occasion on which the speech is to be presented. Be sure that you keep your general purpose for speaking in mind as you limit your topic and formulate your specific purpose.

Project Assignment

Prepare an open list of topics that you find of interest. Begin by listing topics in which you have personal experience. Then add topics concerning your hobbies and special interests. Conclude by listing current events and social problems that intrigue you. Keep your list and add to it every time you think of a new or different topic. Try to add five new topics every week. When you need a topic for a speech assignment, return to your list and select a topic appropriate to your assignment, based on your audience analysis.

At various points in the semester, stop and discuss topics on your list with members of your class. Note the areas of mutual interest and special interests as well as areas of conflict. As time permits, brainstorm topics for other areas and other topics you can add to your list.

References

Bradley, B. E. (1988). *Fundamentals of Speech Communication* (5th ed.). Dubuque, Iowa: Wm. C. Brown Company, Publishers.

Gronbeck, B. E., Ehninger, D., & Monroe, A. H. (1988). *Principles of Speech Communication* (10th brief ed.). Glenview, Illinois: Scott, Foresman and Company.

Lucas, S. E. (1989). *The Art of Public Speaking* (3rd ed.). New York: Random House.

Minnick, W. C. (1983). *Public Speaking* (2nd ed.). Boston: Houghton Mifflin Company.

Nelson, P. E. & Pearson, J. C. (1990). *Confidence in Public Speaking* (4th ed.). Dubuque, Iowa: Wm. C. Brown Company, Publishers.

Samovar, L. A. & Mills, J. (1989). *Oral Communication* (7th ed.). Dubuque, Iowa: Wm. C. Brown Company, Publishers.

Verderber, R. F. (1988). *The Challenge of Effective Speaking* (7th ed.). Belmont, California: Wadsworth Publishing Company.

PROJECT **2**

Outlining the Speech

To get profit without risk, experience without danger, and reward without work, is as impossible as it is to live without being born.
—A.P. Gouthey

The outline of a speech is its blueprint. No other aid is as valuable to a speaker as a well-planned and prepared outline. The ability to put your speech into a stylized format tells your audience members that you are prepared and have considered a number of factors before speaking to them.

Before you begin to write an outline, you will need to understand why you need to outline your speech, the principles of outlining, the techniques of outlining, and the styles of outlines you may be called upon to write.

The outline is the blueprint of the speech—the outline is not the speech. Do not confuse this issue. Often beginning speech students assume that once they have completed the outline, they have completed the speech. In truth, you have completed only the first step in preparing your speech—the step that indicates what you need to include in your speech and what you will exclude. Developing your outline indicates the main topic areas of your speech and the subpoints you plan to use to support your main topic areas, and provides you with a visual image of your speech.

Writing your outline can occur after you have decided both your general purpose and specific purpose, selected your topic, and gathered the majority of the materials for your speech. You may find that you will need to gather more information for your speech after finishing your preliminary outline. On the other hand, you may need to delete some materials from your speech if you find that you have more than can fit in the time limits and other demands of your speech.

In this project we look first at developing your thesis statement. Next, we examine the principles and the techniques of outlining. Finally, we look at some sample outlines for a speech.

Thesis

The point of your speech is stated in one single sentence that clearly tells your audience what you intend to accomplish in your speech. Some books refer to this purpose statement as the "controlling purpose," "thematic purpose," or the "central idea." Other authors refer to this statement as a "purpose statement," a "core statement," the "proposition," or the "thesis." Whatever the label used, and arguments can be offered for each, this statement is the unifying force of the speech, and its precise wording will guide your preparation and your audience's listening. For purposes of this text, we will always refer to this purpose statement as the "thesis."

The thesis is not your specific purpose, but you develop your thesis from your specific purpose. For example, if your specific purpose is to have your audience members understand the effects of radon, you might create a thesis that emphasizes the effects of radon on homes. "Today I will explain the three major effects of radon on residential homes." If your purpose were to get your audience members to have their homes checked for radon, you might word it, "Today I will persuade you to check your home for radon for two reasons."

Without a well-worded thesis statement, you may have a tendency to "ramble" or to "talk around" your topic rather than present a well-thought out and direct speech. A good thesis statement will limit and establish parameters on your topic that will assist you in sticking to your topic. Notice that the preceding statements contain one clear purpose. A thesis statement that said, "Today I will explain radon and its effects on your home," suggests two purposes and will not work for unifying your speech.

How and when do you create your thesis? You should start when you select your topic, and work from there. You may have several tentative thesis statements before finishing your speech. In narrowing your topic, focus first on some specific purpose so you limit your research on the topic. Only after you have researched your topic and have the information available, can you write your final thesis. You may find that you will have to change or adjust your thinking based on your research, but the specific purpose should guide you throughout the research process.

If you are inexperienced as a speaker, begin your thesis statement by stating very matter-of-factly what you intend. A good beginning might be, "Today I will inform you about three aspects of the water diet." This beginning is simple and straightforward. It also incorporates your general and specific purposes. From this statement your audience members know that your general purpose is to inform them; they also know that your specific purpose is to present three aspects of the water diet. Although audience members may know that you do not have time to tell them everything about the water diet, they don't know how much you intend to tell them unless you specify that in your thesis statement. This thesis statement indicates that you will deal with only three aspects of the water diet. As you become more accomplished, you may want to incorporate the three aspects of the water diet into your thesis statement. For example, "Today I will inform you of the constraints, the allowances, and the weight restrictions of the water diet."

Once you have completed your thesis statement, check it carefully to ensure that (1) it is a complete sentence, (2) it contains only one purpose, (3) it is a statement, not a question, and (4) it includes your specific purpose. A sample thesis statement might read, "Today I will persuade you to give blood at the Red Cross for three important reasons." A second variation of this thesis incorporating the three reasons might read, "Today I will persuade you to give blood at the Red Cross to save the life of someone else, to build a reserve for you or a member of your family, and to promote community service."

A thesis statement that has two purposes will confuse some of your audience members and confound the issue you should be addressing. An example of a thesis statement with a double purpose is one like the following: "Today I will inform you of the problems of alcoholism and who has these problems." Notice that this thesis statement not only sounds awkward, but it also suggests that there are two purposes in this speech. One purpose of the speech is to present the problems of alcoholism; the other purpose is to present facts about who is affected by alcoholism. A better thesis statement for this topic would be, "Today I will inform you of two aspects of the problem of alcoholism." A question, such as "Would you like to know more about the problems of alcoholism?" does not tell your audience members that you will speak to them about the topic. Again, your audience members are likely to be confused about your topic and where you are leading them with your speech.

Once your thesis statement has been completed, the rest of your outline can be easily formulated. In attempting to write other parts of the outline before completing your thesis statement, you will likely encounter frustrations and have a tendency to ramble or work your way around the topic, confusing yourself and possibly your audience members. You will probably waste much time trying to complete the rest of your outline if you begin at any place other than your thesis sentence. The focus your thesis statement provides will cut down the amount of time you will need to organize the rest of your speech. By the same token, a poorly stated thesis sentence can make completing your outline difficult, if not nearly impossible.

Principles of Outlining

In formulating your outline, you will need to follow the three principles of outlining. The three principles of outlining are: subordination, division, and parallelism. Let's look at each principle to ascertain (1) what each principle is and (2) how to apply the principle to your outline.

The Principle of Subordination The first principle of outlining is one of isolating main points and subordinate points and organizing the ideas in your speech to represent that intention. Subordination indicates that something is less than or is dependent on something else. In an outline subordinate points are elements (or subpoints) of the main points. These minor points, as they are sometimes called, should equal the major point when they are all put together.

For example, suppose your specific purpose is to inform your audience of the two primary causes of anorexia nervosa. Your main points in the body of the speech would then become those two main causes—pressure to succeed and a determination to control, for example. Your subordinate points would then be those ideas and concepts that support your main points. For example, you might point out that most patients who have anorexia nervosa come from upper middle-class families, are usually females, feel they have little control over their own lives, and so on. These are your "subordinate" points.

The Principle of Division The second principle of outlining is the principle of dividing topics into subordinate areas. Whenever anything is divided, it is segmented into a minimum of two parts. In an outline, when a topic is divided, you must also have a minimum of two parts, thus the reason for the rule that "every 'one' must have a 'two' and every 'A' must have 'B' in an outline. According to the principle, all items in the outline are either undivided or divided into two or more parts. For example, in the speech on anorexia nervosa, the topic was divided into two main causes.

The main ideas can each be subdivided into subordinate points that support each of the main points. For example, the evidence that the patients come from upper-middle-class families could be a subpoint of the first main point (pressure to succeed) and help explain why these people are under extreme pressure. For another example, look at the sample speech "Successful Schools" in Appendix E. Mr. MacAllister indicates that U S West has committed $20 million to support education. The information that follows is his subordinate points and explains how U S West will support education with their $20 million.

The Principle of Parallelism The third principle of outlining is the principle of parallelism. This principle states that all main points in the outline are approximately equal; that all subpoints of a main point are approximately equal; and that the construction of the outline shows their equality. Outlines can be written in two basic styles, as you will see in the next section. The principle of parallelism states that all items in the outline that are approximately equal be shown as equals. Thus, all main points are equal and all subpoints of any main point are equal. These are shown by both the same grammatical structure on the outline and the same form of outline notation. If your outline is a key word outline, for example, then the main points could be represented by words or phrases of the same magnitude (a noun–verb construction, for example; or all nouns). The previous example on anorexia nervosa shows parallel structure in the two main points: pressure to succeed and a determination to control. This example is only slightly more complex than a noun-verb because there is a noun and an infinitive phrase, but it is still parallel because both follow the same pattern.

Techniques of Outlining

Outlines are usually written in one of two different styles: They are either sentence outlines or topic outlines. In sentence outlines each item in the outline is a complete sentence. All main points are written as complete sentences and all subordinate points are written as complete sentences. In topic outlines only key words and phrases are used to represent the ideas you wish to express. These two forms are never mixed. An outline is either a sentence outline or a topic outline, not a combination of the two.

Whether your outline is written as a sentence outline or a topic outline, the mechanics of your outline are the same. Roman numerals (I, II, III, etc.) identify the main sections of your speech. Main points within each section of your speech are identified by capital letters (A, B, C, etc.) Subpoints within main points are identified by Arabic numbers (1, 2, 3, etc.). Examples or sub-subpoints are identified by lowercase letters (a, b, c, etc.). In addition, each subdivision is indented to show the subordination scheme. A typical outline format would look like this:

    I. INTRODUCTION
        A. Main idea number one
        B. Main idea number two
        C. Main idea number three
    II. THESIS
    III. BODY
        A. Main idea number one in support of thesis
          1. Subpoint one in support of A
          2. Subpoint two in support of A
            a. Example one in support of 2
            b. Example two in support of 2
        B. Main idea number two in support of thesis
          1. Subpoint number one in support of B
            a. Example one in support of 1
            b. Example two in support of 1
          2. Subpoint number two in support of B
    IV. CONCLUSION

Recognize that in the preceding example the indentations show the relationships of ideas visually. Notice also that each item in the outline *represents* the totality of the idea you wish to speak about. If you were writing a composition, each item would represent a paragraph or more of composition. In a speech the oral representation should be equal to the written representation. Each item in your outline should represent a paragraph's worth of speech. In general, few outlines need to be more detailed than the previous example.

Sample Outlines

Following are two sample outlines from student projects. The first sample is a sentence outline; the second sample is a topic outline. Notice the principles of outlining and the techniques of outlining identified earlier as they are presented here. Although all aspects are not perfect, you can get a general idea of each of the principles in practice. As you will notice, it is easier to make topic outlines parallel than to make sentence outlines parallel.

SAMPLE SENTENCE OUTLINE

Organ Donation*

    I. INTRODUCTION
        A. Attention-getter: Imagine this conversation.
        B. Credentials: I have worked in a dialysis unit.
        C. Interest: Dialysis affects all of us.
   II. THESIS: Today I will persuade you that organ donation is vital for three reasons.
        PREVIEW: Those three reasons are: (1) There is a shortage of organs available. (2) There are many misconceptions about organ donation. (3) Organ donations improve the quality of life.
  III. BODY
        A. There is a shortage of organs available.
            1. Many patients await heart transplants.
            2. Many patients await liver transplants.
        B. There are many misconceptions about organ donation.
            1. Only young people can donate organs.
            2. Only healthy people can donate organs.
            3. Only wealthy people can afford transplants.
        C. Organ donation improves the quality of life.
            1. Organ donations help patients.
                a. Organ donations help patients psychologically.
                b. Organ donations help patients physically.
            2. Organ donations help families.
                a. Organ donations help families psychologically.
                b. Organ donations help families economically.
  IV. CONCLUSION
        A. Review main points.
            1. There is a shortage of organs available.
            2. There are many misconceptions about organ donation.
            3. Organ donations improve the quality of life.
        B. Closing thought: Most patients wait for a phone call.

SAMPLE TOPIC OUTLINE

Organ Donation*

    I. INTRODUCTION
        A. Attention: Phone call
        B. Credentials: Dialysis unit
        C. Interest: Affects all
   II. THESIS: Today I will persuade you that organ donation is vital for three reasons.
        PREVIEW: Those three reasons are: (1) shortage of organs, (2) misconceptions about donations, and (3) quality of life.
  III. BODY
        A. Shortage of organs
            1. Heart transplants
            2. Liver transplants
        B. Misconceptions about donations
            1. Age
            2. Health
            3. Costs
        C. Quality of life
            1. Help patients
                a. Psychologically
                b. Physically
            2. Help families
                a. Psychologically
                b. Economically

*Outlines by Lisa Griffitts.

IV. CONCLUSION
    A. Review main points
        1. Shortage of organs
        2. Misconceptions about donation
        3. Quality of life
    B. Closing thought: Phone call

Project Assignment

Select a topic from your list of "personal experiences" from Project 1 and prepare both a sentence outline and a topic outline for a speech. Compare the two outlines for completeness and conformity to the style of the different outlines. Make your outlines conform to the principles of division, subordination, and parallelism. Check to make sure that you have a single purpose in your thesis statement, and that you have adjusted to specific requirements of your instructor.

References

Boyd, S. D. & Renz, M. A. (1985). *Organization and Outlining—A Workbook for Students in a Basic Speech Course.* Indianapolis: Bobbs-Merrill Educational Publishing.

Bradley, B. E. (1988). *Fundamentals of Speech Communication* (5th ed.). Dubuque, Iowa: Wm. C. Brown Company, Publishers.

Fletcher, L. (1985). *How to Design and Deliver a Speech* (3rd ed.). New York: Harper & Row, Publishers.

Lucas, S. E. (1989). *The Art of Public Speaking* (3rd ed.). New York: Random House.

Nelson, P. E. & Pearson, J. C. (1990). *Confidence in Public Speaking* (4th ed.). Dubuque, Iowa: Wm. C. Brown Company, Publishers.

Osborn, M. & Osborn, S. (1988). *Public Speaking.* Boston: Houghton Mifflin Company.

Payne, J. & Prentice, D. (1985). *Getting Started in Public Speaking.* Lincolnwood, Illinois: National Textbook Company.

Samovar, L. A. & Mills, J. (1989). *Oral Communication* (7th ed.). Dubuque, Iowa: Wm. C. Brown Company, Publishers.

Schiff, R. L., Kone, H. J., Mosely, J., & Gutierrez, R. (1981). *Communication Strategy: A Guide to Speech Preparation.* Glenview, Illinois: Scott, Foresman and Company.

Sprague, J. & Stuart, D. (1988). *The Speaker's Handbook* (2nd ed.). San Diego: Harcourt Brace Jovanovich.

Verderber, R. F. (1988). *The Challenge of Effective Speaking* (7th ed.). Belmont, California: Wadsworth Publishing Company.

PROJECT 3

The Body of a Speech

Don't apologize. Organize.
—Florynce R. Kennedy

After you have completed the process of selecting a topic and have gathered materials for your speech, you can begin the process of organizing the body of the speech. Projects 3 and 4 concern the organization of the body of the speech and the types of supporting materials you can use to develop the body of the speech. It is important to note at this stage that the body of your speech must be organized before you prepare your introduction or conclusion. If you begin organizing your speech with the introduction, before organizing the body of the speech, you will probably waste time because you are trying to introduce something that does not yet exist. By introducing something that does not exist, you will have difficulty and likely will need to change what you prepare once you have completed the body. It is better to prepare only once. This project presents the value of organization _____ nizational patterns, and finally, a few hints about pre-

in which you thought the speaker was simply "talking
were your thoughts about the speech? The speaker?
·ven interested in the speech. You likely had unpleasant
·came too difficult to make sense of the speech, you
and ceased listening.
ners in making sense of your speech if you organize
one of several organizational patterns. Following a
ws your audience the leisure of concentrating solely
·i also organizing the ideas so they make sense. For
·ll present some new information for your audience

to digest. Your organization should simplify this purpose by making the information fit an existing category of knowledge. In a persuasive speech you should present reasoning and evidence to support your position on an issue that you want your audience to accept. Your organization should facilitate the process of changing the attitudes and behaviors of your audience members.

Imagine that you are listening to a speaker who says, "we really need to consider first what we are going to do about project A. We'll come back to that in a minute. First, let me brief you about the uses of snuff in the United States. But before I do that, I want to tell you what happened on the way to this meeting." How well prepared are you to listen to any of the ideas of this person? Most of us would like to have this person stop on one idea and develop the idea so we could consider it before moving on to the next topic. That is the reason we need organization, so we focus on one topic at a time and in some order that the audience can follow easily.

Organizational Patterns

There are many organizational patterns that might be used to give order to a speech topic. Which pattern you should use will largely be determined by your topic, your audience, and your purpose. The five schemes presented in this project are the most common patterns for most topics. Almost any speech topic will fit into one of these categories.

Chronological Order   The chronological or *time* sequence orders events in the sequence of their occurrence in history. The most frequent use of the chronological pattern is to discuss the first events in an incident and follow with the events that occurred after that, going from the beginning to the end. A typical speech using a chronological pattern is a process speech. All processes have events that must occur before others in order for the process to be completed accurately. In some instances (e.g., a recipe) it might be crucial that the sequence of steps be completed in order because it would be useless for an audience to think in other terms. To discuss baking a cake before mixing the ingredients, for example, would not make sense to any audience.

A speech that you might organize by chronological order might be a speech about the steps in hitting a baseball correctly. If you learn to take your stance correctly, prepare your body to hit the ball, and then swing the bat correctly, you will have more success than if you don't. Telling this process in a chronological order makes more sense than talking about swinging the bat, then talking about preparing your body to swing and taking a stance.

Spatial Order   The spatial, or *space*, sequence orders things as they occur in space. The most frequent use of the spatial pattern is to discuss physical objects or scenes. A typical speech using a spatial order might be a descriptive speech where you would describe what the audience would see, proceeding from left to right, top to bottom, front to back, or some other spatial order. In some instances it might confuse the audience totally to describe an object in any other order than a spatial one—for example, a mountain scene. To discuss the mountain peak, then the foothills, then the left side of the mountain, what was halfway up the mountain, the bottom of the snow line, then what was right of the mountain, would likely confuse the audience rather than clarify what you wanted them to see in their minds.

Problem-Solution Order   The problem-solution sequence arranges a speech into two parts. The first part presents a problem, explains precisely the nature of the problem, and expresses the extent or seriousness of the problem. The second part of the speech presents a solution to the problem and shows how the solution would solve the problem. A typical speech using a problem-solution pattern is a persuasive speech where you are seeking action from the audience.

Note that in certain instances you may present the solution to the problem first and then discuss the problem. You might also discuss the solution to a problem without discussing the problem if your audience is well acquainted with the problem. In some other instances you may need to explain the problem in such depth that you can't talk about the solutions.

A speech topic with which you might use the problem-solution order might be a speech on the educational system in the United States. In the problem section of the speech you might explain the problem of American education and why it is significant. In this section of your speech you might talk about such topics as low test scores, low teacher pay, poor school attendance, low school standards, and so on. In the second section of the speech you would likely present a solution to solve the problem stated in part one. For example, you could propose new standards for graduation from high school, new standards for each grade level, new teacher training standards, more money for exceptional teachers, and so on.

Causal Order The causal order, sometimes presented as cause–effect, is similar to the problem-solution sequence in that you generally divide the speech into two sections. The first part of the speech presents the causes of a problem or event; the second part presents the effects that result from the problem. A typical speech using a causal pattern would be a persuasive speech where you wish to convince or stimulate your audience.

As in the problem-solution order, there may be occasions when you would present the effects before you explained the causes of a specific problem or event. Or you may give a speech including only the causes of a problem or only the effects.

A speech topic with which you might use the causal order would be a speech on interest rates. In this speech you might discuss the causes for high interest rates and then discuss the effects of high interest rates on the national economy. For instance, you might cite as the causes of high interest rates such factors as little money available to borrow, the high level of government debt, and so on. In the second part of this speech you might deal with the effects of high interest rates, such as a small number of new home loans and its effect on the economy, the low investment rates at banks that affect the amount of money saved, and so on.

Topical Order Speeches that cannot be categorized into one of the preceding four sequences can usually be ordered by subtopics. The topic order is probably the most frequently used organizational scheme because it can be used for a speech with any general purpose. The topic order results from dividing a topic into a series of subtopics that derive naturally from the general topic. For example, you could discuss the advantages and disadvantages of an issue, the types or qualities of a subject, the various classes or varieties of a topic, the groups or classifications of an issue, or any other aspects of an issue.

Generally, your topics are ordered from most important to least important or in the opposite order. Consider your topic areas as parts of the whole. You can never discuss every aspect of an issue, so you select the most important aspects and highlight them. A speech falling into a topical order might be a speech on the reasons for abolishing capital punishment in which you select several important reasons and seek to inform your audience about the reasons for abolishing capital punishment or try to persuade your audience that capital punishment should (or should not) be abolished.

Presenting the Body of the Speech

No matter which organizational scheme you use, it is important to remember that you should cover a limited number of topics in depth rather than "skim the surface" and mention a large number of areas or subtopics. Ultimately, the time limits of your speech, the topic itself, and what your audience already knows about your topic will determine the best areas for you to cover in your speech. In most instances two or three well-developed points are superior to five points covered in less detail.

Obviously, you must assume that your speech introduction will prepare your listeners for the speech body. Presentation, which covers everything you do, should not suddenly change simply because you are now discussing the main ideas (the body) of the speech. If you use charts, or other visual aids, your movements should be alert, natural, and coordinate with whatever you are doing and saying (see Project 10). Nothing special is required of your voice except that you speak loudly enough for everyone to hear. Your language should be grammatically correct, and words should be chosen to express specifically and understandably what you want your audience to get from your speech.

A good technique for presenting your points is first to state your point, then identify your support for that point or subpoint. If you have a reference for your support, it is best to present the source for your support before presenting the support itself. You can introduce your references by using expressions such as "According to . . . ," "In her book . . . ," "In an article . . . ," and so on.

Be sure you don't inadvertently forget the last point in your speech body and begin your conclusion, and then with a wave of panic remember the last forgotten point and display fear by your body movements. If you do forget a point, you will achieve the best presentation by keeping your cool, going ahead with the conclusion, and finishing your speech as if you had planned it that way. For sample speech bodies, see the complete speeches in this book. For example, you will find a topical pattern used in Project 12, a spatial pattern used in Project 15, and a chronological pattern used in Project 17. For a sample speech using the problem-solution order, look at the speech by Jack MacAllister in the appendix; for a speech using a causal pattern, look at the Redding speech in the appendix.

Project Assignment

Prepare the outline for a speech you intend to present to the class. In your outline identify your main points, subpoints, and examples for your instructor. Present your outline to your instructor for comments. After you receive comments, revise your speech to improve the areas your instructor suggests. Use the form at the end of the book for your outline.

References

Ayres, J. & Miller, J. (1990). *Effective Public Speaking* (3rd ed.). Dubuque, Iowa: Wm. C. Brown Company, Publishers.

Bradley, B. E. (1988). *Fundamentals of Speech Communication* (5th ed.). Dubuque, Iowa: Wm. C. Brown Company, Publishers.

DeVito, J. A. (1990). *The Elements of Public Speaking* (4th ed.). New York: Harper & Row, Publishers.

Lucas, S. E. (1989). *The Art of Public Speaking* (3rd ed.). New York: Random House.

Nelson, P. E. & Pearson, J. C. (1990). *Confidence in Public Speaking* (4th ed.). Dubuque, Iowa: Wm. C. Brown Company, Publishers.

Osborn, M. & Osborn, S. (1988). *Public Speaking.* Boston: Houghton Mifflin Company.

Sprague, J. & Stuart, D. (1988). *The Speaker's Handbook* (2nd ed.). San Diego: Harcourt Brace Jovanovich.

Verderber, R. F. (1988). *The Challenge of Effective Speaking* (7th ed.). Belmont, California: Wadsworth Publishing Company.

PROJECT **4**

Supporting Materials

Details often kill initiative, but there have been few
successful men who weren't good at details. Don't ignore
details. Lick them.

—William B. Given, Jr.

In making a speech, you must use materials that develop and clarify your thoughts.
Whenever you make a point or present an idea, you must somehow offer evidence that
what you are saying is worthy of belief. To develop and clarify your thoughts and to show
that what you are saying is valid, you need to use supporting materials.

Supporting material may be defined as anything that gives validity to a speaker's
remarks. Authorities often differ in the manner in which they list and classify these
materials; however, for use here we consider four kinds of supporting materials: (1)
examples (real or hypothetical); (2) factual data (facts, figures, statistics); (3) testimony;
and (4) comparisons. In addition, the project explains where to look for supporting
materials and how to use them.

Where to Look for Supporting Materials

The first place to begin a search for supporting materials is with yourself. You are always your
first source of information. Consider what you know about your topic and what experiences
you have had that you can use to add to your speech. What you already know you will not need
to search for. You must always have some personal knowledge of your topic or you do not have
a "right" to speak on that topic. This does not mean that you must be an expert to talk about
a topic, but it does mean that you must have more than a passing interest in the topic.

In some instances you will find your knowledge and experiences about a specific topic are
very meager. In other instances what you know and what you have experienced will be vast and
of great importance to your speech. In both instances list what you know before moving on
to another source of information to find out what you do not know.

A second source of information is other people. You usually will find there are "experts" in most fields in your community. These experts may range from someone who has been working in that area of expertise for a couple of years to maybe someone who has spent years working and studying in the field. An expert need not hold a college degree in a subject to have useful information.

The means for getting information from your experts will be the interview (Project 30). Whether you search this source of information as the second or third source is of little importance, but you should never overlook experts in your local area who have experiences and/or knowledge gained through formal and informal education that could be of value to your speech.

A third source of information is the library. Most communities will have libraries (either school or public) that will have a limited number of references you can use to find the kind of support you need for your speech. Your library search will likely be your most extensive type of research for supporting materials because libraries have more references and a greater store of knowledge than you might find from either your own experiences or knowledge or other community experts.

Since the library search will be your most extensive, you will want to use your time and efforts wisely to maximize your efforts. Always begin your library research by looking for the most recent and most pertinent materials. Usually, you will find periodicals (journals, magazines, and newspapers) have the most current data. These publications are released at regular periods of time and are printed much more frequently than other sources like books. To find this timely information, use the indexes to these sources, such as special subject indexes (*Education Index, Social Sciences Index,* etc.) for journals, the *Reader's Guide to Periodical Literature* for popular magazines, and the *New York Times Index* for newspaper publications. These indexes will lead you to the most recent and most pertinent information on your topic.

Another valuable source will be statistics books. Most libraries will have a number of books like *Statesman's Yearbook, Information Please Almanac,* and *Statistical Reports* that will provide many tables of statistics on almost any topic. Check these sources for the most recent data concerning your topic and for statistics that might not be available in other sources.

You will also want to check the library's supply of books on your topic, and its vertical file. Begin this search with the card catalog or book cataloging system used in your library. If you do not know your library's organizational system, or you can't find the materials you are looking for, ask your reference librarian. You may also need to ask for help in using the vertical file. All libraries have their own methods of filing and cataloging this information.

Supporting Materials to Look For

Once you have begun your search, you must know what you are looking for. Looking does little good if you don't recognize what you need when you see it. This section of Project 4 presents several types of support materials that can be used to develop your points in the body of the speech. Of course, some of this could also be used in the introduction and conclusion to your speech. The primary focus of this section, however, is to acquaint you with the materials you can use for support in the body of your speech.

EXAMPLES

There are several different types of examples that can be used to help your audience better understand what you mean. Examples can be real or hypothetical, long illustrations, short specific instances, extended narratives, or anecdotes. Let's look at each of these examples to understand better how each one can best be used.

Real Examples Real examples are actual instances of events that have occurred. Real examples can come from either personal experiences or the experiences of others you have heard or read about. For example, "Last week as I traveled to St Louis . . ." would represent an example of a personal experience. You might tell of a real experience of someone else by reporting: "Mary McJones reported in the August issue of *Time* magazine that she had experienced . . ." The entire sample speech in Project 13 is a real example.

Hypothetical Examples   Hypothetical examples are best used as instances that *might* occur or have the possibility of occurring. They are not real in that they have not yet occurred as in the real examples. Hypothetical examples frequently start with words such as "if," "imagine," or "suppose." For example, "Imagine yourself sunbathing on a beach of a South Pacific island." "Suppose you were to find yourself on a deserted island in the Pacific and . . ." While these examples may not be real, they can be made pertinent to your speech topic if your audience members see that they could potentially be true. Their value lies not in their truth but in their potential. Audiences sometimes find it difficult to relate to unfamiliar topics, but they can relate to people who have problems they have heard about. If you can't find the real example you need to prove your point, you can illustrate your idea with a hypothetical example.

Illustrations   Illustrations differ from other types of examples in that they are usually longer and more detailed, whereas specific instances are more brief. Sometimes illustrations are presented in the form of extended narratives or as negative examples (what you don't mean). Herbert S. Richey (1977) uses the following illustration in his speech, "The Real Cause of Inflation: Government Services":

> I'd like to talk about modern economics today. I'm sure many of us are already familiar with that. But for those who are not, I can illustrate the theory with a story:
>
> Jed is a part-time farm worker with a flair for applied economics. One day he "borrowed" a country ham from the farmer who employs him . . . without bothering to tell the farmer.
>
> He went downtown and sold the ham to the grocer for $27. Then he used $20 of that money to buy $80 worth of food stamps.
>
> With the food stamps he bought $48 worth of groceries. He used the remaining $32 worth of food stamps to buy back the ham.
>
> Then he returned the ham to the farmer's smokehouse.
>
> So the grocer made a profit, the farmer got his ham back, and Jed has $48 worth of groceries plus $7 in cash.
>
> If you see no flaw in that process, then you are already familiar with modern economics.

The following is a specific instance. Assume that you are discussing the marriages of hollywood actors and actresses:

> Take Joan Collins, for instance, she has been married three times—to actor Maxwell Reed in 1952, to composer-singer Anthony Newley in 1963, and to record producer Ron Kass in 1972. Each marriage has ended in divorce, and nobody can guess how many love affairs she has had.

These types of examples can often prove your point, or get your audience members involved with your topic.

Narratives and Anecdotes   Narratives, like illustrations, are extended examples. A narrative usually recreates a real event and presents it as a story. The anecdote differs from the narrative in that it is usually a hypothetical story as opposed to having been created from a real event, and is usually humorous. An appropriate use of a narrative in a speech would be to explain feelings of people that a series of numbers could not or to stress a particular point. Donald Dedmon (1983) used an anecdote to point out that doing more of what we're doing wrong will not solve a problem. After making his statement, he continued:

> Perhaps, it bears no particular parallel but the story comes to mind of the semi-truck which got stuck going through a tunnel. Tug as they might, struggle as they did, they couldn't move it. The group which gathered about pondered dismantling the truck or digging a higher tunnel. One little boy observing this state of paralyzed thinking asked simply—and solved the problem—"why don't you let the air out of the tires?"

To see how these examples work in a speech, look at the sample speech by W. Charles Redding in the appendix. Professor Redding uses many examples to get his point across.

FACTUAL DATA

Factual data are a second form of support materials. Daily we are surrounded by all kinds of numbers and numerical summaries of events. These numbers can help us to clarify issues or describe the size or scope of an object or event. Factual data are of three different types—facts, figures, and statistics.

Facts   Facts are materials that people generally agree to be true or that can be demonstrated to be true. Things known to have happened or, in some cases, said to have happened may be considered facts. "There are 20 students in this class" is an example of a fact that can be demonstrated to be true or untrue. It is also a fact that in most states anyone over the age of 16 is eligible to apply for a driver's license. It is also a fact that the earth turns such that the sun always rises in the east and sets in the west. Notice that all facts do not have to include numerical data.

Figures   Figures are numbers of anything. A count of objects in a specified category is a figure. For example, the number of cars that pass at Main and Broadway in a one-hour period of time is a figure. Figures are useful support materials when you wish to present "the facts" of a specific case. For example, you may wish to present the population of the state of Oklahoma or the number of people affected by AIDS, the approximate cost for open heart surgery, or any other form of quantitative data. For a good example of the use of figures, look at the sample speech in Project 12 and Project 18.

Statistics   Statistics are systematic compilations of figures that can be used to infer general truths. The difference between a figure and a statistic is that statistics are figures that have been manipulated in some manner. For example, averages and percentages are statistics because the numbers reported must be calculated from figures. An example of the use of a statistic is to report that U.S. citizens eat an average of 15 pounds of salt per year. Note that this example gives no specific figures for any specific citizen that can be verified. All citizens of the United States are classified together as equals and the total pounds of salt consumed by U.S. citizens is then divided equally among them—even for those who are on salt-free diets. There may be someone who eats precisely the average, but we would have a difficult time finding that person. For a good example of the use of statistics, look at the sample speech in Project 19.

TESTIMONY

Testimony is the third general form of support. It consists of what people say when expressing themselves about objects, ideas, events, and people. Testimony may be found in the forms of quotations or paraphrases of recognized authorities in a particular field.

Testimony adds credibility to the speaker, if used correctly. It can also clarify an idea and add interest to a topic. In all cases you should identify the source of the quotation or paraphrase—give credit to the person who made the statement or originated the idea. Unless the quotation is brief, is totally understandable to the audience, and refers directly to the point you wish to make, it is better to paraphrase what someone has said.

In determining which testimony to use, be certain that you check several areas to make sure your testimony will accomplish what you wish. First, make sure that the testimony comes from a source the audience will accept as a recognized authority on the topic. Second, make sure that the testimony you use relates directly to the point you are making. Third, make sure that the testimony is unbiased—that is, the source has no personal gain to make from the statement. There are good examples of the use of testimony in the sample speeches of Projects 12 and 18.

COMPARISONS

A fourth general category for support material is comparisons. Comparisons are used when you are attempting to explain difficult or unfamiliar concepts to your audience. In making comparisons, you must point out the similarities between the new concept and one with which the audience is familiar.

Comparisons may be performed in several recognizable styles. The analogy is probably the most recognizable form of comparison. In fact, it is often defined in literary circles as "an extended comparison." Analogies may be literal, as in the comparison of two brands of cars (a Chevrolet and a Ford), or figurative, cases that are basically unalike, but alike in one special aspect (the sizes of a battleship and football field). Analogies do not prove much to an audience, but they can be used to help clarify unfamiliar concepts and to make new ideas more understandable to your audience.

Two forms of shorter comparisons are metaphors and similes. Metaphors compare objects or concepts by saying that one thing is another. For example, we sometimes refer to a particular car that is not in good working order by saying, "That car is a lemon."

Similes differ from metaphors in that they use the word "like" to make the comparison. For example, "That car runs like a lemon." The metaphor and simile are very similar, but you use the metaphor to make your point stronger—"that child is a pig" is much stronger than saying "that child looks like a pig." Notice that the simile lessens the effect of the comparison, making it less harsh.

Another form of support closely related to the comparison, and often used together with the the comparison, is the contrast. Whereas comparisons point out the similarities between two concepts, contrasts point out the differences. You can contrast the new with the old or the unknown with the known. You can also contrast two new ideas, two old ideas, and so on. By contrasting ideas, you should strive to point out the advantages of one over the other. For an example of the use of a comparison, read the Redding speech in the appendix.

Using Supporting Materials

Whenever you make a point or present an idea in a speech, you need to support your idea by using examples, factual data, testimony, and/or comparisons. Be sure you indicate the source of each of your supports in presenting your speech so that your audience can assess the value of the supporting materials. This project requires you to substantiate your ideas with supporting materials that you may consider a form of evidence.

As you prepare your speech, be sure to prepare and rehearse all materials. All factual data, particularly figures and statistics, should be meticulously rehearsed and semimemorized. If testimony (a quotation) is to be read, it should be largely memorized even though it is written out or you will lose eye contact with your audience more than is appropriate. Should charts, graphs, or other visual aids be used, they must also be carefully prepared and rehearsed. Your supporting materials will be effective in proportion to the care you exercise in selecting, organizing, and rehearsing them.

In presenting your speech, do not announce that you are going to use supporting materials; bring your supporting materials in at the proper time through well-chosen phrases and transitional remarks. It is permissible, sometimes desirable, to say "for example" in preface to an example. You may say "according to . . ." or words such as "in his book . . ." in preface to testimony. In quoting any material, testimony, or otherwise, know it well enough so you can look at your audience a large part of the time.

Project Assignment

Prepare a speech on any subject. In preparing your speech, be sure that you identify a minimum of three different sources of supporting materials (three different books, magazines, etc.) and use two different types of supporting materials (examples, factual data, testimony, comparisons). This assignment may be combined with any other speaking assignment in Units III, IV, V, VI, or VII.

Alternate Project Assignment

Study the speeches in the appendix (or any other source your instructor may indicate) and identify examples of supporting materials used in the speeches. Find an example of each type of support. Be prepared to present your findings to the class with an explanation of the kind of support each represents.

References

Ayres, J. & Miller, J. (1990). *Effective Public Speaking* (3rd ed.). Dubuque, Iowa: Wm. C. Brown Company, Publishers.

Bradley, B. E. (1988). *Fundamentals of Speech Communication* (5th ed.). Dubuque, Iowa: Wm. C. Brown Company, Publishers.

Dedmon, D. (1983). Education: Confirming what we know. *Vital Speeches of the Day, 49,* 14–20.

Devito, J. A. (1990). *The Elements of Public Speaking* (4th ed.). New York: Harper & Row, Publishers.

Gronbeck, B. E., Ehninger, D., & Monroe, A. H. (1988). *Principles of Speech Communication* (10th brief ed.). Glenview, Illinois: Scott, Foresman and Company.

Lucas, S. E. (1989). *The Art of Public Speaking* (3rd ed.). New York: Random House.

Nelson, P. E. & Pearson, J. C. (1990). *Confidence in Public Speaking* (4th ed.). Dubuque, Iowa: Wm. C. Brown Company, Publishers.

Osborn, M. & Osborn, S. (1988). *Public Speaking.* Boston: Houghton Mifflin Company.

Richey, H. S. (1977). The real cause of inflation: Government services. *Vital Speeches of the Day, 43,* 386–389.

Sprague, J. & Stuart, D. (1988). *The Speaker's Handbook* (2nd ed.). San Diego: Harcourt Brace Jovanovich.

Verderber, R. F. (1988). *The Challenge of Effective Speaking* (7th ed.). Belmont, California: Wadsworth Publishing Company.

PROJECT **5**

The Introduction: Getting Your Speech Started

We fail far more often by timidity than by over-daring.
—David Grayson

As with all things in life, a speech must have a beginning, a middle, and an end. In meeting a person for the first time, we desire to make a good first impression so that we become memorable to that person. Just as you want to make a good first impression when meeting someone, you will want to make a good first impression in your speaking. In a speech your introduction makes that first memorable impression on your audience. Prepare it well because you never get a second chance to make a good first impression. This project presents the principles of the introduction, tells how to prepare the introduction, explains how to present the introduction, and presents two sample introductions for you to study.

Principles of the Introduction

Principle One: The first principle of an introduction is to gain the attention of your audience members. As you begin to speak, people often have their minds on several different subjects. Most of your audience members are thinking about something other than your speech. Several students will be giving thought to their own speeches, some other students will be considering an idea from the previous speech, and still others will be thinking about other classes, assignments, other people, and so on. Your first task is to draw their attention to your speech. As Clarence Darrow once said, "Unless a speaker can interest his audience at once, his effort will be a failure." Draw your audience members' attention to your topic at once and you will have a good beginning toward keeping them interested in your speech and topic.

Following are some practical methods for gaining the attention of your audience. These are not the only means for gaining attention, but they are some of the most well-recognized methods for gaining audience attention. None of them is "guaranteed" to work, but each one will offer a different approach to getting your audience members to pay attention to what you have to say on your topic.

24

Startle the Audience   One good method of gaining attention is to startle your listeners. You can do this by using shocking facts—"One out of four of us will die of cancer," or startling statements—"You are all failures." The closer you can make this to your audience, the better. If you say that your topic affects five people in the room, look around and ask which five it will be. You might even ask, "Are you one of the five?" One caution with startling your audience members—be sure that you *startle* them rather than shock them. If you *shock* your listeners, you may never get them back.

One student started to the front of the room to present his speech, fell and ripped a long slit in his leg. As the blood ran onto the floor, and several people became nauseous and panicky because of the blood, the student got up laughing. He had obtained from the first aid instructor an artificial wound and a blood bag that he cut to make it look real. The class never recovered enough from this shock to hear his very valuable speech about binding wounds to prevent further injuries and blood loss before a doctor can take over. *Startle* your audience, but never shock them!

Create Curiosity   A second method of gaining attention is to create curiosity in your audience members. Listeners naturally want to listen when they are curious about something. If you create curiosity in your audience members, they will listen to your speech to become satisfied. One student began her speech by setting up the following conditions:

> Suppose you know of a woman who has several children, the oldest two have died at an early age, another child is mentally retarded and another is severely ill. She now finds out that she is pregnant again and that her husband has a venereal disease. Would you suggest that she have an abortion?

Now you should be curious to find out what the speaker is going to talk about and how you are going to react to the situation just set up for you. When you use the curiosity technique to gain attention, you need to make sure that your speech satisfies your audience members' curiosity. If you do nothing more to satisfy this curiosity, you will have gained little; but if you satisfy your audience members' thirst for knowledge, you will have gained much by stirring their imaginations and making them want to listen to your speech.

Establish Common Ground   In establishing common ground, you relate yourself and your topic to your audience. As audience members, we pay close attention to those people who are like us and those topics that relate closely to us. For example, "We have all driven to campus expecting to park near class, only to find no parking spaces within two miles." In using an attention-getter such as this, you have captured a college class's attention, at least the attention of all those who have driven to campus expecting to find a parking space, only to have to walk several blocks or miles to get to their classes, and reaching class late because all parking spaces were filled. The common bond will hold your audience long enough for you to get into your topic and to provide some important information for the audience.

Tell a Story   Several types of stories can be used to gain attention. Human interest stories tell about people we either know or would like to know. Paul Harvey uses this technique with his program, "The Rest of the Story." Humorous stories are good also because people like to have their funny bones tickled. Almost any story will serve as a good attention-getter as long as it relates directly to your speech topic.

One student began her speech with this story. "Several years ago when my daughter was one, I looked at her and saw her grabbing at her throat. Since I didn't hear any noise coming from her, and my sister had told me about the Heimlick maneuver, I used this technique and a pop-top sprang forth from her mouth. Had I not known this technique, I may have lost my daughter on that day." Now you want to know the rest of her story.

Quote a Noted Authority   Quotations from authorities or from the Bible often gain the attention of audience members. Like stories, quotations must relate directly to your topic if they are to be effective in arousing your audience's attention. In all cases you should set the quotation up for the audience, don't expect the quotation to have interest all by itself. For example, you might begin with the phrase, "When asked whether he would raise taxes, President Bush said, 'Read my lips. No new taxes." You might continue your introduction by saying, "As you all know, there are only two certainties in life—death and taxes. Considering all the technology available today, you may not have to die, but you still have to pay your taxes. Since we must all deal with the issue of taxes almost daily, today. . . ." You can then go into your specific areas of the topic.

Ask a Series of Questions Another good technique is using a series of questions that will get your audience to begin thinking about your topic. Make sure that you use more than one question. One question does not take very long and does little to get the audience members' attention or direct their attention to your topic. In fact, most of them will not have enough time to start thinking about your topic if you don't use at least three questions.

You might begin a speech on wind surfing by asking your audience members: "Have you ever wondered what it would be like to fly like a bird? To soar like an eagle above the clouds and swoop down to earth? Can you imagine what the world looks like from above rather than at ground level? What does man look like from 200 feet in the air?" Now that you have our attention, we will willingly go along on the rest of your journey.

Demonstrate a Process A demonstration can also gain attention. Action or movement of any kind can get your audience's attention and hold it if the action relates to the topic and the audience. When your audience can both see and hear your message, it will most likely remember the message longer and pay more attention during your speech. One student who used a demonstration successfully in an introduction rappelled off the building and through the classroom window to gain attention. Once he was through the window and was able to get free of the ropes, this student began to speak about the adventures to be gained by learning to rappel and how to rappel correctly. Another student began her speech by doing a tap dance in front of the class, then started to explain how we could learn to tap dance quickly and easily at her dance studio.

Another technique very close to the demonstration is the exhibit. Sometimes showing your audience something new and different will also gain its attention. The exhibit differs from the demonstration in that it merely shows what something looks like, whereas the demonstration also shows how something works or how it is done. The exhibit can be used to get people to want to know how something works, which is what your speech would tell them.

One student who used an exhibit successfully was a student who worked in a greenhouse and brought a table arrangement, displayed it, and asked the audience members if they would like to make such arrangements for less than the cost of ordering one from the greenhouse or florist. He then went on to demonstrate the steps in preparing a simple table arrangement for less than half the cost of ordering one from the florist he worked for.

Compliment Your Audience When you are genuinely pleased over the opportunity of speaking before an audience, you may pay the audience members a compliment for their hospitality. This compliment should be tied into the audience's interest in the subject to be discussed, their concern over the issue, and so on. If your presentation doesn't show sincerity, your audience members will not likely maintain their attention or interest in your presentation long.

You may find that the most effective means for gaining attention is a combination of the preceding methods rather than one single method. You should feel free to experiment with combinations to find out what works best for you and your topic. One technique may work well for one topic and be a failure with another, or work with one audience and not with another. Try to find the best technique for your audience, you, and your topic.

Principle Two: A second principle of an introduction is that it should establish your credibility or qualifications to speak on your topic. Your audience members do not always grant you immediate credibility when you announce your topic. Even authorities generally need to remind audiences of their credentials. However, noted authorities such as the President of the

United States or popular local celebrities, do not need to explain to most audiences why they have a right to speak on certain topics.

Establishing your credibility should be done tactfully so you don't sound like a braggart. One student in speaking about child abuse said, "Since my cousin was abused three years ago, I have been studying and reading on the topic of child abuse. Last year I wrote a paper in my composition course on "Detecting Child Abusers." These simple two sentences set up her audience members to accept what she said as an authority in her own right. Although she has no degrees in child abuse, or experience in dealing with child abusers, she does have a right to talk on the topic because of her personal study and interest in the topic.

You must have a "right" to talk on any topic you select to speak on. That right may be gained through personal experience, study, or an intense interest to know more about a specific topic. If you rely on interest, you should have had that interest for more than a week or two or your audience members may well believe your interest began when you decided on your topic, which will likely lessen your credibility rather than strengthen it.

Principle Three: A third principle of an introduction is that you must relate your topic to your audience. In relating to your audience members, you are most interested in arousing their interest so each member of your audience sees some relevance for him- or herself. You must prepare and open the minds of your listeners for the thoughts that are to come. This is particularly necessary if your audience members are hostile or at least not in your favor. You may accomplish this by giving background and historical information so your audience members can and will understand your subject. Also, by tying your topic to your audience members, you can show them the relevance of your topic to their lives.

Some authorities include directing your audience members' attention to your topic as one of the main purposes of the introduction. This includes stating what you intend to accomplish in your speech and previewing the body of your speech. Whether you separate this segment of your speech from the introduction or present it as a part of your introduction, it is important that you tell your listeners what to expect in your speech. This may be accomplished by (1) stating your thesis ("Today I will inform you about two aspects of controlling high blood pressure.") and (2) introducing your main points ("Those two aspects are controlling blood pressure without medication, and controlling blood pressure with medication.").

These statements, whether stated in this precise manner or in another form, should be presented at the very end of the introduction. In this manner they serve as a transition between your introduction and the body of your speech. They will also signal your audience members that the body of your speech is about to begin. Only in rare instances will you want to save your thesis until the end of your speech.

Preparing the Introduction

When you prepare your introduction, keep in mind that what you are preparing paves the way for what is to come later in your speech. However, sometimes it happens that when the chairperson introduces you, she or he says something that forces you to alter your opening remarks. Perhaps, the environment will prompt you to remark about it, or some incident occurring in the audience may require comment. Whatever the circumstances, be prepared to speak impromptu as you feel the occasion demands, then begin your planned introduction by making an easy transition to it.

Your introduction should be built around the purpose you want it to achieve. You alone must decide what this purpose will be. Adapt your introduction to the expected audience, the occasion, and the environment. Be sure that it is also adapted to you, your prestige, and your position in the eyes of your listeners. Without this adaptation, you will not set yourself up for the best speaking opportunity and your best chances for success.

Your wording should be carefully worked out. Rehearse your introduction at least four or five times to fix it well in mind. It should *not* be memorized word for word, although the ideas you wish to present should be practiced many times until you are comfortable with them. Memorizing your introduction word for word may make you sound too mechanical and not interested in your audience members. You may also forget your exact wording and be at a total loss if you can't continue. The best idea is to know and practice what you want to say, but don't memorize specific words.

The introduction to a speech is often prepared last because it can be built around the final draft of the speech. If it were prepared first, the introduction might not merge with and be appropriate to the body of the speech. Also, its length can be determined more advantageously after you have prepared the body of your speech. Ordinarily, it will consume no more than 15 percent of the total time of your speech, and sometimes it will be even less.

Here are a few points to remember when preparing your introduction: Avoid dullness and triteness. Most audiences don't want to hear what they have already heard many times before. In addition, avoid extremely lengthy opening remarks. Remember, the introduction should set up the body of the speech, not present your basic message. False leads that are not followed up, stories that are suggestive or risqué, and stories that are used only to fill time should be avoided, too, so you do not get rejected by your audience members before you even begin the body of your speech.

You will also want to avoid a mere announcement of your topic. If you can't do more than merely state your topic, you haven't done your homework and your audience will know that. Besides, you can't expect your audience members to be interested in your topic simply by your announcing it. Apologies, or remarks that might be construed as apologies, will do little to make a good impression on your audience members. Instead, try to devise a fresh and original approach to your topic that will set the stage for what is to come later in your speech and at the same time bring you and your audience together in a friendly atmosphere.

Presenting the Introduction

An important aspect of your introduction is your behavior before you stand in front of your audience members, and after you get there. If you are sitting on stage in full view of your audience members, you should remain comfortable and calmly alert. People are appraising you while you await your turn to speak. Women speakers should be careful not to cross their legs while seated. Crossing the ankles is permissible, although it is safer to keep both feet on the floor with the knees together. Men should not slouch or sprawl out on the stage. Crossing your legs should also be avoided. This may lead your audience members to believe that you are not necessarily interested in them or in your topic. Remain alert to the other people who are speaking and to the person who is introducing you.

When you are introduced, you should rise easily, without delay or noise, and move to your place before your audience. After arriving, you should allow a few seconds to elapse while you deliberately survey the scene before you and smile at your audience. This suggests to your audience members that you are calm, confident, and pleased to be speaking to them. Then, after addressing the chairperson, if you have not already done so, you are ready to begin your introductory remarks.

You should speak clearly, distinctly, and loudly enough to be heard easily by all audience members. Begin somewhat slowly, then speed up the rate later. This lets your audience members adjust to your vocal patterns slowly and still hear and understand everything you have to say. If you begin too rapidly, your audience members may miss some of the important statements you have to make in setting up your speech.

Beginning speakers sometimes fail to realize that the first words they utter may be their most important ones. Some speakers trust to luck that they will be able to "start their speeches" once they begin speaking. Always plan carefully the introduction of your speech; otherwise you more than likely will have an awkward, poorly organized, and haphazard introduction that will make your audience members uneasy and cause them to lose whatever interest and confidence they may have felt in you and your subject. Let us remind you one more time, your introduction is your first chance to make a good first impression, and you don't get a second chance to make a good first impression.

SAMPLE INTRODUCTION 1

By Steve Keiffer

Drugs

If I asked you as parents, and you as teenagers, to place a pistol to your head and pull the trigger, would you do it? Of course you wouldn't do it, because you cherish life. However, this is what is happening among our teenagers today. Maybe they aren't putting pistols to their heads, but they are killing themselves with drugs.

I have had a deep interest in this topic for some some time now because of a personal friend who took his life due to a drug overdose. My friend was eighteen years of age.

Through my own experience with my friend, and working with teenagers over the past few years, I have found that drugs are becoming the number one enemy of teenagers. Most of you are teenagers, so this will affect you directly. The rest of you have, or will soon have teenage children, so you should also be concerned with the problem of drugs in our society.

Today I will persuade you that drugs are a major problem among teenagers today that must be stopped for three reasons. Those three reasons are: (1) because drugs are readily available to our teens, (2) because drugs are affecting teenagers' abilities to perform, and (3) because drugs are causing the deaths of many teenagers today.

SAMPLE OUTLINE 1

I. INTRODUCTION:
   A. Attention-getter: Pistol
   B. Credentials: Personal experience
   C. Arouse interest: Affects all
II. THESIS: Today I will persuade you that drugs are a major problem among teenagers today that must be stopped for three reasons.
   PREVIEW: Those three reasons are: (1) drugs readily available, (2) drugs affect abilities, and (3) drugs cause deaths.

SAMPLE INTRODUCTION 2

By Janet Rutland

Magic Potion

If I had a "magic potion" that would help you lose weight permanently and keep you healthy and fit, would you drink it? Would you tell others of your magic potion and how it has helped you? Do you drink your daily minimum quantity of "magic potion?" This potion really does exist.

I've been an avid drinker of this magic potion for practically all of my eighteen years, although I must admit that it wasn't always by choice. My parents were thoroughly convinced that drinking this magic potion was essential for a healthy lifestyle and often "pushed" this idea on me. I can often remember my father saying, "daughter, have you had your "magic potion" today?" Well, not quite in those words. Today I am thankful that this habit was instilled in me because I feel as if it has made me a healthier person, and drink eight to ten glasses daily.

This "magic potion" is essential to your life. When you consider that it makes up 60–70% of your body weight, it is obvious that practically every function of your body utilizes some of this "magic potion." In fact, you can't live without my "magic potion."

Today I will persuade you that water is important for your good health by explaining two of the important reasons for drinking water. Those two reasons are: (1) because water aids in permanent weight loss, and (2) because water helps maintain a healthy body chemistry.

SAMPLE OUTLINE 2

I. INTRODUCTION
   A. Attention getter: Curiosity
   B. Credentials: Lifetime
   C. Arouse interest: Essential

II. THESIS: Today I will persuade you that water is important for your good health by explaining two of the important reasons for drinking water.

PREVIEW: These two reasons are: (1) water aids weight loss and (2) water maintains body system.

Project Assignment

Prepare three different introductions, using the suggestions explained in this project as your guidelines. Be sure you gain the attention of your audience, establish your credibility to speak on your topic, and show your audience how they can use what you are about to tell them. Unless your instructor designates otherwise, use only one subject, that is, adoption, that you will introduce in three different ways. If possible, attempt a combination of techniques to gain attention.

References

Ayres, J. & Miller, J. (1990). *Effective Public Speaking* (3rd ed.). Dubuque, Iowa: Wm. C. Brown Company, Publishers.

Bradley, B. E. (1988). *Fundamentals of Speech Communication* (5th ed.). Dubuque, Iowa: Wm. C. Brown Company, Publishers.

DeVito, J. A. (1990). *The Elements of Public Speaking* (4th ed.). New York: Harper & Row, Publishers.

Gregory, H. (1990). *Public Speaking for College and Career* (2nd ed.). New York: McGraw-Hill Book Company.

Lucas, S. E. (1989). *The Art of Public Speaking* (3rd ed.). New York: Random House.

Minnick, W. C. (1983). *Public Speaking* (2nd ed.). Boston: Houghton Mifflin Company.

Nelson, P. E. & Pearson, J. C. (1990). *Confidence in Public Speaking* (4th ed.). Dubuque, Iowa: Wm. C. Brown Company, Publishers.

Osborn, M. & Osborn, S. (1988). *Public Speaking.* Boston: Houghton Mifflin Company.

Sprague, J. & Stuart, D. (1988). *The Speaker's Handbook* (2nd ed.). San Diego: Harcourt Brace Jovanovich.

Verderber, R. F. (1988). *The Challenge of Effective Speaking* (7th ed.). Belmont, California: Wadsworth Publishing Company.

PROJECT 6

The Conclusion: Ending Your Speech

Make sure you have finished speaking before your audience has finished listening. A talk, as Mrs. Hubert Humphrey once reminded her husband, need not be eternal to be immortal.

—Dorothy Sarnoff

Just as no speech would be complete without an introduction, one would also be incomplete without a conclusion. You must find a way of gracefully telling your audience "that's all," "the end," or "I have finished" without sounding like the cartoon character, Porky Pig. The conclusion is also your last chance to remind your audience members of the object of your speech. In addition, just as you want to make a good first impression on your audience members, you also want to leave them with a good last impression.

No doubt you have often heard a speaker stop suddenly, leaving you with a feeling of dangling in midair. You may have wondered why the speaker stopped there, or you may have wanted him or her to pull his or her remarks together so you could grasp the thoughts in their fullness. Surely you have also heard a speaker pass a half dozen stop signs, any one of which should have been a conclusion. Either type of conclusion is poor and represents careless planning.

By working out separate conclusions that demonstrate in themselves various methods of ending a speech, you not only learn how to do them, but you also become more aware of one of the most important parts of every speech, the conclusion.

This project presents the principles of the conclusion, explains how to prepare the conclusion and how to present the conclusion. It also provides a sample conclusion for you to use as a guide in preparing future conclusions.

Principles of the Conclusion

Like the introduction, the conclusion has several principle functions. First, the conclusion should signal the end (or approaching end) of your speech. If there is no signal to the audience

31

that you are about to end, you may take them by surprise and deprive them of that feeling of finality. Some common signals are "In conclusion," "In review," "In summary," or "As I conclude my speech. . . ." Of course, you can be more original, but in doing so you may lose some members of your audience. Unless you are a very accomplished speaker and have a very sophisticated audience, you are safest sticking to the basics. Leave the cute and clever endings to the professional speakers.

Second, the conclusion needs to summarize the main point of the speech. It is more important to summarize your points in some speeches than in others, but in most speeches you *should* tie your ideas together for your audience. Audience members need a brief synopsis of the main ideas you have presented so they can put your ideas into a neat order in their minds. The conclusion serves to remind the audience of these points. Frequently, you will notice that audience members perk up at your signal of concluding. They sit up straighter and pay more attention to what you have to say. This is your opportunity to get your points across even if your audience members missed something during the body of the speech.

The third principle of the conclusion is to bring the speech to an end. Your speech must sound finished when you stop. Sometimes your summary will be sufficient to sound final; at other times you will want to leave the audience members with a "final thought" that gives the speech that final touch and leaves them feeling good about your speech or thinking about what you have said.

The "closing thought" can take several forms. In fact, most techniques used to gain attention in the introduction of the speech can also be used to "close" the speech. Following are some practical and useful methods for closing your speech.

Quotation   A quotation from a recognizable authority or the Bible is a common and effective method for closing a speech. A quotation is especially good if it summarizes your thoughts or provokes others to think about what you have said. A good example of the use of a quotation to conclude a speech comes from a speech by Adlai E. Stevenson (1978) on the death of Sir Winston Churchill. Stevenson said:

> Like the patriarchs of old, he waited on God's judgment and it could be said of him—as of the immortals that went before him—that God magnified him in the fear of his enemies and with his words he made prodigies to cease. He glorified him in the sight of kings and gave him commandments in the sight of his people. He showed him his Glory and sanctified him in his faith. . . .

Story   Stories serve to give speeches a good ending as well as a good beginning. Depending on the type of speech and the nature of your topic, you may want to use a human interest story; a humorous anecdote, or a fictitious story that you create to illustrate your point. Jenkin Lloyd Jones (1973) used a story to end his speech, "Let's Bring Back Dad: A Solid Value System." He said:

> Last year, up on the River in central California, I watched a father osprey at the top of a dead tree teaching his chick how to fish. The father osprey would take off and dive like a plummet into the river in which the whiting were running, come up with a fish, and fly back to the limb, and then the chick would take off and describe a couple of clumsy cartwheels in the air and hit the water with a splash, and less often come up with a fish. And do you know what? I didn't hear that chick say to his father, "Look Dad, you're irrelevant."
>
> Dad was the way of life; Dad was the secret of survival. And if that's good for the osprey nest, then for the sake of our nation and its oncoming generations, let's bring back Dad."

Striking Statement   Sometimes you can't find a quotation that has the exact ring to it you want for your speech or a story that will say what you want, so you must create that striking statement for yourself. Depending on your topic, you may want to make your statement serious or humorous. This is your opportunity to be creative and ingenious. You may not become famous for your ingenuity, but you can display it nonetheless.

An example of a striking statement is this closing by Vernon Jordan (1974) in his speech "Under the Hammer: Freedom, Justice and Dignity." He said:

Yes, black people are asking for the hammer of freedom, the hammer of justice, the hammer of decency; for with that hammer we can build wonders. We can hammer out love and peace, justice, and fairness . . . all over this great land of ours.

A student in a fundamentals of speech class ended her speech on the process of creating latch hook artwork, by saying, "Remember, 'hooking' can be both fun and profitable." Of course, she relied on her audience's ability to catch the double meaning in her striking statement, which made her comment humorous as well as striking. You will also find another example of a striking statement used in the sample speech in Project 20.

Return to the Introduction   A good method of tying a speech together is to refer to something you have said in the introduction. This technique serves to remind the audience not only of the earlier reference, but also to relate the introduction and conclusion to the body of the speech, if you have chosen these references well. One student began her speech with the "curiosity" introduction (see "Create Curiosity, Project 5). She then spoke on the pros and cons of having an abortion. In her conclusion she returned to the introduction by reminding the audience of the conditions she had described. Then she asked, "Did you vote to give the mother an abortion? If you did, you would have killed Beethoven." The speaker's use of the introductory material to tie the speech together also served to give notice of what she thought.

You can find another example of this use of closing in the sample speech by Jack MacAllister in the appendix. You will note that Mr. MacAllister uses a Mark Twain story in the introduction and then returns to the punch line in his closing remarks.

Question   A good ending that will leave your audience members thinking is to ask them a question. For example, "Is this what you really want?" "How long can we let this go on?" "If you could make any change, what would it be?" You can make it a persuasive ending by asking the audience for a specific action. For example, "Please, for the sake of those you leave behind, won't you complete a living will today?" Leaving your audience members with a question, lets them complete your speech independently. For an example of a question ending, look at the sample speech in Project 19.

Challenge   Another good persuasive ending is the challenge. In this ending you call on your audience to perform some action or to fight against all foes. The challenge, then, is an appeal to the fighting spirit within the audience. One student challenged his audience members by saying, "I challenge all of you to follow me to the Red Cross bloodmobile after class to give blood to save the lives of those in need. I'll give my blood to save a life, will you?" Notice that the challenge is present, but also a question. It is a good tactic to combine techniques here as well as in the introduction. The sample speech in Project 21 shows a good example of a challenge to end a speech.

Compliment the Audience   Although it is not one of the the best methods for closing a speech, you could compliment your audience. "Thank-you" and "It was a pleasure speaking to you" are trite expressions that convey little meaning. If you can add some specific detail, you will make the compliment less trite and more useful as a closing. One speaker using this ending effectively closed by saying, "Thank you for inviting me to be your guest on this important occasion of your anniversary. I know I leave enriched by having been here. I hope my remarks have enriched you in some way also." Notice that the triteness is gone from this ending because the speaker has been specific about the occasion and made the remark personal for the audience members. She sounds genuinely interested in the audience and makes them feel closer to her.

All the preceding techniques can be used separately or in combination to make the conclusion sound final. A good technique is to combine the summary with one of the other techniques as a closing thought. Notice that the example used for the challenge also included a question. None of these examples should be considered "sacred" and used exclusively or above any other. None is inherently better than another. You need to select the ending that will best fit you, your topic and your audience.

Preparing a Conclusion

The conclusion should always be one of the most carefully prepared parts of a speech. Just *when* it should be prepared is largely a matter of opinion. Some authorities advise preparing it first because this practice enables you to point your talk toward a predetermined end. Others suggest preparing the conclusion last because this allows you to draw your final words from the full draft of your speech. Regardless of when your conclusion is prepared, all authorities agree that the conclusion must be carefully worded, carefully organized, carefully rehearsed, and, in most cases, *nearly* committed to memory.

The conclusion should be brief, generally not more than one-eighth to one-tenth of the entire speech, and perhaps less, depending on the speech, the speaker, the audience, the occasion, and the environment in which the speech is delivered. A conclusion should never bring in new material, for this creates an undesirable anticlimax and frequently irritates an audience because the speaker runs past a perfect place to stop.

Most of us have heard speakers who have not known how or when to stop speaking. At a recent convention one speaker tried three times to stop his speech, but each attempt was ill-fated and failed to end the speech successfully. Once the speaker started summarizing, but suddenly remembered that he had forgotten an important point, so he inserted, "Oh, yeah, I forgot to mention that as you start the process, . . ." and proceeded to talk another ten minutes about this point from the beginning of his speech. His second attempt to end the speech was aborted when he couldn't get back to his ending. He had tied his last point into his concluding remarks, and couldn't get there without repeating part of his last point. So, to conclude, he almost completely repeated his last point after inserting the part he had omitted. He finally concluded by saying, "I guess I've used up more than my allotted time. I hope you have found it was as useful as I did." As a member of the audience, I wanted the conclusion at least 15 minutes before the speaker got there. On the way out of the room, several audience members commented that he had wasted several good opportunities to shut up. Be sure you don't leave this feeling in your audience.

When preparing your conclusion, you will find no formula that tells which type is best for a given speech. Your own judgment and a critical evaluation of what you want your conclusion to do are the only means for selecting the particular kind you should use. However, because the conclusion is so important, weigh the advantages and adaptability of all types before making your final decision.

Presenting a Conclusion

The importance of the delivery of a conclusion can't be overemphasized. Your total organism—mind, body, and soul—must be harmoniously at work. Eye contact should be direct, gestures and actions appropriate, posture alert, and your voice sincere, distinct, and well articulated. When you move into your conclusion, it should be obvious you are closing your remarks. Your intentions should be so clear that there will be no *need* to say, "In conclusion . . ." However, this or a similar phrase will serve to alert your audience to the fact that you are about to end your speech. This phrase also brings any audience members back to reality who may have drifted off so they hear your final words.

One final caution before closing—when your speech is finished, hold the floor for a second or two. Stand, smiling and looking at your audience as if you are pleased and confident. *Then* return to your chair and seat yourself quietly. Display or frivolity of any kind after the speech may sharply alter any good impressions made while on the platform. Rushing back to your seat will indicate that you did not really wish to speak to your audience. Always leave the audience with the perception that you enjoyed speaking with them. **Never** apologize to the audience as you return to your seat. If you have done poorly, they will recognize it; if not, there is no reason for you to announce it to the audience. In short, do nothing to detract from the impression you have planned to leave with your audience.

SAMPLE CONCLUSION

By Jill Roady

Sample Conclusion

In conclusion, the three main reasons for limiting your exposure to the sun are because the sun causes skin cancer, which is always life threatening; the sun causes heat strokes, which require medical attention; and the sun causes skin disorders, which are uncomfortable and unattractive. An alternative to lying out in the sun too much is this self-tanning cream that I bought at Dillard's for $13. It looks very natural, and it is a lot cheaper than the expenses you may have to pay from lying out in the sun too much. So, in closing, I challenge each of you who like to lie out in the sun all summer to go to a department store and buy a tube of self-tanning cream. Do you really think lying out in the sun is going to make you more attractive if you don't protect yourself? Think about it.

SAMPLE OUTLINE—CONCLUSION

IV. CONCLUSION
  A. Review main points.
    1. Sun causes skin cancer.
    2. Sun causes heat strokes.
    3. Sun causes skin disorders.
  B. Closing thought: Challenge.

Project Assignment

Prepare three different conclusions, using the suggestions discussed in this project as guidelines. Be sure you summarize what you have said as well as tell your audience that you have finished your speech. If possible, use a combination of techniques to close your speech. Unless your instructor designates otherwise, use only one subject, that is, drugs, for which you prepare three different endings. Prepare three conclusions to an imagined speech on the subject.

References

Ayres, J. & Miller, J. (1990). *Effective Public Speaking* (3rd ed.). Dubuque, Iowa: Wm. C. Brown Company, Publishers.

Bradley, B. E. (1988). *Fundamentals of Speech Communication* (5th ed.). Dubuque, Iowa: Wm. C. Brown Company, Publishers.

DeVito, J. A. (1990). *The Elements of Public Speaking* (4th ed.). New York: Harper & Row, Publishers.

Gregory, H. (1990). *Public Speaking for College and Career* (2nd ed.). New York: McGraw-Hill Book Company.

Jones, J. L. (1973). Let's bring back dad: A solid value system. *Vital Speeches of the Day, 39,* 473–476.

Jordan, V. E. Jr. (1974). Under the hammer: Freedom, justice, and dignity. *Vital Speeches of the Day. 40,* 524–544.

Lucas, S. E. (1989). *The Art of Public Speaking* (3rd ed.). New York: Random House.

Nelson, P. E. & Pearson, J. C. (1990). *Confidence in Public Speaking* (4th ed.). Dubuque, Iowa: Wm. C. Brown Company, Publishers.

Osborn, M. & Osborn, S. (1988). *Public Speaking.* Boston: Houghton Mifflin Company.

Sprague, J. & Stuart, D. (1988). *The Speaker's Handbook* (2nd ed.). San Diego: Harcourt Brace Jovanovich.

Stevenson, A. E. (1978). Sir Winston Churchill. In W. A. Linkugel, R. R. Allen, & R. L. Johannesen (eds.). *Contemporary American Speeches* (pp. 273–276). Dubuque, Iowa: Kendall/Hunt Publishing Company.

Verderber, R. F. (1988). *The Challenge of Effective Speaking* (7th ed.). Belmont, California: Wadsworth Publishing Company.

UNIT II

SPEECH DELIVERY

The credit in life does not go to the critic who stands on the sidelines and points out where the strong stumble, but rather, the real credit in life goes to the man who is actually in the arena, whose face may get marred by sweat and dust, who knows great enthusiasm and great devotion and learns to spend himself in a worthy cause, who at best if he wins, knows the thrill of high achievement and if he fails, at least fails while daring greatly, so that in life his place will never be with those very cold and timid souls who know neither victory nor defeat.

Theodore Roosevelt

Project 7: Extemporaneous Delivery
Project 8: Impromptu Delivery
Project 9: Manuscript Delivery
Project 10: Using Visual Aids
Project 11: Nonverbal Presentation
Project 12: Language

Unit II consists of six projects dealing with various aspects of delivery. Do not look on the projects in Unit II as speech *forms,* but rather as *modes* of delivery and aspects of delivery. You should expect to combine the principles in the projects of this unit with the principles of other projects to make a complete project.

Project 7 deals with the principles of an extemporaneous delivery. Do *not* consider this as a speech type, but rather a mode of speech delivery. Likewise, Project 8 deals with the principles of an impromptu delivery. It is *not* a speech type. Project 9 presents the principles of manuscript delivery. Like Projects 7 and 8, this should not be understood as a speech type, but rather as a method of delivering a speech. Project 10 presents the principles of using visual aids during your delivery, and Project 11 covers the nonverbal aspects of your delivery. The final project, Project 12, deals with the principles of language that affect your delivery.

PROJECT 7

Extemporaneous Delivery

> Merit begets confidence, confidence begets enthusiasm,
> enthusiasm conquers the world.
> —Walter Cottingham

Generally, when you are called upon to speak, you will be given some time to prepare what you will say and to rehearse it well in advance. Most audiences do not want you to speak "off the cuff" because they want an organized and coherent set of ideas. In most of your speaking assignments in life you will use an extemporaneous mode of delivery. This project explains the principles of an extemporaneous delivery, how to prepare to deliver a speech extemporaneously, and how to present a speech extemporaneously.

Principles of Extemporaneous Delivery

In style, the extemporaneous delivery fits between the impromptu delivery (presented off the cuff) and the manuscript delivery (read from a carefully prepared script). It is carefully planned, prepared, and rehearsed, much as the manuscript delivery is, but does not have the exact wording or the sound of a composition as the manuscript delivery does. It is also somewhat like the impromptu delivery in that the exact wording is created as you speak and it *sounds* spontaneous—you sound as if you are just talking to your audience about your topic.

The advantages of the extemporaneous mode of delivery over the others are many. First, you have time to research and organize your thoughts. You do not present your speech without preparation nor do you speak without outlining the main and subordinating ideas in the order in which you wish to present them. One of the prime advantages to this mode of delivery is that you do have time to prepare and organize your thoughts.

A second advantage to the extemporaneous mode of delivery is that you can *sound* spontaneous without *being* spontaneous. You definitely want to sound as if you are just talking conversationally with your audience, but you don't want to rely on speaking to your audience without time to organize your thoughts into a coherent presentation. Being spontaneous would make your speech actually be what you could think of at the moment. This does not always work well for including the most important point you need to make to a specific audience.

A third advantage is using your time wisely. In the extemporaneous mode of delivery your time is largely spent in research and rehearsal, not in creating a manuscript or memorizing it. Imagine how long it takes you to create a 1500-word composition. For you to do it correctly would take four or five times longer than preparing an outline of that same material. When you speak it, a 1500-word essay will turn into approximately a ten-minute speech. Now imagine how much time it would take you to memorize that. You should see it would take much longer to prepare a speech in this manner than if you prepared the speech extemporaneously.

A fourth advantage is being yourself. As you look and speak to your audience members, you want to present to them what you are and how you feel about your topic. It is important to good speaking skills that your audience members see and hear *you* and not a façade when you speak. You should not transform your voice and self into someone else when you speak extemporaneously. Practice sounding like your conversational self when you are explaining a concept to a close friend.

Fifth, you have greater flexibility to react and respond to audience feedback when you speak extemporaneously. Because you are not reading from a script, you can maintain better eye contact with your audience members and see when they understand or do not understand you. Likewise, you have the flexibility of moving away from the speaker's stand and approaching your audience, or using visual aids more easily. You also don't have to worry about trying to organize your thoughts as you speak because you have already done that.

One distinct *disadvantage* of the extemporaneous mode of delivery is that you may have a tendency to rely more on notes than necessary. In the impromptu delivery you will rarely have time to make notes, so they do not become much of a problem. In the manuscript delivery you rely on the exact wording of the script in that you "read" from the printed page or have your script committed to memory. For the extemporaneous mode of delivery it is best if you perform with only the notes you can place on a single 3- × 5-inch index card. (You may need two cards if your speech is very lengthy or you have long quotations or many statistics to recall.) On your note card record only key words, such as those in your outline, add any statistics you may need to recall, and put all quotations you want to "read" to your audience. Performing with only these notes will make you sound more spontaneous and conversational to your audience.

Preparing for an Extemporaneous Delivery

Because of the nature of this mode of delivery, you will have time before you speak to research your topic and prepare for its delivery. Following are several suggestions for preparing to deliver a speech extemporaneously.

1. Begin your research well in advance of the day you are to speak. The longer you have, the more familiar you can become with materials with which you may be unfamiliar. Those who wait until the day before the speech so the information will be "fresh in their minds" are asking for trouble. It is more difficult to remember new ideas that are unfamiliar than the ones you have reviewed several days.

   As soon as you receive your speaking assignment, select a topic and begin searching for materials. When you feel that you have sufficient materials, prepare your outline. You may discover that the materials you found do not fit together well, or that you may need more materials. If you do all of this early enough, you will still have time to research more; if you wait until the day before the speech, you may find you do not have sufficient time to do any further research and your speech will suffer from a lack of substance.

2. Prepare the speech well in advance of the day you are to speak. Just as you would not want to wait until the last minute to research your topic, you should not wait to organize your speech either. The longer you have it organized, the longer you will have to see flaws in your organization or to detect changes you would like to make. As in

step 1, you should do this as soon as possible so that you have time to change the organization if you find flaws in it or if it does not fit your subject well. The longer you wait, the less time you have to change anything in your speech.

3. Rehearse your speech several times before you present it, getting the ideas in mind as you want to present them. DO NOT MEMORIZE THE EXACT WORDS YOU WANT TO SAY. Memorizing the exact wording will make you sound artificial or phony to your audience. When rehearsing, be sure you rehearse aloud and simulate the conditions of the actual speech. If you rehearse silently, you aren't allowing your vocal apparatus to practice, and so when you get ready to speak, you may learn that your lips and tongue, and vocal mechanism, don't move in the manner you expected. Try out the phrases on the tongue; see how they feel.

Rehearsing over a period of several days rather than in one long session has the advantage of allowing the ideas to soak in. Don't forget to time your speech as you rehearse. You should detect that each rehearsal is slightly different in time; this shouldn't bother you unless your times are significantly longer or shorter than the assigned time limits of your speech.

Presenting a Speech Extemporaneously

If you have prepared as suggested earlier, you should have the confidence to deliver an outstanding speech. Since you will have prepared a note card or two with your key words and statistics or quotations, don't forget to take your card with you. Refer to it only as you *need* to in order to refresh your memory on the ideas you wish to explain.

Once you are in front of your audience, look back at them, pause, smile, and relax. Be confident in your preparation and rehearsal to carry the speech off well. Sir Francis Drake once said, "Effective speaking is the result of a deep and abiding desire to share your ideas with your listeners." Show your audience you have a desire to communicate a message to them, and they will respond in kind. See yourself succeeding and you will succeed. The calm you display up to this point will tell your audience you are prepared to speak and are confident in your message. All of this is still in preparation to speak. You must be prepared and show your calm and confidence so that when you do begin to speak you will *feel* calm and relaxed as well as present a calm and relaxed picture to your audience.

As you begin to speak, use a clear, distinct voice and use the outline you have planned. Never make any apologies! If there is no need for an apology, your audience will find one inappropriate; if something is wrong, the audience members can figure it out for themselves if they are adept. Be sure you do not speak too rapidly for your audience. Remember, this is the first time they will have heard your message and will need time to digest your words. On the other hand, don't speak so slowly that your audience members feel that it is a drag to listen to you. A good, general rate of speech is about 150 words per minute. Use appropriate bodily actions and gestures for your topic, good grammar, articulation, and pronunciation.

In an extemporaneous delivery you should "converse" with your audience, so use language that is natural and normal for someone of your educational background and level. Be informal. Use contractions and language you use daily, don't try to force formality into your speech or you will place too much pressure on yourself and stifle your conversational style.

There is little fear from extemporaneous delivery if you follow the principles discussed in this project. Prepare well in advance of your speaking situation. Rehearse well, often, and aloud! You may experience some anxiety as the moment to speak approaches, but if you have prepared well and rehearsed well, nothing major can go wrong with your speech. If you feel the need for more help with your anxiety, refer to the section of the appendix dealing with speech anxiety.

Consider your audience members to be on your side. After all, they would much rather see you succeed than fail. See yourself succeeding! One last reminder, if you have prepared and presented your speech extemporaneously, you will always have three speeches: (1) the speech you plan to give, (2) the speech you actually give, and (3) the speech you wish you had given. Your speech will be different every time you rehearse and present it. Expect this, and when you leave out an example or a subordinate point, it will not bother you because you prepared to have a different speech each time you speak.

Project Assignment

Your instructor will assign a speech to be prepared and delivered in the extemporaneous mode. Begin your research well in advance of your speech. Research your topic as suggested in Project 4, finding at least three different types of support from four to six different sources. Prepare your outline as soon as possible so you have plenty of time to rehearse before you speak. Begin practicing your speech several days prior to the date you are to speak, trying several different wordings for ideas and putting the ideas you wish to convey into your mind. NEVER MEMORIZE YOUR WORDING. As you get close to the day to speak, prepare one or two 3- × 5-inch note cards from which you will speak. On the note cards, put only your outline, long quotations, and any statistics you wish to "read" to your audience.

References

Ayres, J. & Miller, J (1990). *Effective Public Speaking.* (3rd ed.). Dubuque, Iowa: Wm. C. Brown Company, Publishers.

Bradley, B. E. (1988). *Fundamentals of Speech Communication* (5th ed.). Dubuque, Iowa: Wm. C. Brown Company, Publishers.

DeVito, J. A. (1990). *The Elements of Public Speaking* (4th ed.). New York: Harper & Row, Publishers.

Gronbeck, B. E., Ehninger, D, & Monroe, A. H. (1988). *Principles of Speech Communication* (10th brief ed.). Glenview, Illinois: Scott, Foresman and Company.

Lucas, S. E. (1989). *The Art of Public Speaking* (3rd ed.). New York: Random House.

Nelson, P. E. & Pearson, J. C. (1990). *Confidence in Public Speaking* (4th ed.). Dubuque, Iowa: Wm. C. Brown Company, Publishers.

Osborn, M. & Osborn, S. (1988). *Public Speaking.* Boston: Houghton Mifflin Company.

Sprague, J. & Stuart, D. (1988). *The Speaker's Handbook* (2nd ed.). San Diego: Harcourt Brace Jovanovich.

Zimmerman, G. I., Owen, J. L., & Seibert, D. R. (1986). *Speech Communication: A Contemporary Introduction* (3rd ed.). St. Paul, Minnesota: West Publishing Company.

PROJECT **8**

Impromptu Delivery

It usually takes more than three weeks to prepare a good impromptu speech.
—Mark Twain

You may be called upon at any moment to "say a few words" or "report" at a meeting. If the specific assignment to speak allows you only a short time to prepare what you will say, you are presenting an impromptu speech. When you speak "off the cuff," or respond to classroom speeches and teacher questions, you are making an impromptu speech. This project explains the principles of impromptu speaking, how to prepare for an impromptu speech, and how to present a speech impromptu.

Principles of the Impromptu Delivery

Impromptu speaking means giving an unrehearsed, unprepared talk. In some classroom situations a person simply selects a subject, goes to the speaker's stand, and begins. At a meeting you may be called on to present a report on a specific topic, or you may be asked to talk on a topic you may not know much about. Other times topics may be suggested by several persons in the audience, a few seconds are given for the speaker to choose the one on which she or he feels best able to speak, then she or he begins. Differences in the manner of selecting a topic are many; however, a fundamental principle of the impromptu mode of delivery is that the ideas voiced about the topic are unprepared and unrehearsed.

The impromptu mode of speech delivery has an advantage over the others in that it takes no rehearsal time or time for researching materials. However, it does have the disadvantage of *being spontaneous;* thus, it sometimes lacks organization. If your speech sounds disorganized, it is probably because you are rambling or talking around your topic or repeating ideas needlessly. If you speak impromptu, you may also make statements that are inappropriate for your audience or situation. Never *plan* to speak impromptu. If you have an opportunity to prepare and rehearse, do so!

Most people at times must present speeches impromptu, on the spur of the moment. Most occasions on which you will be called to speak off the cuff will be those where you already know the materials or have the experience and knowledge of your topic to organize it very quickly. For instance, the boss may ask you to bring others in your work group "up-to-date" on a project you are working on, or on factors that may affect others later. Your background from your work schedule is your research.

Another situation in which you are likely to be called on to make an impromptu speech is in the classroom. Teachers are often calling on students, asking them to tell what they know about a certain topic. The research you do for this type of speech is your homework assignment from the previous day, or some other assignment. Because of your past experiences, you should be able to respond to the teacher and make a coherent response. Notice that this doesn't always call for a formal situation, nor for you to go to the front of the room to talk. This is typical of many impromptu speaking situations.

Preparing for an Impromptu Delivery

Because most impromptu talks you present before an audience will concern a subject with which you are familiar, you need only to organize information and ideas you already possess. Following are listed ten methods for developing an impromptu speech. You should become familiar with these methods so that you can select an appropriate one at an instant notice. Usually, several methods can be used to organize any specific topic. You need to select the most appropriate one or combine several methods to suit best your topic, your specific audience, and your occasion.

All the methods of organization presented here require that you state what your topic will concern in your opening remarks. Next, you will explain what your ideas are and support your ideas with examples, opinions, facts, statistics, and so on. In most instances you will want to summarize your speech before you finish. The following methods deal with the organization of the body of your speech; you must still present an introduction to set up your speech for the audience, and arrive at an ending to conclude your speech gracefully. Keep your topic general.

METHOD #1

(You may begin every impromptu speech with steps 1 and 2 of this method.)

Talk about: 1. The importance of the topic to yourself
2. The importance of the topic to your audience
3. Summarize

METHOD #2

(For a subject that may be discussed on a pro-and-con basis. Example: alcohol, narcotics, taxes, education, etc.)

Talk about: 1. Advantages
2. Disadvantages
3. Summarize

METHOD #3

(For single-word subjects like houses, animals, war, government, jobs, cars, or for the topics mentioned in method #2.)

Talk about: 1. What is wrong with the subject?
2. How can we correct what is wrong?
3. Summarize

METHOD #4

(Many subjects may be restated as problems. Example: If your topic is juvenile delinquency, restate it as a question. For example: What are the causes and effects of juvenile delinquency? Also, see method #9.)

Talk about: 1. The cause(s) of the problem
2. The effect(s) of the problem*
3. Summarize

METHOD #5

(Space or geographical arrangement. Many topics can be discussed under one or more of the suggested orders in this plan. Examples: customs, climate, governments, people, sports, buildings, objects, etc. Or topics listed in preceding methods.)

Talk about: 1. East to west—or
2. North to south—or
3. Top to bottom—or
4. Inside to outside—or
5. Left to right—or
6. Any other spatial arrangement
7. Summarize

METHOD #6

(Chronological or time-sequence arrangement. Trace the order in which something happened. Examples: storms, floods, civilization, attitudes, weddings, invention, books, etc., or topics listed in preceding methods.)

Talk about: 1. The first thing that happened
2. Second thing
3. Third
4. Fourth
5. And so on
6. Summarize

METHOD #7

(Historical approach can be adapted to most subjects. See previous topics.)

Talk about: 1. Past. Give the history or several key events of the past
2. Present. Tell what is happening today
3. Future. Project your ideas into the future
4. Summarize

METHOD #8

(Logical order—may be applied to any subject involving a problem. Example: What should be done about highway accidents? Juvenile delinquency?)

Talk about: 1. Importance of the topic (tell why it is significant)
2. State a problem or problems
3. Discuss a solution or solutions (tell what each will do)
4. Discuss the actions needed to put the solutions into effect
5. Summarize

*Note that you can also reverse this order and talk about effect(s) of a problem first and then talk about the cause(s) of the problem.

METHOD #9

(Point-of-view order. This may be adapted to fit most topics or it may be an adjunct to the previous methods shown. Examples: juvenile delinquency, rats, morals, movies, horses, etc.)

Talk about:
1. Importance to self and audience
2. Point of view of (a):
   a. Doctor
   b. Teacher
   c. Lawyer
   d. Minister
   e. Farmer
   f. Wife
   g. Child
   h. Banker
   i. Carpenter
   j. Etc.
3. Summarize

METHOD #10

(An effective combination method is to . . .)

Talk about:
1. The importance of the topic to your audience and, yourself
2. The history and development of the topic
3. Present conditions pro and con on a local, state, national, or world basis
4. The future developments on the topic
5. What can the audience do regarding the topic?
6. Summarize

Presenting a Speech Impromptu

When you present a speech impromptu, your attitude is the most deciding factor in determining your effectiveness. First, maintain your poise. It is impossible to overemphasize the importance of poise. How do you maintain your poise? Do not fidget in your seat before speaking because you know that you will soon be "on the spot." When called on, rise calmly and take your place before the audience. If you know your topic when you take the platform, begin your remarks calmly, without hurrying, but still have some vigor and force. Also, be sure that you have a plan in mind to develop your thoughts. If you do not know your topic when you rise but are offered several choices after obtaining the floor, stand calmly before your audience and listen carefully to the suggestions. Ask that a topic be repeated or explained if you do not understand it. After you have heard all the proposed subjects, stand calmly, or walk calmly back and forth a few seconds while you decide which one you will talk about. Once your selection is made, decide immediately what method to use in developing it. As your introduction, tell why the subject is important. When you begin to speak, do not make any apology whatsoever. Get on with your speech.

In actually delivering a talk impromptu, you should not start too fast, but rather pick up speed and power as you go along. Aside from this, observe bodily actions and gestures in keeping with the speech situation. Naturally, your articulation, pronunciation, and grammar should be of high standard.

There is little to fear from impromptu speaking if you follow a preconceived method of attack on your subject. Do not allow yourself to become panicky; remember that some nervousness is a good sign of readiness; and realize that your audience will expect nothing extraordinary from you because they too know you are speaking impromptu. Actually, they will be "pulling for you." If you go about your task with poise and determination, your chances of success are exceedingly good. A well-rounded knowledge attained from a consistent reading program will assist you immeasurably.

Project Assignment

In the following space, write three suggested topics for use as impromptu subjects. Avoid such topics as: "What did you do last night?" "A trip to Yellowstone Park." Your instructor may ask you to supply a topic from time to time during the class. Suitable topics for impromptu speaking include: sports, animals, ecology, television, strikes, liquor laws, divorce, narcotics, medicine, college athletics, current events, local politics, and rights. Whenever a new topic comes to mind, add it to your list so that you will always have an up-to-date list of good topics for impromptu speaking.

1. _____
2. _____
3. _____
4. _____
5. _____
6. _____
7. _____
8. _____
9. _____
10. _____

References

Ayres, J & Miller, J. (1990). *Effective Public Speaking* (3rd ed.). Dubuque, Iowa: Wm. C. Brown Company, Publishers.

Bradley, B. E. (1988). *Fundamentals of Speech Communication* (5th ed.). Dubuque, Iowa: Wm. C. Brown Company, Publishers.

Devito, J. A. (1990). *The Elements of Public Speaking* (4th ed.). New York: Harper & Row, Publishers.

Gronbeck, B. E., Ehninger, D., & Monroe, A. H. (1988). *Principles of Speech Communication* (10th brief ed.). Glenview, Illinois: Scott, Foresman and Company.

Lucas, S. E. (1989). *The Art of Public Speaking* (3rd ed.). New York: Random House.

Nelson, P. E. & Pearson, J. C. (1990). *Confidence in Public Speaking* (4th ed.). Dubuque, Iowa: Wm. C. Brown Company, Publishers.

Osborn, M. & Osborn, S. (1988). *Public Speaking.* Boston: Houghton Mifflin Company.

Sprague, J. & Stuart, D. (1988). *The Speaker's Handbook* (2nd ed.). San Diego: Harcourt Brace Jovanovich.

Zimmerman, G. I., Owen, J. L., & Seibert, D. R. (1986) *Speech Communication: A Contemporary Introduction* (3rd ed.) St. Paul, Minnesota: West Publishing Company.

PROJECT *9*

Manuscript Delivery

Being natural beats any performing skill.
—John Updike

On occasion, a speaking situation may be so formal that it demands a formal presentation. Formal presentations usually call for you to write a manuscript and read from the manuscript or present the manuscript from memory. Reading aloud is an art that becomes extremely useful under certain circumstances and at times is demanded. Likewise, a memorized delivery demands skills that are not common to the other methods of speech delivery. This project explains the principles of manuscript delivery, how to prepare a manuscript, the principles of speech composition, how to prepare a written speech, and how to present a manuscript speech.

Principles of Manuscript Delivery

One of the most compelling reasons for preparing a speech manuscript is to have the precise wording that you want. You might need to do this if it is important for you to be quoted accurately. Speakers in this category are high government officials and other individuals who dare not risk others misunderstanding them or misquoting them. Practically all radio and television speeches are presented in manuscript form because of very rigid time limits, station requirements, and the need in some cases for a copy of the script for filing and future reference.

For the same and other reasons, if you are to present a commencement address or a eulogy, you may well prepare a manuscript speech. The formality of these situations and your desire to make precisely the right message for the occasion are other reasons for preparing speech manuscripts. In a eulogy, the emotion of the moment may keep you from speaking well without a script. At a commencement the press may want to have a script to quote from in preparing copy for the paper concerning your remarks.

For most people, however, there are few instances when you should *create* a speech manuscript or *read a speech manuscript.* It is generally not necessary, or required, and usually is not expected of speakers in most speaking situations. If you are inexperienced in public speaking, you may find writing and delivering a manuscript speech more than you are willing, or have time to do. As a rule, do not read your speech except for those special occasions that demand you to be accountable for your every word. The formality of the occasion will dictate when you need to prepare a manuscript.

Because wording is extremely important in a manuscript speech, take the time necessary to create the precise wording or phrasing that says exactly what you mean. Ambiguous wording in this type of speech could cause a serious problem for a diplomat or a politician. Not only is your wording important, but also such other concepts as your style, content, and organization. Sometimes others may tear your speech apart word-by-word if they can get a copy of your manuscript. If you recall, most of our presidential addresses are dissected almost immediately following the speech. This is partially because the press and media have copies of the script before the president even speaks and are able to pick it apart for all kinds of flaws.

Preparing a Manuscript

When you find it necessary to write a speech manuscript, there are several points to consider. First, in preparing your speech, write it so that it sounds as though you were speaking extemporaneously with your audience. Make the speech sound conversational but at the same time observe all the attributes of effective word usage. It is best to type your manuscript double-spaced, using large type and underlining special words. You may even write notes to yourself in the margins.

Second, select your words carefully. Since you have the opportunity of selecting several words for what you mean, be sure the ones you use create the precise meaning you intend. Make frequent use of your thesaurus. Also, make sure you don't create a composition that is to be read. This is still a *speech* you need to compose. Always think of this as an oral presentation. An oral presentation is not the same as a composition. One of the reasons President Reagan was successful as a speaker was that his speeches were written as speeches, not as compositions he just happened to read aloud.

Third, recognize that it takes a great deal of time to write out a speech word for word. You need to begin your speech preparation long before your delivery so you have time to work through the organization, the phrasing, and the selection of words for your speech. Your manuscript should differ from an extemporaneous speech in that you work through the ideas more thoroughly and use more supporting ideas and a more distinct introduction and conclusion. It differs from a composition in that it uses shorter, simpler sentences, less formal language, and more frequent use of personal pronouns.

Begin the process of preparing your manuscript the same way you would begin an extemporaneous speech. That is, start by outlining the ideas you want and the order in which you intend to put these points. Next, start working on the phrasing of the major ideas. Remember to think in terms of your oral presentation, not your composition skills. A good method is to think in terms of "speaking out the speech" rather than "writing it out." As you are preparing your script, think and say the words you would use to tell your best friend. Write down these words, and look at the content later. In fact, you may want to turn on a tape recorder and just talk into it for a while before preparing your script. After you have prepared the major ideas, then start working on your support for the major ideas and the examples that will support what you have said. In this method you are working on small segments of the speech at a time, not trying to work out large segments at a time.

As you prepare your script, think of writing and rewriting. Your rough draft should sound "rough" because you have not polished it yet. Your first draft should never be your last draft. Once you think you have the manuscript completed, read through it aloud as if you were speaking it to your audience. Any parts that don't sound quite right, you should try ad-libbing. Once you find the ideas that sound best for you, replace parts of your script with what you have worked out. Once you replace a segment of the speech, make sure you go back through the entire section to make certain that it fits with what comes before and after it. As a final check on the manuscript, have someone else who is familiar with your topic read your manuscript and evaluate it for you. An unbiased outside observer can always provide you with some possible new insights into your content and style.

Speech Composition

In preparing a manuscript, you will want to follow the principles of "good" speech composition. Following are six suggestions for writing a good speech.

1. Know specifically what *response* you want your audience to give. Your speech, if successful, will get this response.
2. After gathering all needed material and analyzing your audience, *decide what organization you will use*—chronological, spatial, causal, problem-solution, topical, or some other recognizable speech organizational pattern.
3. Use good grammar with sentences averaging between 15 and 25 words in *wording (writing) your speech.* It is best if you use a variety of short, medium, and long sentences rather than all long, medium, or short sentences. Your statements do not have to be complete sentences every time, but they do have to be understandable and correctly put together. Emphasize verbs and concrete nouns while keeping adjectives, adverbs, and prepositional phrases to a minimum.
4. *Keep your words clear (understandable), simple, specific, and accurate.* Do this by using words denoting color, shape, size, direction, and action—all words known by your audience. Your words should average about one and a half syllables per word. Avoid general terms such as wonderful, beautiful, and pretty. Instead, use terms that draw pictures in the minds of your listeners so they will react by saying whatever you describe is "wonderful" or "pretty"—but you don't say it because your audience members will not know what "wonderful" means until you have created such an image in their minds.
5. Use the fewest words possible to make your point. This is known as *economy of words.* If you can, say it with 40 words not 100, then your listeners need not work so hard to decode your meaning. Your listeners will also be more likely to understand your specific meaning if you use economy of words.
6. *Make your speech move ahead toward the conclusion* by careful arrangement of ideas. Present a major idea and explain it with only enough supporting materials to let the audience understand, then move to your next major idea. Usually, two to five main points are sufficient. Place your most important major point first or last; first position may be better in some speeches and last in others, depending on your topic and your audience. Tie your ideas together with "transitions" and "connectives" (when necessary for clarity) by using phrases or sentences to indicate what you have said and/or what you are going to say next, so you advance smoothly from point to point.

How do you know how many major points to use, or when to use transitions and connectives? Only a thorough gathering of materials and *your own judgment* can tell you. The speech will be your creation and will reflect your mind. There is always the possibility you will misjudge your audience, but the preceding suggestions will help reduce mistakes to a minimum. A general rule you might be well advised to follow is, "You are better off developing few points and making them clear than glossing over a large number of points."

You will write a more interesting speech if you select a topic that permits you to include ideas, experiences, and feelings concerning yourself. These should be blended with researched materials to gain your desired response; however, try not to make your manuscript sound like just another research paper. It will also be better if the material reflects something "universal" in interest because many people are concerned with the topic. A speech to stimulate, convince, or get action will likely be more effective as a manuscript speech than a speech of demonstration where your expertise in performing the actions called for is more important. However, many types of speeches, done with discretion and care, can be made interesting and presented effectively as manuscript speeches.

Writing a Manuscript

Whatever you write, *keep it in good taste.*
This speech will be written and presented from manuscript or memory. You have been told to determine your purpose, analyze your audience, gather your material, organize, and write your speech.

1. When gathering materials, you should take notes concerning anything you may use and record each source completely so you are able to list a bibliography.
2. Having done this, you should make a complete outline of the main points and supporting ideas *for the body of your speech only.* This will give you a foundation to build on.
3. Next, you should develop a detailed complete sentence outline showing practically every idea in your speech including your introduction and conclusion; then you will be ready to write word for word because your speech will be organized and your topic limited.
4. You should prepare your introduction and conclusion last. You may collect ideas or make notes for them, but the actual preparation will take place after you complete the body of the speech, so get started preparing the body as early as you can.
5. You should use the following stylistic devices.
   a. Simile: "She was *like* a rose." Simile is a form of comparison generally using "like" or "as" to express a resemblance.
   b. Metaphor: "She *was* a rose." Metaphor is a term or phrase applied to something to which it is not literally applicable or true in order to suggest a resemblance.
   c. Personification: "*Roses smiled* at the morning sun." Personification means an object, not human, behaves like a human. (Roses do not smile; smiling is a human characteristic.)
   d. Specific or concrete words: "The *snarling* dog *foamed* at the mouth while his *bloodshot* eyes *glared* at the man *like a demented tiger.*" Specific or concrete words name, or describe accurately, or show specific or definite action. They may be verbs, adverbs, nouns, or adjectives, but they must be specific, enabling your listener to receive a sensory image of what you say.
   e. You may include additional devices such as direct question, rhetorical question, direct quotation, alliteration, epigram, synecdoche, analogy, antithesis, apostrophe, repetition, restatement, nuance words, allusion, suspense, climax, rhythm, and illustration, if you are familiar with the concepts and how to create a better message with them. These are more advanced techniques and should not be attempted by inexperienced speech writers.
6. Probably you should complete a first draft without delay and then *revise, revise, revise.* Revise, until you have what you want and have met all requirements of style and language. Your completed speech should read with the flavor of your normal speaking vocabulary, not the vocabulary of a stilted academic research paper.
7. You may have to rehearse 15 to 20 times before you master your manuscript well enough to meet audience eye contact requirements—80 to 90 percent of your presentation time.
8. You should avoid the following language choices that are common mistakes when writing your script.
   a. Avoid "catch-all" expressions like "and things like that," "and so forth."
   b. Avoid flowery language that cannot be understood by your audience, or that makes you sound artificial and pretentious.
   c. Avoid trite expressions and figures of speech that do little or nothing to communicate to your audience. Some common trite expressions include: "the pure and simple truth," "other things being equal," "in the twinkling of an eye," "sure as you're born," "over my dead body," and "read my lips." You may have noted some prominent people who have used these expressions rather successfully; however, you should avoid them since they add no content to your speech, and you may be suspect for not having any ideas to bring forth yourself.

d. Avoid slang expressions because they are rarely appropriate for formal speaking situations. Some common examples include: "freak out," "blow his mind," "far out," "it's a gas," "up tight," "turn on," "bummer," and "awesome."

e. Use nouns of general meaning sparingly. Words such as "circumstances," "cases," "instances," "aspects," "factors," "relationships," "attitudes," "etc.," add very little communicative value to any message. Under most circumstances, at least in most cases, the instances in which you use these aspects as factors in a relationship will yield negative attitudes toward you, etc. Notice what "etc." means. It means, I don't have any other ideas, but I feel like I should add something else here.

Presenting a Manuscript Speech

If you find it necessary to present a manuscript speech, there are several points to recall. First, a manuscript speech can be read to the audience or committed to memory and presented word for word from the manuscript. Some textbooks divide the methods of delivery so that the memorized delivery is distinct from the manuscript delivery. The only real distinction between the two is that one is read and the other memorized and recited without the aid of the manuscript. For our purposes here, we consider manuscript to be the generic form of delivery and memorized or read to be the style of presentation. The advantage of memorization is that you don't have to rely on the manuscript and be tied to the pages; however, if your memory fails, you may well forget the entire speech.

Second, you must rehearse your speech thoroughly. If you read your speech, you must be able to look at your audience most of the time. This requires much practice, and in the final analysis it demands that the manuscript be semimemorized. If you present the script memorized, you must spend sufficient time to have the speech totally committed to memory. Rehearsing before a mirror is an excellent way of gaining this proficiency. Nothing short of many hours of going over and over your speech will work, unless you have a photographic memory and can see the speech in your mind.

Third, know your material so well you will not mispronounce or stumble over any words or phrases. At the same time you must avoid developing vocal patterns or stereotyped habits that make you sound artificial. Some speakers depart momentarily from their scripts during reading, thus heightening the extempore effect; but this requires skill and practice and is not recommended for beginners. Always begin your speech without looking at your script. Imagine how you would feel if a speaker began reading, "I'm glad to be here to speak today. I have been awaiting this opportunity for a long time." If you have to read this, can you really mean it?

Fourth, handle your manuscript skillfully. If you plan to use a lectern or speaker's stand, practice with one. Also, practice turning the pages, holding your script, and all the other movements you intend to perform during your presentation. Acting awkward, shuffling your pages, losing your place, turning pages clumsily, holding your script too close or too far away, peering at words, or dropping pages can kill your delivery.

Finally, *observe the preceding points* in conjunction with all other elements of effective public speaking. This includes desirable posture; effective facial, head, arm, and torso gestures; proper use of the voice; and a sincere desire to produce a specific response. Observing these criteria will add to your effectiveness when speaking from a manuscript.

If you intend to speak from memory, here are a few suggestions for trying to memorize your script. Begin by memorizing your key ideas. Don't try to memorize your key ideas word for word, but know your major points in the speech so you can go on to the next point if you get lost during your speech. The main ideas serve as the framework for your speech and the skeleton on which you later attach the flesh.

Once you have the major points learned, then start working on your subpoints. Work through your main points one point at a time, starting with the supports for the first major point. Then learn the examples you intend to use with each subpoint. Once you have learned the subpoints and supports for your first major point, move on to the second point and learn its subpoints and examples. After you have the body of the speech memorized, you should work on the introduction and conclusion. The latter two aspects of the speech will be easier to learn once the rest of the speech has been committed to memory.

Spread your work out over several days. Do not plan to sit down and memorize a complete speech in a few hours. If you do, you may be able to recall it for a short time, but your long-term memory will not have sufficient time to operate completely. Over the period of time in which you are memorizing your manuscript, go over sections of your speech every time you get a few minutes. You don't have to cover the entire speech every time you work on it to be committing ideas to memory.

The advantage to memorizing in this method is that you are learning through your organization rather than word for word. This will help you sound more conversational and should help you recover if your memory fails you at any point in the speech.

Once you have finished your memorizing, you should work on polishing your delivery. This includes planning some specific pauses, maybe changing your volume, pitch, or quality in specific places in the speech. Be cautious about this also. You don't want to look and sound mechanical, so any of these planned actions should *seem* natural and appropriate to the context of your message.

While you are delivering your memorized manuscript speech, it is permissible for you to ad-lib comments as they come to mind or as you react to your situation. Most audience members will not even know if you jump around in your organization if you don't draw attention to it, or unless you sound too scripted. If you sound scripted and then ad-lib a comment, you are likely to sound conversational during the ad-lib, but not during the rest of your speech. This is one of the reasons you want to rehearse so you can sound as if you are carrying on a conversation with your audience throughout the speech.

Project Assignment

Your instructor may assign for you a specific speaking assignment to be delivered in the manuscript mode. As you prepare, write out an outline as if you were preparing an extemporaneous speech. From the outline, prepare your manuscript. As you rehearse, deliver your speech first from your outline and record it. Listen to the recording and compare it with your manuscript. Then as you continue to rehearse, try to sound as if you were speaking extemporaneously. Work until you can sound conversational.

Alternate Project Assignment

Prepare a typewritten, error-free speech following the guidelines here. You will present it word for word from the manuscript while looking at your audience 80 to 90 percent of the time.

Topic: Speaker's choice with instructor's approval
Length: 800–1000 words (six to eight minutes approximately).
Requirements: On the title page list these items.

1. Title of speech (make it interesting)
2. Speaker's name
3. Name and number of this speech class
4. Exact number of words in this speech (count them)
5. Classification of speech: to stimulate, convince, get action, inform, entertain, and so on
6. Type of introduction
7. Type of conclusion
8. Organizational pattern
9. Specific purpose of your speech
10. Bibliography—three or more sources correctly listed

Your instructor may provide a list of other specific limitations and requirements to be included in the assignment.

References

Ayres, J. & Miller, J. (1990). *Effective Public Speaking* (3rd ed.). Dubuque, Iowa: Wm. C. Brown Company, Publishers.

Bradley, B. E. (1988). *Fundamentals of Speech Communication* (5th ed.). Dubuque, Iowa: Wm. C. Brown Company, Publishers.

DeVito, J. A. (1990). *The Elements of Public Speaking* (4th ed.). New York: Harper & Row, Publishers.

Gronbeck, B. E., Ehninger, D., & Monroe, A. H. (1988). *Principles of Speech Communication* (10th brief ed.). Glenview, Illinois: Scott, Foresman and Company.

Lucas, S. E. (1989). *The Art of Public Speaking* (3rd ed.). New York: Random House.

Nelson, P. E. & Pearson, J. C. (1990). *Confidence in Public Speaking* (4th ed.). Dubuque, Iowa: Wm. C. Brown Company, Publishers.

Osborn, M. & Osborn, S. (1988). *Public Speaking.* Boston: Houghton Mifflin Company.

Sprague, J. & Stuart, D. (1988). *The Speaker's Handbook* (2nd ed.). San Diego: Harcourt Brace Jovanovich.

Zimmerman, G. I., Owen, J. L. & Seibert, D. R. (1986). *Speech Communication: A Contemporary Introduction* (3rd ed.). St. Paul, Minnesota: West Publishing Company.

PROJECT **10**

Using Visual Aids

When skillfully combined, pictures, words, and sounds
have the power to evoke emotions, change attitudes, and
motivate actions.
—Jerrold E. Kemp

What's the advantage of using a visual aid? After all, visual aids require a great deal of time and effort to make, they cost money for the materials, and the risk involved is significant. It is simply much easier to give a speech without having to trouble yourself with anything except the speech itself. On the other hand, visual aids can add excitement to any type of speech by enhancing clarity, increasing impact, motivating emotions, and improving persuasiveness. They are especially useful in informing an audience or in demonstrating a process to an audience. This project explains why you should use visual aids, discusses some of the types of visual aids you can use, provides some tips on the construction of visual aids, and explains how to use visual aids.

Principles of Using Visual Aids

The visual aid is a unique form of speech amplification.   A visual aid gives the speech it accompanies a new dimension. Not only can the audience members hear your message, but they can also see it. Visual aids allow you to activate a second sensory receptor in the audience. While we can't *prove* that a picture is worth a thousand words, there is evidence to support the contention that adding the visual dimension to the auditory dimension will increase its effectiveness. For example, Linkugel and Berg (1970) report that:

> when knowledge was imparted to a person by telling alone, the recall three hours later was 70 percent, and three days later, only 10 percent. When imparted by showing alone, the knowledge recall three hours later was 72 percent, and three days later, about 35 percent. A marked improvement. But does this mean that we should stop speaking and just show pictures? Obviously not. When both telling and showing were the teaching tools . . . the recall three hours later was about

85 percent, and three days later, 65 percent. This should emphasize that recall increases markedly by using both speech and pictures.

Other researchers confirm that we learn more from viewing something than by listening alone. Combining both visual and auditory messages may promote clarity and add interest to a speech. A visual aid often saves time also.

Some topics can't be explained well without the use of visual aids. For example, salespeople who wish to sell a product would find it difficult to explain a complicated process or how well a particular machine worked without also giving the "audience" a demonstration. Imagine, for example, a used car salesperson telling you that he or she had a "real beauty" on the back lot that would be perfect for you, but that you couldn't see it until you had bought it. Would you buy the car? Probably not. Remember, the burden on the speaker is to create a clear, concise, and yet precise message. Thus, in some cases, the "show-and-tell" technique may be the best. There are some concepts words alone cannot describe.

Visual aids tend to increase the attention span of audience members. Think back to the last long speech you heard. If the speaker did not use visual aids, how long was your attention span? Would it have increased if the speaker had chosen to break the tedium of listening with a new and different form of material? In general, the more abstract the speech topic, the more a concrete visual aid will help to maintain attention.

The use of visual aids often facilitates a favorable response from an audience. In addition to the intended message of the speaker, the audience members often make references to and recall the messages of the visual aids. For example, audience members often comment about such aspects as the time and effort that went into the materials used to enhance a speech. Such comments may be about the creative nature of the aids or the usefulness to the audience in helping to understand the concepts. This could well help to enhance your credibility with your audience. Other comments concern the speaker's thoughtfulness for the audience because she or he did more than just speak about the topic, or the degree of commitment a speaker may have for a topic. Visual aids support a speaker's ideas by making him or her more believable.

In some instances visual aids may also help increase the audience's ability to retain the speaker's material. If you remember the visual aid, you will probably remember what the speaker said for a longer period of time. For example, Zayas-Baya (1977–1978) reports that we are likely to remember only 10 percent of what we read, 20 percent of what we hear, but 50 percent of what we see and hear. Furthermore, we retain only 10 percent of what we hear but 65 percent of what we see and hear after three days.

We are part of an increasingly visual culture. There is almost no one now who is not a member of the television generation. Most of us either grew up with television or have become a part of the television age and expect that whenever we receive a verbal message it will be complemented with a visual message. We often tune out those speakers who do not provide us with the visual support we desire. The receiver-centered public speaker should recognize the reality of our visual culture and adapt to it. The visual dimension of a speech presentation may be the key factor in achieving your communication goals.

Types of Visual Aids

There are a number of classes of visual aids. Actually, anything that appeals to the visual sense of your audience members can be considered a visual aid. The purpose of this section is to explain more fully the most common types of visual aids. Do not consider this an exhaustive list of visual aid types.

The human body can be used as a visual aid. Often we forget about using people as visual aids because we do not perceive people are similar to objects we may use. A speaker can use his or her own body by using gestures, movements, or attire. The bodies of ourselves or others can also be used, especially in demonstration speeches, as parts of visual aids. For example, instead of just telling your audience members how to swing a golf club, you can show them how to do it. Likewise, you could show them how to use self-defense maneuvers with another person rather than just tell about it and how it is done.

One problem in doing these activities yourself may be that you will run out of breath if the exercise is strenuous. This may affect your delivery. However, if your expertise is of importance to your audience members, the sacrifice may be worth the lessened delivery. For example, several years ago gymnast Jim Hartung wanted to demonstrate some of the fundamentals of gymnastics. His ability to perform the moves for the class was more important than the fact that he couldn't speak and demonstrate simultaneously. After he completed each gymnastic exercise, he explained the concept, and why it was used as a part of the overall routine in the sport.

Objects can be visual aids.   Objects are very good visual aids because they can eliminate distortions the audience may have regarding size, shape, color, or other physical characteristics. A problem with using objects is that they can be too large or too small to be practical as in the case of an airplane or a ship or a small ceramic object. In other cases the object (e.g., nuclear reactor) is not available for presentation. Nevertheless, you will find that when objects are available and appropriate, they can attract attention and clarify a complicated explanation.

Using good objects can show your audience such features as size, shape, color, dimensions, and texture. Bad examples of objects will only serve to confuse your audience members. One student brought a small object to show during one of his speeches. The object could easily be seen in the front of the room, but beyond about two rows, it was not clear. Audience members could discern its size, shape, and color, but the real feature the speaker intended people to see was not visible from a distance. At the conclusion of his speech several students wanted to know more about his visual aid. It became obvious to Jim at that moment that his visual aid had been a hindrance, not an aid. People had not wanted to discuss his ideas, they wanted to figure out what he had brought with him as a visual aid.

Replicas make good visual aids.   Often the real thing (object) is not available, as in the case of the nuclear reactor, but you can use a replica of the real thing and accomplish the same results. In addition, many models have cutaway views or are made of glass or plastic so we can see the functioning of the object as well as what it looks like. Good examples of these are the plastic models of our body parts used as aids in explaining medical functions and replicas of automobile engines to explain the workings of an internal combustion engine. In using models, remember some are very expensive to purchase or rent, and many times they are not available to borrow. They are, however, the only way of explaining and demonstrating some processes, like the functioning of the human heart.

The chalkboard is another popular visual aid.   We sometimes forget that the chalkboard can be used because we see it so often. The chalkboard is one of the most readily accessible visual aids available to students because there is usually one in every classroom. You can readily adapt your writing or drawing to the size of your audience, and the ease of erasure allows for quick alterations to show variations. Using the chalkboard can also cause a problem. Because of its ready access, the chalkboard has been overused and abused. Too often students do not plan better visual aids since they know they have a chalkboard to use. Be cautious that you do not use the chalkboard as a substitute for a better visual aid because you are too lazy to get or create another one. The availability of a chalkboard also tempts unplanned or the spur of the moment use. Haphazard use of a chalkboard is less effective than using no visual aid at all.

Pictures and diagrams also make good visual aids.   Most audience members like to look at pictures. Photographs, paintings, and drawings can often improve your presentation. And, like the chalkboard, they can also be overused, misused, and abused. They could substitute for thought of (or lack of) anything else. This often happens in the classroom when a teacher says you have to use a visual aid during a speech. If your speech is about the workings of the rotary engine and a model is not available, the tendency is to resort to the chalkboard or the use of drawings. The problem with this is that too often the picture or drawing is used instead of taking time to find a model. A better use of pictures would be in conjunction with a speech on the nature of abstract art, or an art technique like shading, sketching, water colors, contrasting, or pictures of an event that could be captured no other way.

Charts and graphs can help to depict statistical and conceptual relationships.   The pie, line, and bar graphs are common charts we use to summarize bulky statistical information in a relatively easy to understand form. The real purpose of the chart or graph is to compress a great deal of information and to show it in a usable and easily interpretable form. To make charts and graphs most understandable, be sure your graphs are used accurately. Pie graphs (see Figure 10-1) show relationships, such as types of garbage in the United States. A good use of such a pie graph would be showing the percent of each type of garbage. Line graphs (see Figure 10-2) show trends, such as the changes in the U.S. population from 1800 to the year 2000. Bar graphs (see Figure 10-3) depict comparisons, like the amount of money spent for military expenditures by several countries at a specific period in history. In addition, charts can be used to demonstrate organizational patterns. For example, they could show the chain of command in an organization (Figure 10-4), the steps in a process (Figure 10-5), or the relationships of objects (Figure 10-6). Again, charts and graphs should not substitute for your lack of anything to say or your lack of anything else; they should *add to* the verbal content of your speech. An example of the misuse or poor use of a chart would be using the main points in your speech as your visual aid on a chart. This is a poor use of a visual aid because there are more important aspects of your topic you can emphasize in most cases. This type of visual aid usually does not "add to" your verbal content and is not much of an "aid" to your audience.

America's Garbage

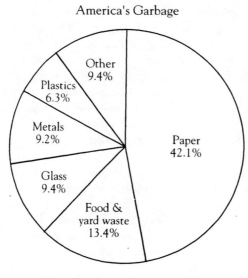

Figure   10-1

Millions of people

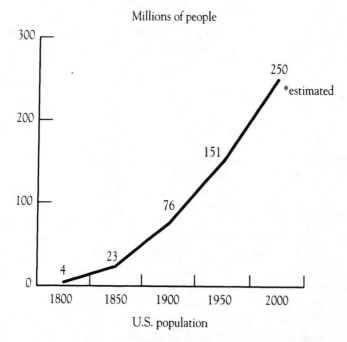

U.S. population

Figure   10-2

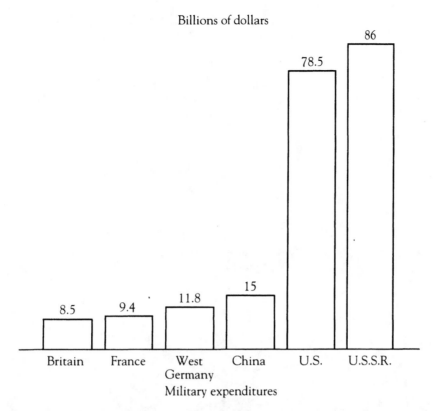

Figure   **10-3**

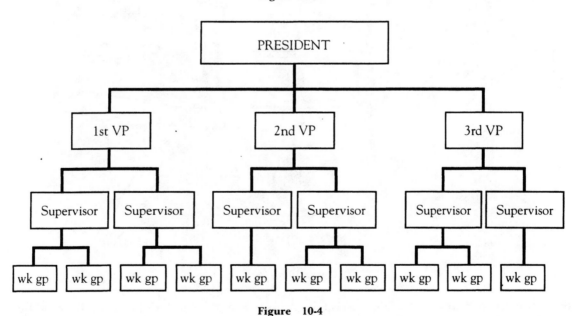

Figure   **10-4**

Maps.   A visual aid very closely allied to charts and graphs is the map. Maps can show dimensions, distances, key elements of a territory, as well as geographical relationships. A properly prepared map should show only what you need to make your explanation. When existent maps are used, they often do not emphasize what you want to show your audience, or show too much. Most road maps are also too small for your audience to see from any distance. Speech topics on weather, travel, transportation, or other geographically oriented topics would make suitable use of a map as a visual aid. (See Figure 10-6.)

Handouts.   Sometimes you will have other materials to "hand out" to your audience. Handouts can range from materials you have copied for the audience to examples or samples

Dewey's Reflective Thinking Process

Step 1: Problem Phase

      A. Identification of problem
      B. Analysis of problem
      C. Analysis of causes

Step 2: Criteria Phase

      A. Principle requirements
      B. Limitations
      C. Importance

Step 3: Solution Phase

      A. Possible solutions
      B. Evaluation of solutions

Step 4: Implementation Phase

Figure   10-5

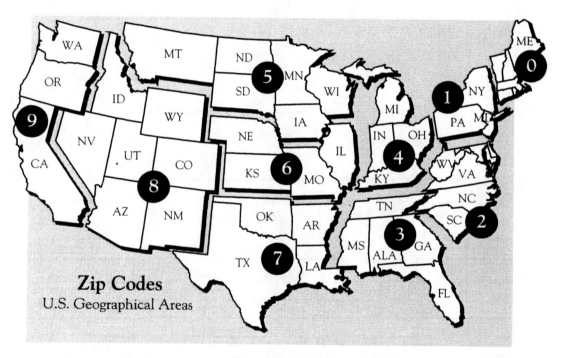

Figure   10-6

of a product you wish your audience to retain. A good use of a handout in a speech would be copies of a living will you would explain or organ donor cards you wish members of the audience to sign. A poor use of a handout would be a copy of your outline or a list of the main points in your speech. Likewise, anything else that either detracts from your speech or does not enhance your topic would be a poor use of a handout.

Electronic media.   Another good visual aid is to use electronic media. Electronic media include slides, filmstrips, videotapes, audiotapes, opaque projectors, and overhead projectors. Although these are all common today, they are probably the most difficult of all visual aids to use well. One of the main factors affecting the use of electronic media is that they can take the emphasis from you and concentrate it on the media object because most require a darkroom to be effective. Electronic media are often misused by beginning speakers who substitute them for verbal messages, much as is done with the chalkboard. In other words, instead of speaking, the beginner may show a film, or some slides, and let the slides tell the message. Only experienced speakers should use electronic devices since something can go wrong (and probably will) at the worst possible moment. When it does, the experienced speaker has a knowledge of what she or he can do, but the inexperienced speaker is at a loss. For most of us the use of electronic media requires either a period of training or a great deal of practice. Electronic media are good aids to know how to use, but don't use them at the expense of your audience, especially in the public speaking situation.

The Construction of Visual Aids

The use of visual aids can help your speech evoke greater interest and understanding, but inadequate preparation or poorly prepared visual aids waste your audience's time, and can bore, exasperate, and even anger an audience if too inappropriate. We offer the following suggestions on the construction of visual aids so you can make your visual aids appropriate for your audience.

Probably the best advice to the beginning speaker is to prepare visual aids well in advance of the speaking situation so they will best enhance your speech. Last minute attempts to find the right pictures, charts, or graphs will frustrate not only you, but may also frustrate your audience members who must suffer through your hastily prepared visuals. An audience can usually sense a lack of careful preparation, so *prepare well in advance.*

It is equally important that you make your visual aid and all of its components *relevant* to your speech. Occasionally, inexperienced speakers fail to get appropriate visual aids and end up throwing in last minute substitutes that are not relevant to the topic. Irrelevant visual aids make you look as if you have thrown in some material as an afterthought simply because the materials were available, not because they pertain to your speech. It is very difficult to "fool" your audience.

When you prepare your visual aids, remember to make your visual aids simple and clear. If you need to make a lengthy explanation about the purpose of your visual aid, it has not been useful for *you* or your *audience.* Audience members should be able to see immediately what you intend. If it is not simple and clear, it is no longer an "aid," but rather a burden you cannot afford as a speaker. It is better to have a series of simple visuals rather than have one complicated visual aid.

Make your visual aids neat and artistic. If they are not, your audience members may well transfer the impression of sloppiness (and possibly other negative attitudes) to you as the presenter of such poor materials. The verbal and nonverbal elements of a message are inseparable and interrelated, so make sure your verbal message is not "messed up" by a sloppy nonverbal visual aid.

The rules for constructing visual aids are very few and simple:

1. *Make your visual aid large enough.* Make your visual aid twice as large as you think it should be. You are much closer to it than your audience members, and to be effective, they must be able to see clearly what you intend. If everyone in your audience can't clearly see your visual aid, you will have wasted your time and efforts. A good rule when making charts is to use a full 24- × 36-inch poster board. Always check the size of your visual aid by standing as far away from it as will be the farthest audience member. If you can see it well, then your audience members should be able to see it also. A good rule is to make your lettering about two inches high. This is generally readable from the back of most classrooms.

2. *Use heavy, dark lines.* Drawing your letters or figures in large-sized print does no good if they are not seen because they are too faint. Again, the rule of thumb is to make your lines twice as heavy (thick) as you think they need to be. If you use colors, be sure to use dark colors. Yellow and other pastel colors can be used to distinguish between features and also to separate important points, but they are of limited use in most charts.

3. *Print, don't write.* Audiences sometimes have difficulty with our handwriting, so the best policy is to print and avoid any confusion. As in the two previous rules, your audience will not consider your visual aid effective if they cannot easily read your

charts. Don't put an unnecessary burden on your audience by writing on charts in a cursive style that may be difficult to read.

4. *Use cardboard or very heavy paper.*   As noted in rule 1, the best advice is to use the standard 24- × 36-inch poster board. Lightweight paper will not stay on an easel or board very well, and is quite easy to see through, which might also cause confusion for your audience. A second alternative is to use the standard 24- × 36-inch art pad and to make sure each page can't be seen through. Using a felt marker will sometimes cause your writing to bleed through to the pages below. If you use a felt marker on art paper, be certain you have an absorbent paper below so it does not bleed onto several sheets and ruin them.

Using Visual Aids

Before using any type of visual aid in a presentation, practice its use. This is a step that is often overlooked. What happens is the speaker practices what to say but only thinks about what to do with the visual aids. Often, the speaker is surprised by some unexpected event, and the use of the visual aid does not come off as it was rehearsed in the mind. To prevent being surprised, practice using your visual aids before you actually have to use them. This should include such small but important tasks as checking to see whether an easel will be available or whether you will have to use the chalkboard; whether there are clips on the chalkboard or if you will need to use tape; whether the poster board will stand by itself or will need holding. You should also practice moving your visual aids if that will be a part of your presentation. In short, rehearse every detail so you know what to expect. In most cases you will detect and be able to correct any problems before they occur.

Since your visual aids can be very powerful speech amplification tools, you should take care to use them to your advantage. The following guidelines should enable you to get the most out of your visual aids.

Don't overdo the use of visual aids.   You may decide that if one visual aid is good, two must be twice as good, and so on. Somewhere there is a point of diminishing returns. Visual aids are a form of *emphasis,* not a form of speaking, so use them to emphasize your verbal message and avoid using them when there is nothing to emphasize. To emphasize everything is to emphasize nothing.

Show your visual aids so everyone in the audience can see them.   Having the most beautiful and imaginative visual aids does not help if everyone in your audience can't see them. Visual aids can be best seen when they are above waist level and slightly in front of you. Be careful you don't inadvertently stand in front of your visual aids. This is easy to do if you place them on an easel or chalkboard. Stand to one side and point with your hand nearest the visual aid. Be sure to allow time for your audience to see whatever it is that you are trying to point out. It is also important that you show only one visual aid at a time. Showing more will only confuse your audience members and divide their attention.

Show your visual aids only when you are talking about them.   If you show your visual aids constantly, people will have a tendency to look at them and not listen to your verbal message. Likewise, you should look at a visual aid only when you make reference to it. Otherwise you will draw undue attention to your visual aid and away from your speech. It is especially important for you to talk to your audience and not to your visual aid. Not only will looking at your audience enhance your delivery, but it will also provide you with feedback from your audience about your visual aid and your speech.

Talk about your visual aids while you are showing them.   Sometimes inexperienced speakers feel that their visual aids are so good that they don't have to say anything about them. If your visual aids are merely put up for your audience to see, no one will know what to look for, and most audience members will miss a large part of your speech trying to find their importance. Point out what your audience members are to see and explain why they are looking at them. In addition, use your visual aids to coincide with the content of your speech. This way, your audience can follow your speech and let your visual aids add to the content of your speech.

Don't pass objects around your audience.   Remember, the point of public speaking is to have everyone focusing attention on the same point at the same time. Having your audience members pass objects around invites chaos. First, everyone is not focusing attention on the same point at the same time, but they also lose many of the points you are making while they are focusing on the object. More often than not, when you pass out materials while you are speaking, you lose control of your audience—lessening your chances of achieving your purpose. Think of the hazards (possible disasters) you may encounter before you decide to pass objects around your audience.

In summary, visual aids can serve a number of important purposes for both you and your audience. However, you must plan their construction and use wisely. The effective speaker knows his or her visual aids well and handles them smoothly, confidently, and with poise. As a result, she or he becomes a more efficient speaker and the audience more efficient listeners.

The decision to use visual aids is an important one. If the decision is yours to make, be sure your visual aids will somehow enhance your speech. That is, they must help clarify, amplify, or improve the comprehension of your speech content by your audience. If, in the classroom situation, you are required to use visual aids, take the same precaution. Do not haphazardly select something to use simply because it fills a requirement. If you feel there is no visual aid available to use, you probably have not thought through your material carefully enough. There is a possible visual aid for nearly every speaking situation.

Next, select an appropriate type of visual aid. Select a visual aid that will be effective (according to your analysis of your audience and material) and that you will feel comfortable using. If you do not feel poised and comfortable with your visual aid, you may need more practice, or you may need to make a change in the visual aid you use. Make yourself comfortable and you will look and feel poised and self-confident.

Finally, practice using your visual aids so you know they can be seen and can enhance your speech, and you can make all necessary movements. In short, **be prepared**. The use of visual aids is not a complicated or risky business if you know what to do and how to do it. Take the time to select and prepare proper visual aids and then practice using them until they are as perfect as your verbal message, and you can count on success.

Project Assignment

Your instructor may assign a specific speech in which one of the requirements is to use a visual aid. Follow the suggestions of this project in preparing and presenting your visual aids. Unless specifically told *not* to prepare and use a visual aid, you should use one any time it will enhance your presentation. Thus, you may use a visual aid every time you speak. Be certain to use visual aids advantageously.

References

Bradley, B. E. (1988). *Fundamentals of Speech Communication* (5th ed.). Dubuque, Iowa: Wm C. Brown Company, Publishers.

Gronbeck, B. E. (1983). *The Articulate Person* (2nd ed.). Glenview, Illinois: Scott, Foresman and Company.

Linkugel, W. & Berg, D. (1970). *A Time to Speak.* Belmont, California: Wadsworth Publishing Company.

Logue, C. M., Freshley, D. L., Gruner, C. R., & Huseman, R. C. (1979). *Speaking: Back to Fundamentals* (2nd ed.). Boston: Allyn & Bacon, Inc.

Lucas, S. E. (1989). *The Art of Public Speaking* (3rd ed.). New York: Random House.

McCabe, B. P., Jr. & Bender, C. C. (1981). *Speaking Is a Practical Matter* (4th ed.). Boston: Allyn & Bacon, Inc.

Nelson, P. E., & Pearson, J. C. (1990). *Confidence in Public Speaking* (4th ed.). Dubuque, Iowa: Wm C. Brown Company, Publishers.

Osborn, M. & Osborn, S. (1988). *Public Speaking.* Boston: Houghton Mifflin Company.

Samovar, L. A. & Mills, J. (1989). *Oral Communication* (7th ed.). Dubuque, Iowa: Wm C. Brown Company, Publishers.

Sprague, J. & Stuart, D. (1988). *The Speaker's Handbook* (2nd ed.). San Diego: Harcourt Brace Jovanovich.

Verderber, R. F. (1982). *The Challenge of Effective Speaking* (5th ed.). Belmont, California: Wadsworth Publishing Company.

Walter, O. M., & Scott, R. L. (1984). *Thinking and Speaking* (5th ed.). New York: Macmillan Publishing Company.

White, E. E. (1984). *Basic Public Speaking.* New York: Macmillan Publishing Company.

Zayas-Baya, E. P. (1977–1978). Instructional media in the total language picture. *International Journal of Instructional Media, 5,* 145–150.

Zimmerman, G. I. (1979). *Public Speaking Today.* St. Paul, Minnesota: West Publishing Company.

PROJECT 11
Nonverbal Presentation

The face is the mirror of the mind, and the eyes, without
speaking, confess the secrets of the heart.
—St. Jerome

Speaking is a total bodily activity. To be really effective, you have to control both your verbal message and your nonverbal presentation. Your feet and legs, your arms and hands, your trunk, your head, your eyes, your eyebrows—every part of your body is a part of your speech. Many beginning speakers do not realize this, although they use total bodily expression all of the time in their normal conversations. Yet they may stand rigidly before an audience when speaking. They move only their vocal cords, their soft palates, tongues, and jaws. Actually, they are only half communicating because they are using only half of their communicating tools. To put all of their speaking power into action, they should include bodily action and gestures. This project is included because it provides an experience which demands that you use bodily actions and gestures and thus improves your speeches through kinesics. Included in this project are explanations of the principles of the nonverbal presentation and the elements of the nonverbal presentation such as personal appearance, physical behavior, and vocal behavior.

Principles of the Nonverbal Presentation

The nonverbal code is one of the two primary codes you can use in communicating any message to an audience. In many instances the message you send with your body language is louder than the message you send with your words. Your unspoken dialogue is a part of every communication you make from a simple "hello" to a passing stranger to the gestures and movements you make during a formal speech presentation. Audiences will look at both and assess what you say and how you say it to determine exactly what you mean.

All of your nonverbal communications affect the way you respond to your audience members and how they respond to you. As you prepare and practice your speech delivery, become aware of your nonverbal messages so they become consistent with your verbal messages. You can also learn a great deal about other speakers by observing their nonverbal communication. Some of their movements and gestures will likely tell you much more about how they feel than their words will.

All nonverbal communication must be understood and interpreted within a context. As an audience member, you must interpret nonverbal cues along with the verbal cues of the speaker to make complete sense of a speaker's message. As a speaker, you will want to work at making your verbal and nonverbal messages complement each other so you send a single, easy-to-understand message to your audience. The setting or situation in which you speak will influence and affect how you present your speech as well as how others interpret what you say both verbally and nonverbally. Your task is to make the messages you send fit the framework of the situation so your audience does not misunderstand what you intend.

Elements of the Nonverbal Presentation

Different authors include varying numbers of elements of the nonverbal code. Burgoon et al. (1989), for example, include kinesics, physical appearance, vocalics, haptics, proxemics, environment, artifacts, and chronemics as the "codes" of nonverbal communication. Some of these elements are even subdivided to include specific areas. For instance, kinesic behaviors are often labeled as emblems, illustrators, affect displays, regulators, and adaptors. All of this can be very intimidating and confusing, to say the least. Some of these terms and some of the nonverbal concepts are more important to public speakers than to others. To avoid confusion, and in order to simplify some of this overwhelming language, we will cover only the most basic aspects of your nonverbal presentation.

In this project, we address only the areas of the nonverbal code that most directly affect public speaking. These areas include: personal appearance, physical behavior and vocal behavior.

PERSONAL APPEARANCE

Do people judge you by the way you appear? Of course they do! Imagine what you would think of someone who appeared before you to make a formal presentation in clothing with holes in the sleeves, knees, or elsewhere. Unless the person were appealing to you for help to buy new clothing or food (or demonstrating a need for helping others), you would probably think the speaker had bad taste and you would likely have little respect for his or her message. The way you appear before your audience is very important to the total message you present. In fact, your audience will see you and begin judging the way you look before they hear a word of your speech.

The clothing you wear should either be neutral or compliment your verbal message. Neutral clothing in a classroom would be clean, untorn clothing that you generally wear to class. In other situations it may include a dress or a suit and tie. Some classes in business and professional speaking demand that students dress according to the dictates of the "corporate world." The key to the clothing you wear is that it be appropriate for the situation in which you are speaking.

You can also wear clothing that compliments your speech. For example, a person making a speech on karate could enhance his or her presentation by wearing a Gi, the official uniform for people who practice karate. Other examples of clothing that compliments a speech are: an ROTC candidate wearing a military uniform while talking about the educational benefits you can get from the military; a nurse in uniform speaking about first aid; a mechanic in uniform speaking about engine repairs or common maintenance practices for the average consumer; a volunteer fireman in uniform, speaking about the benefits of a volunteer fire unit. These are only a few of the possible "uniforms" that could enhance the credibility of a speaker, and thus aid your total presentation.

PHYSICAL BEHAVIOR

Physical behaviors include all the movements of your body as it changes during a speech. This includes such behaviors as posture, movements like walking, gestures, and facial expressions, as well as eye contact. All these behaviors are important to you as a speaker because they are indicators of the total meaning of your speech.

Posture   An important aspect of your nonverbal presentation is your posture. If you stand too rigidly, you will appear stiff and scared of your audience. If you slump or drape yourself over the speaker's stand or lectern, you will appear sloppy and uninterested in your audience. To act interested in your audience and topic, you need to stand up straight with your weight equally distributed on both feet. As you speak, avoid shifting your weight from one hip to the other or crossing and uncrossing your legs. Assuming an erect, but not stiff posture throughout your speech will help you maintain an attitude of alertness and interest in your topic and your audience. It will also avoid giving your audience the appearance of laziness.

Movement   A second factor of physical behavior is movement, or what you do with your entire body during your speech. Movement is characterized by such actions as walking, gesturing, and expressing yourself facially.

If you intend to walk or move about during your speech, you need to make certain that your movements are consistent with the motivations in your speech and do not represent nervous actions. Moving may help your audience keep alert and conscious of your verbal message. On the other hand, standing behind a lectern or speaker's stand may stifle your movements considerably and cause you to appear somewhat stiff and rigid. On some occasions, however, you may be held to the lectern because of the situation or the need to use a stationary microphone. Be cautious in your attempt to use movement in your speech that you don't plan patterned movements. Patterned or planned movements usually look artificial and detract more than they add to a speech.

Gestures can add or detract from your speech, depending on how you use them. Gestures usually refer to the use of your arms and hands as you speak to your audience. Gestures probably cause more problems for beginning speakers than any other movements because there is always a question of what to do with those "things" dangling at the ends of your arms. To be effective, gestures need to be definite and performed in full view of your audience, with enthusiasm. Half-hearted attempts to gesture or gestures partially hidden from your audience are ineffective. The same is true of gestures that are not performed enthusiastically. Enthusiasm, more than any other factor, shows how you feel about your topic and how interested you are in helping your audience better understand your topic.

Beginning speakers sometimes feel awkward or uneasy standing in front of an audience. Standing with your arms pressed to your sides, your hands dangling at the ends, is sure to make you feel uncomfortable. How many times do you stand around talking to other people with your arms pressed to your sides? Probably never. In casual conversations you gesture naturally to emphasize points and help your listeners understand the exact meaning of your words. The same principle applies to public speaking. Get involved with your message and concentrate on communicating your message precisely to your listeners. If you do this, you will begin to use gestures that communicate with your audience, feel natural, and add to your verbal message.

Some common gestures you might want to begin with include those that enumerate (first, second, third, etc.) or emphasize the importance of your point. Another common gesture that works well for beginning speakers is size. You can sometimes show audience members how big or small an object is, or how high or low it is. You should avoid pointing at members of your audience, but a common gesture to show audience members that they are included is to use the open palm up and sweep it from one side of the audience to the other. You use many other similar types of gestures in conversations; practice using them also in your public speaking situations. If you still have difficulty using gestures, read one of the sample speeches in the appendix and imagine what the speaker might be doing with his or her hands—then try doing it yourself.

Facial Expressions   A third important element of movement is facial expressions. Researchers have determined that the face expresses 55 percent of the impact of a message (Mehrabian, 1968; Birdwhistell, 1970). For example, it is difficult (if not impossible) for you to smile and make hateful statements or frown and present a pleasant message. The reason is that your verbal and nonverbal messages are so inconsistent with each other that you have difficulty sending the two conflicting messages. If you don't believe it, try this. Try to look bored and disinterested while attempting to listen attentively to someone speak. You will find it difficult to maintain interest. You can also try the opposite, attempting to show interest in a speaker's points and tune the speaker out. This is very hard to do, if not impossible. In your speeches you need to display your interest and enthusiasm for your topic so you can also excite your audience about your topic.

Eye Contact   A fourth element of physical behavior is eye contact. We separate it here from other aspects of movement because of its extreme importance. Beebe (1974) indicates that good eye contact improves your credibility with your audience. The amount of eye contact you have also reveals how you feel about yourself, your audience, and your topic. Little eye contact indicates that you are unsure of yourself. It also makes you appear distant and untrustworthy to your audience, as well as uninterested in your topic.

Maintaining eye contact does not mean a general scanning of your audience, or facing the audience but looking over their heads. Good eye contact means distributing your eye movements equally to all areas of your audience. In addition, pick out individuals in your audience and address specific comments to them. In this manner you will feel as if you are speaking on a one-to-one basis with the members of your audience and each of them will feel that you are speaking to them. Be cautious that you don't concentrate too much on those listeners you see supporting your message with smiles and nods. It is important to recognize this feedback from your audience, but don't let it control your eye contact. Search out other listeners and attempt to get them to attend to your message also. Ideally, you will hope to establish eye contact with every member of your audience during your speech and maintain eye contact with your audience 80 to 90 percent of the time. Practice will make you feel comfortable with this feeling.

VOCAL BEHAVIOR

Another area of your nonverbal presentation is your vocal behavior. There are several aspects of vocal behavior that need clarification if you are to be effective in delivering your speech so it is easily understood by your audience members. To create more meaningful messages, you need to concentrate on the ideas and feelings you wish to communicate and vary your voice so your audience gets the precise meanings you intend. We look more closely at three aspects of vocal behavior in this section: articulation, pronunciation, and vocal characteristics.

Articulation   Articulation is the forming of sounds in speech. Most errors in articulation fall into three broad categories: addition, omission, and substitution. *Addition* is the adding of sounds to words that are not in the words. For example, many people say "ath-a-lete" for the word "athlete" or "idear" for the word "idea." *Omission* is omitting sounds that should be in the words. For example, many people say "libary" instead of "library," "binness" instead of "business," or "guvmint" instead of "government". *Substitution* is substituting one sound for another. Many of us get lazy and say "git" for "get" or "jist" for "just" and sometimes "wader" for "waiter" or "pitcher" for "picture." Most of these common errors can be corrected by listening more closely to how you speak and making certain you know which sounds are included in the words you use in your speech. If you know you are guilty of articulation errors, use some of the drills in the appendix to help you improve.

Another common problem of articulation is the running of sounds together. Most native speakers of any language will have a natural tendency to run sounds together somewhat. It really becomes a problem when the rate of your speech is such that your audience members can't understand you. For example, look at this conversation between two lazy articulators:

A. Jeet yet?
B. No, ju?

A. Wanna gota John's Place?
B. No, le's gota Cap'n Jack's

Did you understand them? This is what they said:

A. Did you eat yet?
B. No, did you?
A. Do you want to go to John's Place?
B. No, let's go to Captain Jack's

The problem with poor articulation is it may distort the meaning you intend or cause members of your audience to misunderstand what you mean. In some instances you may earn a reputation from your audience as "uneducated" or a "hick." In your attempt to articulate clearly, be cautious that you don't overarticulate because that will make you sound artificial.

Pronunciation   Whereas articulation is the forming of sounds correctly, pronunciation is the ordering of stresses and sounds correctly. "Correct" pronunciation is that accepted by educated people of the region in which you live. Notice that even though most people in the United States speak English, people in different regions of the country accept different pronunciations as "correct." For example, in the New York area it is common to hear an "r" added to words such as "idea" and "draw" so that they become "idear" and "drawr" even by educated people. The same is true for people in the South who speak with a drawl. If you understand these pronunciations, they aren't much of a problem. However, you could be embarrassed with an educated audience that recognizes your errors.

Putting your emphasis on the wrong syllable is also a problem of pronunciation. For example, some people pronounce "thé-a-ter" as "thee-ATÉ-ur." Also, in the South it is not uncommon to hear the word "in-suŕ-ance" pronounced as "in-shurnce" and the word "po-licé" pronounced as "pó lice." Most of us have also added the silent letters in words like "often" and "Illinois." While these pronunciations may not cause your audience to misunderstand you, it may distract from the total message you intend. In addition, errors in pronunciation noticed by your audience could cause your audience members to lower your credibility. In fact, you may even be perceived as uneducated by some people. Always check your pronunciations so you can be certain you pronounce words accurately.

The real problem of mispronunciation is that it affects the way in which your audience members react to you. Second, they may grant you less credibility because of your error; thus, they may not believe or accept what you say. Third, researchers (Mulac and Rudd, 1977) have determined that people who use the "general American" dialect are perceived as more intelligent than people who use an accent, even by those who speak a dialect.

The term "enunciation" is sometimes used to refer to both pronunciation and articulation errors. If someone indicates that you don't enunciate clearly, check to see if your problems are those of articulation, pronunciation, or both so you can correct the problem precisely.

Vocal Characteristics   There are several aspects of the voice that affect speech delivery and may influence the meaning your listeners get from your words. The vocal characteristics over which you have control are: *volume, pitch, rate,* and *pauses.* We will look at each of these separately to see how you can control them to your best advantage.

Volume refers to the relative loudness of your voice. As beginning speakers, you need to remember that you usually speak with people who are within a five-foot radius of you. When you speak before an audience, you have some people sitting much farther away from you. Obviously, if everyone can't hear you, you can't communicate your message to them. Speak loudly enough to be heard by everyone, but not so loudly that you "blast" the people close to you. Also, use variety in your volume. If you get a bit louder on points you wish to stress, your audience members will hear your stress and understand that you feel more strongly about that point.

Pitch is the relative highness or lowness of your voice on the musical scale. People have a general pitch range where they usually speak. When they get up to speak, beginning speakers sometimes limit their general pitch range. Your audience members need to hear your pitch differences so they can understand the distinctions between such common expressions as the "oh" you mean when something surprises you and the "oh" you mean when you are disappointed. Although there are few people who make *no* pitch changes when they speak (referred to as monotone), there are many uninteresting speakers who don't use the full range of their capabilities to express fully what they mean. Remember, variety in your pitch range can also make listening to you more pleasant.

Rate is the relative speed of delivery. There is no "best" rate of delivery you need to concern yourself with, except as it affects your audience. History has recorded excellent speakers who spoke fewer than 100 words per minute (Daniel Webster) as well as some who have spoken as many as 200 words per minute (Dr. Ralph Nichols). A medium rate of 150 words per minute is good because it doesn't sound drawn out and artificially slow, nor is it too rushed. A rapid rate might also make you sound as if you were nervous.

The most important aspect of rate is to adjust to your audience and situation. If your audience members do not know your voice patterns, you should slow down until they adjust; if your topic is new, difficult, or complex, you should also slow down. At the same time, speaking too slowly on simple material may make your audience members begin to think about other things. As in the other aspects of the voice, variety is always a plus.

Pauses are those conscious breaks in your stream of words. Pauses can be used to indicate changes in topics or major points, allow your audience members time to think about an important point or question, and give your speech a sense of timing. Audience members will soon tire of a continuous flow of words, thoughts, and ideas. They will also notice if you fill your breaks with "vocalized pauses" ("um," "er," "uh," and other sounds). Other verbal base-touchers you need to omit include phrases such as, "you know," "you see," "see what I mean," and "OK?" These terms have no content message and do little more than fill speech time. Such fillers often indicate lack of fluency or unpreparedness on your part. Pauses need to be planned so they give a sense of timing to your comments and variety to your flow of words.

Two pauses are especially important to your total presentation—the one before you begin to speak and the one after you finish speaking. Use the pause before you begin to gather your thoughts and to smile at your audience to show your friendliness and warmth toward your audience members. It also displays a sense of self-confidence to your audience. Use the pause at the end of your speech to emphasize your final words and to say, "I've enjoyed speaking with you." It also shows a sense of self-confidence to your audience members by indicating that you don't have to run off and hide from them.

Project Assignment

Create a manuscript for one of your speeches. In the margins of the script indicate the nonverbal cues you plan to use to enhance your speech. Also, note words that may provide you with difficulties in pronunciation or articulation. Mark the script for changes in vocal characteristics. Finally, note any specific language techniques you plan to use in the speech. This assignment may be combined with another project.

Alternate Project Assignment 1

Attend a public speech. As you listen to the speaker, assess the nonverbal communication of the speaker. How does it help enhance or detract from the verbal message? Make the same observations concerning the speaker's vocal behavior. You may make two separate observations and observe one set of behaviors for the first speaker and the other set of behaviors for the second speaker.

Alternative Project Assignment 2

In the appendix there are some exercises designed to help you work on problems of articulation and expression. Select one exercise a day to work on a specific problem you have. Your instructor may select exercises for the entire class to practice with or for specific problems you have with your delivery.

References

Beebe, A. A. (1974). Eye contact: A nonverbal determinant of speaker credibility. *Speech Teacher, 23,* 21–25.

Birdwhistell, R. L. (1970). *Kinesics and Context.* Philadelphia: University of Pennsylvania Press.

Burgoon, J. K., Buller, D. B., & Woodall, W. G. (1989). *Nonverbal Communication: The Unspoken Dialogue.* New York: Harper & Row, Publishers.

Crannell, K. C. (1987). *Voice and Articulation.* Belmont, California: Wadsworth Publishing Company.

DeVito, J. A. (1990). *The Elements of Public Speaking* (4th ed.). New York: Harper & Row, Publishers.

Glenn, E. C., Glenn, P. J., & Forman, S. H. (1984). *Your Voice and Articulation.* New York: Macmillan Publishing Company.

Lucas, S. E. (1989). *The Art of Public Speaking* (3rd ed.). New York: Random House.

Mehrabian, A. (1968). Communication without words. *Psychology Today, 11,* 53.

Mehrabian, A. (1971). Significance of posture and position in the communication of attitude and status relationships. *Psychological Bulletin, 71,* 359–372.

Mehrabian, A. (1971). *Silent Messages.* Belmont, California: Wadsworth Publishing Company.

Modisett, N. F. & Luter, J. G. (1988). *Speaking Clearly* (3rd ed.). Edina, Minnesota: Burgess Publishing.

Mulac, A. & Rudd, M. J. (1977). Effects of selected American regional dialects upon regional audience members. *Communication Monographs, 44,* 185–195.

Nelson, P. E. & Pearson, J. C. (1990). *Confidence in Public Speaking* (4th ed.). Dubuque, Iowa: Wm. C. Brown Company, Publishers.

Osborn, M. & Osborn, S. (1988). *Public Speaking.* Boston: Houghton Mifflin Company.

Sprague, J. & Stuart, D. (1988). *The Speaker's Handbook* (2nd ed.). San Diego: Harcourt Brace Jovanovich.

Verderber, R. F. & Verderber, K. S. (1989). *Interact* (5th ed.). Belmont, California: Wadsworth Publishing Company.

White, E. E. (1984). *Basic Public Speaking.* New York: Macmillan Publishing Company.

PROJECT 12

Language

Eloquence is the power to translate a truth into language perfectly intelligible to the person to whom you speak.
—Ralph Waldo Emerson

Language is your way of reaching the rest of the world. The words you use create ideas in the minds of other people. If the ideas you have in your mind get to the minds of others in the same form, you have communicated; if the ideas are not the same, you have miscommunicated. If you are to communicate with other people, you must select your words carefully so they convey meanings precisely and accurately. Unfortunately, words don't always mean the same thing to different people. Our language is a set of arbitrary symbols that have developed over a period of time, and mean, more or less, different things to different people at different times. This project presents the principles of language, the nature of language, and the elements of language.

The Principles of Language

The effectiveness of a speech sometimes depends a great deal on your choice of language or the words you use. As a speaker you want the words you use to have the precise meaning for others that they have for you. If you think one thing while your audience members think another, and you assume they understand you, you are not communicating with your audience. Miscommunicating with your audience will likely cause you to make a strategic error in judgment. Errors of this nature often cause irreparable damage to your credibility. One student in a fundamentals class several years ago made one of those blunders and was never able to recover and regain the respect of his classmates. This student spoke throughout his speech about using drugs, but never clarified to his audience members that he was speaking about "prescription drugs." Many of his classmates thought he was a "drug addict" and some even suspected he might try to sell them illegal drugs. One student wrote on the teacher evaluations at the end of the semester that the teacher should never have allowed a criminal such as this student to remain in class as he might be hazardous to the entire class and definitely had nothing beneficial to add to the class.

Because we all see the world differently, we tend to describe it and our relationship to it differently. What we see, or choose not to see, affects how we see the world. Of course, this tints our sense of reality a little, and also affects the words we select to use or not use in describing that reality. Our limits of reality also affect our vocabulary to the extent we do not have words to describe some events in our world. If we don't have the words for an event or feeling, we can't express that feeling or describe that event to others, thus limiting our ability to communicate to others our sense of reality.

Imagine, for example, that computers were not a part of your reality. How could you explain to someone else what a computer was? For those who know what a computer is, how limited is your vocabulary? Do you know the meanings of "floppy," "hard disk," "DOS"? If you are a computer programmer, do the words "infinity," "loop," and "toolbox" have different meanings depending on whether or not you are programming?

Words are the tools of a speaker's trade, and few people work with more slippery tools. If a tool is used improperly, or an incorrect one is used, the end product could result in a mess rather than a useful product. One of the main problems of language is that it changes. What was true yesterday, may not be true today. Our world changes much faster than does our language, so we may not always be in touch with the world because we do not have the words to express the changes we have encountered. In the next section of the project we will look at the nature of language, including connotative and denotative meanings and the differences between oral style and written style in language. The final section of the project deals with the elements of language such as clarity, vividness, and appropriateness so you can better select the right word for the right purpose.

The Nature of Language

Language is a set of symbols we arbitrarily use for assigning meaning to the events in our lives. Somewhere, sometime, someone decided we should call those furry creatures we have running around our houses going "meow" "cats." They could well have been called anything else. In fact, if we agreed today to call cats "glips" from now on, we could communicate. When my nephew was about two years old, he didn't say "thank-you." Instead, he said "gami." At first, I didn't understand his language and what he meant, but after his parents told me what he meant by gami, and I had experimented a few times, he and I could communicate very well. Misunderstandings occur not only in cases such as this, but also when we have more than one meaning for a word. The key to using language well is to ensure that you and your audience members are using the same meanings for the words you use.

CONNOTATION AND DENOTATION

Words have two kinds of meaning—connotative and denotative. The denotative meaning of a word is its dictionary meaning. This is a simple matter of looking a word up and applying this literal meaning to the word. Unfortunately, some words in the English language have more than one denotative meaning. As a speaker, you need to find the word that carries the exact meaning you intend. The problem here is that even though you may have the exact dictionary meaning you want, your audience members may not fully understand you because they are using a different dictionary meaning.

Look at the word "hot," for example. If you look in the small intercollegiate dictionary, you are likely to find at least ten different meanings. Think about it. How many ways do you use hot? One meaning is to have a high temperature; another is to have a fiery temper; it also means raging as in a hot battle. What about freshly made, as in hot off the press, or lucky as in hot dice. Maybe you also use hot to mean stolen, as in a hot car. But a hot car could also be one that is fast, couldn't it? What about good looking? Could that apply to a car also? You see, most of these dictionary meanings are easily understood by all of you. But if someone just said that a particular car was "hot" wouldn't you want clarification about which meaning the person was using?

Connotative meanings are more individual and evaluative than are denotative meanings. Connotative meanings suggest the way you feel about a subject. You have positive and negative feelings and when you tie your feelings to these words you are attaching connotative meanings. For example, denotatively a dog is a four-legged domesticated animal, related in ancestry to the wolf. Connotatively, the meaning of dog depends on how you feel about them—a dog may be a friend, a pet, a nuisance, a mangy, flea-ridden brute, or something else, depending on how you feel about dogs, based in part on your past experiences with dogs.

Connotative meanings are very emotional meanings. Gum is a word that brings up many different feelings for different people. Having been a teacher for many years, I have grown to dislike gum on several grounds. My feelings of disgust for gum started much earlier than my teaching career. I used to sit in front of a gum chewer in grade school. Johnny would chew his gum very loudly while I was trying to read, and I found that very distracting since he liked to smack his lips and blow bubbles every once in a while. He also had a disgusting habit of sticking his gum everywhere when he finished chewing it. I sometimes found it on my papers, books, and even in my hair. As a teacher, I was told to enforce the school's "no gum chewing" policy. I detested being a "gum policeman" for every student who wanted to chew gum. I also disliked the gum being stuck to the bottom of the desks in my classroom. As you can see, my experiences have clouded my perception of gum to the point that I don't like it and would find it difficult to see many advantages for continuing the sale of the product.

In selecting the wording for your speeches, think about both the denotative and connotative meanings of the words you select. Your object is to communicate denotatively and connotatively with your audience. You want your audience members to feel the same as you do, or at least to understand what you mean by the words you use. As Donald C. Bryant, a noted speech scholar, has said, "Meanings are in people, not in words."

ORAL LANGUAGE

Oral language is not written language. Sometimes you hear people say, "just write it as you would say it." Don't believe it. Sometimes we talk in single words, phrases, and incomplete sentences. If you were to write like this, you would probably be severely chastised for not knowing how to write properly. Oral language is characterized by the immediacy of your thoughts and expressions. You create oral language as you think the thoughts. Written language is consciously composed after careful thought before it is presented. In fact, sometimes you write, rewrite, and rewrite again before you finish a written composition, but you must make your speech presentation clear the first time. One of the major differences between oral language and written language is that readers have the opportunity to go back and read the passage as many times as they need in order to understand the writer. Listeners must get the message on the first run in most instances.

Oral language is more direct and personal than is written language. This is due in part to the fact that speakers prepare for and speak to specific audiences, whereas writers often prepare for general audiences of readers. Generally, oral language is characterized by shorter words, fewer different words, and more familiar words. We also tend to qualify ourselves more in oral language, or attempt to, than we do in written language and use more personal pronouns. In addition, we use shorter sentences to express ourselves; use more common language, such as contractions and slang; and we add guide words such as *first, next, then,* and so on to help point the way through our speeches.

As we speak, we tend to get more personal than in writing as we add our own personal stories and experiences to our speeches. Oral language is also characterized by more specific and concrete examples than is written language. Written language often relies more on abstract terms and impersonal expressions such as *one, they, a person, she,* or *he.* As we speak, we sometimes say things like, "it seems to me," "what I heard," and "apparently," to suggest that we are not all-knowing. In speech, we also use more repetition than we do in written language. Repetition is a key to helping your audience remember what you have said, but this is not necessary in written communication because you can read and reread as many times as necessary to remember the message.

Occasionally, students want to write out their speeches and then recite them in class so they have perfect control over the speaking situation. These students' speeches are very boring and easy to detect. Because of the differences just discussed, the written speech sounds like a composition delivered from memory. Imagine you are hearing the following two speeches. Which one sounds better to you? Which one was composed and presented to the class as a memorized speech and which one was prepared extemporaneously and spoken to the class without the benefit of a script?

SAMPLE 1

One of the main reasons supporting the importance of information is that it greatly contributes to better decision making on the job. Having an increased knowledge of the alternatives available, the possible costs and advantages of those alternatives, and the experiences of people who have already experimented with the alternatives allows each person to make the best decision possible while decreasing the stress level and decreasing the actual time spent making the decision. Sound decisions rely on current, reliable information.

SAMPLE 2

I realize that abortion is a very controversial issue and that most of you have your own views about the subject. Whether you are for it or against it is of little importance today. Whether we want no abortions or whether we are for "pro-choice," we live in a society where abortion happens everyday. Being a female, I have been reading about the topic since I was old enough to understand what was happening. I became most interested in the topic two years ago when my older sister told me that she was pregnant and was thinking about having an abortion. Now I understand the realities of the issue of abortion. It is not just a topic other people talk about, or that legislators disagree about. I have a real interest in what happens in our society today.

If you selected sample 1 as the composition, you were right. Look closely at the words selected for this composition. There was a conscious effort to choose the right word. Also, notice the impersonal nature of the writing. The author used *people* and *person* rather than *I* or *you,* and the sentences are long and complicated. If you look at the second sample, you will notice all of the short, common words, the personal references, the direct reference to the audience and most of the sentences are short and direct also. As you can see, oral language is not written language. If you are to use language correctly, do not speak as you write, and don't write as you speak because the two are different.

Elements of Language

We have already said that language is a set of symbols that stand for and suggest ideas. We have not discussed any of the aspects of language that you can use to make your speeches better. The following qualities of language are of special importance in the speaking/listening situation because they are the qualities that distinguish competent speakers from the incompetent ones.

CLARITY

An audience must be able to understand what you mean as you speak—your message must be "clear" to the audience. To make your message clear, follow the advice of Abraham Lincoln: "Speak so that the most lowly can understand you, and the rest will have no difficulty." Or as an old minister used to say, "Put the feed down where the lambs can get it, and the old ewes will get some too." How do you do that? Well, the best way is to use simple expressions and concrete, specific terms rather than vague and general expressions. For example, the word "many" is vague and general and provides no specific reference for the audience. More specific and concrete terms would be 90 percent or one million. Likewise, it is more precise to say, "that 1990 red Cadillac convertible" rather than "that rather new-looking car over there."

In attempting to be precise and clear, be cautious that you don't use too many technical terms that your audience members don't understand—terms that only a specialist in your field would understand. By the same token, just because you think your audience members will understand slang, that doesn't mean you should use slang expressions throughout your speech. Slang expressions usually have at least two meanings and the audience will likely wonder which meaning you intend. Use slang expressions sparingly.

Using language your audience members understands is the best policy. Don't try to find new words, or fancy words, to express your ideas. Sometimes the simple, everyday words are the best. *Get* is a perfectly useful word. There is no need to use a thesaurus, nor to think about the other words you could use. In most instances *get* works as well as *obtain, acquire, procure,* or *achieve.* It is also much better than *come into the possession of.* Don't circumvent obvious words like *building* to get to words like *edifice* just to impress your audience with your great vocabulary. Big words and words that are not in your audience members' general vocabulary will tend to confuse rather than impress them. Big words also increase the chances that you will be misunderstood. Speak directly and clearly and you will be understood.

VIVIDNESS

Your language can either be dull and boring or alive and vivid; the latter will create interesting and clear pictures in the minds of your audience members. There are several ways you can make your language more vivid. Here we discuss the use of five strategies for vividness: active verbs, imagery, alliterations, repetition, and parallelism.

Active Verbs   Active verbs make your language more vivid and alive than do passive verbs. "A good time was had by all" is a rather dull way of saying "Everyone had a good time." Generally, avoid verb forms using "have," "to be," and "got."

Action words make your language come alive and move. Action words also make your language more direct in many cases. For example, "The sound of the plane as it sped down the runway was deafening." This is not only awkward, but also passive and not very vivid. Instead, say, "The plane roared down the runway, deafening us." Instead of saying, "It is believed that Mr. Smith paid the bill," or "It is my belief that Mr. Smith paid the bill," say, "I believe Mr. Smith paid the bill." Notice that the final wording is more direct and active. It is also more clear.

Imagery   Create imagery in your language by using words that create sense images in the minds of your audience members. Sense imagery lets your audience members see, hear, feel, smell, or taste what you are talking about.

One way to create sense images for your audience is through the use of figures of speech. Metaphors and similes are the most common figures of speech to use for beginning speakers. Metaphors compare two things that are essentially unalike, but alike in one special manner, without using the word "like." The simile does the same thing, using the word "like." For example, you might compare a person to an animal by saying, "He is a pig." This is a metaphor because you have said that one thing *is* another. If you wish to soften the force of the comparison, you could use a simile by saying, "He looks *like* a pig."

Figures of speech such as the metaphor and simile add color and vividness to your speech. But don't make them too contrived or exaggerated. The associations suggested by similes and metaphors should be simple and easy to understand. If the associations call attention to themselves, they may work against you rather than for you. Make your figures of speech fit your speech message and color it rather than call attention to the language style that you have used.

Alliteration   Use alliterations also to create images. Alliteration is the repetition of the same sound at the beginnings of words. Be cautious that you don't use too many alliterations as that may rob your speech of meaning or interest. John F. Kennedy showed good use of limited alliteration when he said, "We shall pay any price, bear any burden, meet any hardship, support any friend, oppose any foe to assure the survival and success of liberty." The repetition of "p" in *pay* and *price* and "b" in *bear* and *burden,* as well as the "s" in *survival* and *success* are uses of alliteration. Notice also the repetition of "any" throughout the entire passage. For a more complete look at alliteration in Kennedy's speech, read the entire speech, which you can find in *Contemporary American Speeches.*

Repetition   Use repetition to build up intensity and create interest in your audience. Repetition is the repeated use of a word or phrase. Marc Antony in Shakespeare's *Julius Caesar* used repetition successfully as he repeated the phrase "honorable men" frequently. Martin Luther King, Jr. did the same in his "I Have a Dream" speech as he repeated "I have a dream." You can get a better understanding of repetition by reading the entire speech, which you may also find in *Contemporary American Speeches.*

The use of repetition in a speech is not to create words for the speaker, but rather to help audience members understand what is being emphasized, what is important, and what should be remembered. Writers use paragraphs, titles, subheadings, and transitions to help their readers, but speakers do not have these devices to help point out the less than obvious. Remember, you can use the concept of repetition to repeat an idea, but you can also use restatement so your audience members do not get bored with you. Repeat important ideas, but restate what you have said rather than repeat word for word.

Parallelism   Parallelism is the use of related words or phrases. In fact, parallelism might also include the use of repetition. The Kennedy quotation used earlier with alliteration is also an example of the use of parallelism as he used the same structure for his ideas. That structure, "pay any price, bear any burden, meet any hardship, support any friend, oppose any foe" is an example of using parallelism for vividness. Notice that the structure helps you remember as much as the idea itself.

Another example of parallelism comes from Martin Luther King's "I Have a Dream" speech:

> We can never be satisfied as long as our bodies, heavy with the fatigue of travel, cannot gain lodging in the motels of the highways and the hotels of the cities. We cannot be satisfied as long as the Negro's basic mobility is from a smaller ghetto to a larger one.
> We can never be satisfied as long as our children are stripped of their selfhood and robbed of their dignity by signs stating "for whites only." We cannot be satisfied as long as a Negro in Mississippi cannot vote and a Negro in New York believes he has nothing for which to vote. No, we are not satisfied, and we will not be satisfied until justice rolls down like waters and righteousness like a mighty stream."

The structure of King's "We can never be satisfied" to begin each sentence is an example of parallelism. In this case the structure and the words are both repeated. In the Kennedy example the structure is repeated, but not the words; in the King example both the words and the structure are repeated.

If you want your language to be vivid, to hold the attention of your listeners, and to be interesting, use vivid language that will ultimately create a favorable impression on your audience members and make your speech be remembered long after you have finished speaking. Don't be satisfied using only one means of vividness. Practice using all aspects of vividness so you can take your audience members with you rather than pick them up at the end of your speech.

APPROPRIATENESS

To be effective, language also needs to be appropriate—appropriate to your audience, to you, and to your situation. Imagine, if you will, that you are driving down the road and suddenly you see red lights flashing in your rearview mirror. As a good, law-abiding citizen, you pull over and stop. When the officer walks up to your car window, you do not say, "Hey, what's up pig?" because you know that your language would not be appropriate for that audience, for that situation, nor would it be appropriate for you as a speaker who would like to keep from getting a ticket. Appropriateness means good taste and common sense. Avoid slang, jargon, obscenities, or any language that might confuse or offend your audience.

Let's look at some of the factors of appropriateness that may affect how you approach your audience. First, you should avoid slang expressions most of the time. We mentioned earlier that slang is sometimes a part of oral language. It is, but expressions like "awesome" and "rip-off" may not add much clarity to your message. Other expressions, such as "fag," "fox," or "ticked off" may upset some audience members and do more harm than good. While slang can sometimes create color and vividness, it should be used sparingly, and only when you know the effect it will have on your audience members. Remember, communication with your audience members is still the key to effective speaking.

Also, avoid trite expressions. Trite expressions are not offensive to audiences, but they are such overused phrases that they carry little meaning. Some words, such as *tremendous, great, beautiful,* and *lovely,* have been used so much that we don't know what you mean by them. There are also some cliché expressions that have lost meaning through the years. Expressions like *over my dead body, read my lips, last but not least, few and far between, a real trooper, time frame, it stands to reason,* and so on have lost public appeal to the extent that we perceive the speaker as not having anything to say rather than as being cute and clever.

Jargon is also not appropriate in most instances. Avoid jargon that your audience would not understand. It is not appropriate to use a specialized language your audience members don't know if you are trying to communicate with them. Each profession or subject has its own special language. You must use a common language that your audience members can relate to if you are to make your message meaningful to your audience members. If you feel a jargon term is necessary, be sure you define the term so you do not anger or confuse your audience members.

It should go without mentioning that vulgarity is to be avoided. We mention it anyway because it is a part of appropriateness. Vulgar words are crude remarks, sometimes including obscenity and profanity, sometimes merely colloquial expressions. Anything that could upset an audience member because of its questionable nature should be avoided. One of the problems of using vulgarities is that you are often perceived as uneducated and uncouth by audiences if you use them. If you are perceived as unintelligent, you are not likely to make much of an impression on your audience, and not likely to change them if you are trying to persuade them. Off-color language is usually indicative of a low character or one of poor judgment.

In this project we have discussed some of the aspects of language that will help you make your speeches more memorable and understandable by your audience members. If you desire to use language properly, and for the most benefit, pay close attention to your language as you speak. Make sure your language fits the oral style rather than the written style. Be certain that you use the devices of language that will make your audience members like your speech and respond favorably rather than with disgust.

Project Assignment

Using one of the speeches in the appendix, prepare an analysis of the factors of language discussed in this project. First, identify the elements of oral style and written style. Second, what words depend on connotative meanings, and which on specific denotations? Third, point out particular word choices that affect the message. Fourth, point out specific uses of language devices to produce clarity, vividness, and appropriateness.

References

Ayres, J. & Miller, J. (1990). *Effective Public Speaking* (3rd ed.). Dubuque, Iowa: Wm. C. Brown Company, Publishers.

Bradley, B. E. (1988). *Fundamentals of Speech Communication* (5th ed.). Dubuque, Iowa: Wm. C. Brown Company, Publishers.

DeVito, J. A. (1990). *The Elements of Public Speaking* (4th ed.). New York: Harper & Row, Publishers.

Gregory, H. (1990). *Public Speaking for College and Career* (2nd ed.). New York: McGraw-Hill Book Company.

Linkugel, W. A., Allen, R. R., & Johannesen, R. L. (1978). *Contemporary American Speeches* (4th ed.). Dubuque, Iowa: Kendall/Hunt Publishing Company.

Lucas, S. E. (1989). *The Art of Public Speaking* (3rd ed.). New York: Random House.

Nelson, P. E. & Pearson, J. C. (1990). *Confidence in Public Speaking* (4th ed.). Dubuque, Iowa: Wm. C. Brown Company, Publishers.

Osborn, M. & Osborn, S. (1988). *Public Speaking.* Boston: Houghton Mifflin Company.

Samovar, L. A., & Mills, J. (1986). *Oral Communication: Message and Response* (6th ed.). Dubuque, Iowa: Wm. C. Brown Company, Publishers.

Sprague, J. & Stuart, D. (1988). *The Speaker's Handbook* (2nd ed.). San Diego: Harcourt Brace Jovanovich.

Verderber, R. F. & Verderber, K. S. (1989). *Interact* (5th ed.). Belmont, California: Wadsworth Publishing Company.

Wilson, J. F. & Arnold, C. C. (1983). *Public Speaking as a Liberal Act* (5th ed.). Boston: Allyn & Bacon, Inc.

UNIT **III**

THE SPEECH TO INFORM

Details often kill initiative, but there have been few successful men who weren't good at details. Don't ignore details. Lick them.

William B. Given, Jr.

Unit III consists of seven projects designed to provide a variety of experiences in presenting information to audiences. Project 13 deals with the principles of a general speech to inform. Project 14 presents the principles of the personal experience speech; Project 15 the principles of presenting an announcement; Project 16, the principles of describing; Project 17, the principles of defining; and Project 18, the principles of explaining processes. Note that previous principles from Units I and II should be used in conjunction with the projects in Unit III.

PROJECT **13**

The Speech to Inform

What a man does not fully understand is not possessed.

—Johann Wolfgang von Goethe

Whenever something new or different occurs, people like to know the details. As human beings, we are most curious to know who did it, what it was, how it happened, where and when it happened, and why it happened as it did. We want descriptions, special data, an order of events or procedures, causes, and effects. We also like explanations, pictures, and visual aids. We want accurate, specific, nontechnical language so we can understand it clearly and accurately in case we need to explain it to someone else.

We are also curious about the way something works and how it is used. We are interested in history, current events, new and antique products, new processes and discoveries, strange places, as well as foreign countries and their inhabitants. Ordinarily, anything we know little or nothing about interests us, and satisfying our natural curiosity by telling us about it is informative speaking.

Principles of the Speech to Inform

The informative speech provides your audience with a clear understanding of your ideas on a subject. It also arouses interest. This means that your audience members must understand and comprehend fully what you are talking about. Their grasp of a subject should be as complete as you can possibly make it in the time allotted. The information you present should not be offered in such a way that you seem to be attempting to convince audience members that your point of view is the right or best one.

Used sparingly, humor is highly desirable in an informative speech. Usually, there is too little humor in informative speeches; however, you should not attempt to make humor the highlight or focus of your speech. If you do, the purpose of your speech becomes one of entertainment rather than one of informing. As you prepare, keep the informative focus in mind so you don't use humor excessively.

When you conclude, your audience members should feel as if they have received sufficient materials on your subject to understand a new concept better or understand an old topic more fully. In some instances you may want your audience members to look at an old topic in a new light. If you can make them say when they are leaving, "Now I understand that concept; it was certainly cleared up in my mind by that speech," you can be satisfied your speech was informative—just as you intended.

For informative speaking, you should select a subject of interest to yourself and to your listeners. You can do this by thoroughly analyzing your audience—in this case your classmates. You, as the speaker, are charged further with the serious responsibility of knowing what you are talking about—knowing more about it, in fact, than anyone else in your audience does. For this reason, your talk demands that you study several sources of information. Under no circumstances should you be satisfied to glance hurriedly through an article in a popular magazine, jot down a few notes, and toss the periodical aside. This kind of work does not even begin to prepare you to give an informative speech.

Occasions for the informative speech are many. They arise on the lecture platform, in the pulpit, in the classroom, at business meetings—in fact, wherever you find reports are made, instructions given, or ideas presented by means of lectures and discussions you will find informative speeches. The point to bear in mind is that whenever information is disseminated, an occasion for an informative speech arises.

Some topics you might find useful in speaking to inform include:

1. The problems of the aged
2. How to preserve our rivers and streams
3. Jet propulsion
4. Hunting techniques in Africa
5. Trick photography
6. Changing morals
7. The greenhouse effect
8. Acid rain
9. New forms of energy
10. The life of a great person
11. How the stock market works
12. How to predict weather
13. How rain forests affect the United States
14. Native American communication
15. Transportation tomorrow
16. New architectural styles
17. Glasnost
18. U.S. trade deficit
19. Tracing your ancestors
20. Adoption procedures
21. Child abuse (or elderly abuse)
22. Agent orange and its effects
23. Racism in American schools
24. Alternate sources of energy
25. Dealing with oil spills

Preparing a Speech to Inform

To prepare for this speech, or any other speech, you must know and follow certain fundamentals of preparation. These fundamentals consist of the following steps: (1) analyze the occasion, (2) choose your subject, (3) diagnose your audience, (4) gather your material, (5) organize and support your main points with evidence, (6) word your speech by preparing an outline or by writing it out in full or in part (depending on the type of delivery expected of you), and (7) practice aloud. All these aspects of preparation are covered in other projects. If you don't recall what to do for any specific step, review the appropriate project.

If you wish to organize your thoughts logically, decide early what objective you hope to attain and what reaction you want from this particular audience. Next, if you wish, you may divide your discourse into three conventional parts: introduction, body, and conclusion. For more effectiveness, some speakers break down their talks by using various combinations of the following steps: (1) gain attention, (2) make the audience want to hear the ideas, (3) tell why this material is important to your listeners and how it affects them, (4) present ideas, (5) ask the audience to study the topic further or to take some action on it. The time required for any one division of a speech varies greatly; however, more time is given to the presentation of ideas than to any other part.

The wording of your talk may be accomplished by either writing it out in full from the outline or doing considerable practice. In any event, rehearse before a mirror as many times as necessary to fix the proper steps in your mind and the order of their content, along with desirable stage appearance and bodily action. Do not memorize words unless you are asked to use a memorized delivery.

One other point is extremely important—the information you present must be accurate. For accuracy of information you must consult acceptable sources and reliable and competent authorities. Your audience members should know where you got your material—whose research you are citing, whom you are quoting, and so on. You are the person to identify these sources and authorities. You are expected to go even further in this matter of giving information, for you are expected to offer your own conclusions and views and evaluations of your information. All this entails your neat assimilation of all you have pulled together, that is, your entire speech.

A few hints might well be offered at this point. First, include only two or three main points in the body of your speech. Develop these well with examples, illustrations, analogies, and facts. Second, do not be afraid to inject humor and anecdotes into your thoughts to add interest. Be sure these additions are suited to your subject and your audience. Third, be sure your speech moves ahead. Do not allow it to drag. Finally, strive for an interesting introduction and an equally effective conclusion.

Presenting a Speech to Inform

In presenting any speech to inform, you must know your materials and project the impression of confidence in yourself and in your topic. If you have prepared and rehearsed well, you should have the self-confidence to make a good presentation.

Unless instructed to do otherwise, follow the guidelines in Project 7 for using an extemporaneous delivery. In addition, use an easy, energetic presentation. Be enthusiastic and original in what you have to say. Use your hands and body to demonstrate how to do things—make a complete verbal and nonverbal presentation. If possible, use some form of visual aid to make your ideas easily understood and interesting.

The use of notes is somewhat a matter of opinion. If you are adequately prepared, you will not need them because you will speak extemporaneously; this is the most effective method known. If you must refer to notes, they should be short sentences, phrases, or single words that have a particular meaning to you. Whatever notes you use should be brief, concise, meaningful, and entirely familiar. A glance at them should be sufficient to give you their full meaning so you can speak fluently yet logically. Under no circumstances should you have enough notes so you can "read" your speech from your note cards.

Walk to the front of your audience or to the speaker's stand with confidence. Show your audience members that you know your topic and are interested in providing the new information to them. Be enthusiastic. Pause, survey your audience and smile at them.

As you speak, utilize expressive bodily actions and maintain direct eye contact with individual members or small groups of audience members. Be sure you observe the expected time limits and stop when you finish what you have planned to say, no matter how much positive feedback you seem to be receiving. Remember, your conclusion should be as strong and appropriate and as well prepared as your beginning remarks.

SAMPLE SPEECH TO INFORM

By Michele Scott

The Psychology of Color

Would you believe me if I told you that color has an effect on suicide rates? As a matter of fact, overlooking the Thames River in London is a gloomy-looking black bridge known as the Blackfriars Bridge, a favorite leaping off point for despondent citizens. Color consultants studying the situation suggested painting the bridge another, more soothing, color. The bridge was repainted and immediately the suicide figures declined.

Many ancient people believed that color possessed magical powers. I have researched and studied the psychology of color and found that even today we all assume a link between color and our minds. The optimist, we say, views the world through "rose-colored glasses." While when sad, a person is in a "blue" mood. A jealous person is said to see "green." And now, scientists are discovering that certain colors do, indeed, have a profound influence on our bodies, moods, and behaviors. Today I will inform you of three aspects of color that affect all of us. Those three aspects are: (1) the concept of color, (2) the effects of color on moods, and (3) the psychological differences of colors.

First, what is the concept of color? "Colors are electromagnetic wave bands of energy," says Alexander Schauss, director of the American Institute for Biosocial Research in Tacoma, Washington. "Each color has its own wavelength and can be duplicated by combining two other colors or wavelengths. The wave bands stimulate chemicals in your eye, sending impulses or messages to the pituitary glands near the brain. These are master endocrine glands that regulate hormones and other physiological systems in the body."

Stimulated by response to colors, glandular activities can alter moods, speed up heart rates, and increase brain activity. As you can see from the previous statement, the colors that surround us can affect our hormones and the secretions in our bloodstream. These secretions also affect our moods and affect the way we react and respond to other people and the situations in which we find ourselves.

Second, our moods are affected by the colors around us. In general, dark colors strike us as heavy and foreboding, while light colors seem not only cheerful, but physically light as well. Bonnie Bender, color marketing manager at Pittsburgh Paints, and an authority on color psychology, reports that in an experiment testing the psychological effects of paint on worker productivity, researchers painted heavy boxes white and light boxes black. Workmen had considerably more trouble lifting the light black boxes than the heavy white ones.

Marcella Graham, medical technologist, color consultant and interior designer, described an equally dramatic example of the use of color to lift depression and stimulate activity. Called in for a consultation on staff and patient apathy in a hospital, she found the whole place painted light and medium chocolate brown and two shades of grey-green. Graham advised painting the hospital, floor by floor, using pumpkin orange, strawberry pink, emerald green and lavender. (Simply putting in pink curtains and orange bedspreads would not do it; color has to be massive to produce its effects.) Patient response to the brilliant colors was immediate and positive. Elderly men shaved and dressed to get out of bed each day. Female patients began circulating and visiting in the halls and requested powder, combs, lipstick, and stockings. Even staff morale picked up.

And third, colors exert a powerful force on our mental and physical health; therefore, it is important to know about their psychological influences. Here is a spectrum of colorful facts. Consider how your color environment affects how you react and respond to others.

The color red creates the effect of anxiety. The red family includes everything from maroon to crimson to pink (although pink-red mixed with white seems to have properties of its own). Several years ago, Robert Gerard, then a doctoral candidate at the University of California, studied the physiological reaction of people in a colored room, measuring blood pressure, respiration rate, heartbeat, muscle activity, eyeblinks, and brain waves. The rate of activity of all these indicators went up in a red room. Brain-wave activity, which showed an immediate response, stayed high for more than ten minutes. People who were already anxious found red even more disturbing than those who were previously calm. When the same people went into a blue room, all the physical indicators went down.

Pink is restful; it can even convey a purity that makes people reluctant to damage it. In a study done by graduate students at Texas Wesleyan College, Fort Worth, children kept in different-colored corrals were given a variety of playthings, including paints and crayons. The children eagerly decorated all the corral walls except the pink ones, which remained virtually spotless. When the researchers regrouped the children to see if those youngsters who painted the most graffiti would behave differently in another group, the results were confirmed. Pink walls effectively kept off graffiti.

A study of 153 men at the U.S. Naval Correctional Center showed that a particular shade known as Baker-Miller pink can curb aggressive tendencies and actually reduce physical strength. When prisons began using Baker-Miller pink, some were able to lower the number of guards on duty. At latest count, says Schauss, more than 1400 hospitals and correctional institutions in America are using pink for its tranquilizing effects.

Blue evokes a mood of tranquility and serenity. Almost any shade of blue will do it, from cobalt to sky blue to sapphire. An intriguing new study done at the University of Alberta, Edmonton, Canada, investigated the effect of a blue surrounding on a class of behaviorally disturbed children, some of whom were blind. The researchers first measured the kids' baseline heart rates, respiration, and other physiological indicators. Then the walls of the classroom were painted light and dark blue. All the physical indicators went down, and the children became noticeably calmer—even the blind children! Researchers and teachers who observed the children during the one-month ''blue-paint'' period were amazed at how calm they were. When the classrooms were repainted their original brown and yellow, the children's heart rates, respiration, and pulse went back up and hyperactivity resumed.

''The fact that the blind children experienced this effect provides strong evidence that color has a direct biochemical pathway to the brain,'' Schauss says, ''it works as long as the retina of the eye is attached to the brain. However, if a blind child closes his eyes so that color cannot strike the retina, the effect won't work.''

Yellow lifts spirits and makes people feel peppy and optimistic. It is the color of highest visibility; if you glance quickly at a collage of colors, yellow will be the first one you perceive. Tests show that yellow raises blood pressure, pulse, and respiration, although not as consistently as red does.

The energizing effect of yellow was illustrated in a study by a Swedish scientist, Oscar Brunler, PhD. Mice placed in slate-blue boxes became listless and inactive. When Brunler switched them to yellow boxes, they became alert and active.

Yellow's activating properties work on humans, too. Watch of the Color Association reports that a study involving preschool children under age five showed that out of a roomful of toys, children most frequently grabbed the yellow ones. According to Bender, a telephone company found that when the interior of a phone booth was painted yellow, people finished their conversations faster and freed the booth for other customers.

In conclusion, today, I have explained to you three aspects of color: First, colors are electromagnetic wave bands of energy, each having its own wave length, which is sent as a message to the brain. Second, our moods are affected both positively and negatively by our perceptions of the colors that surround us. And third, we learned that colors have different psychological influences upon us. For example, they can irritate us, soothe, speed up or slow down heart rates, depress us, or cheer us up.

In closing, the next time you are trying to decide what color to use, whether it be your clothing, your room, or something else, I suggest that you consider how it will ''color'' your thinking as it colors your world.

SAMPLE OUTLINE—SPEECH TO INFORM

1. INTRODUCTION
   A. Attention-getter: Questions
   B. Credentials: Research/Study
   C. Arouse Interest: All affected
II. THESIS: Today I will inform you about three aspects of color that affect all of us.
   PREVIEW: Those three aspects are: (1) the concept of color, (2) the effects of color on moods, and (3) the psychological effects of color.
III. BODY
   A. The concept of color
      1. Electromagnetic wavebands of energy
      2. Stimulates gland
   B. The effects of color on moods
      1. Dark and light colors
      2. Lifts depression
   C. The psychological effects of color
      1. Red effects
      2. Pink effects
      3. Blue effects
      4. Yellow effects

IV. CONCLUSION
    A. Review main points
        1. The concept of color
        2. The effects of color on moods
        3. The psychological effects of color
    B. Closing: Consider color

PRINTED SOURCES OF INFORMATION

Give complete information for each source. When the author's name, the title of the article, or the date is not listed, write "none listed."

1. Author's name __None listed__

    Title of article __"How Color Goes to Your Head"__

    Book or magazine containing article __*Science Digest*__

    _____ Date of publication __December 1984__

    Chapters and/or pages containing material __p. 24__

2. Author's name __Kane, Leslie__

    Title of article __"The Power of Color"__

    Book or magazine containing article __*Health*__

    _____ Date of publication __July 1982__

    Chapters and/or pages containing material __p. 154__

3. Author's name __Morgan, James__

    Title of article __"Seeing Red, Feeling Blue, and Other Color Facts"__

    Book or magazine containing article __*Good Housekeeping*__

    _____ Date of publication __April 1983__

    Chapters and/or pages containing material __p. 227__

4. Author's name __Ponte, Louella__

    Title of article __"How Color Affects Your Moods and Health"__

    Book or magazine containing article __*Reader's Digest*__

    _____ Date of publication __July 1982__

    Chapters and/or pages containing material __p. 93__

5. Author's name __None listed__

    Title of article __"The Psychology of Color"__

    Book or magazine containing article __*Forest for Home Economics*__

    _____ Date of publication __October 1982__

    Chapters and/or pages containing material __p. 62__

Project Assignment

Prepare and present a four- to six-minute speech designed primarily to inform your audience on a topic on which they have little information. Use the skills presented in Project 4 for finding supporting materials to develop the body of your speech. Be sure you select a topic in which you can draw upon your own knowledge as well as finding support through interviews and library research.

Your instructor may require specific types of supporting materials or a specific number of library references for your speech. If you are not presented a specific number of sources, be sure that you use at least three different sources and at least three different types of supporting materials. Check also to ensure that your topic will fit within the time limitations and any other requirements your teacher may place on this assignment.

Organize the body of your speech according to one of the accepted organizational patterns discussed in Project 3. Your introduction and conclusion should conform to the standards set forth in Projects 5 and 6; and your delivery needs to conform to the standards set forth in Project 7, or any other requirement set by your instructor. Any needed visual aids should be prepared in accordance with Project 10.

References

Ayres, J. & Miller, J. (1990). *Effective Public Speaking* (3rd ed.). Dubuque, Iowa: Wm. C. Brown Company, Publishers.

Bradley, B.E. (1988). *Fundamentals of Speech Communication* (5th ed.). Dubuque, Iowa: Wm. C. Brown Company, Publishers.

Jeffrey, R. C. & Peterson, O. (1988). *Speech, A Basic Text* (3rd ed.). New York: Harper & Row, Publishers.

Lucas, S. E. (1989). *The Art of Public Speaking* (3rd ed.). New York: Random House.

Minnick, W. C. (1983). *Public Speaking* (2nd ed.). Boston: Houghton Mifflin Company.

Mudd, C. S. & Sillars, M. O. (1985). *Speech Content and Communication* (5th ed.). New York: Harper & Row, Publishers.

Nelson, P. E. & Pearson, J. C. (1990). *Confidence in Public Speaking* (4th ed.). Dubuque, Iowa: Wm. C. Brown Company, Publishers.

Ochs, D. J. & Winkler, A. C. (1983) *A Brief Introduction to Speech* (2nd ed.). New York: Harcourt Brace Jovanovich.

Osborn, M. & Osborn, S. (1988). *Public Speaking.* Boston: Houghton Mifflin Company.

Samovar, L. A. & Mills, J. (1989) *Oral Communication* (7th ed.). Dubuque, Iowa: Wm. C. Brown Company, Publishers.

Sprague, J. & Stuart, D. (1988). *The Speaker's Handbook* (2nd ed.). San Diego: Harcourt Brace Jovanovich.

Verderber, R. F. (1988). *The Challenge of Effective Speaking* (7th ed.). Belmont, California: Wadsworth Publishing Company.

Zimmerman, G. I., Owen, J. L., & Seibert, D. R. (1986). *Speech Communication: A Contemporary Introduction* (3rd ed.). St. Paul, Minnesota: West Publishing Company.

PROJECT **14**

The Personal Experience Speech

> There are really only three types of people: those who make things happen, those who watch things happen, and those who say, "What happened?"
>
> —Ann Landers

You take a step forward in your speaking experience when you present a personal experience speech. Although this speech is essentially about yourself, it still requires definite preparation and interesting presentation. You should learn the importance of these two requirements early in your speech training. Aside from becoming acquainted with these aspects of speech making, you should feel increased confidence and poise as a result of this speech experience. Your ease before the group will improve noticeably. By giving your best to this speech, you will achieve credible improvement and a desirable personal satisfaction. This project presents the principles of relating personal experiences, preparing the personal experience speech, presenting the personal experience speech, and a sample personal experience speech.

Principles of the Personal Experience Speech

Every day of your life you have experiences only you can relate to someone else. In presenting a personal experience speech, you gain practice in speaking while talking about something only you can tell. Thus, you speak as the only authority. The personal experience speech can be a confidence builder since no one can dispute your evidence and you can maintain calm about speaking because all you need to do is to recall the events of your experience as they occurred.

If the experience was funny or amusing but had no "lesson" to be learned, you could plan to entertain your audience members as well as inform them. On the other hand, if your experience did have a "lesson" for life or was serious in nature, you could inform your audience members, and possibly convince them to change their behaviors. Your primary objective in both speeches would be to relate the experience to your audience so others could relate to your experience, and maybe learn a valuable lesson in life.

86

A personal experience speech requires that you select a topic that would be of interest to your audience because of the "special nature" of the experience. The special nature of your speech might be the uniqueness of the experience, like spending a vacation in some exotic foreign culture or a special lesson you learned—how much your family really loves you, for example. Ordinary, everyday experiences we can all recall having had, like a trip to the grocery store or a zoo in town, or some uneventful vacation will not make good personal experience speeches since they lack that special nature needed to make your audience members interested.

Some topics of interest for personal experience speeches include:

1. An accident
2. The big fire
3. Falling through ice
4. Nearly drowning
5. The "big game"
6. A day in the U.S. Army
7. Aboard a ship
8. Climbing a mountain
9. Saving a life
10. Sailing a boat
11. My first sky dive
12. A robbery
13. A flying lesson
14. A chemical experiment
15. An interesting job
16. Professional wrestling
17. Carnival rackets
18. A ski contest
19. A great book or movie
20. Building a new deck
21. Living with cancer
22. Living in a wheelchair
23. Living in a foreign country
24. An Indian powwow
25. Any experience of special interest

Preparing a Personal Experience Speech

In preparing a personal experience speech, you should probably as the first and most important step select an interesting and exciting topic. Let's assume you know generally what is expected of you when you give your speech. Let's assume, too, you have your purpose constantly before you—to inform your audience members about your experience. Now develop your speech in the following order:

1. *Outline your speech in considerable detail.*   This means you must set up the order of the events you want to talk about. Be sure your outline places these events in their most effective order throughout your talk. Since experiences occur in chronological order, that usually works best in this type of speech. A little thought about arrangement will tell you how to place your ideas. In arranging what you will talk about, include your own personal feelings and reactions, the activities of other persons or animals, and objects that made your experience thrilling, exciting, or funny. This will add interest.
2. *Practice your speech aloud.* You can do this before friends and in front of a mirror. Do this until you have memorized *the sequence of events,* not the words you will use to tell your experience. You will naturally tend to memorize certain words and phrases and this is all right. But do not under any circumstances memorize the whole speech word for word. Every time you rehearse you will tell the same things, but never with exactly the same words. Each rehearsal will set the pattern of your speech more firmly in mind, until after several practices (the number depends on the individual), you will be able

to present your speech with full confidence and the knowledge that you know what you are going to say. Remember, you need to know the events you are going to talk about and describe, but you do not want to memorize the words you are going to use.

3. *Make a final evaluation of your speech before marking it "ready for presentation."* Ask yourself the following questions and be sure your speech answers each question adequately.

   a. Does your speech merely list a series of persons, places, and things? (Vitalize these persons and things by describing what happened and by pointing out unusual or exciting incidents, such as dangers or humorous occurrences.) Avoid unnecessary details.

   b. Is your speech about you only? If so, you can improve it by talking about the influences that were operating in your presence. For example, if you rescued a drowning man, do not be satisfied to say, "I jumped in and pulled him out." Tell what he was doing; describe his struggles; tell about the depth of the water, the distance from shore; recount your fears and other feelings as you pulled him toward shore; tell how the current almost took you under; demonstrate the way you held him by the hair; and so on. Emphasize such items as your fatigue and near exhaustion as you fought to stay afloat. If you do this, your experience will be much more interesting to listen to and will tell your audience members much more than the fact that you saved a man's life.

   c. Do you have a curiosity-arousing introduction, one that catches the attention of your audience members? Does it establish your credibility and let your audience members know what to expect?

   d. Do you have a conclusion? A speech is never finished without one. Be sure you summarize what you have said about your experience, and make some final statement to which your audience members can relate. Your final statement should relate the "lesson" you learned and want your audience members to learn also.

Presenting a Personal Experience Speech

Your attitude regarding yourself and your audience will exert a marked influence upon you and your listeners. You should have a sincere desire to inform your audience about your experience. If it is information that you earnestly desire to give your audience members, concentrate on making them *understand* what you are telling them. If you intend to provide entertainment as well as inform your audience members, strive to give them enjoyment by amusing them and causing them to smile—and perhaps even laugh.

You should never feel that what you have to say is simply not interesting and never was, which is the attitude of some students. Consider for a moment the child who runs toward you eagerly, grasps your hand, and excitedly tells you about a big dog two doors down the street. Her story no doubt captures your interest; yet there is nothing inherently interesting about a big dog you have seen many times. Why, then, are you interested? The answer lies largely in the extreme desire of the child to tell you something. She wants you to understand her, and therein lies the basic secret of giving information to which people will listen attentively. You must have a sincere desire to make your audience members understand you and enjoy what you are saying.

Demonstrate the points you can by bodily actions and gestures. Let your arms and hands gesture whenever you feel an impulse to do so; otherwise your hands may hang comfortably at your side or rest easily on a tabletop or chair back. Be calm about putting your hands anywhere. Feel free to change your stage position by moving laterally a few feet. This will cause attention to be drawn to your presentation.

Use your voice normally and conversationally. Talk earnestly and loudly enough to be heard by everyone present. If you are truly interested in your experience and truly desire your audience members to understand you, your voice modulation and force will take care of themselves very well. Get involved with your topic and act as if you are enjoying making your presentation and you will likely present yourself and your experience interestingly.

If you use speaking notes, observe a ten-word maximum. Use large handwriting so you can read your notes easily. Use a 3- × 5-inch note card so it will fit nicely in the palm of your hand. When referring to your notes, raise them to a level that permits you to glance at them without bowing your head. Do not try to hide your notes or act ashamed of using them. They are your map. Use them as a guide rather than as a crutch and your audience members will not notice they are present.

SAMPLE PERSONAL EXPERIENCE SPEECH

By Clint McGaha

The Disappearing Car Incident

Has your car ever been stolen? Have you ever walked outside from a store or shopping mall to get into your car only to find that it was gone? Can you imagine how you would feel if you couldn't find your car where you left it? I remember well the feeling I had back in July of 1988 when I went to the exact location I had left my car only to find out that it was missing. Yet, if I had only done one simple thing, I would have saved myself a very unfortunate mishap. Therefore, you may be interested in knowing what that simple thing was in order to prevent a similar experience from happening to you.

Today I will explain two aspects of my disappearing car incident. Those two aspects are: (1) losing my car, and (2) finding my car.

First, it all happened as I was driving to work on that hot July day. Since I didn't have air-conditioning in my car, and the drive from home to work took thirty minutes, I got thirsty along the way. Even though I was running behind schedule, I desperately wanted a peach Zeltzer Seltzer. So I decided to stop at the McAnally's convenience store at the corner of 16th and Mississippi.

As I turned off the road, I noticed several cars directly in front of the store which caused me to park in the north extremity of the parking area. I then jumped out of my car, ran inside the store, snatched the "Zeltzer" and hurried to the checkout stand. The whole process could not have taken more than a minute.

After handing the cashier the exact change, I rushed outside to get in my car so I could rush on to work, but to my utter disbelief, my car had disappeared. I could not find my car anywhere near the store, nor could I see someone driving away in it.

I stood in total amazement, thinking how stupid I had been for leaving the keys in my car. I again turned a complete 360 degrees looking everywhere for a sign of my car. It could not be seen. I was so perplexed I almost didn't notice a teenage boy walking toward me. All I could think about was "How will I ever find my car?"

It was at this point that events began to unfold which would lead me to finding my car. These are events that I still remember as if they were yesterday. This is how I found my car.

It was at this point that the teenager I mentioned earlier approached me and asked, "Do you drive a yellow Chevette?" I excitedly answered "Yes!" hoping he might have seen who had stolen my car, or he might have some information as to where my car might be. I was half right—he did have some information on the whereabouts of my car. In fact, his account of this story might be more exciting than mine. This is how his story might have gone:

"I was driving up Sixteenth Street on the way to my apartment when suddenly this idiot in a yellow Chevette began driving in reverse toward me. I honked repeatedly, thinking he would stop, but the car kept coming at me. Then I noticed that there was no driver in the car. It was too late for me to move—the collision was unavoidable. The Chevette smashed into the front of my car, then swerved onto a side street before finally stopping. I couldn't imagine who would let a car roll down a hill, but I decided whoever he was must be at McAnally's. So I drove up to the store, and as I pulled into the parking lot, I noticed a young man who stood looking as if his car had just disappeared."

After the teenager told me what had happened, he drove me to my car to survey the damages. Luckily, no people were injured, and, of course, my clunker sustained no damages. I was not so lucky with his silver, 1987 Mazda RX7. It sustained considerable frame damage which resulted in costing me close to five hundred dollars.

In conclusion, I now realize that if I had done only one simple thing, I would have avoided this whole terrifying experience of walking outside to find my car missing. I could also have avoided the embarrassing experience of having my car roll down a hill and hit another vehicle. Even though it is not known whether I left my car in neutral or if it slipped out of gear, which it had done before, it would not have mattered if I had used my parking brake. So, in closing, I encourage you to remember when driving, not only to wear your seat belt and be a defensive driver in order to protect yourself, others, and your car, but also to remember the little things when you get out of your car also. Like setting your parking brake. I learned that it can be just as crucial as the other aspects of driving.

Sample Outline—Personal Experience Speech

I. Introduction
    A. Attention-getter: Questions
    B. Credentials: July 1988
    C. Arouse interest: Similar incident
II. THESIS: Today I will explain two aspects of my disappearing car incident.
    PREVIEW: Those two aspects are: (1) losing my car and (2) finding my car.
III. BODY
    A. Losing my car
        1. Driving to work
        2. Stopping at McAnally's
        3. Disappearance of car
    B. Finding my car
        1. Teenager
        2. Story
        3. Damages
IV. CONCLUSION
    A. Summary
        1. Losing my car
        2. Finding my car
    B. Closing: Set brake

Project Assignment

Select a personal experience from your life that interests you and that can be made to interest your audience. Prepare a two- to four-minute speech in which your general purpose is to inform your audience. Whatever you decide to talk about should be vivid in your memory and close enough in time that you can recall it well. Be sure that you are doing more than just relating a series of events in your experience. You will want to leave your audience with some "lesson" to be learned from your experience.

Organize your speech using a chronological or other logical order that your audience members can follow easily. Start by writing down the series of events in your experience. Group the events into two or three points that you can make about your experience—not a list of events. Then prepare an introduction that will gain attention, and direct your audience members to your topic. Don't forget to prepare a suitable conclusion that will remind your audience members of your experience but will also remind them of the lesson you learned from your experience.

References

Ayres, J. & Miller, J. (1990). *Effective Public Speaking* (3rd ed.). Dubuque, Iowa: Wm. C. Brown Company, Publishers.

Bradley, B. E. (1988). *Fundamentals of Speech Communication* (5th ed.). Dubuque, Iowa: Wm. C. Brown Company, Publishers.

DeVito, J. A. (1990). *The Elements of Public Speaking* (4th ed.). New York: Harper & Row, Publishers.

Gronbeck, B. E., Ehninger, D., & Monroe, A. H. (1988). *Principles of Speech Communication* (10th brief ed.). Glenview, Illinois: Scott, Foresman and Company.

Lucas, S. E. (1989). *The Art of Public Speaking* (3rd ed.). New York: Random House.

Nelson, P. E. & Pearson, J. C. (1990). *Confidence in Public Speaking* (4th ed.). Dubuque, Iowa: Wm. C. Brown Company, Publishers.

Zimmerman, G. I., Owen, J. L. & Seibert, D. R. (1986). *Speech Communication: A Contemporary Introduction* (3rd ed.). St. Paul, Minnesota: West Publishing Company.

PROJECT **15**

The Announcement

Speech was made to open man to man, and not to hide
him; to promote commerce, and not betray it.
—David Lloyd

Each year people make many millions of announcements. Each year many other people who hear these announcements are left in a confused state of mind because the information presented was poorly organized, obscure, or incomplete. Often, as a result, attendance at clubs, schools, churches, and other organizations has been disappointing. It is true that you can't force people to attend a gathering, but it is just as true that you can increase attendance by making absolutely certain everyone within hearing distance of your voice is fully informed about the event you are announcing.

Principles of Making an Announcement

An announcement is a presentation of information. It is brief, concise, to the point, and pertinent. It tells specifically about something in the past (who won a prize or an award), about events to occur immediately (the governor will appear on campus today, or there will be an important committee meeting following adjournment of the business meeting), or in the near future (a dance to be sponsored next week). An announcement should be crystal-clear in meaning, contain all necessary and helpful data, be stated in easily understandable terms, and be heard by everyone present.

Occasions for the use of announcements arise at practically every kind of meeting. In addition, radio and television have offered a convenient medium for making announcements. You will find announcements are made around you every day.

You may use the following suggestions as bases for announcements:

1. A school or civic election
2. A school or business meeting
3. A skating party tomorrow night

4. A picnic next week
5. A school or community play next week
6. A football game
7. A basketball game
8. A convention
9. A special sale
10. A new schedule
11. A lecture
12. A new schedule for classes
13. A hunting expedition
14. A ski meet
15. The showing/demonstration of a new car
16. The introduction of a new product
17. New closing hours for the library
18. A bowling tournament
19. A special hearing
20. A special meeting to decide an issue.

Preparing an Announcement

The chief purpose of an announcement is to inform. An announcement is an informative presentation *about* the event, not a sales pitch for audience members to attend the event. Be sure you don't confuse the two speeches as you prepare your materials. Organize the main points of your announcement into a meaningful order for your audience members. Have an interesting introduction and a strong conclusion, as well as good organization of the other necessary material.

Your first job will be to gather information. Be sure to secure this information from authentic and authoritative sources. Do not rely on hearsay. Be absolutely certain your data are accurate and correct to the last detail. If there is any doubt at all, recheck the material before presenting your announcement. It is your responsibility to have all the last minute information available. Ascertain whether any changes have occurred since you first received your information.

As you are gathering your materials for your announcement, be sure you find out these details: What is the event (name)? When is the event (day, date, and time)? Where is the event? Who is sponsoring the event? In addition, you may want to find out any special details that may affect your audience members such as costs, benefits, limitations on time to make arrangements, limitations on numbers available or eligibility requirements, or any other factors that might affect when and how people will respond. In some instances you may want to describe the purpose of the event—as in a dance to honor a group, an event to raise money for orphans, and so on. In making your announcement, you may not need to use all the information listed here, but you will need to collect, or at least consider, all these elements as possibly important to your announcement.

The organization of your announcement is important. Begin preparing your introduction as you would the introduction to any other speech. You will need to get the attention of your audience members and turn their attention toward your topic. Next, you will want to present the information you have collected in a logical sequence, often giving the most important point first, followed by the rest of your announcement in order of importance. For example, show that the event is timely and opportune. If there are known or probable objections, refute them impersonally; however, avoid going into a defensive debate or offering a long list of excuses for the action your announcement proposes.

Name the exact place of the event and its location. Tell how to get there, if this is necessary, and indicate the advantage of the place. Give the date, the day, and the exact hour, including beginning time as well as anticipated ending time. If there is an admission charge, state the price or prices. If desirable, tell about the reasonableness of the charges and where the money will go, especially when the project is a worthy one. If there are tickets, tell where, when, and how they may be secured. If reserved seats are available, explain any special conditions concerning them.

Finally, summarize your announcement by restating the occasion, the place, the time, and the admission, making sure you don't make a sales pitch for people to attend the event. Not all the collected information should be included in every announcement. Your own judgment will tell you what should be omitted or included. Generally, you will want to include sufficient information to last at least a minute, but you will not want to go much over a minute in making your announcement. Instead of saying, "I thank you" when you finish, it's better to say, "We hope to see you there," or words to that effect.

Prepare notes for use in making your announcement so nothing essential will be omitted. Use 3- × 5-inch note cards that will fit easily into the palm of your hand. Make your notes brief, orderly, and legible. Rehearse them until you have everything well in mind. Remember, you want to tell this announcement to your audience, not read it to them.

Presenting an Announcement

Your attitude should be one of alertness and politeness. There will be no great need for bodily action other than that which naturally accompanies what you have to say. Speak clearly and distinctly. All places, dates, days, and times must be articulated so there can be no misunderstanding by your audience members.

Since most announcements are important enough for all audience members to hear them well, you will not want to speak from your seat. Go to the front of your audience where all audience members can see you as well as hear you. Never get "trapped" in the back of the audience, in an obscure corner, or elsewhere among the crowd. Go to the front and stand near the center of your audience.

Observe good posture. Pause until you have gained the attention of your audience. Your first words should be heard by everyone. In some cases you may need to raise your hand or rap on a table to get attention. However, do not attempt to talk above crowd noises if the audience is slow to respond. When referring to your notes, hold them up so you can see them and still keep your eyes on the audience; avoid talking to the floor. When you finish, go back to your seat unostentatiously. There should be no display in your entire performance. Pleasantness and the desire to be understood are enough.

SAMPLE ANNOUNCEMENTS

By James Paschall

(Sample 1)

attention   Have you ever dreamed of being a star? Have you imagined what the applause would be like when you took your bow? Or you accepted your award for your starring role? Maybe your time for stardom has finally arrived because now you have the opportunity to start on that starring role.

who, what,   The East Central Theatre Department will be holding tryouts for its production of
when, where,   Thornton Wilder's "Our Town" on Monday and Tuesday, October 2nd at 4:30 and October
details   3rd, at 7:30 in Science Hall 124. All East Central University students are encouraged to try out for the play.

Reading sheets can be picked up between 9:00 A.M. and 5:00 P.M. in the Theatre Office, Science Hall, 101 between now and October 2nd. You will be expected to read from at least two scenes, and be available for rehearsals from October 4 through the production dates of November 8 to November 11.

benefits to   This is a prime time for those of you who have dreams and aspirations of becoming
listeners   stars on TV or the stage. This may be the production that starts you on your way to fame and fortune. Even if you don't plan a career in theatre, this may be your opportunity to have fun and work on the stage here at ECU.

summary   Remember, Tryouts for "Our Town" will be held October 2nd and 3rd in Science Hall 124. All students are eligible to try out and to work on the production. Break a leg.

(SAMPLE 2)

attention   The leaves are changing colors. There's a slight chill in the air. Fall is definitely here, and that means football. I know all of you are rabid football fans, and want to support the home team and root the team on to another state championship.

who, what,
when, where   The Ada High Cougars will be hosting the Seminole Chieftains this Friday night at Norris Field. In Friday night's game, our Cougars will be working on going undefeated in District play for the third consecutive year. Once we win the district, as many of you know, we will be heading for our 14th state championship. The team needs your support as they work for that goal.

          Kickoff is at 8:00 P.M., but you will want to arrive early so you can get a good seat in the student cheering section. We have a special section that has been set aside on the east side of the stadium, Section C. That's about the 50-yard line.

Cost   Tickets will be on sale at the gate for one dollar for students, and two dollars for adults. Your activity tickets are good for a fifty percent reduced rate for this special game. Bring your parents and other family members to cheer on the Cougars.

Summary   Come out and show your true Ada High spirit Friday night at Norris Field. Remember, your activity ticket is good for a reduced rate, and we have a special section set aside for students. Support the Cougars and their march to the state championships. Go Cougars!

Project Assignment

Prepare two announcements on different topics using the list in this project as a basis. Make sure that your announcements are complete, yet brief. As you develop your announcements, be certain that you include the answers to the questions: Who? What? When? Where? Why? and How? Also, remember to include the special details such as prices, limitations, and benefits to your audience members. Make sure your introduction gains attention and gets your audience members turned to your topic. Your conclusion should review the most important aspects of your announcement. You will need only two to three minutes for both announcements. Follow any other specific instructions your instructor may provide.

References

Fletcher, L. (1988). *Speaking to Succeed in Business, Industry, Professions.* New York: Harper & Row, Publishers.

Stone, J. & Bachner, J. (1978). *Speaking Up, A Book for Every Woman Who Wants to Speak Effectively.* New York: McGraw-Hill Book Company.

PROJECT 16

The Speech of Description

I attribute the little I know to my not having been
ashamed to ask for information, and to my rule of
conversing with all descriptions of men on those topics
that form their own peculiar professions and pursuits.

—John Locke

Whenever someone says, "I saw . . ." you want to know what it looked like. It matters
little whether someone has seen a place, an event, another person or an object, chances
are you want a description so you can see in your own mind what the other person saw.
As a speaker it is to your advantage to know how most effectively to describe people,
places, events, and objects so your listeners clearly see what you describe. This project
presents the principles of the speech of description, preparing a speech of description,
presenting a speech of description, and finally, a sample speech of description.

Principles of the Speech of Description

Often in an informative speech you will need both to show and tell your audience what you
are talking about. The goal of any informative speech is to provide a clear, accurate, and
informative "picture" of your topic. The speech of description is a specific type of informative
speech, the primary goal of which is to give your audience a clear mental picture of a person,
place, object, or event. Description is the tool used to provide that clear, accurate picture.
Speeches of pure description are rare; however, the technique of describing is used in almost
all speeches. As you read this project, see how you can apply principles to descriptions that
you need to present. Also, return to this project when you need to present descriptions for
other speeches.

Description helps your audience members classify or categorize items into a meaningful
structure. Description appeals strongly to the senses. Your audience members want to know
what size something is—its length, width, depth, height, and so on. They also want to know
the shape of the object—is it square, circular, oblong, triangular, or some other shape? Another

descriptive aspect that helps to classify an object is the composition of the object—wood, glass, aluminum, and so on. Sometimes it is important to know the color, weight, or condition of an object. For example, a rusty, green, 20-year-old Ford looks much different from a new green Ford direct from the showroom floor.

Some suggested topics for descriptive speeches include:

1. An unusual person
2. A natural phenomenon (a tornado)
3. Cave formations
4. Oktoberfest in _____ (any city)
5. The Statue of Liberty
6. The Pacific (or Atlantic) Ocean
7. Marine life
8. A riot
9. A night in Las Vegas
10. Open-heart surgery
11. A ski slope
12. A Hawaiian sunset
13. A mountain view
14. Some rare animal
15. A cruise ship
16. A specific beach
17. An antique (car, furniture, coin)
18. The great oak tree
19. Unusual landscape
20. A foreign country

Preparing a Speech of Description

The preparation for a speech of description generally follows the guidelines of the Speech to Inform (Project 13). The distinction between this speech and Project 13 is the focus of the assignment. Project 13 deals with informing in general, whereas this project deals with the specific aspects of description as they apply to informing.

First, this speech must focus on a specific, mentally visible person, place, object, or event. To be visible in the minds of your audience members, what you describe must be specific and concrete. Your audience members can't see "love," for example, but they *can* see the Statue of Liberty. In selecting a topic to describe, recall the suggestions for Selecting Topics (Project 1) and the requirements for informative speeches (Project 13).

The second focus of the descriptive speech preparation is its organization. Since the objective of your assignment is to present a clear, accurate mental picture to your audience, a spatial order as described in Project 3 will often be the most successful. For example, you might describe the Statue of Liberty from top to bottom or from bottom to top. On the other hand, you might use a topical pattern if you describe the texture, its construction material and its size, or some other aspect. Once you decide on the specific aspects to describe for your audience members, forming your outline and the basis of your speech will be easy.

A third focus of description is to select the specific descriptive elements you will present. Remember, you will not be able to present everything there is to know about the person, place, object, or event you will describe. If you do, you will violate the rule of presenting "new" material to your audience. Another potential problem is that you will create "information overload" for your audience members by presenting more information than they can digest. In addition, you probably will not have enough time to present everything, given the time limits on most speeches. So select aspects that are new to your audience and those that help create a sensory image for your audience. Then present a mental picture so vivid that your audience members can actually "see" what you describe.

Presenting a Speech of Description

Since this is an informative speech, it should be presented in the same manner as any other informative speech. Use an extemporaneous method of delivery for this type of speech so you can maintain eye contact with your audience members, and thus adjust to their feedback.

Drawing mental pictures can become dull if you don't maintain enthusiasm and energy in your presentation. Sometimes visual aids can be very helpful for your audience members to see general details that you describe and for you to help point out the relationships between the parts of the whole object or their relative locations.

As you speak, be sure your audience members note your sincere desire to present this specific description for them. Determine how your audience members can use the information and present your speech so you fulfill this need in your audience. Be conversational, but speak loudly enough for everyone to hear you easily without straining.

SAMPLE DESCRIPTIVE SPEECH

By Susie Pearson

The Elm Tree

In the early days of the frontier, two identical tracks could be seen running along side by side through the dusty, rocky crevices of the mountains and over soft green blankets of clover in the valleys across the United States. What mighty object could have endured such rugged miles? The wagon wheel, made from the strong, stone-hard wood of the elm tree. For ten years I made use of the elm tree in my own backyard, but not in the form of a wagon wheel. In the hot, sticky summer afternoons when the smell of freshly mowed grass was heavy in the air, I would sit in the cool shade of the elm tree and watch my cats play in its limbs.

You, too, might have an elm tree in your yard, and just don't know what it is. At any rate, elm trees are common in many parts of the United States as shade trees today, although many have been destroyed by Dutch Elm disease.

Today, I will describe the three main parts of the elm tree in my backyard. These three main parts are the root system, the trunk, and the limbs.

First, I will describe the root system of the elm tree. The root system started from a single seed no bigger than the eraser on the end of your pencil. From that seed, a carrot-shaped tap root formed. Over the years, the tap root thrust its way downward through the hard soil to the inner depth of the earth in search of a supply of cool water to quench its thirst. From this tap root stem millions of coarse, tiny root hairs intertwining their way through the pebbles and dirt in the upper layers of the soil in search of additional water and nutrients.

From this complicated network of roots, shooting upward, out of the ground, is the second part of the elm tree—the trunk. The trunk is shaped like a three-leaf clover and often the trunk of a mature tree measures three feet in diameter. It is covered with an armor of rough, knobby dark brown-gray bark. Underneath the bark is an aromatic slimy syrup-like substance which is sometimes used to soothe irritated throats. In the very core of the trunk you can find the stone-hard wood from which wagon wheels were made. The main trunk stands six to seven feet high and then branches out into the third main part of the tree—the limbs.

Usually, three major limbs rise upward from the mighty trunk. Growing from these three limbs are hundreds of smaller limbs towering up to fifty feet high and spreading outward into a twenty-foot span. The limbs are covered with the same rough, knobby bark as that of the trunk. From these limbs stem small twigs covered with smooth light-gray bark. In the winter the tree limbs are decorated with tiny reddish-brown buds. In the summer, they wear a brilliant green headdress of almond teardrop-shaped leaves that have sawtooth edges.

In conclusion, I have described for you the three main parts of the elm tree. First was the tap root, with its millions of coarse, tiny hairs that stretches well into the earth for the tree's nutrients. Second was the clover-shaped trunk, covered with knobby dark, brown-gray bark ranging up to three feet in diameter. Third was the limbs which often reach fifty feet high and spread out twenty feet or more with their shade.

In closing, the next time you are stretched out on a lawn chair in the shade of your favorite shade tree and something hits you on the top of the head, when you look up to see what flew over, take a good look at the tree also. You should be able to tell if it's an elm tree.

SAMPLE OUTLINE—DESCRIPTIVE SPEECH

I. Introduction
    A. Attention-getter: Wagon wheel
    B. Credentials: Ten years
    C. Arouse interest: You

II. THESIS: Today I will describe the three main parts of the elm tree in my backyard.
    PREVIEW: These three main parts are: (1) roots, (2) trunk, and (3) limbs.

III. Body
    A. Roots
        1. Seed
        2. Tap
        3. Network
    B. Trunk
        1. Clover-shaped
        2. Diameter
        3. Texture
    C. Limbs
        1. Height
        2. Span
        3. Foliage

IV. Conclusion
    A. Review main points
        1. Roots
        2. Trunk
        3. Limbs
    B. Closing: Look

Project Assignment

Prepare and present a two- to four-minute speech describing a person, a place, an object, or an event. Unless otherwise instructed, write out only an outline so that you speak extemporaneously. A copy of the outline should be presented to your instructor before you begin to speak. As you prepare and present your speech, give special attention to language that creates clear, accurate mental pictures for your audience. Remember, your purpose is to make what you are describing clear and vivid in the minds of your audience members.

In preparing for this assignment, begin with your personal knowledge of the object you are preparing to describe. Go back and look at the object again, if you can. Or close your eyes and transport yourself to the object and time in your past so you can resee it in your mind. Be sure that your organization of the body of the speech follows a logical pattern that your audience members can easily follow. Be especially enthusiastic in your presentation of the speech so your audience members can also get excited about your topic.

References

Bradley, B. E. (1988). *Fundamentals of Speech Communication* (5th ed.). Dubuque, Iowa: Wm. C. Brown Company, Publishers.

Fetzer, R. C. & Vogel, R. A. (1982). *Designing Messages: A Guide for Creative Speakers.* Chicago: Science Research Associates, Inc.

Minnick, W. C. (1983). *Public Speaking* (2nd ed.). Boston: Houghton Mifflin Company.

Ochs, D. J. & Winkler, A. C. (1983). *A Brief Introduction to Speech* (2nd ed.). New York: Harcourt Brace Jovanovich.

Verderber, R. F. (1988). *The Challenge of Effective Speaking* (7th ed.). Belmont, California: Wadsworth Publishing Company.

PROJECT **17**

The Speech of Definition

New truths begin as heresies and end as superstitions.
—Thomas Huxley

Whenever someone talks to you about a concept that may be interpreted in more than one manner, you seek a definition. In seeking a definition, you try to determine which of several possible interpretations you are supposed to use in understanding what the other person intends. Definitions are the means by which we make sense of our world. This project presents the principles of definition, preparing the speech of definition, presenting the speech of definition, and a sample speech of definition.

Principles of Definition

The primary purpose of definition is to clarify meaning. Only after the speaker and audience share a common meaning can understanding take place. In some instances, you may need to devote an entire speech to definition so you are certain your audience members understand your concept. However, most speeches are not totally devoted to definition—only a portion of your speech explains the concept and the rest of the speech presents some other form or aspect of speaking. The principles in both cases are the same, whether you present an entire speech of definition or a definition within another speech.

You use words every day that you feel may need no explanation—no definition. Whenever there is any doubt about the meaning of a word, or there is ambiguity because a word has two or more meanings, you need to spend time defining precisely what you mean. Whenever you use a word your audience members may not fully understand, you need to define. Unless you and your audience members share a common definition of the concepts you are talking about, you are not communicating.

Some topics suitable for speeches of definition include terms like:

1. Liberal, moderate, conservative
2. Cryogenics or cryosurgery

   3. Autism
   4. Somatology
   5. New slang expressions (like bad, awesome)
   6. A foreign word frequently heard (like fiat, coup, faux pas)
   7. Computer terminology (floppy disk, program, DOS)
   8. Terms usually heard as letters (ESP, AIDS, LSD)
   9. Syndromes (Downs syndrome, Stockholm syndrome)
  10. The origin (etymology) of any word
  11. A word with an unusual meaning (aglet, zarf)
  12. The unusual meaning of a common word (low, mill, ward)
  13. A word used in a specific sense (fei, port, talisman)
  14. Terms from the news (like glasnost, perestroika, apartheid, greenhouse effect)
  15. Common concepts that have specialized meanings (like cholesterol, low fat, unsaturated fat, illegal drug, abuse, inflation)

Preparing a Speech of Definition

There are several acceptable methods for preparing a speech of definition. The method you use will depend a great deal on the concept you intend to define, the information available to you, and what your audience already knows. The five most common methods of defining are: (1) etymology, (2) classification, (3) comparisons, (4) synonyms and antonyms, and (5) uses.

Etymology   The etymology of a word is its origin or history. In some instances it will be helpful or meaningful for your audience members to know how a word has evolved through history or has maintained its original meaning because of some historical event or reference. One word that has changed its meaning considerably over the years is "calculate," which can be traced back to the Latin "calculus," meaning pebble. This reference is possibly a reference to the use of pebbles in counting at that time in history. An example of a word that has retained much of its original meaning over the years is "narrate" and its forms such as narration and narrative. These words come from the Latin word "narrare," which means to relate or tell.

Classification   A second method of defining is through classifying a word. When you classify a word, you put it into a class or group and tell how it is similar and how it is different from the other members of that classification. One student used classification to define "Barn Owl." He explained how the Barn Owl was like other owls and how it differed and was distinguished from other owls. Definitions of biological and zoological terms fit this type of definition very well.

Comparisons   Audience members have difficulty with the unknown. One method of defining that will help them understand the unknown is to compare it with the known. Comparisons point out similarities between two concepts. Contrasts, which point out differences, can also help. Comparisons work best with abstract terms like "liberal." In this case comparisons with "moderates" and "conservatives" may well tell your audience members exactly what you mean when other forms of definition might not.

Synonym and Antonym   When you define by synonym, you use words that have the same or almost the same meaning. When you define by antonym, you use words with the opposite meaning. Defining by synonym and antonym is a special form of comparison and contrast and works only if your audience members are familiar with the synonyms and antonyms you use. For example, let's say you would like to define the word "Heaven" using synonyms and antonyms. Synonyms include, "paradise, the abode of God, dwelling place of the righteous after death, our eternal home, the afterworld, afterlife," and so on. To define "Heaven" using antonyms, you could use "hell, hades, the underworld, eternal agony," and so on. These single words are only examples of synonyms and antonyms that can be used. As a speaker, you will need to explain the relationships of the terms.

Uses   A final method of defining is to explain the *use* of an object. Sometimes people will not understand a term but will understand the function of the object. When you explain a word in terms of its use or function, your audience members can quickly comprehend your message. For example, many people would not know a *zarf* by name. On the other hand, most people will quickly understand what you were defining if you explained that a *zarf* is the holder for a handleless coffee cup. Most of us have seen and used a zarf at one time or another.

Definitions should be brief and to the point if they are to communicate. Even speeches of definition need to be short to prevent your audience members from becoming bored. Remember, the purpose of a definition is to share a common meaning with your audience. Often in speeches of definition you will want to use a combination of methods to make sure you and your audience members are working on the same meanings. The combination of methods allows for greater coverage of a term and helps a larger segment of your audience to understand the term or concept you are defining.

Presenting a Speech of Definition

Because definition by itself is not very exciting, you must present your definition as enthusiastically and as interestingly as you can. Be energetic and original in what you say. Make your audience members feel that it is important for them to understand your definition. In doing this, you will need to show your audience members how they can use the word and its meaning to better advantage. Simply telling audience members that they will be better off knowing what you tell them will not be sufficient. In some instances you can tell your audience members that understanding the term will save time, money, or possibly a life. In other instances it may simply be a case of more complete understanding of your speech or someone else's speech, or for those important games of trivia.

Whenever possible, use visual aids with your speech of definition—pictures, charts, or anything that will create interest in your definition, your speech, or communication and aid you in getting and maintaining audience attention. Don't expect your visual aid to make your speech interesting for you, but use it to help you *increase* interest. In most instances you will not want to use a poster or chart simply to show the spelling of the word; however, in some instances, as with a foreign word or phrase where the spelling and pronunciation are significantly different from the English, this may well help you.

As you get up to speak, use all of your bodily movements, eye contact, and vocal techniques to convey to your audience that you are confident. Observe the time limits and stop when your speech is finished—don't ramble on. Make your conclusion strong and appropriate to your preceding remarks. In fact, a good, strong conclusion can sometimes save an otherwise uninteresting definition.

SAMPLE DEFINITION SPEECH

By Steven Jones

Aglets

Today we are going to play the role of spermologer. No, we are not going to be studying sperm, but rather odd facts such as words with little known meanings. I am a part-time spermologer whose interest was stimulated while reading *Boyd's Book of Odd Facts,* Chapter 14, "Words and Meanings." The hobby has come in very handy during the current fad of pursuing trivia. Our word for today is *aglet,* an object that I see many of you brought plenty of today.

Today, I will define "aglet" for you by looking at two aspects of the word. Those two aspects are: (1) the origin of the word, (2) the use or purpose of the aglet.

First, what is the origin of the word "aglet?" The word "aglet" in its current form is derived from the Middle French word aguillette, spelled a-g-u-i-l-l-e-t-t-e, which means diminutive. This word in turn was derived from the Old French word aguille, spelled a-g-u-i-l-l-e, which means needle. Finally, aguille was derived from the Latin word acus, spelled a-c-u-s, which also means needle. Thus the word "aglet" literally means "a diminutive needle."

What is an "aglet," you are still asking? An aglet is the little piece of plastic or metal at the end of your shoelace. Additionally, an aglet may be any substance that forms a sheath around the end of a string, lace, cord, or rope.

Second, what purpose does the "aglet" serve? That is pretty obvious. As a sheath, the aglet prevents the lace or cord from unraveling at the end. This makes the lace or cord very easy to handle. But, more importantly, the aglet allows the end of the lace to be used as a needle. This means the lace can easily be slipped through the holes in your shoe or boot, or any other hole as needed.

Hopefully, for all you new found spermologers and trivia buffs, you now have a new word to test on your friends. The word is *aglet*. It is the name of the little piece of plastic at the end of your shoelace. Its purpose is to allow the lace to be handled easily, as a needle would be, which is sufficiently compatible with its origin. Go forth and spread the word.

SAMPLE OUTLINE—DEFINITION SPEECH

1. Introduction
    A. Attention-getter: Spermologer
    B. Credibility: Interest and study
    C. Arouse interest: Trivia
II. THESIS: Today I will define "aglet" by looking at two aspects of the word.
    PREVIEW: Those two aspects are: (1) the origin of the word and (2) the use or purpose of the aglet.
III. BODY (main points and supporting materials)
    A. Origin of aglet
        1. Middle French—"aguillette"
        2. Old French—"aguille"
        3. Latin—"acus"
    B. Use of the aglet
        1. Prevents unraveling
        2. Acts like a needle
IV. Conclusion
    A. Review main points
        1. Origin of aglet
        2. Use of aglet
    B. Closing thought: Spread word

References

Boyd, L. M. (1979). Words and meanings. *Boyd's Book of Odd Facts.* New York: New American Library. *World Book Encyclopedia Dictionary.* (1972). Chicago: World Book, Inc.

Project Assignment

Prepare and present a two- to four-minute speech of definition. Select a word or concept that your audience members will not fully understand by merely hearing it. That is, select a word or concept that has several possible interpretations, is new, possibly has a vague meaning, or has an unusual definition. Select the method(s) of defining that will most clearly explain what you mean to convey to your audience members in terms they will readily understand.

In preparing for this assignment, begin with your personal knowledge of the term you are preparing to define. Then go to authoritative sources like dictionaries, dictionaries of synonyms, and other specialized sources. Be sure your organization of the body of the speech follows a logical pattern your audience members can easily follow. Sometimes using a pattern that follows your methods of defining will work well. Be especially enthusiastic in your presentation of the speech so your audience members can also get excited about your topic. Unless you show some enthusiasm for your term, your audience members will not likely be very interested.

References

Bradley, B. E. (1988). *Fundamentals of Speech Communication* (5th ed.). Dubuque, Iowa: Wm. C. Brown Company, Publishers.

Fetzer, R. C. & Vogel, R. A. (1982). *Designing Messages: A Guide for Creative Speakers.* Chicago: Science Research Associates, Inc.

Nelson, P. E. & Pearson, J. C. (1990). *Confidence in Public Speaking* (4th ed.). Dubuque, Iowa: Wm. C. Brown Company, Publishers.

Verderber, R. F. (1988). *The Challenge of Effective Speaking* (7th ed.). Belmont, California: Wadsworth Publishing Company.

Walter, O. M. & Scott, R. L. (1984). *Thinking and Speaking* (5th ed.). New York: Macmillan Publishing Company.

PROJECT **18**

Explaining Processes

Most human beings would rather suffer permanently
without a talent than to endure the temporary pain of
acquiring it.

—Whiting

Almost every day someone wants to know how to do something, how to make something, or how something works. When you make this type of explanation your audience members will understand better and be able to perform the function better if they can also *see* how you perform each step. In explaining the process, however, you need to do more than simply show and tell. You need to *demonstrate* the steps of the process, which involves both the physical and mental skills involved in completing the process. This project explains the principles of the process speech, preparing process speeches, presenting process speeches, and a sample process speech.

Principles of Process Speeches

The process speech appears deceptively simple. All you must do is select a topic you know well and tell your audience members how to perform the steps, right? This is what makes the process speech deceptive. However, most students seem to approach the process speech in this manner. If you know your topic well, you may leave out important steps or skip necessary explanations that your audience members need to perform the process successfully for themselves. On the other hand, if you don't know the process well enough, you will likely omit or skip steps or explanations your audience members need to complete the process.

The process speech is more than a simple "show-and-tell" project like you used to present in kindergarten. You must do more than simply *display* some object as you talk about it, you must demonstrate its function or show a process. If you talk about glass etching, for example, you need to do more than show the audience a piece of blank glass and one with an etching. You need to demonstrate the steps in preparing the glass, putting the design on the glass, and preparing the glass for display. The purpose is more specific than merely informing the audience about the process because you must show the use or application of the materials you are demonstrating.

In selecting a process to demonstrate to your audience, be cautious that you don't select one that is too simple (one the audience already knows, like how to tie your shoes) or one that is too complex for them (one the audience members could not comprehend within the time limits, like how a nuclear reactor works). You need a topic that will fit within your time limits without rushing it or stretching it, and one that meets the requirements for an informative speech. Some topics suitable for a "process" speech include:

1. How to perform some athletic feat (throw a football, swing a golf club, break a board, etc.)
2. How to build a bird house, aquarium, porch swing, and so on.
3. How to make flies for fishermen, puppets, and so on.
4. How to sew, knit, crochet, macramé, and so on
5. How to select, cut, or grade meat
6. How to perform CPR
7. How to perform card trick(s)
8. How to play a musical instrument
9. How to transform some "old" object into something useful
10. How to perform any craft such as ceramics, glass etching, painting, and so on.
11. The process of decision making in some event such as Napoleon's defeat, Bay of Pigs, *Challenger* shuttle disaster, and so on
12. The process of a specific law from inception to law (ERA, tax revision, etc.)
13. The appeal process in a specific court case (*Roe* v. *Wade*, school prayer, etc.)
14. Some scientific process such as photosynthesis, fission, fusion, and so on.
15. Any other process relating to your major field of study (a business process, a computing process, a teaching process, etc.)
16. Each of the preceding topics could be turned into a "how-not-to" topic

Generally, avoid topics dealing with cooking because we can all read and follow recipes. Also, avoid simple topics like how to iron clothing or wrap gifts. These topics are so simple we will gain little, if anything, from them. Use your time and your audience members' time more wisely.

Preparing a Process Speech

After you have selected your topic, the first step in preparing your speech is for you to complete the process to determine how much time it takes and to list the steps and substeps for yourself. You may decide the pattern of organization at this time also. Generally, process speeches use the chronological pattern as the steps must be completed in a specific order to complete the product or perform the process correctly. For example, if you were demonstrating the glass etching process, and you applied the acid first, your process would not complete the product successfully. In some other instances you may use a topical order because your steps do not need to be completed in a specific order, as in a speech about a business process where it doesn't matter which step you perform first, second, or third.

A second consideration in preparing your process speech is the preparation of your visual aids. Some topics, such as knitting or macramé, for example, will require that you prepare some of the steps ahead of your presentation because you don't have time to complete the entire process during your speech. If you were demonstrating the process of making a bird feeder, you might need to cut out pieces ahead of time; or if you were arranging flowers, you might need to have several arrangements in partial stages of completion so you could demonstrate the steps of the process without *completing* all the steps. In both of these instances you would need a completed sample to show the finished product to your audience since it is unlikely that you could demonstrate all the steps and complete the product in front of your audiences' eyes within the time limits.

In some instances you may need to group the steps of your process. You should never have more than three or four steps to your process because that is all your audience can remember. If you have a lengthy process that includes 12 or 15 steps, you can group the steps as substeps of larger categories. For example, if you were building a birdhouse, step 1 could be gathering or preparing your materials; step 2, assembling your materials; and step 3, finishing your birdhouse. All substeps such as what to gather and sizes to prepare would be placed under step 1. The steps of assembling, such as which pieces need to be placed together first, and the process of gluing or nailing, and so on would be placed under step 2, and what you finish the house with (paint or varnish) and the steps of putting a hanger on it, would be grouped under step 3.

Once you feel you have your demonstration prepared, perform it again to make sure it fits your time limits. As you rehearse, always use the visual aids you plan to use as you demonstrate the process. Perform every detail as you rehearse or you will likely forget something during your presentation. Another reason for rehearsing what you plan to do is to ensure that your presentation goes smoothly. If you just think through or "mock" your real actions, you will likely have some unforeseen difficulty in the actual presentation before your audience. Rehearsing allows you the opportunity to foresee any problems you might have in front of your audience.

Rehearse details or particulars of the process to tell your audience members as you perform lengthy steps of the process. Your audience will want to hear you talk about what you are doing and your reasons for doing it. You can also add cautions and variations of your technique to fill spaces while you finish intricate steps. For example, you could say, "now here is the tricky part," or "If you're not careful . . ." or "It is most important at this point for you to . . ." Sometimes it will also help your audience members if you show both left- and right-handed strategies, if they are different.

Presenting a Process Speech

As with other speeches to inform, your objective is to present new information to your audience. Since the information is new, your audience members may have difficulty remembering your ideas. So, help them by grouping your ideas into easy-to-remember points and repeat these steps. Be sure you state your points simply and in as few words as possible. If you have lengthy points or words that have no meaning for your audience members, they will not easily remember your speech and you will have missed one of the important aspects of informative speaking.

Don't rush your speaking or the movements you make in showing intricate manipulations. If you are demonstrating knitting or Karate moves, you will need to go through the steps in slow motion so your audience members can see how the movements are orchestrated. Then you will want to speed the movement up a bit, and finally go through the steps at normal speed. If you perform at only slow motion or normal speed, you will not have given a completely understandable demonstration.

Be sure you keep all visual aids and demonstrations in front of you and in full view of your audience. If your audience members can't see what you are showing them, they will not be able to understand or perform your process on their own. In most instances you will want your audience members to be able to perform the steps of your process for themselves in the future. If your process is one that audience members are merely to "understand," as in the process of an historical event, you will still want to present some form of visual aid that will help audience members remember your process.

Be enthusiastic and interesting in your presentation. If you act excited about your topic, your audience members will also get interested and excited. Maintain as much direct eye contact with your audience members as possible. As you are demonstrating, look at your visual aids to locate yourself, but then look back at your audience members and speak as much as you can to get their feedback. You need to see from them whether they understand your explanations. If you concentrate on your visual aids, you can't see the audience reactions and will not know if you have been understood.

Keep your presentation within the time limits. Keep your speech and demonstration moving along steadily—don't let a step bog you down or create "silent" spots. If a step is not working out as you had planned, stop forcing it after several tries and tell your audience what is supposed to happen and move on to the next step of the process. Sometimes the excitement of performing the steps of the process in front of an audience will make it more difficult to do all steps as smoothly as you would in the privacy of your home with no one watching you. Finish your demonstration as enthusiastically as you began. A good way to end your demonstration is to remind your audience members of the steps necessary to complete the process and how they can use the information for themselves.

SAMPLE PROCESS SPEECH

By Lynn McNeill

Making Covered-Wagon Mailboxes

What do ropes have in common with a mailbox? What do brooms have in common with a mailbox? For that matter, what do flour sacks have in common with a mailbox? If your answers are: "I have no idea." let me assure you there can be a connection.

Two and one half years ago my husband and I started a woodcraft business in our backyard. A year later we developed a plan for a covered-wagon mailbox. This product has been so successful we have sold over forty, probably closer to fifty, some of which have gone to Texas, Louisiana, Illinois and Oklahoma.

Today I will demonstrate the three main steps to painting a covered-wagon mailbox. These three steps are: (1) gathering materials, (2) painting the base, and (3) painting the design.

First, let me begin with the materials you will need. These materials are very basic. I use water-based enamel paint. These paints usually cost $2.25 and last about one year. I use very inexpensive paint brushes which can be bought at any Walmart or Kmart for about $1 each. I also use toothpicks occasionally for the small detail work on the base. You must use a galvanized, rural mailbox in order for the paint to stick. The last materials I use are the "clean-up" items. These consist of water and paper towels. After you have gathered all of your materials, you are ready to begin step two.

Step two consists of painting the base. First, you paint black horizontal lines the width of the base (show this). Be sure you leave about one inch between each line. Next you paint black, staggered, vertical lines between each horizontal line forming individual pieces of lumber (show this). When these two steps are finished, simply take the end of your paint brush and dip it into the black paint, and make small dots at each end of the "lumber" pieces (show this). This gives the illusion that the boards have nails. You are now ready for the second phase of the base, painting the "hanging items."

The "hanging items" can range from ropes to soup kettles. Anything that the pioneers would have used crossing the plains would be appropriate. Today I will demonstrate how to paint a broom onto the base. I usually paint the handle green in order for it to contrast with the boards (show this). After I have painted a vertical green line down a portion of the base, I take the red and yellow paint, swirl the colors together, and paint the "straw" onto the top of the broom. When this is finished, I go back and paint a small black line between the straw and the broom handle in order to achieve the look of a "hanger." (Show this.) When I have painted six to eight items on the base, I am ready for step three.

Step three consists of painting the mailbox itself. On each mailbox you have the flag side and the opposite side. I usually begin on the flag side which, for the most part, consists of the name and address. This can be anywhere from one line to seven lines, depending on what the owner wants printed here. I have already painted the name and address on this particular box to save time. Now I will finish this side by painting a small design beside the name. The color scheme of this particular mailbox is the individual's company colors. So I have painted the name and address in black and will do the design in yellow.

I am now ready to paint the opposite side. This is my favorite side because I can use my imagination more. I have two ways of painting the opposite side—patterned or unpatterned. The patterned scheme is simply filling in the blanks. I trace around a pattern and paint in the design. I prefer painting nonpatterned. This allows me to use my imagination more and create scenes or slogans to fit the individual. On this mailbox I am painting the slogan "Hay Van Manufacturing" in black print and will finish by placing small black lines underneath these words (show this). After this is completed, I am finished with this particular mailbox, and need to let it dry for about one hour.

In conclusion, let me remind you of the three steps in painting a covered-wagon mailbox. First, gather all of your materials. Don't forget to collect paints, brushes, mailbox and cleanup supplies. Second, paint the base of the mailbox. As you do, make the base look like boards nailed together. Finally, you paint the mailbox itself. Plan what you need to put on each side of the mailbox and center it so it looks neat and readable from a distance.

The next time you go out to your boring mailbox and pull down the boring lid, or perhaps you have a post office mailbox and you have to climb those many steps everyday, remember what you could have with an exciting covered-wagon mailbox. And when you reach in and pull out a bill, you can feel more enthusiasm with a new covered-wagon mailbox. ("Oh look! A bill! How exciting!")

SAMPLE OUTLINE—PROCESS SPEECH

I. Introduction
   A. Attention-getter: Curiosity
   B. Credentials: Two and one half years
   C. Arouse interest: Fun, money-maker
II. THESIS: Today I will demonstrate the three steps in painting a covered-wagon mailbox.
   PREVIEW: These three steps are: (1) gathering materials, (2) painting base, and (3) painting mailbox.
III. Body
   A. Gathering materials
     1. Mailbox
     2. Paint supplies
     3. Cleaning supplies
   B. Painting base
     1. Lumber
     2. Hanging items
   C. Painting mailbox
     1. Flag side
     2. Opposite side
IV. Conclusion
   A. Review main points
     1. Gathering materials
     2. Painting base
     3. Painting mailbox
   B. Closing thought: Humorous ending

Project Assignment

Prepare and present a four- to six-minute process speech in which you demonstrate how to do something, how to make something, or how something works. Unless otherwise instructed, prepare and work only from an outline so that you speak extemporaneously. A copy of your outline should be presented to your instructor before you speak. Give special attention to a clear organization of steps that your audience members will find easy to remember.

As you prepare your speech, be sure that you plan verbal descriptions of what you are showing your audience members as well as presenting the process visually. Sequencing the steps in your process will be just as important as showing the steps themselves. As you rehearse this speech, be sure you rehearse both what you will say and what you will do.

Your introduction should gain attention, establish your right to talk about your topic, and arouse your audience members' interest in your speech. As you prepare your conclusion, be sure you review the steps in the process for your audience members, and make a final statement to close. Remember, you are trying to teach your process to audience members who do not know this process well. Include as many details and cautions as necessary so people can leave your presentation and perform the operation on their own.

References

Ayres, J. & Miller, J. (1990). *Effective Public Speaking* (3rd ed.). Dubuque, Iowa: Wm. C. Brown Company, Publishers.

Bradley, B. E. (1988). *Fundamentals of Speech Communication* (5th ed.). Dubuque, Iowa: Wm. Brown Company, Publishers.

Fetzer, R. C. & Vogel, R. A. (1982). *Designing Messages: A Guide for Creative Speakers.* Chicago: Science Research Associates, Inc.

Lucas, S. E. (1989). *The Art of Public Speaking* (3rd ed.). New York: Random House.

Minnick, W. C. (1983). *Public Speaking* (2nd ed.). Boston: Houghton Mifflin Company.

Nelson, P. E. & Pearson, J. C. (1990). *Confidence in Public Speaking* (4th ed.). Dubuque, Iowa: Wm. C. Brown Company, Publishers.

Verderber, R. F. (1988). *The Challenge of Effective Speaking* (7th ed.). Belmont, California: Wadsworth Publishing Company.

Zimmerman, G. I., Owen, J. L., & Seibert, D. R. (1986). *Speech Communication: A Contemporary Introduction* (3rd ed.). St. Paul, Minnesota: West Publishing Company.

UNIT **IV**

THE SPEECH TO PERSUADE

There is nothing more difficult to take in hand, more perilous to conduct, or more uncertain in its success than to take the lead in the introduction of a new order to things.

Jean-Jacques Rousseau

Project 19:   The Speech to Convince
Project 20:   The Speech to Stimulate
Project 21:   The Speech to Get Action

Unit IV consists of three projects designed to provide several different experiences in persuading audiences. Project 19 presents the principles of "The Speech to Convince." The objective of this project is to get the audience to accept your proposals willingly. Project 20, "The Speech to Stimulate," is designed to stir up the audience so that it wants something done. The distinction between these two projects is very subtle, and is intended to provide variety in projects rather than a great distinction between two types of persuasion. The "Speech to Get Action," Project 21, differs from the first two persuasive speeches in that it concentrates on the action the speaker desires the audience to take. Again, the distinction is very subtle, and is a matter of degree rather than a different type of persuasion.

PROJECT 19

The Speech to Convince

> The best way to get on in the world is to make people
> believe it's to their advantage to help you.
> —Jean de La Bruyère

We are bombarded daily by all kinds of persuasive messages that try to get us to do or think in a specific manner. Sometimes we are pulled in several directions at the same time. When people try to persuade us, they want us to be convinced so our behaviors are consistent with our ideas. Actually, very few people do what someone else wants unless they are convinced. In fact, Samuel Butler once said, "A man convinced against his will is of the same opinion still." You may do what others want if you have to, but this does not mean you have been convinced it is the right thing to do. Because you want to learn to convince people rather than coerce them into doing what you want, this project presents the principles of the speech to convince, preparing a speech to convince, presenting a speech to convince, and a sample speech to convince.

Principles of the Speech to Convince

The objective of the speech to convince is to get your audience members to agree with your belief, attitude, or opinion. Through the use of logic, evidence, and emotion you work to secure the *willing* acceptance of your proposal by your audience members. If you are to get audience members to agree to your concepts willingly, you must present sufficient logic and evidence to persuade them that you are right. An important aspect of convincing an audience is to get them to accept your proposal willingly. You do not coerce or threaten audience members with consequences if they don't accept your position. Instead, the skillful speaker uses the available means of persuasion and allows the audience members the freedom to agree or not agree without fear of retribution. For example, the block bully may get the other kids on the block to agree with him, but they do so out of fear rather than through conviction that he is right. Very few kids on the block will be his "friend" without coercion, unless they get something in return. The same is true of the boss who tells people who work for him or her to perform an undesirable task or be fired. People may perform the task rather than be fired, but they are not likely to be convinced about the task because they were coerced rather than persuaded.

The arguments you offer to convince your audience must be based on sound reasoning and good, unbiased evidence. You base your reasoning on the evidence (factual data, statistics, and expert testimony) you have available. It is usually wise to appeal to the basic emotions of your audience members, such as appealing to love of country, self-preservation, desire for recognition, desire for adventure, loyalty, political beliefs, religion, and the like. This necessitates a thorough analysis of your audience so you may base your appeal on their beliefs and attitudes. It also means you must present your logic and evidence in such a way that it will direct their thinking through channels they can readily follow and accept.

The speech to convince can be used almost anytime you want to secure audience agreement. The speech to convince is used in virtually every organization at some time. For instance, any time there is a difference of opinion and people try to get other members to agree to their point you have a speech to convince. You reach many daily decisions by convincing other people that you are right—for example, you argue against going to Mickey's for lunch because you heard they use soybean substitute in their meat; you convince a friend to take you to a party because you need a ride and the other person doesn't know where the party is to be held, and so on.

The ultimate goal of the speech to convince is simply to get your audience members to share your position. Therefore, a sales talk is not a speech to convince because your purpose in a sales talk is to get your audience members to take the action of giving you money for your product. Naturally, a certain amount of convincing precedes your request for money, but your *ultimate goal* is to get a specific amount of money in return for your product. You really do not care whether the audience members change their minds, just so you get their money. We may conclude, then, that a speech to convince is not a sales talk, nor is it primarily to stimulate or arouse your audience members about your topic; it is one in which your purpose is to change another person's mind about something on which there is definite disagreement.

Some topics suitable for speeches to convince include:

1. All U.S. citizens capable of working should be provided jobs.
2. All efforts at altering the natural genetic process should be controlled by international agreements.
3. Anyone who receives welfare payments ought to repay the government by performing services for local, state, or federal government agencies.
4. There should (or should not) be control of nuclear space weapons.
5. All U.S. citizens should (or should not) pay a flat tax rate for all taxes.
6. The federal government should (should not) institute a national lottery.
7. Every mentally able person should be legally compelled to attend school until he or she completes high school.
8. Outer space travel regulations should be established by international agreements.
9. Family size should be limited by law.
10. Mercy killings should be legalized nationally.
11. Strikes should be prohibited by law.
12. Compulsory arbitration of all labor disputes should be established by law.
13. Gambling should be legalized nationally.
14. Antipollution laws should be made stronger and strictly enforced.
15. Welfare should be abolished.
16. Day-care centers for children of working mothers should be run by the state.
17. Test-tube babies should be government controlled.
18. All known dope addicts should be committed to special hospitals for treatment.
19. Nuclear warfare should be outlawed.
20. Human cloning should be regulated by law.

Preparing a Speech to Convince

In preparing the speech to convince, remember your goal is to get people to agree with you. Eventually, you may wish to change their actions, but your sole purpose in this speech is to secure agreement. This is not an easy task, but it is not impossible. To achieve the "convincing effect," you need to look carefully into the organization of your speech. In Project 3 two patterns of organization suitable for persuasive speeches were presented—the problem-solution order and the causal order. Either one can be used to convince an audience, as well as the topical order, which would show the reasons you have for your audience to be convinced.

The suggested steps that follow do not apply to all speeches to convince, but you should *consider* the following areas if you use a problem-solution order:

1. *Give a history of the problem.* Discuss the events leading up to the present time that make the topic important. Tell why it is significant for your audience members to hear the discussion you are about to present. (Do not spend too much time on the history; you have other points to cover.)

2. *Discuss the present-day effects of the problem.* Give examples, illustrations, facts, and views of authorities that clearly bring out the situation you are talking about. These are musts if you wish to be convincing.

3. *Discuss the factors that brought about the effects you listed in point 2.* Here again, you must present examples, illustrations, facts, and views of authorities to prove your points. Be sure you show how these factors brought about the effects you mentioned.

4. *List possible solutions to the problem.* Discuss briefly the various alternatives that could be taken, but show that they are not effective enough to solve your problem. Give evidence for your statements: examples, illustrations, authorities' views, facts, and analogies.

5. *Give your solution to the problem.* Show why your solution is the best answer. Present your evidence and the reason for believing as you do. This must not be simply your opinion. It must be logical reasoning backed up by evidence from other authorities.

6. *Show how your proposal will benefit your audience members.* This is the real meat of your entire speech, if you have completed each preceding step up to this point. Here is where you must convince. You definitely need to show your listeners how they will benefit from your proposal—for example, how they will make more money, be safer from an enemy, live longer, be happier, get better roads, get better schools, have lower taxes, or buy cheaper groceries. In other words, your listeners must see clearly and vividly that your proposal will help them. They must concur on this point.

7. *Answer the question, what, if anything, do you want your audience members to do about the solution you propose?* Here is the proof of your effectiveness. You now tell your audience members what you want them to accept. If you have been convincing up to this point, they will probably go along with you; if not, you have "stumbled" somewhere in your speech. You may ask your audience members to write to their congressional representatives, to vote for or against a bill, to give money to charity, to attend a rally, or to clean up their town. You suggest the action for them but you do not argue for its performance since this would lead into a speech to get action.

If you use a causal order, consider the following areas:

1. *Give a history of the problem.* See the explanation of this point on the problem-solution organization.

2. *Discuss the causes of the problem.* Give examples, illustrations, facts, and views of authorities to point out the nature of the problem and the extent of the causes of the problem.

3. *Demonstrate that the causes produce certain effects.* Show the conditions needed for a cause–effect relationship. For example, you could show that the increasing rise in the national debt continues to lessen the money available for housing loans and could eventually make it impossible for young couples to own homes.

4. *Show the effects produced.* Use the testimony of experts, statistics, and examples to show that the effects result from the causes you pointed out earlier. Here is where you can secure conviction.

The preceding procedure can be reversed also so that effects are presented first.

If you do not wish to follow the preceding methods, here is another method that accomplishes the same end but is described differently:

1. *State your proposition in the introduction* (thesis).
2. *Give a history of the problem that brought up the proposal* you are asking to be adopted.
3. *Show that your proposal is needed.* Offer evidence that establishes the need for your proposal. No other proposal (solution) will do. For example, there is too much violence on television. This violence is leading to a more violent society. There can be no other solution than to reduce the number of violent acts that can be shown during a particular viewing period.
4. *Show that your proposition is practical.* Give evidence to prove that it will do what you say it will. In other words, show that it will work. In the case of violence on television you must show that reducing the number of violent acts will reduce the number of violent crimes committed in society.
5. *Show that your proposition is desirable.* Give evidence showing the results of your proposition. Show the benefits of your proposal and their contributions to society, or how they reduce certain harms. For example, you can show that reducing the number of violent crimes on television not only reduces the number of violent crimes in society, but also increases the quality of life in America and enables television to make better use of its programming. Of course, you must then show the examples of this working. You might show how other countries use television for educational purposes, like using soap operas to reduce the spread of AIDS and other diseases.
6. *Conclude your speech with a final statement in support of your proposal.*

Note: If you are opposed to a certain proposal, you may establish your point of view (convince your audience) by offering arguments that show any one of the following to be true:

1. The proposition is not needed.   (Give evidence.)
2. The proposition is not practical.   (Give evidence.)
3. The proposition is not desirable.   (Give evidence.)

Of course, if you can establish all three of these points, you will be more convincing than if you prove only one. For this speech, follow the same procedures just outlined, but convince your audience members to reject a specific proposal rather than to adopt it.

You will face untold difficulty from your audience members if you fail to have the body of your speech properly organized and if all your points are not supported by evidence. The best guarantee of success in a speech to convince is to have your speech carefully prepared. In addition to a well-organized speech with points supported by evidence, you must have a well-constructed introduction and a strong conclusion. However, just having volumes of evidence, a clear-cut organization, and vivid language will not be sufficient to convince most audiences. You must also deliver your speech confidently and well, without excessive use of notes, if anyone is to be convinced that *you* are convinced about your own proposal.

Presenting a Speech to Convince

In general, present your speech frankly, enthusiastically, and energetically for the most desirable results. You may use a reasonable amount of emotion; however, it should not be overdone. Excessive emotion can sometimes be interpreted as a substitute for evidence or a lack of general support for your proposal. If you use emotional appeals, be sure you use them in conjunction with other forms of evidence.

Your bodily action should suit the words you utter and be such an integral part of your overall presentation that no attention is directed toward it. Vigor and intensity should characterize your bodily action. Show by your verbal and nonverbal presentation that you are convinced and you feel that you are offering the best proposal for all—not just yourself. If you get wrapped up in your subject, and show your enthusiasm for your proposal, you are likely to use natural-looking bodily actions that support your verbal presentation.

Your voice should reflect sincere belief in your views and, through inflection and modulation, carry the ring of truth and personal conviction. Utilize sufficient force to convey sound and meaning to all audience members. If you do any less, you may be perceived as a phony, or at least less than honest and sincere in your proposal. If you say you are concerned, your voice must sound concerned. If you speak with a soft voice, you may not convince audience members that you have strong convictions about your proposal.

Naturally your presentation will vary according to the occasion, the size of the room, the acoustics, and the type of audience before whom you give your speech. You would not speak to a small group of business people in the same manner as you would address a large political gathering, for example. Adapt your verbal, vocal, and nonverbal aspects of delivery to the specific conditions under which you are speaking.

SAMPLE SPEECH TO CONVINCE

By Elizabeth Wookey

Donate Blood to the American Red Cross

According to the Norman, Oklahoma American Red Cross, 250 units of blood are required each day. This does not include times of disaster, such as burn victims, tornadoes, and multiple car accidents. This blood is distributed to fifty-six different hospitals. If the Red Cross is unable to get two hundred fifty units of blood donated each day, they will not be able to supply the hospitals with the amount of blood that is needed for that day. In January of this year, blood transfusions went up two hundred units because the hospitals were full of patients who required blood transfusions. That means they needed four hundred fifty units of blood donated each day for that month.

I have been interested in donating blood for three or four years. I have also done extensive research on how you can become a donor, as well as the procedure that the Red Cross goes through.

This could affect everyone here today. Some time in the future, you may need to have a blood transfusion. How would you feel if the doctors and nurses came into your room and told you that there wasn't any blood for your blood transfusion, because no one was willing to give a little time and blood to save your life? I would hate to think that I was so selfish that I wouldn't give a little bit of myself to save someone else's life.

Today I will persuade you to donate blood to the American Red Cross for three reasons. Those three reasons are: First, because it is a simple procedure; second, because there is no cost; and third, because it saves lives.

First, you should give blood because it is a simple procedure. Anyone can be a donor. Everyone, however, must pass a health history test before the Red Cross will take a blood donation from them. This health history test consists of questions about your own medical history. You must be between the ages of seventeen and sixty-five. You must weigh at least one hundred ten pounds, and you cannot be taking any medications at the time that you donate blood. If you have been taking penicillin, you must have been off it for at least two days before you come in to give blood because it can be passed to the recipient through your blood.

In addition, a person cannot be a donor if she or he has ever had hepatitis or has ever been exposed to it. Hepatitis can also be passed on to the recipient through your blood. You cannot be sick with a cold or any other illness at the time that you want to be a donor because this will drain all of your energy and it will also take longer for your body to recover. If you have high blood pressure, the Red Cross will absolutely not let you donate blood because it would be extremely hazardous to your own health. Nor can you donate blood if you are pregnant or nursing a child. You must wait until six months after your baby has stopped nursing.

The last question on the health history test asks if you have any history of complications while donating blood. They are looking for problems such as fainting or convulsions as a result of giving blood. In some situations, they will go ahead and let you donate blood if the only complication you had was fainting. In other situations, you will not be allowed to give blood at that time.

When you go to donate blood, it is recommended that you eat at least four hours before the time of donating; this is to keep you from fainting. After you have given blood, Red Cross volunteers feed you chips, cookies, and pop or orange juice because your body needs carbohydrates, sugar, and caffeine immediately after you have given a pint of blood. This helps to restore your body with energy.

Donating blood also takes a little bit of your own personal time. We all could give up a little bit of our own personal time that we aren't doing anything important with to save someone else's life. We all would want someone to take a little time to save our lives.

Second, there is no cost to you to donate blood. You have nothing to lose but a little bit of blood which your body will replenish in two weeks. The American Red Cross will let people donate blood only every fifty-six days. This is to protect you from giving up too much of your blood and causing you to get sick, or not recover from colds and other illnesses. The Red Cross is thinking of the donor first, not just collecting blood. They will not risk your health to just get another donation.

People who have a low iron content in their blood will be asked to wait to donate blood when their iron content is higher. A woman's iron content must be at least thirty-eight percent and a man's must be at least forty-two percent. This is also to protect the donor from being susceptible to any illnesses.

According to Richard Schubert, President of the American Red Cross, no one can contract AIDS from donating blood because everything is sterile and used only once. Everything is thrown away and destroyed after it has been used so that no one can get it when it is no longer sterile. According to Deborah Gregson, Shawnee American Red Cross, volunteer blood is the best. No one who has AIDS or has been exposed to AIDS will go to donate blood. That is because the blood is always tested before it is used.

There is also no medical cost for the donor. Donors don't have to pay for the donation or any of the testing. The recipient has to pay for all testing and processing of the blood, but the blood itself doesn't cost them anything. If people need more blood than the hospital has, then the hospital calls the Norman Red Cross where an extra supply of blood is kept. The recipient doesn't have to pay for the extra blood because it was also donated. They do have to pay for the testing and processing of the blood as well as the other blood.

Third, donated blood saves lives. There are many people in hospitals who are waiting for donated blood. They will die without it. Some of these people cannot afford to pay for blood transfusions and this is their only hope of living. Ms. Gregson said that if no people are willing to give a little bit of themselves, then all of these people will die. They need our help now, and we may need their help some time. We could all be in that same situation and we would want someone to take a little time to save our life, so we all should do the same for them.

In conclusion, let me summarize my three points. First, I told you donating blood was a simple procedure. Anyone can do it. Donating blood takes only a little bit of your time and a little bit of yourself. Second, there is no cost to you as a donor. The blood is free for the recipient, except for the cost of testing and processing the blood. There is no cost for donors. In fact, you get free food after you donate. Third, donated blood will save many lives this year. There are many people who need your blood and this is the only way that they can receive that life-saving blood.

In closing, I ask you, please, will you go with me right now and donate blood to the American Red Cross? Donations are being taken now in the Student Union. You can save at least one life by giving a little of yourself. Won't you do that little bit?

SAMPLE OUTLINE—SPEECH TO CONVINCE

I. INTRODUCTION
    A. Attention-getter: Facts
    B. Credibility: Interest/Research
    C. Arouse interest: Affects everyone
II. THESIS: Today I will persuade you to donate blood to the American Red Cross for three reasons.
    PREVIEW: Those three reasons are: (1) simple procedure, (2) no cost, (3) saves lives.
III. BODY
    A. Simple procedure
       1. Health history
       2. Personal time
    B. No cost
       1. Nothing to lose
       2. No medical cost
    C. Saves lives
       1. People waiting
       2. People die without blood
IV. CONCLUSION
    A. Summary
       1. Simple procedure
       2. No cost
       3. Saves lives
    B. Closing: Go give blood

References

Gregson, Deborah. (1987). Red Cross Volunteer, Interviewed by Elizabeth Wookey, April 25.
Facts About AIDS and Drug Abuse. (1986) American Red Cross. October, pp. 1–4.
Schubert, Richard. (1985). *American Red Cross AIDS Public Education Program.* December, pp. 1–4.
Schubert, Richard. (1986) *AIDS Fact Sheet.* Video.

Project Assignment

Prepare and present a six- to eight-minute speech in which your purpose is to convince your audience on an important issue to you. Your objective should not be to secure action from the audience, but rather to get them to agree with your position. Select evidence that will produce sound reasoning through logic or emotion. It is essential that you appeal to interests of your audience.

As you prepare for this speech, pay close attention to your audience analysis and what you know about your audience members. Gather materials that will support your position. You will want facts, statistics, examples, and support from authorities to prove your proposal. You will also want to know what opponents of your position say, so you are prepared to defend your position to opponents and contradict their major arguments.

Your introduction will need to gain attention, establish strong credentials for you, and direct your audience's interest to your topic. Do a good job of relating your topic to your audience members by showing them that your topic affects them. Your conclusion should review your major reasons, or evidence, to reprove your position. Call for your audience members to adopt your proposal as you close.

Your delivery must be convincing if you are to convince your audience. Anything that might detract from your delivery should be resolved before you speak. Act confidently, convincingly, and dynamically toward your proposition.

References

Ayres, J. & Miller, J. (1990). *Effective Public Speaking* (3rd ed.). Dubuque, Iowa: Wm. C. Brown Company, Publishers.

Bradley, B. E. (1988). *Fundamentals of Speech Communication* (5th ed.). Dubuque, Iowa: Wm. C. Brown Company, Publishers.

Devito, J. A. (1990). *The Elements of Public Speaking* (4th ed.). New York: Harper & Row, Publishers.

Heun, R. & Heun, L. (1986). *Public Speaking* (2nd ed.). St. Paul, Minnesota: West Publishing Company.

Hybels, S. & Weaver, R. L. II. (1986). *Speech Communication.* New York: Random House.

Jeffrey, R. C. & Peterson, O. (1988). *Speech, A Basic Text* (3rd ed.). New York: Harper & Row, Publishers.

Minnick, W. C. (1983). *Public Speaking* (2nd ed.). Boston: Houghton Mifflin Company.

Nelson, P. E. & Pearson, J. C. (1990). *Confidence in Public Speaking* (4th ed.). Dubuque, Iowa: Wm. C. Brown Company, Publishers.

Ochs, D. J. & Winkler, A. C. (1983). *A Brief Introduction to Speech* (2nd ed.). New York: Harcourt Brace Jovanovich.

Osborn, M. & Osborn, S. (1988). *Public Speaking.* Boston: Houghton Mifflin Company.

Sprague, J. & Stuart, D. (1988). *The Speaker's Handbook* (2nd ed.). San Diego: Harcourt Brace Jovanovich.

Verderber, R. F. (1988). *The Challenge of Effective Speaking* (7th ed.). Belmont, California: Wadsworth Publishing Company.

Walter, O. M. & Scott, R. L. (1984). *Thinking and Speaking* (5th ed.). New York: Macmillan Publishing Company.

PROJECT **20**

The Speech to Stimulate

> If all my talents and powers were to be taken from me by
> some inscrutable Providence, and I had my choice of
> keeping but one, I would unhesitatingly ask to be allowed
> to keep the power of speaking, for through it, I would
> quickly recover all the rest.
>
> —Daniel Webster

When people get concerned about an issue, they want others also to be aroused or stimulated. Often a speaker appeals to audience members to do something, to change their minds, to give consideration to an idea, but fails to stir them sufficiently to provoke them to action. If you want to stir audience members or get them aroused about an important issue, it is to your advantage to learn the methods and approaches that cause audiences to be stimulated by speech. This project provides an opportunity for you to practice arousing or stimulating an audience as it presents the principles of the speech to stimulate, preparing a speech to stimulate, presenting a speech to stimulate, and a sample speech to stimulate.

Principles of the Speech to Stimulate

The primary purpose of the speech to stimulate is to arouse enthusiasm or heighten audience emotion about an issue. In addition, the speech to stimulate should make your audience members more aware of a problem, a condition, or a situation. Audience members should become so concerned about your problem, condition, or situation that they become stirred up and aroused enough to do something to change conditions on their own.

A recent example of people becoming stirred and stimulated to do something is the case of the students in China during the summer of 1989. People in both China and the United States became excited about the conditions in China. The speeches in China led to students' protests of the government. The situation also stirred up people in the United States to do something. In fact, Congress voted to allow Chinese students to remain in this country when

118

their studies were finished. President Bush was apparently not stimulated to act in the same fashion as he vetoed the bill.

The techniques of the speech to stimulate are frequently used in commencement addresses, conventions, rallies, pep meetings, sales promotions, and religious gatherings. Another common form to many athletes is the pep talk by the coach between halves of a game, or at an important time out. The coach attempts to stimulate players to change their behaviors so the team can prevent scores from the opposing team or score points for their team, or both.

If you fulfill your purpose, your speech will have touched the emotions and influenced the intellect of your audience members such that they will feel impelled (or compelled) to adopt new attitudes and/or take action that you suggest. The coach's purpose in the pep talk, as suggested earlier, is to compel the team to "take charge" of the game and play hard enough to win. To succeed in stimulating your audience members, you will need to use vivid language, project obvious sincerity and enthusiasm, and appeal to some basic drive of your audience members. In the case of the students in China it was a drive for freedom that was the cause that they were willing to live and die for; in the case of the athletic team it was a sense of pride in winning, or some other similar value.

Stimulation is often achieved by catchy slogans, concreteness, specific examples, illustrations, contrasts, and facts. A good example of a speech to stimulate using the preceding techniques is a speech to "Save the Whales," or any other environmental factor, for that matter. Many people still recall the "Greenpeace" symbol of that campaign some years ago, as well as the recordings "Songs of the Humpback Whale." There are all sorts of examples of whale killings and statistics on the number of whales killed at any one time. Another more recent example is the recent presidential campaign issue over funding childcare for families with children. Both candidates wanted to fund some sort of childcare, but the issue developed over how it would be funded and run.

The nature of the speech to stimulate demands that you be aroused and stirred, as well as be vigorous. It calls for enthusiasm, energy, force, power, and spirit; the quantity and quality of your vigor depend on the response you seek from your audience members. Most of all it requires that you be sincere. Imagine, if you will, a coach who says to the team, "I don't care if we win this game. I just want to give you some experience playing the game and learning the rules of the game." This coach is not very likely to stimulate this team to go out and do more than "play." Likewise, imagine the students in China rallying for one day and saying to the government, "we don't care whether you make changes or not—we just want to be out here today and demonstrate. We hope you see our side of this issue." Again, the vigor of the speech shows how deeply concerned you are about the conditions or issues you talk about.

Regardless of what kind of speech you present, it should always possess sincerity. Of all the many kinds of speeches, none demands sincerity from you more than the speech intended to stimulate or arouse. Therefore, place sincerity foremost in your thinking as you select a topic suitable for you and your audience. What issue can genuinely get you aroused and about which can you be most sincere and enthusiastic?

Some topics suitable for speeches to stimulate include:

1. Drugs—our greatest enemy
2. Welfare pay—the great American "ripoff"
3. Congress is squandering our money
4. The electoral college—a system outdated
5. The two-party system—a sham
6. Taxes punish people for working hard
7. Professional athletes—too much pay
8. Crime—our greatest threat
9. The American Indian—a dying race
10. Energy alternatives—it's now or never
11. Unemployment pay—unfair to those who work
12. Farming the oceans—a must for the future
13. Freedom of the press—myth or reality
14. Government waste is ruining our economy

15. Higher education—a must for the year 2000
16. Space weapons—the only deterrent to Russia
17. The penal system—no useful purpose
18. Social Security—an institution of the past
19. Congressional "wrong-doing"
20. Any campaign—Community Chest, Red Cross, Scouts, Salvation Army, election, and so on.

Preparing a Speech to Stimulate

Basically, you will prepare this speech according to the steps followed in preparing any speech. It is essential that you give more than passing attention to your purpose—to stimulate. This purpose will be behind every statement you utter, superimposed on your entire construction; hence, it must receive first consideration. If you don't make this consideration, your speech will likely fall short of your desired intent.

Having made yourself keenly aware of your purpose, set about achieving this purpose. Naturally, your attention turns to organization. Generally, you should use the problem-solution or causal order as you organize your ideas. For more information on these, see Projects 3 and 19. You may also use a topical order as you present subareas of your general topic.

We will assume that you have gathered your materials and are ready to arrange them in the various divisions of your outline. First, as always, think of organizing the main body of your remarks. In arranging your main points, remember that your language is of utmost importance. Word pictures and graphic illustrations must be presented with vivid phraseology that will call up definite associations in the minds of your listeners. You may also use slogans and catchy phrases to make your ideas remain with your audience. Be concrete and specific by naming persons and places for which the speech calls. Avoid the abstract and intangible when giving examples, illustrations, and facts. This does not mean you are to employ needless detail, but your ideas must be aimed to hit their mark and make a strong impact.

For example, if you wish to stimulate the legalization of certain drugs, you can't talk about or present examples about "drugs" in general. You must present facts, examples, and illustrations concerning the drugs you want legalized. If the legalization of marijuana is your topic, don't use information concerning other drugs and try to relate it to marijuana. This is abstract and intangible, and you will likely do little more than upset members of your audience. At best, they will not be able to connect the two concepts.

You may also use comparisons and contrasts as a means of clarifying your thoughts and pointing up their significance. Comparisons and contrasts have the advantage of relating your topic to other concepts your audience members may know better than your topic. For example, the legalization of marijuana can be compared with the legalization of alcohol years ago. You can also contrast the legalization of marijuana with the legalization of prescription drugs or other drugs like cocaine.

Certainly throughout your entire speech you will appeal to the basic drives in people: needing security, saving or making money, keeping the home intact, gaining recognition, enjoying social position, maintaining a cleaner city or town, knowing new experiences, and so on. In other words, you touch your listeners' pride and patriotism, their pocketbooks and bank accounts, their sympathies, their family and home affections—yes, even their fighting spirit. Relate to the issues that affect your audience members.

Once you have stimulated your audience members—have thoroughly aroused them—you can point out how their thinking or conduct may be affected by the ideas you are advancing. That is, you can tell them that the conditions you present need not be this way forever. There are solutions to the dilemma you present. However, the speech to stimulate does not call for action in the sense that you are asking for contributions, votes, and so on. So, be cautious that all you do is suggest that conditions can be changed, don't call for the action or challenge your audience members to take specific actions that you may desire.

You will want to organize your introduction for this speech late in the process. As before, you will construct it after certain other parts of your speech are completed, but certainly you will give it close attention before your speech is fully prepared. If you do not begin with a strong attention-getting statement and direct your speech to the audience members, showing them how important it is to them, you may fail in the entire speech.

Presenting a Speech to Stimulate

A forceful, dynamic, and energetic presentation should be used unless you are speaking on a solemn occasion calling for reverence, devotion, or deep feeling. In this case your voice and manner should be an animated and sincere projection of your ideas, accompanied by appropriate bodily actions and gestures. On other occasions you should show that you are alive with your subject, full of it, and eager to share it with others. Above all, you must be sincere and earnest. Remember, your audience members will reflect your activity and eloquence. They will be just as lively or as solemn as you stimulate them to be.

SAMPLE SPEECH TO STIMULATE

By Karen R. Nick

Why You should Vote

Did you know that only five people in this room are expected to go and vote in the next election? That's only 25% of us, which is a minority; however, that minority will be electing the people who will direct all our lives in the coming years. I am personally a registered voter and have voted in a local election. In addition, I have studied the American Government and politics in five different classes over the past several years.

As a college student, you are probably like me in that you feel you are old enough to do anything you want without anyone telling you what to do. If you don't consider going to vote, then you are allowing other people to determine which leaders will be deciding political issues for you—like how much tax you will pay and what is legal or illegal for you to do.

Today I will convince you that you should vote for two reasons. Those two reasons are: (1) because voting is your privilege, and (2) because voting is your duty.

First, voting is your privilege because you live in a free country where you are able to vote and because you are able to elect the officials you want to represent you.

Because you live in America, you can vote if you are a citizen over eighteen years of age. Other factors, such as race, religion, or IQ do not matter. Also, your vote has as much influence as the President's vote or the little old lady down the street. Of course, it counts only if you exercise it because you also have the privilege of refraining from voting. When I remember that our forefathers gave their lives to give me the freedoms I have, it is almost impossible for me not to use the privilege of voting.

According to the book, *The Rights of Candidates and Voters,* voting grants to all citizens the power to elect those persons who make decisions affecting their lives. This statement shows the importance of elected officials. These officials include local, state, and national officials.

Of the state and local elections, the Governor's race almost always has the biggest voter turnout. The other elections, such as County Commissioner and City Council Members, have very low voter turnouts which is difficult to understand because the local government affects people more directly than the national government or the state government. The city in which you live is run by the local government. The local government keeps roads in good repair, raises and lowers our taxes, and controls utility rates that affect each of us more directly than the state or federal government.

The national government is important because it handles our foreign correspondence. We are able to elect officials according to whether we are for peace talks and anti-nuclear defense, or the Star Wars program and a large defense budget. Our personal opinions are expressed through the people we vote for. Both kinds of elections are privileges that we have and that we should take advantage of more than we do.

In addition to being a privilege, voting is a duty to all Americans. As former President Lyndon B. Johnson said, "Voting is the first duty of democracy." An even more forceful statement can be found in the book, *The American Voter.* "Voting is absolutely necessary in a democracy. Without it, leaders would be appointed rather than elected and this could become a communist country." This harsh statement sounds blown out of proportion, but consider this: According to the *U.S. Government Current Population Report,* in November 1985 only 72% of the eligible voters in this country were registered to vote, and only 59% voted.

There are several reasons why people don't vote. A chart in the *Daily Oklahoman* on December 8, 1980 showed some of these reasons: 42% indicated that they were not registered; 17% disliked the candidates running; 8% were sick; 5% were not interested in the election; 4% were new in town; 3% were out of town; 3% were at work; 2% had miscellaneous other reasons; and 10% had more than one specific reason. As you can see, these excuses are products of apathy. People simply aren't concerned with the government and how it's run. When the time comes that too few people care, there won't be elections. When that happens, democracy will be gone. And then, what is to stop communism from stepping in? To keep our democracy, we must decide to do our duty and vote.

It is also our duty to vote in order to establish our future and the future of our children. We should always strive for excellence and vote for the candidate we feel is most qualified. The 26th Amendment lowered the voting age from 21 to 18; therefore, we can begin to establish our future national, state, and city government when we are eighteen years old. In order to do this, we must follow closely the various political campaigns so that we know who the best qualified candidates are and who will best represent our views. We need to also think about the future of our families and children that we have or will have.

Our economy and our foreign relations are always established in a building block form. Each government administration affects the economy and foreign relations. This can be good or bad; thus it either helps the next administration or starts the next administration in a rut. By electing good officials we can make improvements on these important issues and make the United States a better place for our children.

In conclusion, I would like to remind you of the two reasons you should vote. First, voting is our privilege because we live in a free country where our forefathers fought to give us this privilege. Also, we are able to choose the people we want to govern us. Second, voting is our duty because it is necessary in maintaining a democracy. If people don't vote, we may end up as a communist nation. It is also our duty to establish our future and the future of our children by electing competent leaders who will improve America.

I have given you several issues to consider when you decide to vote or not to vote. Because of the facts I have just given you, you should not be able to consider staying home from the voting polls come election day. In closing, let me remind you that the majority of us like to gripe about the government; but remember, those who don't vote lose their right to gripe about the people who are running the government.

SAMPLE OUTLINE—SPEECH TO STIMULATE

   I. INTRODUCTION
      A. Attention-getter: Five votes
      B. Credentials: Five classes
      C. Arouse interest: Independence
  II. THESIS: Today I will convince you that you should vote for two reasons.
      PREVIEW: Those two reasons are: (1) voting is your privilege and (2) voting is your duty.
 III. BODY
      A. Voting is your privilege
         1. Free country
         2. Elected officials
            a. Local
            b. National
      B. Voting is your duty
         1. Keeps democracy
         2. Establishes future
            a. For ourselves
            b. For children
 IV. CONCLUSION
      A. Summary
         1. Privilege
         2. Duty
      B. Closing: No vote—no gripe

References

Bohle, Bruce (1967). *The Home Book of American Quotations* New York: Dodd, Mead & Company. p. 429, No. 12.
Campbell, Angus. (1980). *The American Voter.* Chicago: University of Chicago Press. pp. 90–91.
Burt, Neuborne, & Eisenberg, Arthur, (1976). *The Rights of Candidates and Voters.* pp. 23, 59.
Reasons for Not Voting. *The Daily Oklahoman,* December 8, 1980, p. 24.
U.S. Department of Agriculture. (1985). *Current Population Reports. November 1985,* p. 20.

Project Assignment

Prepare and present a three- to five-minute speech to stimulate. Your purpose is to arouse and stir the audience's emotions concerning your topic. Your objective should *not* be to secure action from the audience, but rather to stimulate them to understand more about a problem that exists.

As you prepare for this speech, pay close attention to your audience analysis and what you know about your audience members. Gather materials that will stimulate and arouse your audience members. You will want facts, statistics, and examples to prove your position and excite your audience members.

Your introduction will need to gain attention, establish your credentials, and direct your audience's interest to your topic. Do a good job of relating your topic to your audience members by showing them that your topic affects them. Your conclusion should review your major points and reprove your position. Use an emotional appeal to stimulate your audience members to want to do something.

Your delivery must be dynamic if you are to stimulate your audience. Anything that might detract from your delivery should be resolved before you speak. Act confidently, convincingly, and dynamically toward your topic.

References

Ayres, J. & Miller, J. (1990). *Effective Public Speaking* (3rd ed.). Dubuque, Iowa: Wm. C. Brown Company, Publishers.

Bradley, B. E. (1988). *Fundamentals of Speech Communication* (5th ed.). Dubuque, Iowa: Wm. C. Brown Company, Publishers.

Devito, J. A. (1990). *The Elements of Public Speaking* (4th ed.). New York: Harper & Row, Publishers.

Heun, R. & Heun, L. (1986). *Public Speaking* (2nd ed.). St. Paul, Minnesota: West Publishing Company.

Hybels, S. & Weaver, R. L. II. (1986). *Speech Communication.* New York: Random House.

Mudd, C. S. & Sillars, M. O. (1985). *Speech Content and Communication* (5th ed.). New York: Harper & Row, Publishers.

Nelson, P. E. & Pearson, J. C. (1990). *Confidence in Public Speaking* (4th ed.). Dubuque, Iowa: Wm. C. Brown Company, Publishers.

Osborn, M. & Osborn, S. (1988). *Public Speaking.* Boston: Houghton Mifflin Company.

Pace, R. W., Peterson, B. D., & Burnett, M. D. (1979). *Techniques for Effective Communication.* Reading, Massachusetts: Addison-Wesley.

Rodman, G. (1986). *Public Speaking* (3rd ed.). New York: Holt, Rinehart and Winston, Inc.

Samovar, L. A. & Mills, J. (1989). *Oral Communication* (7th ed.). Dubuque, Iowa: Wm. C. Brown Company, Publishers.

Verderber, R. F. (1988). *The Challenge of Effective Speaking* (7th ed.). Belmont, California: Wadsworth Publishing Company.

PROJECT **21**

The Speech to Get Action

Leadership is the ability to get men to do what they don't
want to do and like it.
—Harry Truman

There are times when you speak to convince an audience or to stimulate them. However, most often you will probably want your audience members to take some action as a result of your speech. People tend to resent being *told* to do something; therefore, you have to approach a request for action in a persuasive manner. If you want to get the right response from your audience, you will need to know how to organize your speech and what to include in your appeals to your audience. This project presents the principles of the speech to get action, tells you how to prepare and present a speech to get action so your audience members will *want* to do what you suggest, and presents a sample speech to get action.

Principles of the Speech to Get Action

In the speech to get action you attempt to get your audience members to perform a certain action, either immediately following your speech or at some specified time later. This speech stresses the action to be taken, such as spend money or perform volunteer service, and differs from the other persuasive speeches in its focus on the persuasive situation. In the speech to convince your purpose was to get your audience members to agree mentally with your thoughts; in the speech to stimulate your purpose was to get your audience members stirred up to want to do something; in this speech you suggest and even call for specific action from your audience members.

More specifically, the purpose of the speech to get action is to present ideas, suggestions, and arguments in such a manner that your audience members will believe so strongly what you tell them that they will actually carry out your suggestions. To accomplish this objective, you must present information that convinces your audience members by facts, logic, and emotions to do what you suggest. You must stimulate and arouse your audience members to feel they want to do something. Tell them what to do and stress the action to take. You may point out what will happen if audience members do not take action and what will happen if they do. Of course, you will show what your audience members stand to gain by doing what you suggest.

You may have noticed that this speech includes the principles discussed in the two previous projects. It includes the principles of convincing as well as stimulating audience members because you must convince and stimulate them before you can call on them to perform specific behaviors. This means that you must be more complete and thorough in this persuasive message.

Remember, this speech is successful only if your audience members actually do what you want. Because this is true, you may need to spend an ample amount of time showing your audience members that you share common beliefs or attitudes with them. You may also need to spend more time researching your topic and using expert testimony to prove your position so you can convince your audience members to do what you want.

Naturally, you must prepare thoroughly to ensure you master both general and detailed information which you deliver with vigor and confidence. If you are to move your audience members to action, you must be firmly convinced of what you are saying. If you do not project that conviction through your sincerity and delivery, you are not likely to be successful. There is no room for pretense in the speech to get action. Remember, this is the *ultimate goal* of persuasion.

Occasions for the speech to get action are common. Among the most common occasions are political rallies for a particular candidate, a party platform, or a party issue. In civic meetings people are urged to give money for worthy causes or to sign petitions. At labor conventions and meetings workers are urged to vote to strike and/or picket a company. At religious gatherings men and women are told to cease iniquitous activities, to join the church, to tithe, and so on. Sales people insist that people purchase their products. Teachers lecture their students on the desirability of more study. Whenever you ask other people to do something, you have delivered a speech to activate.

Some topics suitable for speeches to get action include:

1. Sign a petition
2. Form a neighborhood watch team
3. Put welfare cheaters out of business
4. Start a tutoring program
5. Organize a group to entertain at rest homes
6. Join a recycling movement
7. Write your congressional representative about certain legislation
8. Promote the four-day workweek
9. Give one day's time to help clean up the city park (or perform some other civic duty)
10. Sign a living will
11. Promote the televising of courtroom procedures
12. Join a group to prevent consumer rip-off
13. Form an antinoise campaign
14. Propose a program for helping the aged in your community
15. Join a "Big Buddy" program
16. Join a local campaign for or against any significant issue
17. Organize a group to give blood at the local Red Cross chapter
18. Organize a group to aid child abusers
19. Join a group to help drug abusers
20. Organize a local campaign for gay rights, feminine equality, and so on

Preparing a Speech to Get Action

First, decide exactly what action you will ask your audience to take. This must be definite. It must not be a generalized or hazy idea about some vague action. Until you know absolutely and positively the specific action you want, you are not ready to begin preparing your speech. Thus, a complete sentence statement of your specific purpose is required. Write it out so you can have it before you throughout your entire preparation. For example, "I want my audience members to do something for Senator Snoot." is very vague and general. By contrast, "I want my audience members to contribute money and time in support of Senator Snoot in her campaign for reelection" is more specific.

Having decided on the action you want from your audience members, organize your speech as follows:

1. Tell generally and in some detail what is now happening in regard to the subject you are talking about. Give facts, examples, illustrations, and testimony to make your ideas clear, but do not spend too much time on this part of your speech. For example, you could show that while the majority of voters in her district support Senator Snoot for reelection, she has not received enough campaign contributions to finance the trips she must make. And that workers are needed to help prepare mailings to potential voters.

2. Show how this is affecting the lives of your listeners. Show definitely that it is costing them money, damaging their community, retarding their personal advancement, endangering their lives or their children's lives, giving them a bad name, and that it is unsanitary, detrimental to community progress, and so on. (Use whatever appeals are necessary and appropriate to make your audience members see that they are affected personally. Be sure to give evidence to support your appeals or you may not persuade anyone. Make your point clear but do not overwork it.) For example, you could show that if Senator Snoot is not reelected, her opponent will surely change the way life goes on in your community as you know it. Look at specific campaign promises and differences in issues between the two candidates. Prove that it is in the best interests of your audience members that Senator Snoot be reelected.

3. Show what can be done to correct or change the situation, and indicate the action necessary for your audience members to take. The action you suggest at this time and your arguments to show that it should be taken will make up the major portion of your speech. For example:

   a. Show how your audience members will benefit personally and/or as a group if they take the actions you suggest. Be specific in pointing out what they stand to gain from the action. You may want to show how beneficial and helpful it will be to them, or you may want to appeal to their desire for money and wealth, security, fame, social status, prestige, or recognition. It is at this point that your audience members must be convinced. If your audience members believe they will actually receive all the benefits you mention, it is a pretty safe bet they will follow your suggestions. If it sounds too good to be true, it probably is. It is not necessary to get unanimous action, but only enough to make your efforts worthwhile.

   b. Show how easy it will be for audience members to take the action you propose. The easier it is to do, the more likely your audience members will do it. Consider your own situation. If someone asks you for money, you think in terms of the amount he or she wants. If you are asked for a dollar, you are more likely to donate that than if you are asked for $100.

   c. Show that audience members can afford it if money or goods are suggested. Again, the less the "cost," the more likely your audience members are to see that they *can* afford the cost. If what you are asking is considerable, you may need to show how audience members can pay a little at a time, and that it takes a small amount per day. Car sales and other such purchases are often placed on a dollars per day rate, so people can see that they can afford what they want.

   d. Show your audience members how they can spare the time if it takes time. You may need to break down the time into small units and show that it will take only "minutes per day" for audience members to do what you want. The ads you see on television for "toning your body" use this technique to show that you do have the time to get in shape.

    e. Tell audience members specifically when to do it. You should be specific in giving people the date and the time you need their actions completed. In some instances you will want to give an arbitrary date, but most of the time you will need to get actions completed by a certain date if they are to be helpful. Take the campaign help, for instance. It would do little good to have people call for supporters after a candidate has lost or to donate rides after the polls close.

    f. Tell audience members where to do it. Name the exact location and give directions about how to get there, if they are necessary. If you want people to work out of "campaign headquarters," you may need to give an address for those who have not been there. Under other conditions you will want people to congregate or show up to work at a specific location. If this is not a well-known spot in the community, you may need to tell people how to get there.

    g. Tell audience members what equipment will be needed (if any). Under some conditions you will want people to bring equipment or materials with them that will be needed for the task at hand. For example, if you are holding a car wash and people need to bring hoses, rags, chamois clothes, and so on with them, you need to make this clear. Likewise, you must let them know if all they need to do is show up because everything will be furnished.

    h. Give the names and addresses of specific persons to contact. Tell your audience members when to make the contacts—the hours those persons are available. In some cases phone numbers and addresses should be available; in other cases it will be a "sign up now" situation in which you want the people who are present and no others need apply.

    i. If a petition is to be signed, have several copies available, together with pens and pencils to be passed around. If the petitions are available, you are more likely to get signatures than if people have to track down the petitions or find another person to get to sign the petition. Remember, people will take the path of least resistance.

    j. Tell how to perform the action if there is any question about it. In most instances your audience members will clearly know what to do and how to do it; on other occasions you may need to explain. New activities and processes take explanations for the audience to do them correctly.

4. Reiterate briefly the "bad things" that will happen if your audience members do not take the action you suggest, then contrast this by repeating the "good things" that will follow if they do as you say. Conclude with well-planned remarks, stating your confidence that they will do the right thing. You can either call for action by your audience members or challenge them to follow your lead.

Presenting the Speech to Get Action

In this speech, as in any speech, you will find it advantageous to be both sincere and personally convinced of what you want your audience members to do. Be confident, poised, at ease, alert, appropriately dressed, and friendly. Naturally, your enthusiasm and vigor will be geared to the occasion, the audience, the environment, and your own style of speaking. Earnestness is also desirable.

    You must adjust your bodily actions and gestures to all the elements of the speaking situation. Older and better educated audiences do not want as much vigor and activity as do less enlightened and younger groups. Speak accordingly.

    Your language should be clear, vivid, and easily understood. The words should be "picture words" that tell or describe your ideas so well that your listeners immediately picture in their minds what you are talking about. Simple, descriptive language that brings up memories, images, and matters close to your listeners' way of living is most effective. There should be no display of vocabulary, no use of "dollar words" just for the sake of sounding important. The concern that counts most is language that says something your audience members can readily understand.

Say "we" when speaking to your audience. If you constantly refer to your listeners as "you," they may, and usually do, wonder what you yourself are going to do about the action you are asking them to take. If you say "we" instead of "you," the audience immediately includes you as one of them, and sees you also taking the actions you are asking them to do. This "common ground" technique works well in a variety of situations.

On many occasions when action is sought from a group, certain persons in the audience agree beforehand to do what you ask as soon as you ask for it. In this way they lead off and set the pace, thus inducing others to follow. Sometimes people are "planted" in the audience, or demonstrations are prearranged, to do certain things that will influence the audience. A good example of this is the deafening fanfare, parading, beating of drums, and waving of signs at political conventions. All this is designed to get action of a very specific nature—vote for a specific candidate. Generally, it is a significant part of the nominating speech in national conventions. The ethics and effectiveness of this type of activity may be open to question; however, the fact remains that it is done. You must decide for yourself whether you wish to use it as part of your presentation.

Other methods can be used to influence the behavior of audience members so they will respond as you desire. For example, you can exhibit charts and drawings, pictures, diagrams, and graphs; you may show movies and any other visual aids that enhance your message. Sometimes group singing is used to get the audience in a receptive mood. Printed matter is handed out to audience members as they enter the speaking situation. It is usually unwise, however, to distribute anything *during* your speech because it will draw audience members' attention away from what you are saying, as well as create a noisy disturbance.

If material is to be distributed, do it before you start speaking or after you conclude. If it is done before, be sure your audience members have sufficient time to examine the materials and satisfy their curiosity before you begin. You can then refer later to a specific portion of the materials that you ask them to read with you. If the material is distributed after you finish speaking, be prepared to answer questions or to discuss it if any questions arise.

SAMPLE SPEECH TO GET ACTION

By Dani Duncan

Inhumanity to Man's Best Friend

"You see one in every community, a dog tied day-after-day to a back porch or back fence, lying lonely on a pad of bare, packed dirt. The water bowl—if there is one—is usually empty or just out of reach. Abandoned, but chained up, backyard dogs can't move to comfort, shelter, or companionship. In winter they shiver; in summer they languish . . . year 'round they suffer!" These words by Author Ralph Dressen describe the plight of many animals.

I have lived on a farm all of my life—18 years. I have grown up taking proper care of different kinds of animals. Recently, I read several articles pertaining to the welfare of animals. What I read made me see red as I learned about the ways other people were treating their pets.

The story that I told you just a moment ago about the "backyard dog" is not an uncommon one. We have all seen dogs either chained up or abandoned on the side of the road—left to fend for themselves after having been fed by humans all of their lives. And I'm sure most of us have wondered what we can do to help these unwanted friends in need. We *can* help these animals that are being abandoned or abused with little or no cost.

Today I will persuade you to alleviate any inhumane acts toward animals for two reasons. These two reasons are: (1) because it prevents cruelty to animals, and (2) because it improves their living conditions.

First, it prevents cruelty to animals. One way it helps prevent cruelty is by ending suffering. If we see someone beating or abusing an animal, we should do our best to stop it. If it is someone in our neighborhood, chances are we know the person and what extent of action we would need to take to prevent this from happening again. Even if you don't know the people involved, you need to intervene to prevent the animal from suffering.

We can also bring aid to the suffering animal. If the people who are making animals suffer are your neighbors, and you know that they don't have enough money to supply their pets with proper meals, you can save your table scraps and tell your other neighbors to do the same and then give the scraps to the animals. Do something to keep the animal healthy and to prevent it from starving to death.

You can also educate people. We need to tell other people whom we see with pets to be kind to them and to treat their pets like a part of the family. Inform people that according to Katharine Brant, author of "Cats and Dogs," a pet owners' publication, the fact is that animals feel—not only physical responses to pain, hunger, cold, and disease, but they also feel emotions like fear, anxiety, depression, and love. This is either not recognized by a great number of people, or worse yet, they don't care. They ignore the feelings of their pets. We must help educate people to the facts.

Second, we can improve the living conditions of our pets. One way we can do this is by finding shelter for them. If the people in our neighborhoods do not like to be told that they are being cruel to their animals by starving them, chaining them up, or beating them, and if they don't heed your "friendly" advice on how to take care of their pets properly, you can simply call PAWS—Pontotoc County Animal Welfare Shelter. The shelter will see to it that people take proper care of their pets. If you tell the shelter about the situation, they will take action to help the animals in your neighborhood. In some situations, PAWS will take animals and shelter them at their shelter in Ada. In other cases, they will educate people in the proper care for their pets.

According to a 1988 PAWS pamphlet, and the shelter supervisor, PAWS workers and volunteers pride themselves on the fact that they do everything possible to find loving, compatible individuals and families to adopt unwanted animals. PAWS also assists owners in finding and regaining their lost pets. PAWS is a busy place since it is the only animal shelter in Pontotoc County.

In conclusion, let me remind you of the two reasons you should take action to alleviate animal suffering. First, it will help prevent cruelty to animals. If you stop people from abusing their pets by helping feed them and by helping to educate pet owners, you are helping a friend. Second, you can improve the living conditions of pets which are not being properly cared for. If you have no other recourse, you can call PAWS here in Ada at 332-5233, and they will help save the lives of suffering animals, as well as find deserving homes for unwanted pets.

In closing, I challenge you to help prevent cruelty to animals whenever you see it happening. And if you want to see how good the conditions are at PAWS, they are holding an open house this weekend at the Ada Shelter. Who knows, maybe you can even go and adopt a pet and friend for life. The Shelter almost always has pets that need homes.

SAMPLE OUTLINE—SPEECH TO GET ACTION

   I.   Introduction
         A. Attention-getter: Quote
         B. Credentials: 18 years
         C. Arouse interest: Personal reference
  II.   THESIS: Today I will persuade you to alleviate any inhumane acts toward animals for two reasons.
         PREVIEW: Those two reasons are: (1) prevent cruelty and (2) improve living conditions.
 III.   BODY
         A. Prevent cruelty
            1. Stop suffering
            2. Bring aid
            3. Educate people
         B. Improve living conditions
            1. Find shelter
            2. Find companions
 IV.   CONCLUSION
         A. Review main points
            1. Prevent cruelty
            2. Improve living conditions
         B. Closing: Challenge

References

Brant, Katharine. (1987). Cats and Dogs. *The Animals' Agenda,* March 1, p. 34.
Dressen, Ralph. (1988). The Backyard Dog. *The Animals' Agenda,* October 1, p. 21.
PAWS. (1988). *What Is PAWS?* March, pp. 1–2.

Project Assignment

Prepare and present a six- to eight-minute speech to get action in which you call on your audience members to take some specific action. Use the means of persuasion to convince people that your action is the correct course for the future. Pay close attention to the means of persuasion.

As you prepare for this speech, pay close attention to your audience analysis and what you know about your audience members. Gather materials that will stimulate and arouse your audience members. Even though your purpose is to move them to action, you will need to convince them of your position before they will take action. You will want facts, statistics, and examples to prove your position and to excite your audience members. Usually, two or three well-developed reasons for doing something are better than a larger number of undeveloped or less-supported reasons.

Your introduction will need to gain attention, establish your credentials, and direct your audience's interest to your topic. Do a good job of relating your topic to your audience members by showing that your topic affects them. Your conclusion should review your major points and reprove your position. Your closing remarks should be your call for specific action, hopefully to be completed as soon as you finish speaking. You may ask your audience members to do what you want, or you may challenge them to follow your example.

Deliver your speech in an energetic, sincere manner if you intend to stimulate your audience to want to do what you suggest. Use visual aids and examples that will make your point as clearly as you can. Act confidently, convincingly, and dynamically toward your topic.

References

Bormann, E. G. & Bormann, N. C. (1985). *Speech Communication: A Basic Approach* (4th ed.). New York: Harper & Row, Publishers.

Devito, J. A. (1990). *The Elements of Public Speaking* (4th ed.). New York: Harper & Row, Publishers.

Hopper, R. & Whitehead, J. L. (1979). *Communication Concepts and Skills.* New York: Harper & Row, Publishers.

Hybels, S. & Weaver, R. L. II. (1979). *Speech Communication* (2nd ed.). New York: Van Nostrand Publishing Company.

Mudd, C. S. & Sillars, M. O. (1985). *Speech Content and Communication* (5th ed.). New York: Harper & Row, Publishers.

Nelson, P. E. & Pearson, J. C. (1990). *Confidence in Public Speaking* (4th ed.). Dubuque, Iowa: Wm. C. Brown Company, Publisher.

Ochs, D. J. & Winkler, A. C. (1983). *A Brief Introduction to Speech* (2nd ed.). New York: Harcourt Brace Jovanovich.

Osborn, M. & Osborn, S. (1988). *Public Speaking.* Boston: Houghton Mifflin Company.

Rodman, G. (1986). *Public Speaking* (3rd ed.). New York: Holt, Rinehart and Winston, Inc.

Samovar, L. A. & Mills, J. (1989). *Oral Communication* (7th ed.). Dubuque, Iowa: Wm. C. Brown Company, Publishers.

Verderber, R. F. (1988). *The Challenge of Effective Speaking* (7th ed.). Belmont, California: Wadsworth Publishing Company.

UNIT V
THE SPEECH TO ENTERTAIN

There is no pleasure in having nothing to do: The fun is in having lots to do and not doing it.

Mary W. Little

Project 22: Sources of Humor
Project 23: Humorous Speeches
Project 24: The After-Dinner Speech
Project 25: The Master/Mistress of Ceremonies

Unit V consists of four projects dealing with entertaining speeches. Project 22 presents a series of sources of humor that may be utilized in the remaining three projects. Project 23, the "Humorous Speech," presents the principles of presenting a humorous speech. The "After-Dinner Speech," Project 24, differs from the humorous speech in that it prepares you for a specific speaking assignment in the dinner setting. The final project in Unit V, Project 25, presents the principles of being a master/mistress of ceremonies. While this project is not a specific speech, it does encompass the skills involved in entertaining an audience at various levels.

PROJECT 22
Sources of Humor

Be sincere. Be simple in words, manners and gestures. Amuse as well as instruct. If you can make a man laugh, you can make him think and make him like and believe you.

—Alfred E. Smith

A well-developed sense of humor is a valuable asset for any speaker. If your audience members perceive you as humorous, they will also perceive you as genial, likable, and believable. Humor, and more specifically, a good sense of humor is one of the speaker skills that will almost always stand you in good stead with your audience members. In fact, William Penn is reported to have said, "Where judgment has wit to express it, there is the best orator." This project presents the principal sources of humor and some suggestions for using humor appropriately.

Principal Sources of Humor

Humor is often listed as a "factor of attention" for speakers. When people laugh, they attend to the source that provoked the laughter. In fact, there are few techniques you can use that will serve to hold your audience's attention as well as humor. It is little wonder, then, that textbooks often promote the use of humor to begin speeches and develop the support for the body of the speech, as well as to end speeches. There is probably no other aspect of speaking that could serve better than humor to put your audience members at ease and to make them more open to receive your message. As long as it is in good taste and provides pleasure and enjoyment to your audience, make judicious use of humor.

The occasions for using humor in a speech are varied. You may need to speak to a club, to an assembly, or in an after-dinner occasion where you will need to use some humor or to make your topic light. While some speeches do not have humor as their primary purpose, it may help if at some point in your otherwise serious speech, you use some form of humor to break the serious mood. As long as you use humor appropriately, adapt it to your audience and occasion, and understand the reasons people laugh, you should feel comfortable in using the sources of humor.

Why is something funny? Why do people contract their facial muscles and alter their breathing into that pattern known as laughter? This project provides a variety of sources of humor to help explain some of the reasons we laugh or find things funny and amusing. It does not, however, serve to provide a *theory of humor.* The main purpose of this project is to provide examples of some of the circumstances that make people laugh or be entertained. By no means is this an exhaustive list of the sources of humor, it provides only the most frequently used sources of humor.

OVERSTATEMENT OR EXAGGERATION

Overstatement or exaggeration is an effective humorous technique because it takes common or ordinary events in life and distorts them until they become ridiculous. When your point is exaggerated sufficiently, it becomes funny. The fellow in the restaurant who asks for a rare steak, and then says to the waitress, "Just slice me a piece of meat as the cow runs through the kitchen," is making use of exaggeration to get his point across to the waitress that he wants the outside of his meat seared and the center left cool.

Another example of overstatement or exaggeration comes from Fred Lindemann, a Yankee turned Texan. Fred delights in telling Yankees that things are really not bigger in Texas. People just use different names. For example, a mosquito in Texas is called a humming-bird in any other part of the country. Notice that it is the exaggeration of the common notion about Texas and Texans that makes us smile or chuckle at this example. Distortion works only if your distortion results in making your point ridiculous.

UNDERSTATEMENT

Understatement is the opposite of overstatement. Instead of exaggerating, you treat a subject in such simple terms that it is ridiculous—make less of something than there is. An example of understatement also comes from the restaurant. The waiter, trying to please his customers, walked up to a table of customers busily eating their steaks. The waiter asked, "How did you find your steak?" The disgruntled customer turned and replied, "Oh, quite by mistake. I just moved the parsley twig, and there it was."

There are several stories told about President Calvin Coolidge that show the use of understatement. President Coolidge was known to many people as "Silent Cal" because he was not known to speak much. To demonstrate this, the story is told of a woman who had been seated next to the president at a state dinner one evening. She chattered and talked all evening, trying to get President Coolidge to talk. Finally, in total desperation, she turned to the president and said, "Mr. President, you just have to talk to me. You see, I have a bet with my husband that I can get you to say more than two words."

Calmly, the President turned to the lady and replied, "You lose."

In another incident, President Coolidge had just returned from church one morning and was being questioned by Mrs. Coolidge.

"What did the minister talk about?" asked Mrs. Coolidge.

"Sin," said the president.

"Well, what did he have to say about it?"

"He's against it."

Be cautious when using both overstatement and understatement. In order to provoke humor, your distortion must still have a sense of reality to it. If there were not a grain of sense in any of the preceding situations, there would be no humor. It is the possibility that they could be true that makes us want to believe them, and at the same time laugh at their ridiculous nature.

PUN OR PLAY ON WORDS

Puns make use of the multiple meanings of words to create humor. One way of making a pun is to use the unusual meaning for a word instead of its literal or usual meaning. To be humorous your audience must share the multiple meanings of the word with you. You may also use language in an unusual manner to create a pun. For example, you could use words that sound alike to substitute for each other.

Shakespeare made generous use of puns throughout his plays. In *Julius Caesar* he makes use of the double meaning of several words used during his time. For example, a cobbler could mean one who makes shoes, or a bungler of things; the sound for "sole" and "soul" are the same, as are "all" and "awl." Notice also the double meaning for the word "out." In the first scene of the play, this exchange takes place:

> MARULLUS: You sir, what trade are you?
> 2ND COMMONER: Truly, sir, in respect of a fine working man, I am but as you would say, a cobbler.
> MARULLUS: But what trade are thou? Answer me, directly.
> 2ND COMMONER: A trade sir, that I hope I may use with a safe conscience; which is, indeed, sir, a mender of bad soles.
> MARULLUS: What trade, thou Knave? Thou naughty knave, what trade?
> 2ND COMMONER: Nay, I beseech you, sir, be not out with me; yet, if you be out, sir, I can mend you.
> MARULLUS: What meanest thou by that? Mend me thou saucy fellow!
> 2ND COMMONER: Why, sir, cobble you.
> FLAVIUS: Thou art a cobbler, art thou?
> 2ND COMMONER: Truly sir, all that I live by is with the awl; I meddle with no tradesman's matters, nor women's matters, but with awl.

Shakespeare uses the two meanings for "cobbler," "out" and the sounds for "sole" (soul) and "all" (awl) to confuse and actually create humor in the situation.

Another example of the use of language to create a play on words is this story of Mark Twain. Checking into a hotel in Canada, Twain noticed that the person who had arrived just ahead of him had written on the hotel register: "Baron von Blank and Valet."

Not to be outdone by this show of elegance, Twain wrote: "Mark Twain and valise."

Here is another use of play on words. Two men were in the midst of a very heated argument when one of the men raised his voice and thundered, "My argument is absolutely sound."

"Yes," replied his opponent, "Your argument is sound—all sound."

Many other comedy routines have been based on the use of puns. Abbott and Costello made their entire reputations based on the use of play on words. "Who's on First" is a classic of the first magnitude. Here is another gem from an Abbott and Costello routine:

> ABBOTT: I've got heart trouble. I guess I'll just have to lie around.
> COSTELLO: You're just about the best liar around these parts.

IRONY AND SARCASM

Irony makes use of unusual turns in language, a twist of events, or conditions that are the opposite of what you actually expect. As one author noted, "It is irony when a minister's child raises hell." Another example of a case of irony is the hopeful politician who began his speech, "Ladies and gentlemen, before I begin my address I have something important to say." That's ironic because most of us would expect his address to be important. Hopefully, he did too.

Sarcasm is closely related to irony in that the speaker says the opposite of what she or he means or pokes fun at someone or something. For example, the person who dislikes an art object you have just purchased but says, "I just love your taste in art," uses sarcasm. Of course, it can be a dangerous risk with humor if the humor is lost or people do not understand that you are using sarcasm. It is easy to be misunderstood and to offend people with sarcastic remarks. Make limited and cautious use of sarcasm.

UNEXPECTED TWISTS

Stories that take an unusual turn or have an unusual twist often are a source of humor. Examples of this type of humor seem to be headed in one direction but take a sudden turn at the end, catching the audience by surprise. The following story takes one of those unexpected twists:

> A well-known evangelist came to town to speak and the auditorium was packed. For the better part of an hour, the famous man denounced the evils of drink, his impassioned denunciations taking in the distillers and sellers, as well as the imbibers.
>
> The large audience was enthralled with the fiery speech, but no one was more fascinated than a young man who had entered the auditorium only to get in out of the rain, and who was hearing the great evangelist for the first time.
>
> As he was concluding his lecture, the famed evangelist thundered, "Who has the largest bank account? I'll tell you who—the liquor store owner, that's who! And who lives in the finest house and in the most exclusive neighborhood? Again, the liquor store owner! Who buys his wife mink coats, Cadillacs and jewels? The liquor store owner! And who is keeping him in all this luxury? You, the working men and women who spend their hard-earned money for all that whiskey, wine and beer!"
>
> At the close of the sermon, the young man who had been so enthralled with the evangelist rushed to the speaker's platform and grasped his hand. "Thank-you! Oh, thank you" he cried. "You are indeed an inspiring man!"
>
> "Then you are saved?" asked the the great evangelist. "You've decided to give up drinking?"
>
> "Well, no, not that," explained the young man. "But I'm going right out and buy a liquor store."

Notice that the story starts you going in one direction, and at the end changes directions. We are led to believe that the evangelist will perform his duties and "save" the young man because of our past knowledge and experiences of evangelists. When the young man indicates that he will go out and buy a liquor store, the tables have been turned on the evangelist.

ABSURDITY

Another source of humor is the absurd. If you can make a thing or story so ridiculous that it is totally absurd, you can often create humor. In fact, many of the common jokes that we pass around are of this type. If you are old enough to remember the "elephant jokes" of a few years ago, you know what kind of humor is involved. If not, the recent trend in "frog jokes" are in the same mold—totally absurd.

Following is another example of absurdity:

> There was a contest to raise money at the county fair: A strong man had squeezed a lemon dry, and a prize was offered to anyone who could get another drop from it. Many men tried, but the lemon did not yield another drop. Finally, a little man said he could squeeze more juice from the lemon. Amid the laughter of the group, the little man was handed the dry lemon. He took it into his hand and squeezed a jet of juice from it. "Extraordinary! Marvelous!" the onlookers shouted. "Not at all," the little man replied, "You see, I work for the IRS."

Sometimes absurdity is expressed through the use of incongruity. Incongruity is the use of people and events, or the two are so totally out of place that the parts don't fit together. Any time you mix a bit of the exotic with the ordinary, the expensive with the cheap, you have incongruity. It is the collision between incompatible events that makes the story funny.

The following story is an example of incongruity:

> President Franklin D. Roosevelt was asked by his secretary whether he had heard that one of his old friends was saying negative things about him. Roosevelt replied, "Is that so? When did this happen?"

His secretary said, "Oh, the past few weeks."
Roosevelt leaned back in his chair, took a puff from his cigarette, blew out a thoughtful ring or two, and said, "That is strange. I don't recall ever doing him any favors."

Another example of the incompatible nature of events occurred recently as two young college students were heard discussing the one's dog.

"My dog has no nose."
"How does he smell?"
"Terrible."

ANECDOTES

Anecdotes are probably the most well known, as well as the most often used, source of humor. Anecdotes dramatize events, usually with scene, setting, character description, and dialogue. What makes anecdotes funny is that there is usually some unusual twist or turn of events as the story progresses. Many of the best anecdotes, however, come from real-life examples.

It must be remembered that any anecdote, as with any other sources of humor, must relate to the topic you are discussing. If the point of the anecdote does not coincide with the point you wish to make as a speaker, you have probably lost the point. A story for its own sake or for the sake of humor alone, does little to enhance your speech.

Mark Twain was both a marvelous storyteller and the subject of many an anecdote. The following example is a typical Twain tale:

Mark Twain was attending a meeting where a missionary had been invited to speak. Twain was deeply impressed. Later he related: "The preacher's voice was beautiful. He told us about the sufferings of the natives, and he pleaded for help with such simplicity that I mentally doubled the 50 cents I had intended to put in the plate. He described the pitiful misery of those savages so vividly that the dollar I had in mind gradually rose to five. Then that preacher continued, and I felt that all the cash I carried on me would be insufficient, and I decided to write a large check."

"Then he went on," added Twain. "He went on and on and on about the dreadful state of those natives, and I abandoned the idea of the check. And he went on. And I got back to five dollars. And he went on, and I got back to four, two, one. And still he went on. And when the plate came around . . . I took 10 cents out of it."

Twain's tale would be a useful one for making a point about brevity or the judicious use of time. It would be out of place in most other circumstances and would not fit the topic under discussion.

MALAPROPISM

Malapropism is using big words, but using the wrong word for what you mean. Usually, the word you use is very close in sound to the word you intend. Many television shows have used the malapropism for a character who is trying to impress others with his or her knowledge. In one episode of "The Andy Griffith Show" Barney tells some of the boys that if they don't mend their ways they'll be "incarcerated." Opey doesn't know what "incarcerated" means, so he asks and one of the other boys replies that when you are incarcerated, the doctor gives you a shot. Barney to the rescue says, "No, that's innarculated."

What makes the malapropism funny is that the audience knows the word the speaker intends, but the speaker must appear to be unaware of the mistake. Archie Bunker was a master at using malapropisms. His ridiculous misuse of words made his humor on "All in the Family" funny. During the election campaign last fall one politician made good use of a malapropism when he said, "My opponent's party produces a great defect on this country."

QUIPS/WIT

A final source of humor is the quip or use of the wit in making humorous remarks about a subject. Many comedians make use of the quip in monologues when they make such comments as: "Is anybody breathing out there?" "Oh, you *are* a cold one tonight." "What's the matter, did you have to pay to get in here?" "Will the lady who just laughed please stop. It might wake everyone up." Quips of this nature tend to be very mundane and should be used sparingly.

On the other hand, quips can produce genuine humor and catch the audience up in the mood of the situation. President Reagan used a quip very effectively during the 1984 debates when asked about the age issue. He said, "I won't make the fact that Mr. Mondale is so young an issue."

This witty remark undoubtedly earned Reagan some support as people saw him as having a sense of humor. Be aware of trying too hard to use witty remarks. President Bush did this in the 1988 campaign, and lessened his following somewhat. It became too obvious that he was trying to use a witty remark, and the remark was inappropriate at the spot where it was used.

Using Humor Appropriately

To be effective, whether your speech is one primarily to inform, to persuade, or to entertain, your humor must be used judiciously and appropriately. One speaker forgot this important note when he began an important business meeting. He said, "Did you hear about the duck who walked into a restaurant, ordered a seven-course meal and asked the waiter to put it on his bill? Well, today I'm going to be talking with you about the company's new five-year plan." This speaker tried to use humor, but forgot that he should relate his humor to his topic. His humor was inappropriate for his occasion. Eugene E. White (1984) lists the following nine cautions in using humor. They are excellent suggestions and ought to be observed. He says:

1. *Do not poke embarrassing fun at any person or minority groups in the audience.* (Any time you use humor at the expense of others, you are treading on dangerous territory.)
2. *Instead of ridiculing individuals or minorities present in the audience, perhaps poke a little fun at yourself.* (The key here is to use a little self-deprecating humor—only enough to show that you are human.)
3. *Avoid off-color humor.* (Since the potential is always present for offending people, simply avoid this type of humor.)
4. *Be brief.* (Remember, you want to leave your audience *wanting more*— not *less*—of you.)
5. *Be enjoyable.* (Humor should provide a pleasing sensation for your audience. Act as if you are enjoying yourself, and your audience probably will also.)
6. *Consider humor as a spice or tonic, not a staple.* (Just as you can overdo anything else, you can also overdo humor. Even in a speech to entertain, you need to make a point.)
7. *Use only relevant humor.* (If your humor doesn't fit the situation you are involved in, you have wasted a good opportunity to communicate with your audience.)
8. *Avoid stale material.* (More than in any other area, humor must be fresh. If you repeat only jokes or stories everyone has heard, you'll bore your audience. Adapt any material to fit **you and your** situation.)
9. *Learn to use types of humor other than stories, puns and anecdotes.* (Variety is the spice **of life!** For appropriate variety, use a number of the previous sources of humor.)

Project Assignment

Read a speech your instructor may assign or select one with humor in it and identify the sources of humor used by the author. As an alternative (or in addition to the assignment, listen to a humorous presentation (Bill Cosby, Bob Hope, "Saturday Night Live," or some other appropriate comedy routine/show) and identify the sources of humor used to entertain the audience. As you identify the sources of humor, also note the appropriateness of the humor. In some instances you may find someone who has violated one of the principles of using humor. If he or she has (and some comedians do), how did you react to the humor and the comedian?

References

Ayres, J. & Miller, J. (1990). *Effective Public Speaking* (3rd ed.). Dubuque, Iowa: Wm. C. Brown Company, Publishers.

Capp, G. R., Capp, C. C., & Capp, G. R., Jr. (1990). *Basic Oral Communication* (5th ed.). Englewood Cliff, New Jersey: Prentice-Hall, Inc.

DeVito, J. A. (1990). *The Elements of Public Speaking* (4th ed.). New York: Harper & Row, Publishers.

Gronbeck, B. E., Ehninger, D., & Monroe, A. H. (1988). *Principles of Speech Communication* (10th brief ed.). Glenview, Illinois: Scott, Foresman and Company.

Heun, R. & Heun, L. (1986). *Public Speaking* (2nd ed.). St. Paul, Minnesota: West Publishing Company.

Jabush, D. M. (1985). *Public speaking: A Transactional Approach.* Boston: Allyn & Bacon, Inc.

Minnick, W. C. (1983). *Public Speaking* (2nd ed.). Boston: Houghton Mifflin Company.

Samovar, L. A. & Mills, J. (1989). *Oral Communication* (7th ed.). Dubuque, Iowa: Wm. C. Brown Company, Publishers.

Sprague, J. & Stuart, D. (1988). *The Speaker's Handbook* (2nd ed.). San Diego: Harcourt Brace Jovanovich.

Walter, O. M. & Scott, R. L. (1984). *Thinking and Speaking* (5th ed.). New York: Macmillan Publishing Company.

White, E. E. (1984). *Basic Public Speaking.* New York: Macmillan Publishing Company.

PROJECT **23**
Humorous Speeches

The most perfect humor and irony is generally quite
unconscious.
—Samuel Butler

Humor is a topic that deserves more attention than it generally receives in speech. We
use humor to gain attention in speeches, to illuminate examples in the body of the speech,
and to conclude speeches. Because humor is so prevalent in speeches, we often forget
that it is difficult to present a humorous speech. In fact, some people confuse a humorous
speech with a comedy routine; nothing could be further from the truth. A humorous
speech is one of the most difficult speeches to present because it requires the use of
several sources of humor and must give the impression of being "off-hand" rather than
calculated and precise. This project presents the principles of the humorous speech,
preparing a humorous speech, presenting a humorous speech, and a sample humorous
speech for you to study.

Principles of the Humorous Speech

The humorous speech, sometimes simply called "the speech to entertain," should be fun and
entertaining to both you and your audience members. The objective of the humorous speech
is to amuse, entertain, or otherwise divert the attention of your audience members from the
rigors of everyday living. This type of speech may be separated from speeches to inform and
speeches to persuade by the intent of the speaker. Humorous speeches can inform and persuade, but your primary purpose is to entertain, or amuse your audience members and relax
them through the use of humor. Notice that you may entertain your audience without being
a comedian.

In this project we are concerned with the humorous speech as opposed to a general
speech to entertain. The speech to entertain is more generic and includes a number of methods
of entertaining, one of which is humor. For example, you could entertain your audience by

reading to them, telling them a story, or performing any number of other acts. The humorous speech, on the other hand, seeks to entertain the audience through the use of humor. It is a specific form of entertaining speech, which focuses on the sources of humor from Project 22.

Although humor is the primary ingredient of a humorous speech, the speech is more than a series of funny jokes or unrelated "one-liners" such as you might hear on the "The Comedy Club" or "The Johnny Carson Show." Your speech must be built around a theme or topic and developed as a speech. If you do not prepare in this manner, you have a comedy routine rather than a speech. Everything must be directly related to your topic or it doesn't fit in your speech.

Humorous speeches are meant to be light, original, and in good taste. This means that you do not expect your audience members to take your comments seriously. Obviously, death is a serious topic, but it could be treated lightly in a humorous speech. For instance, my grandfather used to say, "Don't take life too seriously because you can't get out of it alive anyway." Generally, you will not want to use death or any other similar serious topic as your humorous topic unless it fits well with your audience members and a common situation.

To have a good humorous speech, you must use originality and good taste in your speech. Originality in a humorous speech means that you must find your own unique approach to your topic. You "create" a new way for your audience to view your topic. This does not mean you must *create* all of your information for yourself. You may borrow from other people, as I did from my grandfather earlier. Good taste means you use good judgment in your materials and your approach to your topic. In general, anything that embarrasses or makes your audience members uncomfortable will not be in good taste. Material that is risqué, vulgar, or sexist, or suggests prejudice of any form is also in bad taste.

A second purpose of the humorous speech is to get your audience members to laugh so they relax and forget their cares and worries. On the other hand, don't be too surprised if everyone does not think the story, pun, or anecdote you thought was hilarious, was as funny as you did. Because of our different backgrounds, experiences, and senses of humor, we all react differently to the various sources of humor. The humor of any situation depends on the timing, use of words, bodily actions, voice, and so forth of the speaker at a particular moment in time. And what provokes only an inward smile in you may cause someone else to laugh loudly, snicker, or chuckle, depending on that person's inclination at the moment. Remember, the mood of audience members at the time of your speech may greatly affect how they respond to you and to your sources of humor. You cannot control everyone in your audience, nor can you control the "funny bones" of others to ensure laughter when you attempt to be funny. What you do is to take your best shot at it, using the sources of humor, and take what you get.

How do you make something funny? Someone once said that humor is usually achieved by following a main road, hitting a few bumps, skidding around a bit, getting stuck in a mud hole, and having a flat tire, all the time keeping to the main highway. Thus, when you arrive at your destination, you have traveled a straight road but you have had a pleasant time doing it. If you can take a direct route to your destination and have fun doing it, you will probably have a humorous speech.

Generally, humorous speeches are given at dinners, meetings, special assemblies, parties, and other special occasions where serious speeches would be inappropriate and out of harmony with the mood of the occasion.

Some topics suitable for humorous speeches include:

1. How to be a howling success
2. How to be popular in college
3. Night life in a dormitory
4. Today's fashions
5. How to tell a joke
6. Bringing up father/mother
7. Playing the class clown
8. The lazy way to weight loss
9. Neighborhood bullies
10. Double dating
11. Modern art, dance (or some other custom)

12. The modern robot
13. Computerized dating
14. Dogs and the people they own
15. Advertising's game
16. Kid brothers (sisters)
17. Alibis
18. Tourists
19. Politicians and what they mean
20. A new and humorous manner of looking at any object or situation

Preparing a Humorous Speech

As in the preparation of any good speech, you must pay particular attention to your organization of points, arrangement of materials, and rehearsal. As you prepare, keep your general purpose—to entertain—clearly in mind. Make the rest of your speech subservient to that purpose.

In addition to your general purpose, you will need to consider four important points. First, make your material relevant to your audience and your topic. If your material does not appeal to your audience members, and they can't relate to your humor, it will be lost. For example, if you are speaking to other students, pick out topics that students can relate to, like family and school situations; if you are talking to a group of business leaders, select a topic related to business, like customers relations, selling, profits, or rising costs.

Second, keep your humorous speech funny. You must put yourself in a humorous mood and frame of mind as you prepare and present your speech. You must also keep a sense of good taste about your humor. You will want to avoid using offensive material that would not be perceived as funny by your audience members. Generally, any material that is sexist or racist, or shows prejudice in any way should be avoided. You will recognize the material as offensive if it belittles or puts down any segment of society. For example, "Polock" jokes or stories that make fun of women, men, or ethnic minorities put other people down.

Third, use a variety of sources of humor. Project 22 presents nine sources of humor—don't be afraid to use all of them. In addition, your humor must be appropriate to your topic and your audience. If you are to appeal to your audience members, select sources of humor that would appeal to them. The same speech and sources of humor would not necessarily appeal equally to your local church group and a local labor union. While the same topic and general theme may fit two totally different audiences, you may need to change the examples and illustrations you use, and possibly even the sources of humor. Some audiences, for example, may not have the background to understand an overstatement or an understatement, or the fact that a statement was sarcastic. Your task is to determine what your audience members *will* understand and perceive as funny.

Fourth, you can't maintain a humorous mood for a long time. Generally, humorous speeches are brief and to the point. Just as audience members can tire of serious material, they can also tire of laughing too much. By the same token, it is difficult for you to maintain a humorous atmosphere for any length of time. It is better for you to select two or three major aspects of your topic and illustrate them than to develop four or five points in less detail. You should always leave your audience members wanting more of you rather than less.

There are also cautions that you must apply to the preparation of the humorous speech. First, be sure you don't let your speech turn into a series of unrelated funny stories or one-liners. Neither should your speech consist of one long story. Second, exaggerations or episodes used as illustrations must be related to the theme of your speech or in some way assist you in making your point. Third, while you may want to adapt your opening remarks to slips of the tongue made by other speakers, do not overuse this device because it will become tiresome and boring for your audience.

In actually setting up the humorous speech, follow the principles that would apply for any speech. Develop the body of your speech first. Do this by making a point and then telling two or three humorous stories or anecdotes, or by using other forms of humor. Repeat this procedure for all of your points, making sure that you develop your remarks point by point in logical order. Finish your speech by preparing a clever and interesting introduction and an appropriate and memorable conclusion.

You should recognize that a humorous speech does what every other speech does, and in addition—this is important—utilizes materials that in themselves carry and imply humor. Your selection of these humorous materials, their arrangement in the speech, and the words and physical activity you use to present them are what achieve the effect of entertainment.

Some of you may ask, "How do I know my speech will be entertaining?" You don't! Just prepare what you think the audience will consider funny and present it the best you can. Others of you will simply know that your speech is funny. If you find that people don't laugh as you had anticipated, just remember, the only assurance you have that your speech is entertaining is that you have prepared it well. The degree of entertainment value in your speech depends a great deal on how well you know your audience members and are able to adapt your speech to them.

It is difficult to select, organize words, and rehearse a speech of humor, but you must do all these things. Your own ingenuity and intelligence are the only assets you have in preparing a humorous speech. Use these inherent personal resources well and you will have little to worry about. There is no quick, easy method for preparing a humorous speech.

Presenting a Humorous Speech

The humorous speech is characterized generally by a lively presentation. You may be whimsical, facetious, happy, or jovial, or you may embody a mixture of these moods. Be pleasant, of course! Your entire bearing and decorum should visibly reflect the feelings and tenor of your remarks. Only through a careful preparation and rigorous rehearsal will you be able to present this image to your audience members.

The speech should progress with a smooth forward motion. Avoid delays and hesitations, except those employed for a special effect. If there is laughter, refrain from resuming your speech until you can be heard. Usually this is at the moment *just before* the laughter stops. *Never* laugh at your own jokes or indicate that you think you are funny. However, you should enjoy your audience and yourself, and let this be obvious.

One of the greatest dangers for you as an inexperienced speaker is to prolong your anecdotes, jokes and stories, or the whole speech if you see the audience enjoying it. This may also happen because you forget to keep moving or because you have not prepared your speech properly. You should always have several ending places that you can use to end your speech if you see that your audience is becoming bored or restless. It is also possible that nervousness may cause you to have memory lapses or become confused.

You should always strive to hit your punch lines when they are hot and then move on to the next ones. Keep the pace moving! Battista must have been thinking of the humorous speech when he said, "a good speaker is one who rises to the occasion and promptly sits down." One of the worst experiences you can have is to drag out your speech because you are enjoying it too much.

Be sure you don't announce your attempts at humor. Your audience members will tell you when they have noted your attempts to be funny. They will acknowledge when your speech was funny by smiling or laughing if they catch on. If not, you may have material they do not perceive as funny, your humor may have escaped them, or you may have some inappropriate humor. You will need to decide what happened after you finish your speech; not during the presentation of your speech.

Good humor often depends on timing. Build up to your punch lines and deliver the lines at the right instant for maximum impact. Note how a slight pause just before the line will sometimes heighten its impact also. Listen to some professional comedians to see how they handle punch lines to get the most of their humor. Be sure you deliver your punch lines so everyone can hear them. Don't let your voice fall or rush the line so it gets missed by your audience members.

Sometimes humor can be best heightened and punctuated with your physical delivery. Any bodily movements you intend should be controlled and appropriate for your intent and audience. Give special attention to your facial expressions and gross bodily movements. You can also use posture and small bodily movements and gestures to help enhance your presentation. Since your face is the part of your body most frequently used and observed in the speech, make the most of your facial expressions to help your audience members better comprehend your humor. Rather than making physical movements the object of your humor, in most instances you will want to use it to underscore your verbal message. Remember, your verbal message is usually the most important aspect of your speech.

SAMPLE HUMOROUS SPEECH

By Dina L. Kemper

Dieting

Have you ever noticed that there are more people who talk about going on a diet than actually do? Ever notice that dieting is like the weather? Everyone talks about it, but no one ever does anything about it. In fact, do any of you actually know anyone who has gone on a diet, and stayed on the diet long enough to lose more than a pound? I know from personal experience that it is very difficult to go on a diet and stay on a diet. I actually start a new diet every week—I just can't stay on a diet. I am sure that all of us in this room have either said we were going on a diet, or we've known someone who has, so I'm sure you will want to know the "facts of dieting" from Dina Kemper.

Today I will present two reasons people find it difficult to begin and stay on a diet. Those two reasons are: (1) because of rationalization; and (2) because of peer pressure.

First, one of the main reasons people find it hard to begin diets is because of rationalization. Let me give you a hypothetical example of rationalization at its best. I feel I need to lose weight, so I decide that *tomorrow* I will begin my diet. (Notice I didn't start today. That's too easy.) Pleased with myself, I sit down on the couch, grab the remote control, and then I turn on the TV. Click. And then it happens. I've had the "experience." You've had the "experience." We have all had the "experience." A Christian Children's Fund commercial is on TV. You know the one I'm talking about. The one where Sally Struthers urges you to send money to the fund so starving children in Ethiopia can be fed. And then they show the pictures of the children. You see starving, malnourished, potbellied children who are crying because they are hungry. Their big, brown eyes plead with you. "I know you are starting a diet tomorrow, but how can you let the food in your refrigerator and cabinets go to waste when I am starving?"

Overcome by emotion, I run into the kitchen, and I start gorging myself with cupcakes, cookies, and ice cream. I rationalize to myself, "I may be overweight, but I can't let this food go to waste when there are starving children in the world." And I fail to begin my diet once more.

Another reason people find it difficult to begin and stay on diets is because of peer pressure. Imagine, if you will, a Monday morning and I am trying to get ready for class. I try and try to pull on my jeans, and then I begin to cry. "M-m-my j-j-jeans don't fit an-an-anymore. M-m-my hips are too wide, and my thighs are t-t-too fat. I'm go-goin' on a d-diet!" I go through the whole day without cheating on my diet. Five o'clock rolls around, and I'm feeling good. Then, my roommate bursts into the room, and says, "You want to go to Mazzios' Pizza with us?" I reply, "NO, I'm on a diet. Besides, I don't need food to have a good time." I then begin to do my homework. Later that night (about 2:00 A.M.), I hear a barely audible voice say, "Dina-a-a-a. Di-i-i-na-a-a. Time to go on a doughnut run."

"Aw, Come on. You know I'm on a diet. Besides, I need to finish my homework."

"But you've been working hard all night. You deserve a break."

"Yeah, I do, don't I? No, no. I'm staying on my diet."

"I'm buying."

"Well, ok. Let me get my jacket."

As you can see, peer pressure makes it very difficult to stay on a diet. Especially when the other person is buying. Besides, I don't want to hurt other people's feelings. I really must do my duty and go with my friends when they need my help.

Today I have shown you two reasons people find it difficult to begin and stay on diets. First, because of rationalization. It seems that we will find any reason to not go on a diet. Second, we bow to peer pressure. It is almost impossible to not yield to the pressure of friends who need your help. In closing, I would like to leave you with my theory on dieting. Never do today what you can put off until tomorrow.

SAMPLE OUTLINE—HUMOROUS SPEECH

   I. Introduction
      A. Attention getter: Questions
      B. Credentials: Personal experience
      C. Arouse interest: All know
  II. THESIS: Today I will present two reasons people find it difficult to begin and stay on a diet.
      PREVIEW: Those two reasons are: (1) because of rationalization and (2) because of peer pressure.
 III. BODY
      A. Because of rationalization
         1. Hypothetical example
         2. Emotional outcome
      B. Because of peer pressure
         1. Start diet
         2. Help friends
 IV. CONCLUSION
      A. Review main points
         1. Because of rationalization
         2. Because of peer pressure
      B. Closing: Twist

Project Assignment

Prepare and present a three- to five-minute humorous speech on a topic of your choice. Be sure that your topic and sources of humor are adapted directly to your audience. You should use a minimum of three sources of humor in your speech. Be sure you have selected a topic that is appropriate for you, your audience members, and your occasion.

As you prepare your materials for this speech, don't be afraid to borrow from other sources and make it your own. The use of stories, hypothetical examples, and real instances of behavior will make your speech more interesting than will materials with which your audience members will have difficulty identifying. Make your materials as novel or unusual as you can so they aren't the same things we hear everyday.

Organize your speech as you would any other speech. Find an order of topics that is logical and can be followed easily by your audience members. Since this is a speech, you need to make points with your audience. You don't want to have one long point about a topic, but rather a series of two or three points that will leave your audience members with a message.

Create a strong introduction that will not only introduce your topic, but will also get the audience's attention and establish your right to speak on this topic. Your conclusion should finish your speech on a high note and leave your audience members feeling good about your speech. A final witty remark is a good closing for this speech.

Practice your delivery until you feel comfortable using your humor. You can practice parts of your speech without practicing the entire speech. Make sure your bodily movements are consistent with your verbal message unless they are used for comedic effect. Above all, enjoy yourself.

References

Gronbeck, B. E., Ehninger, D., & Monroe, A. H. (1988). *Principles of Speech Communication* (10th brief ed.). Glenview, Illinois: Scott, Foresman and Company.
Heun, R. & Heun, L. (1986). *Public Speaking* (2nd ed.). St. Paul, Minnesota: West Publishing Company.
Hunt, G. T. (1987). *Public Speaking* (2nd ed.). Englewood Cliffs, New Jersey: Prentice-Hall, Inc.

PROJECT **24**

The After-Dinner Speech

> Honest good humor is the oil and wind of a merry meeting, and there is no jovial companionship equal to that where the jokes are rather small, and the laughter abundant.
>
> —Washington Irving

The most common form of speech to entertain is the after-dinner speech. In fact, speeches to entertain are often called "after-dinner speeches" because they are used as entertainment after dinner meetings. Recognize that speeches to entertain do not necessarily have to be humorous; however, they are usually light in nature, as opposed to being serious. After a fulfilling meal, people generally are in no mood to listen to reasoned arguments or ingest much new information. Instead, they want to relax and be entertained—they want to hear something that will divert their attention from the cares and worries of the day.

As a rule, listeners expect an after-dinner speaker to do more than string together a series of jokes or one-liners. The after-dinner speech is not a comedy routine, but rather a speech with a focus on a particular topic. Humor can be used generously in an after-dinner speech, but your audience members should easily recognize your theme or at least become aware of some idea you intend to make light of. In this project you will learn more of the principles of the after-dinner speech, learn how to prepare and present an after-dinner speech, and read an after-dinner sample speech.

Principles of the After-Dinner Speech

The main purpose of the after-dinner speech is to entertain your audience. In most instances you will be concerned with your ability to get your audience members to relax and enjoy your speech and the event that surrounds your speech. Most after-dinner speakers make generous use of humor to entertain their audiences because most people are entertained by humor—that is, they enjoy and are relaxed by the effects of humor. However, humor is not the focus of this speech as it was in Project 23. The focus of this project is entertainment.

While the after-dinner speech is not focused on the use of humor, the employment of humor in an after-dinner speech is a possibility. This skill in the entertaining speech is a skill that needs practice. Few people are funny in and of themselves. Even comedians make use of the sources of humor discussed earlier (Project 22), and most spend a great deal of time practicing and perfecting their skills before they become professionals.

Sometimes beginning speakers assume that humor is not good (or at least not successful) if the audience isn't rocking with laughter or rolling in the aisles. The truth is some humor is meant to provoke only a smile. Audience members can be entertained—that is, enjoy and be relaxed—with only an inward sense of pleasure. As a speaker, you should decide not only what sources of humor, if any, to include, but also the degree of pleasure you wish to provide. If you prepare so your audience members only smile at some of your lightheartedness, you can understand their feedback and know that they were pleased and enjoyed your speech.

In most instances the after-dinner speech is short, to the point, and genial. Your audience members have had a good meal and are in no mood to hear lengthy speeches or ones they need to think about deeply in order to understand. Because they are already in a good mood from the meal and friendly conversation, you must be prepared to continue the genial mood and add to the atmosphere. Avoid anything that causes gloom or bad feelings in your audience. While you may not know everything that may cause any member to become less optimistic or less friendly, you should avoid anything that you are sure will not add to the joyousness of the occasion.

What makes a topic entertaining rather than serious is the speaker's use or treatment of the topic. Again, Project 22 can help you greatly in determining how to make serious topics light, as well as provide you with sources of humor. Some ideas, such as anecdotes, are not created, but rather are borrowed from other sources. Use the sources of humor to create sense (or nonsense) for your audience. Avoid any attempts at "private" or "inside" jokes that the majority of your audience would not understand. To be entertaining, ideas must be easily understood and well within the bounds of appropriateness.

Appropriateness and thematic development of your topic are probably the two most important aspects of the after-dinner speech. Any topic or subject that embarrasses or offends your audience members is not likely to entertain or allow them to have a good time. Likewise, if your audience members cannot tell that you have a theme and your points fit together, they may find it difficult to sustain their interest and attention. Develop your theme through your development of points and subpoints as you would in any other type of speech. After all, this is a speech—not a comedy routine, even though its focus is on entertaining your audience.

Almost any topic can be entertaining. The best topics for after-dinner speeches are those with which both you and your audience members are familiar. If you take commonplace ideas and give them a new twist or perspective, you are talking about topics your audience members understand and can react to.

Some topics suitable for after-dinner speeches include:*

1. Campus life (any aspect of)
2. Taking tests
3. The annual budget
4. If I were King (Queen)
5. Gadgets—our greatest enemy
6. On becoming "user-friendly"
7. Silence is not always golden
8. My first day on the job
9. The last days of a single person
10. How to win friends and influence their money
11. Why I read the small print
12. Ten years from now
13. Advertisements

*Please note, if a dinner has a particular theme, you should select a speech topic in keeping with that theme.

14. TV programs
15. Income taxes are too simple
16. First dates, blind dates, or double dates
17. The Devil made me do it
18. Home remedies
19. Weekend "sportaters"
20. Absentminded professors (students)

Preparing the After-Dinner Speech

In preparing the after-dinner speech, follow the suggestions given in Project 3 for speech organization. Plan to speak extemporaneously, with minimal use of notes, if you are to be most effective. This is a speech that you definitely do not want to present from a manuscript. If you attempt to be entertaining, and have to read to your audience, the chances of being entertaining are lessened considerably.

The preparations for this speech are little different from those of any other speech. If your thoughts are humorous, prepare much as you would a humorous speech; reread the preceding projects on sources of humor (Project 22) and the humorous speech (Project 23). Follow the procedures of Project 23 or one of the other recognized procedures for speeches to inform or to persuade that have been presented in Units III and IV.

A number of formats are acceptable for the after-dinner speech. First, you could adopt the format used for other speeches in this text. You gain attention, establish credibility, and arouse audience interest. Then state your purpose in a thesis statement. Next, develop the body of your speech through a series of points that are supported by illustrations, examples, anecdotes, and so on. Finally, conclude your speech by summarizing or relating a story to repeat your major point. Try to leave your audience with a good feeling by making them laugh one last time.

Gronbeck, Ehninger, and Monroe (1988) also provide a suitable pattern for organizing the after-dinner speech. The authors suggest that you follow these four steps:

1. Relate a story or anecdote, present an illustration, or quote an appropriate passage.
2. State the essential idea or point of view implied by your opening remarks.
3. Follow with a series of additional stories, anecdotes, quips, or illustrations that amplify or illuminate your central idea. Arrange those supporting materials so they are thematically or tonally coherent.
4. Close with a striking restatement of the central point you have developed. As in Step 1, you may use another quotation, or one final story that clinches and epitomizes your speech as a whole.

It is not necessary and certainly not always advisable for you to plan to tell a joke on the toastmaster or master/mistress of ceremonies, regardless of what the toastmaster may do in the way of introduction. If the occasion calls for humor, be ready to meet it. If there is any doubt as to what to do, play it safe. Good taste never offends. As for risqué stories, leave them home. If you do not have a good, clean story that packs a wallop, you have not tried to find one. The world has a great storehouse of humorous and clean stories for all who want them, and they are excellent for after-dinner speeches. If you can't think of one or find one in your reading, talk with your friends, they are an excellent source for stories.

Most libraries have several books filled with stories for after-dinner speakers. Some common book titles for searching for appropriate stories and anecdotes include: *A Complete Treasury of Stories for Public Speakers; A Dictionary of Wit, Wisdom and Satire; A Treasury of Laughter; Speaker's Handbook of Epigrams and Witticisms; The Public Speaker's Treasury Chest; The Speaker's Treasure of Stories for All Occasions; Toastmaster's Treasury;* and *Lifetime Speaker's Encyclopedia.*

To complete the preparation of your after-dinner speech, practice it aloud several times so you can present it without notes, if possible. It is a good idea to ask one or more friends to hear you in rehearsal, but before you take their advice or criticisms too literally, give some thought to their suggestions and the reliability of their advice. Sometimes your friends may be too eager to criticize and not provide helpful hints. At other times they may not consider your situation carefully enough as they judge only their relationship with you. You must ultimately decide what is appropriate and useful in your own speech.

Presenting the After-Dinner Speech

After-dinner speeches are prepared and practiced so well that you never have to grope for words or your next idea. Be careful, however, that you don't let the thoroughness of your preparation affect the spontaneity of your speech. If you use humor, be sure you wait for the laughter to *almost* stop before progressing, and make your audience members believe that your ideas come "on-the-spot." Notes will tend to destroy the informal and casual atmosphere that you have created already, so in most cases prepare to speak without the use of notes.

The delivery of your after-dinner speech is vital to its success. As you know from listening to professional comedians, a sense of timing is essential. A punch line that doesn't fit at the exact moment, a speaker who doesn't wait for the audience to catch up, or an inappropriate pause can cause you to lose the mood of any situation. Your success is often based on your degree of preparation and rehearsal.

Your presentation should be lively, but reflect the atmosphere already created. Generally, simple organization, graphic word pictures, sufficient humor, lively and animated delivery, and a forward movement of ideas characterize after-dinner speeches.

Your voice and bodily actions should be in harmony with the occasion and your environment. Chances are you will not need to talk loudly to be heard, nor will you be permitted much bodily action because of space limitations and arrangements. Take care when you rise to speak that you don't scrape your chair noisily on the floor or fall over backward and make yourself appear awkward and clumsy. To prevent this, see that your chair is far enough away from the table so you can rise easily. When the chairperson, master/mistress of ceremonies, or president introduces you, rise and address the speaker according to his or her position: "Madame President," "Mr. Chairman," and the like. Also acknowledge the rest of your audience with a comment that includes them in your speech. Some common acknowledgments include: "and fellow class members," "and fellow business associates," and "honored guests, relatives, and associates."

Keep your remarks in line with the occasion and purpose of your speech, ad-lib and improvise as the situation demands. Retain your sense of humor, and use it when appropriate. Above all, observe your time limits. Remember, the program committee has allotted you only a certain amount of time. Don't violate your time limit simply because you are having a good time or your audience members seem to be responding well to your speech. A violation of their expectations on time can well destroy any joy and happiness you may have instilled in your audience. Many an after-dinner speaker has spoiled an excellent speech by not knowing when to stop. Use the old comedian standard of leaving your audience wanting more of you, not less.

SAMPLE AFTER-DINNER SPEECH

By Gerald Vinson

What's in a Name?

"What's in a name? That which we call a rose by any other name will smell the same." Juliet was more concerned with Romeo's last name than his first, but I disagree with her. There is something to a name, especially our first names.

Until recently I was not very satisfied with my first name, and I bet there are many of you who aren't too happy with yours. Are you one of those who cringes every time the teacher calls the official roll?

Today I'll discuss three aspects of first names: First, name connotations; second, name originations, and third, name solution.

First, names have connotations. We associate certain physical types to names. If you name your son *Rock* and he grows up to be five feet-two and weighs 247 pounds, he's not a *Rock,* he's a boulder—maybe half a mountain.

Then there's *Lance*. Lance should be the athletic type: tall, handsome and well-tanned. What happens if Lance turns out like Rock?

Have any of you guys ever been on a blind date? Let's assume I set you up with *Raquel,* a girl you know nothing about. Raquel will bring all kinds of pleasant images to your mind. You can't wait to see Raquel. But at the last moment Raquel gets sick, so I substitute *Ethyl,* another girl you know nothing about. Or Gertrude! Or Agnes! or better yet, Gladys!! Will you be as excited to see these women as you were to see Raquel? I'll bet not!

And Women, you're no better than the men. How anxious are you to have a blind date with a Robert, a David, a Mark, or a Brian? How about if his name was Homer? or Herman? or Clarence? or Ralph? or *Arlie?* I'll bet none of you would show up for those dates if you found out the name ahead of time. You would conveniently get sick or be called out of town at the last moment.

My first name is *Gerald*. I know, you all call me Jerry, but my real name is GERALD. Sounds rather plain, doesn't it? If it were ice cream, it would be plain vanilla; and it's not very romantic. Can you imagine Juliet saying, "Oh *Gerald,* oh *Gerald*. Wherefore art thou, *Gerald?*"

I have had trouble with my name from the outset. In the first grade I couldn't spell it. I soon noticed that I was the only kid in school named Gerald. There were many Larrys, Davids, Bobs, (sometimes called Robert) Jims, and Johns. But I was the only Gerald.

That wasn't the worst. At that time, before everyone had a TV, all of us kids went to the Saturday Matinee. One of the cartoons was about a goofy little kid who couldn't talk. He made all kinds of noises. You know what *his* name was? *Gerald Mc Boing-Boing!!!!* It's not fun being called "Gerald Mc Boing-Boing," but that's who I was whenever my classmates wanted to make fun of me, or recalled the cartoon character with the name *Gerald*. Is it any wonder that I adopted the nickname, Jerry?

How do we get our names? Obviously, our parents stick us with them. I mean, give them to us. They name us after relatives they admire, or ones who have some money and who might give it to them if there were a family namesake. Movie stars and sports figures are also good sources for names. Other parents prefer Biblical characters.

I prefer literary characters. I named my daughter *Lara,* after a character in *Dr. Zhivago*. If she had been a boy, her name would have been "Jason." Jason is my favorite Greek hero. He has all the characteristics I admire in a man. He's handsome, brave, ruthless with women, and treacherous when necessary.

What's the solution to being misnamed? It's easy. At birth every child would be given a number, his/her social security number. So, my name would have been "573-56-5980 Vinson." This would have been my name until I got old enough to choose a name for myself. If this were the case, today my name would be Jason Vinson. Of course, you can see some problems with allowing children to select their own names. One parent allows a child to select a name at eight and other parents make their children wait until later. You could be the *last* kid on the block to get a name. And if the government got wind of what was happening, they would soon create a law on the legal age for selecting a name. Then there would have to be a license fee and a tax for filing the name, etc. You know how it is with politicians—anything to tax!!

So, you see there *is* something to a name. Names have connotations; our parents often stick us with unwanted names, and there is a solution to the problem, which will probably never be put into effect. But I want to leave all of you misnamed people with some consolation. Your name may surprise you as much as mine did me. Go to the library and look in the *Dictionary of Given Names*. I looked up "Gerald." It means "bold warrior or good spear thrower." I never knew I could throw a spear. By the way, Jerry comes from "Jeremias," which is from the Biblical Jeremiah. It means "anointed one or chosen of God."

Gerald or Jerry, I can't lose. My real problem is living up to either one of these names.

SAMPLE OUTLINE—AFTER-DINNER SPEECH

   I. Introduction
      A. Attention-getter: Shakespeare
      B. Credentials: My name
      C. Arouse interest: "Roll call"
  II. THESIS: Today I will discuss three aspects of first names.
      PREVIEW: Those three aspects are: (1) name connotations, (2) name originations, and (3) name solution.
 III. BODY
      A. Name connotations
        1. Associations
          a. Rock
          b. Lance

         2. Blind date
            a. Raquel
            b. Ethyl
            c. Robert
            d. Homer
         3. My name
            a. Ordinary
            b. Early difficulty
      B. Name originations
         1. Relatives
         2. Popular figures
         3. Biblical characters
         4. Literary figures
      C. Name solution
         1. Use number
         2. Select name
   IV. Conclusion
      A. Review
         1. Name connotations
         2. Name originations
         3. Name solution
      B. Closing thought: Consolation

Project Assignment

Prepare and present a three- to five-minute "after-dinner" speech on a topic of interest to both you and your audience. Be sure you use a variety of supports and sources of humor, if humor is a part of your speech. Your instructor may require that you use a specific number of sources of humor. Be sure your speech is in *good taste.* Avoid anything risqué.

As you prepare your materials for this speech, don't be afraid to borrow from other sources and make it your own. The use of stories, hypothetical examples, and real instances of behavior will make your speech more interesting than will materials with which your audience members will have difficulty identifying. Make your materials as novel or unusual as you can, so they aren't the same things we hear everyday.

Organize your speech as you would any other speech. Find an order of topics that is logical and can be followed easily by your audience members. Since this is a speech, you will need to make points with your audience. You don't want to have one long point about a topic, but rather a series of two or three points that will leave your audience members with a message.

Create a strong introduction that will not only introduce your topic, but will also get the audience's attention and establish your right to speak on this topic. Your conclusion should finish your speech on a high note and leave your audience members feeling good about your speech. A final witty remark is a good closing for this speech.

Practice your delivery until you feel comfortable. You can practice parts of your speech without practicing your entire speech. Make sure your bodily movements are consistent with your verbal message unless they are used for comedic effect. Above all, enjoy yourself!

References

Ayres, J. & Miller, J. (1990). *Effective Public Speaking* (3rd ed.). Dubuque, Iowa: Wm. C. Brown Company, Publishers.

Gronbeck, B. E., Ehninger, D., & Monroe, A. H. (1988). *Principles of Speech Communication* (10th brief ed.). Glenview, Illinois: Scott, Foresman and Company.

Heun, R. & Heun, L. (1986). *Public Speaking* (2nd ed.). St. Paul, Minnesota: West Publishing Company.

Hunt, G. T. (1987). *Public Speaking* (2nd ed.). Englewood Cliffs, New Jersey: Prentice-Hall, Inc.

Minnick, W. C. (1983). *Public Speaking* (2nd ed.). Boston: Houghton Mifflin Company.

Samovar, L. A. & Mills, J. (1989). *Oral Communication* (7th.). Dubuque, Iowa: Wm. C. Brown Company, Publishers.

Wilson, J. F. & Arnold, C. C. (1983). *Public Speaking as a Liberal Art* (5th ed.). Boston: Allyn & Bacon, Inc.

PROJECT **25**

The Master/Mistress of Ceremonies

> . . . when you know to laugh and when to look upon things as too absurd to take seriously, the other person is ashamed to carry through even if he was serious about it.
>
> —Eleanor Roosevelt

When someone serves to coordinate the activities of a program, you have an MC (master or mistress of ceremonies). Sometimes called a toastmaster, host, or hostess, the MC generally provides the transitions between speakers, introduces speakers and entertaining numbers, and generally ties a program together.

Probably no speaking task requires more skill or speaking talent nor receives as little attention as the duties of the MC. Because of its showcase appearance, the MC is often looked at as a glamorous job. If you do your job well, no one notices; but if you falter in the least, everyone is sure to take notice.

This project explains what the MC does, how to prepare to be an MC, and how to perform as an MC. The assignment for this project differs from the assignments of other projects in that it must be combined with other projects to work. The MC can't work by him- or herself.

Principles of Master/Mistress of Ceremonies

The MC serves to unify a program. As the MC, you begin the program, keep it moving, and end it. Everything that happens during the program is your responsibility. During the process of a program you may present any number of speeches and kinds of speeches. It is customary, for example, for the MC to present a speech of welcome at the beginning of the program. Sometimes toasts are expected as part of the ceremonies. As the MC, your responsibility is to present the first toast or to organize the order of toasts, and arrange for others who will present toasts.

During the program the MC usually ties speakers and events together by introducing speakers and events as well as by presenting (and possibly accepting) gifts or awards. In other

151

instances it is possible that you will have to present other types of speeches such as announce-ments, reports, and humorous speeches. Almost always the MC must make the closing remarks. As the MC, you should be prepared to present most of your material extemporaneously; however, the situation is very changeable, so you must also be prepared to speak impromptu when the situation demands.

In addition to being prepared to present many different types of speeches, the MC is also responsible for getting the program together and seeing that all arrangements are made before the program begins. Some typical duties that the MC must attend to include the following: First, the MC may determine the seating arrangements for speakers, especially at the head table; sometimes the MC helps determine the seating arrangements for guests also. Second, the MC usually determines the order of the program and when to perform each task. For example, the MC must decide when to "open" the program—should it be done before the meal or after the meal? Are toasts to be made during the meal? Who will make which toasts? When should the speeches (program) begin? There are no "rules" for making these kinds of deci-sions, and sometimes the decision-making process is a joint venture with a small group of organization members. Sometimes you will have sole discretion in making those decisions. At other times the decisions become a part of timing because of certain time constraints—you have only one hour to accomplish your program, for instance.

Third, it is the duty of the MC to greet the speakers as they arrive and generally provide some conversation during the waiting time before the program begins and to introduce the guests to other members of the organization. Sometimes the MC even selects the speakers; at other times the selection process is not one of the duties of the MC. It is your responsibility to know or find out which of these duties are expected of you and which decisions will be made by a committee or other segment of the organization.

As an MC, be prepared for last minute changes. When unexpected changes in events, speakers, or program occur, you need to be prepared to adjust to the changes as needed and be able to make some impromptu presentations. For example, if a guest is late in arriving, be willing to shift program orders to accommodate the guest. The same is true if someone needs to leave early. In some instances you may have a last-minute change in guest speakers, so you will need to prepare a new introduction. As an MC, be prepared to adjust quickly.

Preparing to Be a Master/Mistress of Ceremonies

Because the MC performs a variety of duties during a program, the preparations must follow the dictates of several speeches. As the MC, you are responsible for getting things started, keeping the program moving, and closing the meeting. All that occurs between the opening and closing are your responsibility.

Sometimes the MC has other responsibilities within the organization. These duties must also be maintained. If you are an officer, prepare to handle the duties of your office first so these duties do not interfere with your responsibilities as MC. If you are chairperson for a committee (or a committee member), be sure your duties are accounted for also. Once you have accounted for your official organizational duties, you can begin to prepare for the responsibilities of an MC.

As in preparing for any speaking situation, it may work to your advantage to outline the program and then the "body" of the presentation before you prepare your introduction and conclusion. In some instances, however, your welcome (the opening) may be an established custom and its preparation may be your first and easiest task. It is essential for you to remember that your purposes as MC are to: (1) get things started, (2) keep the program moving, and (3) close the meeting. Resist any temptation during your preparation to think the audience has come to hear you. Whatever the occasion, you are *not* the featured speaker, so you will not want to "spotlight" yourself or your speeches.

In preparing your welcome, refer to Project 37. Remember to start *on time.* Then greet your guests and fellow members. Briefly make your remarks welcoming all present, and, if appropriate, introduce any special guests. Never let your welcome be presented impromptu.

Plan the wording carefully as your beginning is likely to set the mood for the entire program. If you are serious or humorous, the atmosphere will thus have been set for the occasion. In most instances the "after-dinner" or light and relatively informal or casual aire would be most appropriate.

Once the program is under way, it is your responsibility to keep things moving. Try to avoid long gaps of time between events, but you don't want to rush things too quickly either. At a dinner or banquet you don't want to have people eating their main course while the guest is speaking. On the other hand, you don't want people waiting for a speaker long after they have completed their dessert. It is best to prepare a time schedule for your entire program, check the schedule with your caterer and speakers, and then stick to it as closely as you can.

Next, prepare your introductions and transitional remarks so they tie your program together and provide continuity. When you speak, make your comments brief and related to the speeches or events that have just occurred or are about to take place. As you arrange the program, have a reason for putting one event or speaker first, another second, and so on. This will help to provide continuity and your audience members can see connections between speakers. In some instances you may need to provide impromptu remarks to tie one speaker's presentation to the next speaker.

As you introduce speakers, follow the instructions in Project 31. Remember, it is your responsibility in introducing speakers to arouse interest in the speaker and the speaker's topic. Try to get the audience to look forward to the presentation. Again, be brief—avoid *lengthy* introductions. If your introduction is too long, you may find yourself in a predicament by having used too much of the speaker's time. If it is too short, you will not have properly prepared your audience members for the speaker.

Finally, as you prepare for the closing, return to Project 32 and review the suggestions for the farewell speech. While the two are not synonymous, there are similarities. Even the best program needs some sense of finality. Don't simply dismiss your audience, you need to take a few seconds to thank your audience members and tie the program to them one final time. Plan a way of tying the program to something in the future, and point out the benefits of having attended the meeting.

On some occasions you may also need to prepare yourself for either presenting or receiving awards or gifts. On those occasions you need to review Project 36. As in the other speeches by the MC, these speeches are generally brief. Don't try to tell everything the person has done to deserve the gift or award, but rather highlight the honoree and stimulate the audience to appreciate the person being honored.

As you can see, the preparation for acting as MC is very extensive and needs careful planning. Nothing should be left to chance. On the other hand, you should also prepare to speak, change, and adapt to the circumstances of the situation at hand. Adapt to the specific remarks of the speakers.

Performing as a Master/Mistress of Ceremonies

If you have prepared properly, the task of performing as MC will be relatively easy. One aspect to which you generally want to donate time is using good humor to project the lightness of the occasion. If the event is one of a serious nature, then work on projecting that mood and the goodwill of your organization.

It is sometimes customary now for an MC to present a monologue to begin a program. If you do, it is usually as a humorous reference to the events of the day or personalities, much as Bob Hope and Johnny Carson do. Make your monologue brief also (no more than five minutes) and related to a theme for either your banquet or your speaker.

Make your introduction of speakers and guests brief and follow a left to right or right to left order. You may, if there is a head table, introduce guests from the outer edge to the center or lectern. Since your audience members do not want, and you don't have time to do a complete biographical sketch of each guest, you should introduce the person by presenting the person's name, making a statement to relate why that person is a special guest and deserves an introduction or recognition. Try to make your audience members and your guests comfortably acquainted. If you are not well recognized by your audience, you may need to introduce yourself also. Generally, however, the MC is a well-known and respected member of the organization and needs little introduction. As you make introductions, it is generally accepted that your audience applaud each individual. If no one begins the applause, you as the MC, should begin.

As you introduce speakers, give the person's name, even though the audience just heard it, and then give the pertinent information about the speaker and the speech. It is good to repeat the speaker's name again to complete the introduction. A good statement is "And now, here he is, Mr. John Doe." Always lead the applause, greet the speaker at the speaker's stand with a handshake, and then take your seat smartly, focusing your undivided attention on the speaker. Lead the applause again at the conclusion of the speech. A sincere thanks to the speaker and a brief reference to the speech are always welcome. For example, "Thank you, Ms. Jane Doe, for those encouraging words about new opportunities for all of us."

Never attempt to make a rebuttal speech on the speaker's remarks or attempt to justify comments by the speaker. Let the speech stand on its own merits or demerits. Move immediately to the next event or speaker on the program until the end, when you give your closing remarks.

Closing remarks should be brief and signal the end of the banquet or dinner. Generally, thank everyone for attending and especially mention special guests and/or speakers. In some instances the president or some other leader will want to make the closing remarks. If this is your duty, be sure you know all persons to be thanked before the audience, then conclude with a brief statement, such as: "Thank you all. Drive carefully. Good night." This will signal the end of the program and serve to dismiss the audience to talk and/or leave.

As a follow-up to your program, stop and shake hands and thank all of your guest speakers again. Let them know you are pleased with their performance and appreciate their help in making your job easy and enjoyable. Wait until all guests have departed before leaving. It is generally rude and impolite for the MC to leave the banquet or dinner before the special guests have departed. As the MC, your job is one of public relations and goodwill. You should do everything you can to make this program and your organization look good to the organizational members as well as to your guests.

Project Assignment

Your instructor may assign you to serve as an MC for the speeches in your class on a particular day. Review the principles and ascertain the exact nature of your duties. Review the projects appropriate to your duties, as assigned. Prepare to welcome your guest speakers and introduce them, as a minimum.

Begin by determining the scope of your assignment and gathering all the materials you need. Organize your materials so each presentation fits the constraints of the duties of that assignment. Prepare to speak extemporaneously, but adjust and speak impromptu if necessary.

References

Sprague, J. & Stuart, D. (1988). *The Speaker's Handbook* (2nd ed.). San Diego: Harcourt Brace Jovanovich.

UNIT **VI**

SPEAKING IN BUSINESS AND PROFESSIONAL SETTINGS

Achievement is the knowledge that you have studied and worked hard and done the best that is in you. Success is being praised by others, and that's nice, too, but not as important or satisfying. Always aim for achievement and forget about success.

Helen Hayes

Unit VI consists of five projects that relate specifically to speaking in the business and professional settings. These projects are either of the informative or persuasive type, but will be used mostly by persons in business or in professional settings rather than in general informative or persuasive speaking situations. Project 26 is the report, and presents the principles of reporting. Project 27 presents the principles of preparing and presenting briefings. Making proposals is the topic of Project 28. Project 29 is the sales talk and presents the principles of making sales speeches of various types. The final project is the interview, Project 30.

PROJECT 26

Reports

The learning and knowledge we have is, at most, very
little compared with that which we are ignorant of.

—Plato

"As the significance and complexity of projects increase, the time available to a speaker
to explain thoroughly these projects to appropriate groups often decreases. A speaker
may have 10 minutes to explain a simple project but may be allowed only 20 minutes to
explain a project a hundred times as complex. It is therefore important that a speaker be
able to analyze data and reduce them to their significant elements, avoiding both meaningless generalities and confusing detail. Perhaps nowhere is the need to be precise
greater than in the special report."

The preceding statement was made by a well-known educator who through experience
has learned the importance of the special report. Students will do well to follow his advice
in learning how to prepare and present a report. To help you do this, this project presents
the principles of reports, preparing and organizing reports, presenting reports, and a
sample report.

Principles of Reports

The report is an informative speech prepared because someone or a group of individuals needs
certain definite and specific information. It generally requires an investigation of literature or
on-the-spot conditions involving original research, or a combination of both types of information. Its purpose is to provide a clear understanding of all the data, factual information, and
recommendations that are contained in it.

The report may concern the financial condition of a business, information on engineer-
ing, personnel, labor conditions, salaries, wages, marketing, distribution, or many other aspects of business, or conditions relating to any type of enterprise or situation. A report may
pertain to past events or to present conditions; or it may be an investigation made solely for
the purpose of providing information on which to base future action.

In a report you should make no efforts to persuade or influence the actions or beliefs of your audience members. You may make recommendations at the conclusion of your report if you feel they are wanted or needed; they generally provide the basis for future action or change of belief. Your purpose, however, is not to persuade with your report. Your purpose is simply to report the facts of the situation.

Incomplete reports may be presented at various stages in the development of a project. There are two kinds. The first is a *preliminary report,* which is limited to incomplete data covering your project only as far as the investigation has gone or during the beginning stages of a project. It may include an outline of plans for further investigation or suggestions about whether the organization should proceed with plans on the project.

The second type of incomplete report is a *progress report,* which is made during the progress of a project to tell of the accomplishments thus far in the investigation. It generally presents more extensive information than the preliminary report, tentative conclusions about the progress of the project, and further plans about the investigation. Progress reports are usually given when a leader wants to know if a work team is progressing on schedule, or if they need help, extended deadlines, more materials, and so on. At other times the progress report is used simply to keep interested members of the organization up-to-date on the achievements of long-term projects. In most instances you will want to report what has been done up to this point, what problems and delays have occurred, and what the future anticipations for the project are. Honesty is the best policy in this report. A delay or potential problem reported at this time could save your company time and money later if the delay is remedied or the problem is avoided by immediate action.

Occasions for reports arise any time special information is needed. Such reports are made to business managements and to governing bodies of any organization, whether civic, religious, educational, financial, agricultural, governmental, political, or otherwise.

Some topics suitable for reports include:

1. Report on attendance at local football games for the past five seasons. Is a new stadium needed?
2. Is present athletic equipment adequate?
3. How much money is needed to operate the school during the coming year?
4. Should the teaching staff of your school/college be increased?
5. Should more parking space be provided for student and faculty cars?
6. Should the school cafeteria be enlarged?
7. Is student housing adequate?
8. Should more money be provided for publication of the school paper?
9. Is the number of tardy students large enough so that they should be penalized for tardiness?
10. Should dormitory regulations be changed?
11. Report on library (school or public) conditions to determine whether a new library is needed.
12. Should a traffic light be placed at a certain intersection?
13. Should the city's main street be widened?
14. What is the present condition of the fire department?
15. Would it be advisable to provide more water for the city?
16. Are city traffic regulations adequate?
17. Should the city purchase land for a new park?
18. Should a new school health program be established?
19. What is the status of property taxes?
20. Should the city help fund the new hospital?

Preparing a Report

In preparing a report, bear in mind that your purpose is to present data, other information, conclusions (tentative or final), interpretations, and recommendations so your listeners will have a clear understanding of all your information. You are not to attempt to persuade or get action from them. You simply lay the results of your findings before your audience in the most understandable way possible.

Equally important is the fact that most special reporting is done because someone (a group of persons, a leader, or a business) needs to secure certain specific information so others may proceed with new actions, continue their present actions, or cease unproductive actions. What you discover, as the reporter, may form the basis of future actions by a management team or by the company president. Hence, it is of utmost importance that your report be complete and accurate.

A reliable method for preparing your report might be as follows. Learn specifically what you are supposed to investigate and for what your report will be used. You can see at a glance that you will have to do two things. First, you need to find out what information is required by the group to whom you must report. Second, you must search out all the information before drawing up your report. An example might be, "Should the Blank Oil Company buy a certain property and construct a service station on the site?" Here it would be necessary to investigate all the costs of acquiring the property and to become familiar with building restrictions, fire protection, tax rates, adjoining businesses, competitive neighborhood stations, the number of motor vehicles passing the location daily, and so on. After finding answers for these questions, you would prepare your report.

Or, as another example, suppose a factory needed to learn the number of man-hours lost because of sickness and injuries among employees over a three-month period. Their problem is whether they should set up, equip, and staff more first-aid stations in the factory. You can easily visualize the task of investigation. Here you will not try to count sick people as they leave the factory, but you will go to the company books and search for the needed information for a previous three-month period. In this case you will examine records. This is comparable to investigating literature in a library to secure needed information. You will prepare your report after your information is collected.

You can gather investigatory data by correspondence, reading, personal interviews, field investigation, and laboratory research. A combination of all these methods is often required if you are to collect the best and most accurate information for your report.

Organizing the Report

We now consider the organization of your report. Since the organization of most reports is similar, the following plan is recommended:

    I. INTRODUCTION
        A. Prepare your introduction. (This may be done last.)
        B. State the reasons for your report. (A brief history may be included.)
        C. State the purpose of your report and the problem you were investigating. Be specific.
        D. Name your sources of data. Be specific for all sources.
        E. Explain clearly your method of securing data. Tell about special records that you examined, identify persons you interviewed, and state where and when. Describe any special tools, equipment, instruments, or other mechanical devices you used in getting data. State places, times, dates, and anything else relevant to describing your method of securing information.
        F. State generally what the main ideas in your report will concern.

(Select only the essential elements from these areas that must be included in your report. Some reports will demand that you cover all areas, others will require only a few of the preceding items.)

    II. BODY
        A. Present your first main finding.
            1. Give a subfinding—if there is one—to substantiate your first main finding.
            2. Give another subfinding—if there is one—to substantiate your first main finding.

    B. Present your second main finding.
       1. Give a subfinding—if there is one—to substantiate your second main finding.
          a. Present data to verify your subfinding.
          b. Present further support for your subfinding.
       2. Give another subfinding—if there is one—to substantiate your second main finding.
          a. Present data to verify this subfinding
          b. Present further support for your subfinding

Present as many more main findings and subfindings as necessary.

   III. CONCLUSION
     A. Summarize your findings.
     B. Summarize the significance of your findings.
     C. When requested, make recommendations regarding the problem you were investigating. You may recommend that further investigation should be made or that certain action should or should not be taken, or you may combine the two. (Do not strive to have your recommendations adopted. Other persons will decide this on the basis of your complete report.)

In organizing your material, select only the main findings or your summaries of them and list them in order of significance and importance. Often the people who listen to a report are interested only in the main ideas it contains. Hence, an oral report does not contain much detail. Too much detail will probably be more confusing than clarifying because people simply can't grasp everything that is presented. A written version of the oral report, including all details, should be prepared for study at a later date.

Presenting a Report

In your oral report, as in any speech, you should observe all the elements that contribute to effective speaking. Everything should be well prepared and well rehearsed. Your language should be clear and vivid. It is probable that you will make your report to a group of specialists who will understand the terminology and technical terms you may use. However, if your audience is composed of laypeople, you must use understandable, nontechnical language. It is also probable that interest in your report will be more than average because persons who are concerned about the special information you have will make up your audience. This should not be interpreted to mean that your report should be dry and dull. Rather, your efforts should be directed toward using language that is descriptive, concrete, and concise so complete understanding can be gained. Make your report as interesting as possible.

If diagrams, charts, graphs, and other illustrations are used, they should be ready for instant use during your report. You should be entirely familiar with them. They should be placed so everyone in your audience can see them easily, and they should be large enough to be easily read. Review the principles of using visual aids (Project 10) before presenting your report. It should help you in both preparing and presenting your charts, graphs, and so on.

Talk audibly and clearly. Your voice should be distinct, well articulated, and loud enough for all to hear easily. Speak at a speed that can readily be followed and comprehended: A speaking rate of 125 to 150 words per minute is generally about right. Naturally, you should sound both confident and pleasant, as well as conversational. You should never sound as if you have memorized and are reciting your written report. Under no circumstances should you ever read your written report to your audience. If you do, you may lose your credibility with your company president or the management group listening to your report.

After your report is concluded, be prepared to answer questions from your audience members if the occasion permits. It is also desirable to have written copies of your report available for those who want them. Usually, the president, and possibly a vice-president who is significantly affected, will want written copies of your report. Not all members will want nor will they need copies of your written report.

Some of the other common types of reports that you may be asked to present from time to time include the following:

1. *The Sales Report.* In the sales report you describe the sales you have made. You include all information relative to the sale—data regarding the time of day when the sale was made, place, office conditions, general environment, method used in making the sale, statistical information, and any special features or unique aspects of the sale. This type of report concerns a limited group and is unique because it deals only with sales and those who are involved in a "sales" work group.

2. *The Committee Report.* In the committee report the chairperson usually speaks for a committee. The chairperson acts as spokesperson for the group. In this type of report you must include all essential findings and recommendations that your committee adopted. Before the chairperson makes the final report, it is sometimes wise to have the committee approve the report to make sure that all necessary information has been included. The committee report should present important details and deliberations that contribute to a clearer understanding of the committee's actions. Each item should be clear and to the point. Often it is a good plan to number or letter the individual items of the report. Recommendations should be held to a minimum; six or seven are generally more than sufficient. The entire report should be logically arranged.

   Frequently, the committee delegates full authority to the chairperson to present the report without their final approval. In this case strict impartiality on the part of the chairperson should be carefully observed. A written copy of the report is usually desirable so that a permanent record of the committee findings will be on file.

3. *The Personal Experience Report.* The personal experience report gives the time, place, and description of the situation and environment in which personal experiences occurred. All such events should be accurately and objectively reported in the proper sequence. The individual making this report should recount these events as they were experienced, show their significance to each other, and show any relationship that exists among them. An example of a personal experience report is a police officer's report to a superior officer about the capture of a criminal.

SAMPLE REPORT

By Janna Storey

Communication Apprehension

It was my first time. I'll never forget how scared I was. Thoughts of doubt kept rushing through my mind. "I can't do this. I'm too nervous. I'll make such a fool of myself. Why me?" Finally, I realized that other people had survived this first time experience and that I could survive also. I took a deep breath, gave myself a pep talk, and began to take the first step. The first step always seems to be the most difficult. After finally realizing that I could go through with it, I walked to the front of the room and began my first speech.

That first speech was almost ten years ago and I am still alive to talk about it today. Of course, I have also taken several speech classes where I have learned the skills of speaking in public.

Most of you have experienced some type of communication apprehension during your lives. This apprehension may have come during a speech, such as mine was, or it may have occurred during a conversation or a group discussion. Communication apprehension is an equal opportunity concept and does not select only certain people to "hit."

Today, I will inform you of two aspects of communication apprehension. Those two aspects are: its universality and potential solutions.

First, communication apprehension is universal. No one is exempt from having the symptoms of communication apprehension. If you get sweaty palms and butterflies in your stomach when you speak in front of an audience, or you find it difficult to talk to a certain individual, or to speak up in a group, you aren't alone. This feeling of anxiety is known as communication apprehension and is experienced by over one-half of beginning speakers. James McCroskey, a well-known communication researcher, defines communication apprehension as, "an individual's level of fear or anxiety associated with either real or anticipated communication with another person or persons." Consistent with McCroskey, Daly and Sorensen, two other communication researchers, contend that people experiencing communication apprehension "avoid communication if possible or suffer a variety of anxiety-type feelings when forced to communicate."

This feeling of anxiety that we call "communication apprehension" is common to many people. As the old saying goes, "misery loves company." If you have been feeling that you are the only one in your class who gets trembling hands and a weak stomach at the very thought of giving a speech, you couldn't be more wrong. In fact, you are part of the majority. Recently, I took a poll of students in an Introduction to Speech Communication class. Of the sixty students surveyed, ninety percent reported some form of nervousness about giving a public speech. Even Sir Winston Churchill and Abraham Lincoln have confessed to having had communication apprehension. The major difference in the effect stage fright has on a beginner and on an experienced speaker comes from how each handles the nervousness once it occurs. This idea of handling a fear of speaking, leads to possible steps in learning to control this anxiety dilemma.

As a beginning speaker, you are likely to imagine that the best way to deal with communication apprehension is to rid yourself of it. According to McCroskey, a limited amount of anxiety can be helpful. The trick is to control that amount—not to do away with it entirely. The next question, then, is "How do I go about controlling my speech anxiety?"

Second, let's look at some potential solutions to speech anxiety. One step in controlling speech anxiety is to pick a topic of interest. According to James Winans, one of the masters of speech communication in the United States, "To interest an audience, the speaker should aim to hold his hearers with a minimum of effort on their part; for whatever energy goes into mere effort to attend is lost to consideration of the subject matter." So, interest along with attention is a must for any speech. Any time you are interested in your topic, it is easier for you to speak on that topic.

After selecting a topic of interest, thorough preparation is needed. O'Connor, author of a popular speech textbook, states that, "most stage fright comes from a fear of not succeeding in front of the audience." Making sure that you are prepared may be easier if you follow these simple steps:

1. Study your topic.
2. Analyze the needs of your audience.
3. Research and outline the ideas of your speech.
4. Rehearse your presentation.

O'Connor also suggests that thorough preparation not only can give you the right level of confidence before your speech begins, but it can also support you once you have started speaking.

The final element I will discuss concerning how to control your speech anxiety is relaxation. Relaxation techniques will help you to reduce the physical symptoms of communication apprehension. After interviewing five speech instructors, I gathered information on how to encourage students to relax. All five of the instructors interviewed, agreed that exercising before speaking was a necessary ice-breaker for anxiety. These instructors referred to this type of exercise as "speech aerobics." Speech aerobics is a warm-up activity performed prior to a student giving his/her speech. The class can perform these exercises as a group, or an individual can do speech aerobics on his/her own. A few ideas for speech aerobics include:

1. Stand up. Reach as high as you can with your arms over your head. Then let your arms fall to your sides.
2. Force yourself to yawn widely several times. Fill your lungs with air each time by breathing deeply.
3. Let your head hang down as far as possible on your chest for several moments. Then slowly rotate it in a full circle, at the same time allowing your eyelids to droop lazily. Repeat this several times.

These techniques may also be done privately to reduce your anxiety level. An important consideration to remember when you are thinking about speech apprehension is that audiences tend to be very sympathetic. When you are an audience member, how many times have you wanted to see the speaker fail? Probably, the most common answer would be none. Audiences want to see their speakers succeed, not fail.

In conclusion, the next time you feel weak and nervous about giving a speech, don't panic. Remember that you aren't alone. Communication apprehension is a common feeling. It is universal, but there are ways to control your anxiety. Remember to select a topic that interests you, prepare thoroughly, and do your speech aerobics.

In closing, instead of thinking "I *have* to give a speech," it might be better if you think, "I have a speech to *give.*"

SAMPLE REPORT OUTLINE

I.   INTRODUCTION
    A. Attention-getter: Story
    B. Credentials: Speech classes
    C. Arouse interest: You

  II. THESIS: Today I will inform you of two aspects of communication apprehension.
      PREVIEW: Those two aspects are: (1) its universality and (2) potential solutions.
  III. BODY
     A. Its universality
       1. Definition
       2. Common
       3. Control
     B. Potential solutions
       1. Topic
       2. Preparation
       3. Exercises
  IV. CONCLUSION
     A. Review main points
       1. Universality
       2. Solutions
     B. Closing: Speech to give

References

Beatty, Michael J., Behnke, Ralph R., & McCallum, Karin. (1978). Situational determinants of communication apprehension. *Communication Monographs, 45.* 188–191.

Butler, J. F. (1986). Personality characteristics of subjects high and low in apprehension about communication. *Perceptual and Motor Skills, 62,* 895–898.

McCroskey, James C. (1970). Measures of communication-bound anxiety. *Speech Monographs, 37,* 269–277.

O'Connor, J. Regis. (1988). *Speech: Exploring Communication.* Englewood Cliffs, New Jersey: Prentice-Hall, Inc.

Winans, J. A. (1943). The sense of communication. *Southern Speech Journal, 9,* 3–11.

Project Assignment

Prepare a four- to five-minute report on one of the topics listed earlier, or on any other suitable topic that your instructor approves. Prepare an outline on the form at the end of this book and be prepared to speak extemporaneously to your audience. Concentrate on presenting information rather than trying to influence or affect your audience's beliefs.

Depending on the type of report you are giving, collect the information you need to complete your report. Learn what you need to know about the project under investigation. As you organize your findings, use one of the recognized patterns from Project 3 to describe the history of the project, the present developments, and future considerations.

Prepare an introduction that will gain attention, show your involvement with the project, and motivate your listeners to want to hear your report. Your conclusion should summarize your findings and close with something of interest to your audience. Develop appropriate visual aids to help you explain your report to your audience.

References

Gibson, J. W. & Cornwell, C. (1979). *Creative Speech Communication.* New York: Macmillan Publishing Company.

Rodman, G. (1986). *Public Speaking* (3rd ed.). New York: Holt, Rinehart and Winston, Inc.

PROJECT **27**

The Briefing

There can be too much of a good thing. For instance,
throwing one end of a rope to a person who is drowning
is good. Throwing both ends is too much.

—Anonymous

This is the age of briefings. We hear about briefings every day. For example, the president
or some other government agent receives a briefing. There are briefings in the military
before most maneuvers. In business, the boss wants a briefing on an upcoming meeting
or on a recent company operation. In other areas we have become used to the "brief
guide," "the brief handbook," and the "brief edition." The brief has become the favorite
form of presentational speaking for many people. Because of its increased use, this
project presents the principles of the briefing, preparing a briefing, presenting a briefing,
and a sample briefing for study.

Principles of the Briefing

The briefing is a special form of informative speaking in which the recipient is concerned with
a specific report about a particular operation. As such, the briefing may be more limited than
the other forms of informative speaking. Many briefings are for exclusive audiences. In some
instances it may be a small audience of a few people or maybe only one person, like the
President of the United States, a business executive like the company president or a foreman,
or for a military general. In other instances the briefing may be for larger audiences, like the
workers who will be operating new equipment or implementing a new procedure for the
company, or for the soldiers who will be performing the military operations.

Another special feature of the briefing is that the information is to be presented to people
of a definite group. The audience members generally have considerable knowledge on the topic
of the briefing, so there is no need to waste time with background information or what leads
up to the briefing. The area of concentration is only the new details that members of this group
do not have—recent developments, for example.

The major purpose of the briefing is to give someone who knows about a specific operation more updated data concerning recent events involving the operation. For example, in the military, briefings are usually presented to members of a combat team immediately before the operation to bring them up-to-date on the latest developments in the area and to prepare them with the specifics of their mission. In business, a briefing may be given to the people who are to install new equipment or begin a new procedure. One reason that the president, or any other leader, wants a briefing is so hours are not wasted in reading extensive reports. Effective leaders want to use their time efficiently and to the benefit of the entire organization. If time is saved by hearing the specific details of progress rather than reading a report, the leader can better gauge how to alter progress and make midcourse corrections as well as to keep the organization running smoothly.

A second principle of a briefing is to update everyone on the current conditions that affect the group's operations. In the case of the president, he may know the generalities of definite government action that is impending or has just been completed and needs to be updated on events since his last briefing. In a business, the company may have a new procedure, some new equipment being installed, or material available on a new concept, and the company president needs an update on the implementation of the new procedure and its effects so far, the progress of the installation of the new equipment, or a report on the new concept. In all instances it is the job of the briefer to make a very short report of the specific data that the leader does not already know. As noted previously, there should be no wasted time or effort for the leader.

Preparing a Briefing

Debaters and lawyers have been preparing briefings for years. They know that the best preparation for presenting a briefing is to read all the significant material available. Gather all materials and read them once through to get the main points from each one. The reason for this is that you will be preparing all the main points from your sources and not just reviewing each one independently. You will want to prepare a single, unified report of the topic, not individual reports of each of your authorities.

Once you have determined the main points of your topic, create an outline of the topics you could include in your briefing. When you have completed this outline, read it carefully and determine which of the issues are essential to the brief and which are already known to your audience members. Remember, your task is to save the time of those you are briefing. You will not want to waste their time by presenting facts and information they already know. You will also want to make sure you are presenting "new information." Unless you are doing this, you are not informative, nor are you presenting a brief.

Because of your very limited time and the nature of your presentation, you should strive to be as clear as possible in presenting all your ideas. Try to waste no meeting time in attempting to explain what you mean by any terms, details, or omissions from your briefing. Also, it is your objective to instill understanding in your audience in the brief time you have available. Leaders are most interested in group productivity, and to them time is money and not to be wasted. However, you should never sacrifice comprehension for brevity. After all, your goal is to save others the task of looking up facts or having to make on-site inspections for themselves.

Once you have all of your information gathered, it is critical for you to put your information into an outline format so you will be assured of presenting your information in an organized manner. Just as with any other speech, you should begin by preparing your thesis first. Once you have determined your thesis, it will be easier to determine which materials to include in your briefing and which materials to leave out.

A simple thesis is, "Today I will explain the three steps we have taken to install the new degreasing equipment. The three steps are: (1) removing the outdated equipment, (2) cleaning the installation area, and (3) redesigning the equipment room." Now it will be easy to fit all the new information in these three areas you have selected for presentation. This outline can be easily rearranged and details changed to accommodate different audiences. For instance, let's say you have to present a briefing to the Board of Directors on the progress of equipment installation and to the crew leaders of the work crews who will be operating the new equipment. Since both audiences will not want the same information, your outline can be easily changed to fit each audience.

The briefing to the Board of Directors will likely be an *informational briefing,* where you attempt to familiarize the board members on the general conduct of the business. They probably will not be interested in the details of the new equipment installation and your decision-making process unless it has become a problem. For example, they don't care about how you decided what to do or when and where to put the new equipment. Their main concern is total company output and productivity. What must be done to get the plant back in operation, and how soon this plant will be back in full operation.

The group of crew leaders, on the other hand, would likely be interested in more details of how the equipment setup was decided and how it will affect their work crews. This latter briefing may take the form of an *instructional briefing.* One of the main differences between these two briefings is that in the latter it is more important that your audience members remember what you say because they will have to pass this information on to other people or use it in their daily work. In this instructional briefing you must rearrange the information so it most closely meets the demands and needs of the crew leaders. In this situation you may have to sacrifice some brevity for the comprehension of your information by the crew leaders. You may also have to use more repetition, illustrations, examples, visual aids, and other techniques to help clarify your message and make it memorable.

In fact, you may not be able to complete this briefing without some form of visual aid. Your ability to construct and use visual aids effectively may well determine whether your audience members understand you. If your audience members can see complex ideas on a visual aid, your task of presenting your information may be greatly simplified. Good visual aids will also help your audience members remember what you said much longer. If you need to, review the materials in Project 10 on using visual aids.

It is important at this stage in developing your briefing that you decide which type of briefing your situation demands, and supply the appropriate information for that type of briefing. In some instances you may need to persuade your audience members that your plan of attack is appropriate, accurate, or the best line of attack. Knowing your purpose is critical to the proper preparation of your briefing.

Once you have the body of your briefing prepared, you need to turn your attentions to the introduction and conclusion. Because it is a speech, the briefing needs an introduction and a conclusion. Return to those projects if you need help in preparing either one.

Remember, in all briefings your information must be factual, orderly, concise, honest, clear, and strictly objective. You should strive in all cases to present only the background material that is essential for your audience members to understand your message easily. Do not add any extraneous material of dubious importance, no matter how colorful or interesting you may find it.

Presenting a Briefing

The rules for presenting a briefing are the same as those of presenting an informative speech. To be most effective, this speech should be presented in an extemporaneous manner. Scripted briefings may be asked for following an oral presentation, but the oral presentation should never be delivered based on a written form. As an oral briefer, you must make sure your audience members understand what you say. If you do not keep good eye contact with your audience, you will not fully understand the degree to which your audience members are following your message. Your presentation should also be active. That is, you will need to maintain the full attention of your audience members during your entire presentation. It should sound like a conversation with your audience. If you get too formal, you may lose some of your audience members.

As you talk, remember that your audience members can't go back and reread what you have said if they don't understand you. In most instances you are going to be their sole source of information. If you have prepared to present your brief orally, you will have prepared only an outline from which you will present your information. Since the true test of your success in this project is what your audience members can take away with them, your oral presentation skills will have to be at their best. No matter how brilliantly you have researched your materials and prepared your outline, if your audience members do not listen to you or they do not understand you, all your brilliance will be lost. So, present your briefing as though this information is from firsthand, personal knowledge (which it will be if you have prepared well in advance). In instances where you need to use someone else as a reference, do so as if this were an expository address. For instance, you may say, "according to John Doe, the construction engineer, we will begin the process of removing equipment on Tuesday." Whenever it is appropriate, cite the sources of your information to help your audience know you are not just "talking," but "talking with authority."

Never go over the time limits imposed on you from the person(s) requesting the briefing. If your audience members want more information or wish to spend more time discussing the matter with you, they will control the meeting time after your presentation has been completed. Any violations of the expected time limits by you could be grounds for a reprimand from your supervisor or the party requesting the briefing.

Briefly, the obstacles of presenting a briefing are the same problems as those of any formal speaking situation. Your success or failure will likely be determined by your ability to analyze your audience accurately, prepare your information precisely, and deliver your speech clearly and convincingly. Remember, the purpose of the briefing is to save time and money for others; if you prepare adequately, you will have saved rather than wasted the time of others.

One last point to remember: The persons who are briefed often want to ask questions after you have finished your presentation. Be prepared to answer questions that will clarify what you have said or extend a point you may have made. In certain instances the persons who are briefed may want to know more than you have presented, or may become intrigued by some comment and desire to pursue a more lengthy discussion of the issue. Be prepared to spend the time necessary to satisfy their "information hunger."

SAMPLE BRIEFING

By Susan Jacobs

Accounting Skills

I brought with me today some good news and some bad news. The good news is that if you were to open a CPA practice today, you could earn sixty dollars an hour for your services. The bad news is that you would have to share that with each of your employees. If your business were successful and you had several clients, that hourly fee could accumulate to quite a salary, even after deducting your employees' wages.

I plan to be a CPA when I graduate from college. I have been working for three years on that degree, and I feel that I know some of the skills and abilities that are needed to be a successful CPA.

Some of you are also working toward degrees in accounting. To be successful accountants, you'll need some skills. I am going to tell you about some of those skills so that you can make sure you possess them when you're ready to start your career.

Today, I will explain to you the three most important skills to have in order to become a successful accountant. These skills are: (1) the ability to communicate, (2) the ability to use your knowledge, and (3) the ability to use computers.

The most important skill we can possess as accountants is the ability to communicate on an interpersonal level. In a public practice, we will be dealing with clients of all kinds. In my interview with Keith Morrison, a CPA here in Ada, I learned that our ability to communicate will determine our success or failure in the business world. How well we meet the demands and handle the problems of our clients will decide our fate.

The communication demands that we will face in business will include oral communication with clients and written communication with certain agencies. In dealing with clients, we will speak with individuals about their tax returns and company representatives about their books. We will also spend time writing to various agencies, such as the Internal Revenue Service, the Oklahoma Tax Commission, regulatory agencies, and insurance agencies. According to Mr. Morrison, the whole objective of the accounting process is to communicate information to the end user. If we can't do that, we're not going to succeed in accounting.

One of the problems Mr. Morrison runs into is when a client comes in with a problem, but the client isn't sure what the problem is, or she or he isn't quite sure how to explain it. We as accountants have to understand the problem before we can help the client. We must be good listeners so that we know which questions to ask. By asking the right questions, we can figure out the problem. We can waste a lot of time by failing to communicate effectively.

The second most important skill is the ability to use the knowledge we have acquired while pursuing our accounting degrees. Mr. Morrison believes that we'll have the knowledge that we need from the courses we are required to take, but whether we can apply that knowledge will depend on our attitudes. We must get training and experience in order to apply our knowledge and get the best results.

The third most important skill we must have is the ability to use computers in our accounting capacity. A mere familiarity will not be enough. We must be able to deal with computers, function with them, be able to communicate with them in a sense, and be able to get along with them. Programming skills aren't essential, but they would be helpful. They would enable us to be more familiar with the computer. We must feel comfortable with computers and not be afraid of them. We must be able to combine our accounting knowledge with our computer knowledge to master the business applications.

In conclusion, there is more to being a successful accountant than obtaining a degree. We must be able to communicate with our clients on an interpersonal level. We must be able to get to the root of their problems, and we must able a able to communicate to them the information they need whether orally or in writing. We must be able to apply the knowledge we've acquired while pursuing our degrees in order to get the best results from the training and experience we pick up along the way. And we must have an understanding of computers and how they function in the business world so that we can combine our accounting with the computer and master the business applications.

We all want to be successful in our careers. We must sharpen our skills and make the most of our knowledge, and we will succeed.

SAMPLE OUTLINE—BRIEFING

I.   INTRODUCTION
   A. Attention-getter: Joke
   B. Credentials: Three years
   C. Arouse interest: Use
II. THESIS: Today I will explain the three most important skills to have in order to become a successful accountant.
   PREVIEW: Those three skills are: (1) ability to use communication, (2) ability to use knowledge, and (3) ability to use computers.
III. BODY
   A. Ability to use communication
      1. Communication demands
      2. Communication problems
   B. Ability to use knowledge
   C. Ability to use computers
IV. CONCLUSION
   A. Summary
      1. Ability to use communication
      2. Ability to use knowledge
      3. Ability to use computers
   B. Closing: Relate to audience

Project Assignment

Prepare and present a five- to seven-minute briefing on a topic of interest to both you and your audience. Be sure you check with your instructor for specific details of your assignment.

Prepare for your briefing by collecting all the information you will need to complete your project. Then begin by outlining the major points you need to present, based on your audience. Once you have the body completed, you may begin on your introduction. Be sure you gain attention, relate your topic to your audience members, and establish your credentials. Your conclusion should review the main points you have made in the briefing, and make your audience feel complete.

Alternate Assignment

Combine this assignment with the interview. Interview someone who holds a job like the one you want in five years. Find out what communication skills you will need to know to become a competent candidate for that job. Then prepare a briefing in which you report to the class on the important communication skills for your future and what classes you will need to take.

References

Berko, R. M., Wolvin, A. D. & Curtis, B. (1990). *This Business of Communicating* (4th ed). Dubuque, Iowa: Wm. C. Brown Company, Publishers.

Berko, R. M., Wolvin, A. D., & Wolvin, D. R. (1988). *Communicating: A Social and Career Focus* (4th ed.). Boston: Houghton Mifflin Company.

Dance, F. E. X. & Zak-Dance, C. C. (1986). *Public Speaking.* New York: Harper & Row, Publishers.

Loney, G. M. (1959). *Briefing and Conference Techniques.* New York: McGraw-Hill Book Company.

Military Briefings. (1985). In *Staff Skills, Roles, and Relationships,* a manual by Combined Arms and Services Staff School, Fort Leavenworth, Kansas, pp. 91–102.

PROJECT **28**

The Proposal

Life's a tough proposition, and the first hundred years
are the hardest.
—Wilson Mizner

Every day you propose things to others. You propose such activities as a plan of action for your company or group of friends or a place to have lunch. You also propose that others follow some popular trend, wear a particular clothing fashion, or a hairstyle, plus many other actions. The proposal is a part of your everyday life. Knowing how to make better proposals will help you be more persuasive and understandable, and you will likely get what you want more often. This project presents the principles of the proposal, preparing the proposal; presenting the proposal, and a sample proposal for study.

Principles of the Proposal

The proposal is a persuasive speech in which you usually attempt to secure audience action—you have a plan and want others to go along with your plan. In some instances you may simply present information for others to listen to, but generally your object is to get others to go along with your plan of action because you feel it is the best alternative. Because of your purpose, this speech is similar to the "Speech to Get Action" (Project 21) and the "Sales Talk" (Project 29). The main differences are that the speech to get action is more generic and does not necessarily help you propose a plan of action. The sales talk is more specific in that it deals with selling a specific product or service. For example, you might propose that your club or an organization to which you belong sell Christmas candles to raise money for a group project. Generically, you are trying to get action from the group with your proposal. Technically, you are also "selling" your organization members on your plan. If this were a sales talk, you would be attempting to sell individual members of your audience the Christmas candles. As you can see, there are similarities in preparing a speech to get action, a sales talk, and a proposal.

Whenever you prepare a proposal, you must first know to whom the proposal will be

169

presented, who will be evaluating your proposal, and who the decision makers will be. In typical everyday situations such as going to lunch or a movie you know your audience members very well and know what motivates them. You will need to know the same information when you propose a course of action for your company or work group. If you propose a course of action for your work group, and the work group does not have the authority to make the changes without the company president's approval, you may not have made the right proposal. In this instance your proposal would have been best presented to your work group, and if they accepted it, you should then present a proposal to the next level in your company, progressing until you can make your proposal to the company president, who can act on the proposal. In this sequence of steps you may need to make several different proposals to secure the actions you desire. What will sway your work group may be totally unmotivating for your supervisor or the company president. In each case you must present the specific aspects of your proposal that will satisfy the needs of your audience members.

One of the most significant reasons proposals fail is that either the presenter has not adequately analyzed who the audience members are or has misanalyzed what will motivate the audience members to accept the desired action. Another possible reason that a proposal may fail to secure the proper reaction is presenting the wrong proposal information to the audience.

In determining what will motivate your audience members, think in terms of typical motivators. Most people are motivated by money or profit. Remember, time is also money for some people. So, if your proposal will make money, save money, or show some increase in profit, you stand a better chance of getting others to accept your proposal. This is true for individuals as well as for companies and organizations. Efficiency is also a good motivator. We Americans like efficiency and pride ourselves on our efficiency. We can be motivated by someone showing us how we can be more efficient or by proving to us that we are inefficient.

Other audience members will respond to the degree of risk involved in your proposal. If the risks are low and the chances for success high, it is easier to persuade your audience members than if the odds are reversed. Some people respond and react better to "new," "creative," and "innovative," proposals. They want unique and different proposals. This is one of the techniques often used by advertisers who are trying to get consumers to try their products. Look at the number of advertisements that use words like "new," "improved," and some form of futuristic reference to get you to buy their products. Some proposals contain the actual words; others suggest the creative and innovative aspects of their products.

You may also use the Maslow hierarchy of needs (Maslow, 1954) to find out which needs in the audience are unmet and attempt to fulfill these deficiencies. While you may not be able to identify a level of needs for all audience members, you may determine which human needs will be motivational for your audience. Maslow's needs hierarchy include: (1) physiological needs (concerns related to one's health and well-being, such as food and drink); (2) safety needs (personal security and protection, such as housing); (3) love and belonging (concerns related to being loved and belonging to social groups, such as your friendships); (4) esteem (held in high regard by your fellow companions—respect); and (5) self-actualization (striving for ultimate personal fulfillment, actions that you do to please yourself).

Obviously, the ideas presented are not the only aspects of audience motivation; they are presented here only as suggestions for looking at audience motivations before you prepare your proposal. Your task as the presenter of the proposal is to know which person(s) you are persuading and what motives him or her, or them, and to prepare a proposal that will respond to the unmet needs or respond to the motivations of your audience members.

As in other projects, consider the following topics for proposals as the starting place for you to begin brainstorming for a topic suitable to speak on. These suggestions are meant to whet your appetite and get the juices flowing so you can create the best idea for you and your audience.

1. Propose that your group support a local charity.
2. Propose that your organization donate time for community cleanup.
3. Propose that your club adopt a highway.
4. Propose that your group donate money to the hospital building fund.
5. Propose that your organization host a traveling show.

6. Propose that your club organize a benefit for the homeless in the city.
7. Propose that your work group alter its method of operation.
8. Propose that your work group join a company project.
9. Propose that your work group support a company charity drive.
10. Propose that your company adopt a set of new work rules.
11. Propose that your company change hours of operation to "flex time" to accommodate more of its workers.
12. Propose that your company establish a day-care center for workers' children.
13. Propose that your company change its training program.
14. Propose that your company purchase a new computer system, or other new equipment.
15. Propose that your company hire a "Consumer Relations Director."

Preparing the Proposal

As with other types of oral presentations, it is critical that your proposal be organized clearly so it is easy to follow. Most generally, people do not want or have time for lengthy, cumbersome proposals. You must be aware of the time available for your proposal. If you are allowed only five minutes to make your presentation, organize so you are able to include all pertinent facts in your presentation. If you have been given a longer period of time to present your proposal, you will need to give careful attention to the number of details you can include. Once you have adequately analyzed your audience and determined what will motivate individual members of your audience, you need to secure adequate supporting facts for your proposal.

One method of preparing for your proposal is to review Project 21, the "Speech to Get Action." This project will help you organize your presentation in a simple four-step process to get action from your audience. Another effective method of organizing a proposal is the "state-your-case-and-prove-it" method. This organizational pattern follows the topical organization scheme (Project 3) in which you assert a position and then follow it up with proof. In this organizational pattern you begin with a conclusion you have drawn (and which you assert to your audience). Your conclusion is justified through your use of specific arguments (proof) that your conclusion is valid.

Sometimes your audience members will be generally aware of your proposal before you present it officially and will bring with them preconceived notions as to the actions that they should take. If they are predisposed in your favor, it will be advantageous to your proposal. However, if your audience members are predisposed against your proposal, you will need to overcome their predisposition by presenting information that will be new and different from what they already know.

In preparing your introduction, you need to establish your topic and your credibility, and make sure that your audience members know how your proposal will affect them. If your topic is well known to your audience members, or has been the topic of much discussion, you may need to justify to your audience members why your proposal needs to be considered or reconsidered. For example, is there new information available? Have recent events changed the conditions? Has there been a continuing controversy that needs to be settled? All of these are merely suggestions of ideas that will help you relate your topic to your audience.

Presenting the Proposal

Prepare to speak extemporaneously (Project 7). In most instances you will find that the majority of your audience members will be upper echelon management, who are highly intelligent and should easily understand your proposal. Begin your presentation as you would any other persuasive speech. Make sure you stress your credentials or your "right to speak" on the topic. If your audience members already know this information, stress your recent work that they may not know about. You will also want to stress the importance of your topic to your audience members. You must adapt to the audience depending on whether you work for a large organization where you may not be well known or for a small company where everyone knows you. Arouse interest so your audience members will be eager to adopt your proposal. Remember, most of your audience members will know the organization well, so you can use technical terms and some organizational jargon.

Throughout your presentation, you must clearly state your proposal and relate your supporting materials to your thesis. Make your statements sound sincere. You must sound personally convinced that your proposal is the right course of action or your audience will not be convinced. In that case they will probably not approve your proposal. Avoid any apologies for not knowing something or for not preparing more thoroughly. If you are not prepared, or you have not learned what you need to know, your audience members will find out if they are astute; if not, there is no sense in telling them what your inadequacies are. Imagine how you would respond to a speaker who began, "I'm not really ready for this proposal, but I guess I have to make it today, ready or not. So, here goes." Are you willing to accept this proposal? Probably not.

As you speak make your bodily actions and movements consistent with your verbal message. If your nonverbal message is not as clear and confident-appearing as your verbal message, you may counteract the effects of your verbal message. Remember, saying "we" will remind your audience members that you are a part of them and that your proposal affects you as well as it does them. Never separate yourself from your audience verbally or nonverbally. In fact, you will do best if you can speak without the use of notes and without a speaker's stand so you can get physically close to your audience members. This not only tells the audience that you are interested and concerned, but shows it as well.

If you can do so, also prepare some visual aids that will enhance your presentation and bring you and your audience members closer together. Generally, using visual aids such as charts, drawings, pictures, diagrams, and graphs will also increase audience interest in your presentation (see Project 10). Information that is new or unique or will graphically demonstrate changes that your proposal will produce will work best in getting your audience members to accept your proposal.

In concluding your proposal, do more than *repeat* your contentions. You must highlight the significance and importance of your arguments. If you *restate* your contentions rather than repeat what you have said, your audience will not be bored with your arguments. In closing your presentation, encourage your audience members to reflect on the advantages of your proposal and the arguments you have presented. You might call for a specific action if you feel that people are ready to act on your proposal—or that action taken now would certainly be in favor of your proposal. If this is inappropriate, close by picturing the future with your proposal in operation. Always leave your audience with a favorable impression of both you and your proposal.

SAMPLE PROPOSAL

By Shirley Windsor

Every Litter Bit Hurts

Have you ever felt lost in your own office? Lost because of clutter on the desk, on the floor, around your feet? Granted some of it is our own fault but as professional people who have earned office positions, we also anticipate some reasonable help from maintenance to keep business running smoothly.

Recently there have been numerous complaints about articles missing from offices. I have also been one of those persons who has been complaining because of losses from my office. Generally, these complaints promote an atmosphere of mistrust between our office staffs and maintenance employees. The complaints about the maintenance of the building include those of missed areas as well as those of poorly cleaned areas. The time we spend registering complaints about cleaning could be better used working on uncompleted projects.

I propose that we enlist the aid of maintenance in establishing a time schedule for individual office cleanup. This proposal is very simple, costs the company nothing, but could save much money in lost documents, lost property, and lost credibility. The most difficult aspect of this proposal is that it will require a cooperative effort from each of us who occupies an office. That means that each of us must make a personal sacrifice to ensure the security of his/her own office.

Since all of us are involved in special projects of sensitive natures, I recommend that maintenance schedule the cleaning of individual offices while office personnel are in the office area. If no projects of a sensitive nature are pending, office personnel have the option of being present during the cleaning process.

This procedure would entail setting up a time schedule when maintenance would be allowed into the specific sensitive areas during joint working hours. A meeting between office employees and maintenance management could easily be arranged. Cooperation between specific area coordinators in the building would enhance the effectiveness of practical aspects of time and work for maintenance employees.

As for the missing of primary areas of the building, I propose that each manager be responsible for determining that all areas of his/her staff have been cleaned daily. Any area, such as a restroom, a work area, or a staff meeting room, can be reported to the supervisor, who contacts the director of maintenance and the missed area can be cleaned immediately.

It is a known fact that a pleasing office appearance and atmosphere enhances productivity and customer relations. The enactment of this proposal would ensure project security, provide efficiency, success, and satisfaction within the work area, as well as promote public relations between ourselves and maintenance personnel.

Project Assignment

Prepare and present a seven- to ten-minute proposal in which you propose a specific course of action or change in activities for your company, work group, or some organization to which you belong. (Your instructor may specify which one you must prepare.) Use your analysis of audience motivation to prepare a proposal that will make your audience members want to adopt your proposal. Pay close attention to the details of the presentation so you are convincing.

As you prepare for your proposal, pay close attention to your audience analysis and what you know about your audience members. Gather materials that will stimulate and arouse them. Even though your purpose is to propose a plan of action, you will need to convince your audience members of your position before you can get them to take action on it. You will want facts, statistics, and examples, to prove your position, and to excite your audience members. Usually, two or three well-developed reasons for doing something are better than a larger number of undeveloped or less-supported reasons.

Your introduction will need to gain attention, establish your credentials, and direct your audience's interest to your topic. Do a good job of relating your topic to your audience members by showing them that your proposal affects them. Your conclusion should highlight the significance and importance of your arguments. Your closing remarks should encourage your audience members to reflect on the advantages of your proposal and the arguments you have presented.

Deliver your speech in an energetic, sincere manner if you intend to stimulate your audience to accept your proposal. Use visual aids and examples that will make your point as clearly as possible. Act confidently, convincingly, and dynamically toward your proposal.

References

Andrews, P. H. & Baird, J. E. Jr. (1986). *Communication for Business and the Professions.* Dubuque, Iowa: Wm C. Brown Company, Publishers.

Maslow, A. H. (1954). *Motivation and Personality.* New York: Harper & Row, Publishers.

PROJECT **29**

The Sales Talk

Men willingly believe what they wish.
—Julius Caesar

You are confronted every day by the "sales talk." Either you are trying to influence the thinking, feeling, or actions of others or they are trying to influence yours. Whether you are trying to get others to agree with you, buy something from you, or like you, you are "selling." Salesmanship is the most obvious application of persuasive communication. Some people confuse the "selling" as disseminating information; others think of it as coercion. Neither of these aspects of persuasion is accurate. To sell something (either a product, service, or yourself), you must make the object of the sale attractive to your buyers and the best of a limited number of options they have. Zelko and Dance (1978) said, "all discourse is persuasion; all communication is influence." This makes it difficult to think of any speech act as anything but selling, in the broadest sense.

In a narrower sense, selling and the sales talk generally refer to the situation in which you try to sell an object or service to a person or group of persons in exchange for their money. It is in this narrower sense that this project is concerned. The aim of this project is to provide you with an experience of selling a product or service to a group, either collectively or individually. We will look closely at the principles of the sales talk, preparing a sales talk, and presenting a sales talk. Finally, you can read a sample sales talk.

Principles of the Sales talk

The sales talk is essentially a persuasive speech in which you attempt to secure audience action—you attempt to persuade your audience members to buy your product or service. In some instances you may actually take orders at the conclusion of your talk; in other instances you may only stimulate interest in your product so people will buy it when they see it on display. In most instances it is better if you have the product available for immediate delivery. In either

174

case your purpose is to sell by stimulating your customers to want what you have for sale and to be willing to part with their money for it.

To sell to your listeners, you must begin by establishing a confident and friendly atmosphere. This is basically a question of do you get "a foot in the door" or a "door in the face"? If your customer is to have confidence in your product or service, you must project your own confidence in that product or service. Likewise, anything but a friendly atmosphere will likely suggest to prospects that you are more interested in their money than in their welfare. A warm, friendly greeting and a smile will do more toward promoting a sale than almost anything else you can say or do.

In addition, you must be thoroughly familiar with your product or service if you intend to sell your audience members on it. Nothing is more frustrating to a buyer than to find a salesperson who doesn't know his or her product. You should be able and willing to speak about and answer questions regarding the production, manufacturer, cost, terms of sale, guarantees, repairs, cost of upkeep, use, and other such matters about your product. You should also know how to meet objections, answer questions, and/or make comparisons with major competitors. Assume that your audience members have other options than to buy from you—yours is not the only store in town, nor the only product on the market. Anticipate those options and attempt to counteract them during your sales talk.

Another important principle of the sales talk is to know your audience members well. Find out as much as you can about your audience so you know what their needs, problems, and motivations are. Only when you know your audience members well can you determine how to approach them. It is not always possible to find out everything you may want to know about your audience, but you should find out as much as possible. Remember, the purpose of finding out this information is to determine how to prepare and present your message for the most effect.

You will be most successful if you can fulfill a need of your audience members or solve a problem they have. Some basic needs you might fulfill are: (1) physical needs such as food, drink, and sleep; (2) safety needs such as a home, or safety from natural disasters, and so on; (3) social needs such as having contact with people and having friends; (4) esteem needs such as recognition for achievement; and (5) self-actualization needs—anything that makes you happy about yourself.

Selling is the process of getting others to do what you want because they want to do it. Obviously, the ultimate goal of the process of selling is to get the audience to "buy." Occasions for the sales talk are many; any time you appear before one or more people for the purpose of selling (getting others to buy or do something that is your idea, not theirs), you make a sales talk. And just as often, you must sell yourself as well as your product or service. You must appear to have your audience's welfare in mind—not just fattening your own purse.

Some topics suitable for a sales talk include:

1. Selling tickets to a movie, play, concert, and so on
2. Selling an item of clothing
3. Selling real estate or other property, oil stock, and so on
4. Selling insurance of any kind.
5. Selling a piece of personal property (a car, radio, stereo, bicycle, and so on)
6. Selling a piece of sports equipment (a football, a bat, a glove, a tennis racquet, and so on)
7. Selling old or rare objects (coins, stamps, antiques, and so on)
8. Selling a specific service (mow lawns, clean, paint, guide, and so on)
9. Selling a product of a hobby (key chains, belts, paintings, and so on)
10. Selling a product or service of someone else—that is, serve as a broker

Preparing a Sales Talk

Follow the regular steps of preparation for any speech. Pay particular attention to your analysis of your audience. It could be fatal to misjudge your prospective buyers. You should know as much as possible about such items as their probable incomes, credit ratings, occupations, religion, education, and local beliefs. A wise seller will find out what competing products the audience members have heard about from other salespeople and be familiar enough with those products to make comparisons favorable to his or her product.

It is advisable to demonstrate whatever you are selling, if possible. This means you must know how to show your product or service to its best advantage. Be sure it looks good and works well. A dirty or drab appearance can make an audience less receptive to your product; likewise, a machine that does not work will not sell. When you can, let your audience try it out for themselves so they can see that there is no trick. For example, let them drive the car so they know it runs well. Can you imagine anyone buying a used car from "Honest Sam's Used Car Lot" if old Sam says "I've got this beauty in the shop now. You can't see it or drive it, but I'll make you a good deal on it now. Sight unseen." I doubt many people would buy this car. Likewise, whether your product is old or new, let your customers see and test the product, or see the service, for themselves. Not only does this show your honesty with your prospective buyers, but it also lets your product sell itself.

As you consider your credibility, determine what your audience members know about you personally and what they will attribute to you because of prior experiences with salespeople. If your audience members have negative attitudes toward salespeople, in general, you must determine how best to establish yourself as competent and trustworthy. Although there are more dimensions of credibility than competence and trust, these are probably the two most essential factors in selling. Audience members will not buy from a person who does not appear to know the facts about his or her product, nor from someone who does not give the impression of being honest.

The organization of the sales talk should be carefully thought out. Several acceptable methods are available to choose from. Berko, Wolvin, and Curtis (1990) recommend a four-step approach. In their approach you first establish a confident and friendly atmosphere. Second, you focus attention on the prospect's problem or need. Third, you solve the problem or fulfill the need by linking product features to customer benefits. Fourth, you make the buying easy by encouraging minor decisions about color, model, and so on throughout your talk—major decisions to buy are gradual.

Bell (1984), as well as other authorities, recommends the Motivated Sequence for selling a product. The Motivated Sequence is a five-step process. The first step is an *attention step* in which you get the attention of your audience members and make them *want* to listen. Step two is a *need step* in which you show your audience members that there is a problem or a "need" that begs to be fulfilled. Step three is the *satisfaction step* in which you present your solution to the problem or fulfill the need. Step four is the *visualization step* in which your audience members picture themselves enjoying the results of the solution. Step five is the *action step* in which you request your audience members to buy and they resolve to buy your product or service.

Another organizational scheme is the **AIDS** pattern of Shipp (1980). AIDS is an acronym for the four steps of the pattern:

A = Get **A**ttention

I = Arouse **I**nterest

D = Stimulate **D**esire

S = Get the **S**ale

Step one is an *attention* step in which you get the attention of your audience members. Step two is the *interest* step in which you attempt to arouse your audience members' interest in your product or service. Step three is for stimulating a *desire* in your audience members for your product or service. Step four is getting your audience members to commit to the *sale*.

As you can see, the Berko et al. method, the Motivated Sequence suggested by Bell, and the AIDS method of Shipp are all very similar and contain the same basic approach to selling your product. All three approaches suggest that you get the attention of your audience members, as well as steps in which you establish a need for your product, and show how your product or service fills audience needs and how you stimulate your audience members to buy.

A final plan for organizing your sales talk is the following four-step approach: First, present information about *yourself and your product.* Who are you? What position do you hold? How long have you been with this company? Why did you choose to work for it? What is the name of the company? How old is it? Is it a nationwide organization? Is it financially sound? Is it reliable? Does it stand behind its products? Does it guarantee its products? Does it quibble over an adjustment if a customer asks for one? Does it have a large dealer organization? Can you get parts and repairs quickly if these are needed? Is it constantly improving its products? Does it test all its products before placing them on the market? How large is its business? What special recommendations does it have?

It may not be necessary to answer all these questions; however, many of them will be asked. In answering them, give information that establishes you as a reputable salesperson and your company as a reputable firm.

Now that you have laid the groundwork, you are ready to *show and explain the goods* you have for sale. The nature of the article or service you are selling will determine how you do this. Probably the first thing you need to do is to explain the purpose of your product or service. Then explain and demonstrate how it operates. In doing this, be sure to play up the advantages of your product or service, special features, new improvements, economy of operation, dependability, beauty, ease of handling, and so on. Give enough detail to be clear but not so much that you confuse your listeners.

At this point you have established yourself and your company, and you have explained and demonstrated your product. Your next step—*showing how your product will benefit its purchasers*—requires careful analysis of your audience members. You must know their wants and needs to show them vividly how your product or service satisfies these wants and needs. If your product is a tractor, a farmer will do his work more easily and economically by using it. If it is a correspondence course, the buyer will make more money, gain prestige, secure advancement from the course. If you are selling a service, you need to show that no one else has the quality of service, nor is it as inexpensive. Be sure you don't use the word "cheap." Whatever you are selling, show your audience members the advantages and benefits of purchasing it. Sometimes it is helpful to mention the names of other persons who have bought the product or service from you and are now enjoying owning it—especially if your audience members know these people.

And now comes the last step. How can they *buy it?* Where? When? Who stocks it if you carry only samples? How much does it cost? Do you sell on the installment plan? What are the carrying charges? How much do you require as a down payment? How many months are allowed to pay for it? What is the monthly payment? Or is it sold only for cash? Is any discount allowed for cash? What special inducement is offered to those who buy now? How much can they save? Will future prices be higher? Do you take trade-ins? How much allowance is made on a trade-in? Make it as easy and simple as possible to buy the goods or service you are selling. Be sure your explanations are clear and exact. Do not use misleading terms or give wrong impressions. If your sales tactics will not stand a full, complete, and candid examination, you will be wise to change your policies or your product.

Presenting a Sales Talk

To be effective, your sales talk must be presented in an interesting and enthusiastic manner. One method of making your presentation more interesting is by using visual aids to help your audience members visualize how their lives would be better with the product or service. In some instances you may not be able to sell your product or service without a demonstration. Would *you* buy a vacuum cleaner or the used car from "Honest Sam" without seeing it operate or operating it yourself? Would you contract with a lawn service without seeing the quality of the work the service claims? Probably not, unless you get a "money-back guarantee" in writing if you do not like the product or service.

Another method of making your presentation more interesting is by involving your audience members in your presentation. Your audience members' participation in the presentation will make them feel more as if you care about them. Let them see, hold, and use the product themselves. Convincing audience members that your product is "simple to use" is much easier if they can use it themselves and see that it is indeed easy to use. "Sampling" the product will always help to show that you have nothing to hide.

Look good; be good. Have a neat and pleasing appearance, plus a friendly and polite attitude. These points are extremely important. Be direct, but avoid being "smart" or using questionable stories to impress your audience members. Put the group at ease and get on with your speech. Your manner should be conversational, your voice easily heard by all, but not strained. Have your speech thoroughly in mind. Do *not* use notes. Obviously, you will have difficulty selling your product or service if you have to consult notes in order to remember what you want to say about it. You also want to avoid sounding as if you have a "canned" speech. If you sound like you have memorized lines, your audience members will tend not to believe what you say. This is not a simple "commercial" for your product—it is a sales talk.

Your bodily actions should be suitable for holding attention, making transitions, and demonstrating what you are selling. Be sure you communicate with your eyes. If you don't look at your audience members, they will perceive that you are not being honest with them. Eye contact may be the most important nonverbal clue your audience members may have to your sincerity. It is also a good indication as to how your audience members are reacting to you and your product. Mauser (1977) suggests that the eyes are so telling that if you see your audience's eyes widening, it is time to try to close the sale. On the other hand, if they are narrowing, probably you are not selling the right features, or filling the right needs of your audience members.

Your language, of course, should be simple, descriptive, vivid, and devoid of technical terms. If you speak in technical terms or with undue complications, your audience members will not understand and will likely believe they cannot handle the product themselves. If your language is not descriptive and vivid, your audience members also will not fully understand your product and may confuse what you intend. In all your explanations, be thorough and clear.

You can use a wide variety of visual aids to help present your sales talk. Flip charts, graphs, and portfolios have been used for years. Think in terms of what will make your product most sellable and use a variety of aids. Some other aids that can be used include: facsimiles, photographs, illustrations, advertisements, catalogs, kits, and audio visual aids such as slides, films, recordings, and so on.

In using charts, pictures, diagrams, or the article itself, your familiarity with them should be so great that you can point out any part of your product while retaining a position that permits focusing your attention on your audience. In answering questions, be as clear as possible and be sure your questioner is satisfied with the information you give.

Special Hints: Do not knock your competitors or their products; it is better to praise them. If you offer any special inducements to encourage buying your product, be sure to present them at the appropriate time—usually while you are attempting to get the sale. After concluding your talk, allow your audience members time to ask questions. Some may want to ask questions during your speech. In this case be sure to answer them clearly; however, do not turn the sales talk into a question-and-answer session before describing what you plan to sell.

SAMPLE SALES TALK

By Hardy Patton

Why Obtain the Services of a CPA?

Spring Break, isn't it great? You've been sitting in the classroom listening to lectures, recording notes, and taking tests for approximately eight weeks. Thoughts of Padre Island or Colorado ski runs cross your mind. I know I look forward to Spring Break every year, but picture for a second a nice, normal spring day during the week preceding Spring Break. You return to your room from classes, looking for your stored tennis racquet. You open the bottom drawer of your dresser and what do you see? Believe it or not, you see your unfinished tax return. It's due shortly, only two days away, so you quickly try to complete it.

You consider the facts: You had a part-time job and earned $2,500, you took 23 credit hours during the year, and you're twenty years old. You ask yourself, do I have to file? Can I claim myself as an exemption? Am I able to allow my parents to claim me as a dependent? Finally, you ask yourself, can all of this just wait until I return from Spring Break? The answer to this last question is no! The IRS, Internal Revenue Service, waits for no one.

As a Senior Accounting major, presently interviewing with international accounting firms and preparing to take the CPA exam next year, I will convince you to enlist the services of a Certified Public Accountant to solve your accounting problems so you can be on your way to a great Spring Break.

First, a CPA is qualified to aid you in your accounting problems. A CPA, like most professionals, must complete a four-year plan of education including the fields of business law, tax, and general financial accounting. These fields of study include such specific topics as consolidated statements, auditing, cost accounting, and federal income tax accounting. All of these topics of study must be mastered thoroughly because they are all tested on the CPA exam.

This brings me to my second point. A CPA must pass the Certified Public Accountant's exam. This is a comprehensive, three-day exam over almost all of your accounting and law college classwork. According to the State Examiner's board, only 10% of all college graduates pass this test on the first try. After passing the test, a CPA must pursue a minimum of 60 hours of continuing education every three years. Those hours are usually required outside of the workplace, forcing CPAs to give up their weekends and evenings occasionally to meet this requirement.

All of this education and testing helps prepare each CPA for a variety of fields. First, they can perform audits. You might ask yourself, why do I need an audit? Well, have you ever considered opening your own business? Someday you may need an audit to convince a bank to give you a loan to get started in that business, or to expand it. A CPA is the only person who is really qualified to perform such an audit.

CPAs can also be used as consultants. If you ever have a question about whether to invest in a specific stock, call your CPA. The CPA can either tell you the answer, give you advice, or lead you to someone who does know the answer. Individual CPAs are like the rest of us, they each have their own specific interests and follow them, but they know other CPAs with other interests and can help you find the answers to your questions.

Finally, CPAs can prepare your tax returns. This is a problem that affects us all, even college students. With all the new tax laws, the practice of preparing a simple tax return has become very complicated, but your CPA can help you solve that problem. Your CPA can also answer those other important questions that I didn't answer for you earlier. The reason I didn't answer them was that there is no one simple answer that will fit each of your situations. You need to see your CPA to get the right answers to fit your situation.

In conclusion, let me summarize what I have said. A CPA is educated, tested, and then educated some more to qualify as an active CPA. Also, a CPA is trained to help you in a number of areas, including auditing, consulting, and tax preparation. Therefore, if you have an accounting problem, don't be shy, just look in the yellow pages. You will never be sorry you did, and you just might have a chance to go on your Spring Break.

SAMPLE OUTLINE—SALES TALK

    I. INTRODUCTION
        A. Attention-getter: Spring break
        B. Credentials: Senior
        C. Arouse interest: Tax return
    II. THESIS: Today I will convince you to enlist the services of a Certified Public Accountant to solve your accounting problems.
    III. BODY
        A. CPA is qualified
            1. Class requirements
            2. CPA exam
            3. Continuing education
        B. CPA is helpful
            1. Audits
            2. Tax returns
            3. Consultants
    IV. CONCLUSION
        A. Review main points
            1. CPA is qualified
            2. CPA is helpful
        B. Closing: Spring break

Project Assignment

Prepare and present a five- to seven-minute sales talk in which you attempt to sell a real or imagined product or service to your audience. Research your product as well as that of your competitors so you can highlight your product well. Use visual aids to help sell your product also.

As you prepare for your sales talk, pay close attention to your audience analysis and what you know about your audience members. Consider the needs of your audience members that you can fulfill with your product or service. Even though your purpose is to sell your product or service, you will need to convince your audience members that you have a good product or service before you can get them to buy. You will want facts, statistics, and examples to prove your product or service and to interest your audience members.

Your introduction will need to gain attention, establish your credentials, and direct your audience's interest to your product or service. Do a good job of relating your topic to your audience members by showing them how you can affect their lives. Your conclusion should review your major selling points and reprove your product or service. Your closing remarks should be your call for a sale, hopefully to be completed as soon as you finish speaking.

Deliver your sales talk in an energetic, sincere manner if you intend to stimulate your audience members to buy. Use visual aids and examples that will help your product or service sell itself. Act confidently, convincingly, and dynamically toward your product or service.

Alternate Project Assignment

As an alternative to the previous assignment, you might try to sell a product or service that no one would want (e.g., an old tennis shoe with a hole in the toe). If you are given this assignment, you must be serious about selling your product. Treat your product as seriously as you would a real product, which your audience members could easily see the use for. With this product, you must concentrate more on creating a need and use for your product. Don't be afraid to become creative. If fact, the more creative, the better. Follow the preceding suggestions for preparing and presenting your sales talk.

References

Bell, C. B. (1984). *Speaking in Business: A Basic Survival Guide.* Dubuque, Iowa: Kendall/Hunt Publishing Company.

Berko, R. M., Wolvin, A. D. & Curtis B. (1990). *This Business of Communicating* (4th ed.). Dubuque, Iowa: Wm. C. Brown Company, Publishers.

Hamilton, C. & Parker, C. (1987). *Communicating for Results: A Guide for Business and the Professions* (2nd ed). Belmont, California: Wadsworth Publishing Company.

Kossen, S. (1988). *Creative Selling Today* (3rd ed.). New York: Harper & Row, Publishers.

Manning, G. L. & Reece, B. L. (1987). *Selling Today: A Personal Approach* (3rd ed.). Boston: Allyn & Bacon, Inc.

Martin, R. C., Robinson, K. F., & Tomlinson, R. C. (1963). *Practical Speech for Modern Business.* New York: Appleton-Century-Crofts.

Mauser, F. F. (1977). *Selling: A Self-Management Approach.* New York:/ Harcourt Brace Jovanovich.

Pederson, C. A. & Wright, M. D. (1987). *Selling: Principles and Methods* (9th ed.). Homewood, Illinois: Richard D. Irwin, Inc.

Shipp, R. D. (1980). *Practical Selling.* Boston: Houghton Mifflin Company.

Zelko, H. P. & Dance, F. E. X. (1978). *Business and Professional Speech Communication* (2nd ed.). New York: Holt, Rinehart and Winston, Inc.

PROJECT 30

The Interview

by

Robert Greenstreet

Many speakers limit themselves by unnecessarily restricting their preparation. They research what they can find in the library, often failing to take full advantage of academic and community resources. The interview provides a vehicle for improving speech preparation. Effective interviewers may gather information unavailable in written form. They may also get immediate feedback on their understanding of the topics they have chosen. To gain these benefits, the interview must be conducted skillfully. This project includes the principles of the interview, preparing for an interview, conducting an interview, and a sample interview schedule to study.

Principles of the Interview

Like conversation, an interview involves communication between two parties. Unlike conversation, the interview is always purposeful. At least one party (frequently both) has some purpose in mind; something she or he wants to accomplish. You will probably want to gather information, or you may want to inform or persuade your interviewee.

Like a speech, an interview has three basic parts. In the opening the interviewer (the person conducting the interview) and the interviewee (the person being interviewed) become comfortable with each other. As an interviewer you will probably want to introduce yourself, thank the interviewee for meeting with you, and explain what you hope to accomplish. The substantive portion of the interview consists of the question-answer process. Most likely both of you will ask and answer questions. The closing provides an opportunity for the interviewer to sum up what has been communicated and for both parties to clarify, correct, or amend statements they have made. The closing should also answer the question "What happens next?" Of course, you will also want to express your appreciation for the other's time and effort.

Like a speech, the interview has structure. It is not random. You will introduce an area of questioning with a primary question, and follow it up with secondary questions. Secondary questions should help you gain a fuller understanding of both the area in question and the interviewee's previous response. Your list of questions to ask is called an agenda. Your agenda will probably consist of both open and closed questions. Open questions call for an elaborated response, a response of several words (possibly an explanation). Closed questions may usually be answered in a few words, often with a single word (yes or no, true or false). An agenda beginning with open questions and moving to increasingly more closed questions follows a funnel organizational pattern. An agenda beginning with closed questions and moving to increasingly more open questions uses the inverted funnel organization. Some interviews consist entirely of open questions (or closed questions). These use tunnel organization.

Preparing for an Interview

You will probably use the interview to help you prepare for your speeches. Interviews can help you gather information, verify information, and focus your understanding. The interview should be integrated into your preparation. That is, it should complement, rather than substitute for, other research. Your first step in preparing to interview, then, is to begin researching your chosen speech subject.

As you gain understanding of your subject, you will be able to develop a list of potential interviewees who may be able to provide helpful insights to further your understanding. As you research, write down your questions. As your list of questions develops, ask yourself "Who might be able to help answer these?" Let's assume you are planning to talk about drunk driving. Your library research provides you with a wealth of information, but nothing about your local community. You wonder, "Does this happen here? How often? Are people injured? How seriously? What happens to drunk drivers here? Are they punished? Can they be rehabilitated? Why do they drink and drive? Are there any local programs to curtail drunk driving?" Local law enforcement officials (city police, county sheriff, state patrol) should be able to answer some of your questions. The local hospital, clinic, ambulance service, or emergency room might also facilitate your understanding. In talking with representatives of these agencies, you are likely to take your understanding beyond impersonal statistics as you begin to realize what those figures mean in human terms. You might want to interview one or two people who have driven while drunk. Where would you find them? Those willing to talk would probably be involved in some sort of rehabilitation program such as Alcoholics Anonymous. State agencies, hospitals, churches, and community service agencies are also likely places to locate substance abuse counselors. Your school counselor can probably also provide some information (though, of course, names of his or her counselees will be kept confidential). In every community you should be able to create a list of more potential interviewees than you will have time to consult.

Your next step is to prioritize your list. Whom do you most want to interview? Put that name first on your list. Be sure to list everyone you feel could be helpful in developing your understanding of the subject. Because all of those people have demands on their time, many of them may be unable to meet with you at a time convenient for you. Start at the top of your list and telephone until you set up an interview. Record the time, date, and location for the interview.

Your next task is to review your list of questions so you can organize them into an agenda. Consider the areas you want to discuss. Organize your questions under each area into primary and secondary questions, with secondary questions grouped under the primary questions they develop. Review the working of your questions—will your interviewee understand what you want? If not, reword your question.

Conducting an Interview

Dress carefully and neatly, at a level appropriate to your interviewee and the setting. Your clothes and grooming should help you communicate with your interviewee. Be a few minutes early for the interview (but expect to wait until the appointed time).

Try to be as polite and respectful as possible during your interview. That does not mean you should be apologetic or subservient. A professional, courteous attitude is appropriate. You are the interviewer; it is your responsibility to control the interview. If your interviewee tends to ramble or get off the subject, you should ask closed, direct questions to focus the interview. If your interviewee is reticent, more open questions might encourage more lengthy responses.

Unless you are trained in shorthand, you may experience some difficulty in recording answers to your questions. An inconspicuous portable tape recorder can provide an accurate record of the interview, but many people become nervous when being recorded (which influences their answers). You may also need to stop and turn the tape over or switch tapes. If you use a recorder, you will want to be sure its use does not bother your interviewee. It is best to ask the interviewee before you begin. Be certain the equipment works, and take extra tapes and batteries. Even if you use a recorder you will want to take notes. Taking notes demonstrates your interest and encourages helpful responses. It also helps you concentrate and focuses your attention in a way that helps you ask responsive secondary questions. Do not attempt to record every word of every response. Try to record enough key words to leave you with the basic idea the interviewee communicated.

After the interview you should review your notes (or the tape) and excerpt material appropriate to your speech. This material should be filed with your other speech support materials. You should also write a note of appreciation to your interviewee.

SAMPLE INTERVIEW SCHEDULE

Subject: Drinking and Driving
Interviewee: Wilma Skritch, High School Counselor

1. Do you deal with students who drink and drive?
   1.1 How many times in the past school year?
   1.2 Are the number of cases increasing?
2. Is there a particular type of student who drinks and drives?
   2.1 Are more of them men than women?
   2.2 Does the incidence of drinking and driving peak in a particular age group?
   2.3 Can you provide a psychological profile of the typical student who drinks and drives?
      2.31 What is his or her mood at the time?
      2.32 Why does he or she do it?
3. What problems do these students face?
   3.1 Are they prosecuted?
   3.2 Do they lose their licenses?
   3.3 Does the school take any action?
   3.4 What potential penalties do they face?
4. Does the school offer any programs for these students?
   4.1 Are the programs designed to rehabilitate or prevent?
   4.2 Do they work?
   4.3 What does the program involve?
   4.4 Who runs the program?
5. If you had your way, what would you do to solve the problem?

Project Assignment

Prepare an agenda and a list of interviewees for interviews on your speech subject. After your instructor has reviewed your agenda and list, schedule and conduct an interview. Write a brief report of your interview. In your report tell what happened (how you conducted the interview), and discuss the value of the interview in your speech preparation.

References

Berko, R. M., Wolvin, A. D. & Wolvin, D. R. (1988). *Communicating: A Social and Career Focus* (4th ed.). Boston: Houghton Mifflin Company.

Brooks, W. D. & Heath, R. W. (1988). *Speech Communication* (3rd ed.). Dubuque: Wm. C. Brown Company, Publishers.

Downs, C. W., Smeyak, G. P. & Martin, E. (1980). *Professional Interviewing*. New York: Harper & Row, Publishers.

Stewart, C. J. & Cash, W. B. Jr. (1988). *Interviewing: Principles and Practices* (5th ed.). Dubuque: Wm. C. Brown Company, Publishers.

UNIT VII

SPECIAL OCCASION SPEECHES

Public speaking requires a lot of preparation. There's just no way around it—you have to do your homework. A speaker may be very well informed, but if he hasn't thought out exactly what he wants to say *today, to this audience,* he has no business taking up other people's valuable time.

Lee Iacocca

Project 31: Introducing a Speaker
Project 32: The Farewell Speech
Project 33: The Eulogy
Project 34: The Dedication or Commemorative Speech
Project 35: The Critical Response Review
Project 36: Presenting and Accepting a Gift or Award
Project 37: The Welcome Speech and Response
Project 38: The Nominating Speech and Acceptance
Project 39: Radio and Television Speaking

Unit VII consists of nine projects for speaking on special occasions. All of these projects will technically fit into one of the other categories in Units III, IV, or V, but because of their special nature, they are placed in this special unit. Project 31 presents the principles of introducing a speaker, a frequent task in daily life. Project 32 presents the principles of the farewell speech. Project 33 presents the principles of the eulogy—to honor or commemorate someone living or dead. The dedication speech is the topic of Project 34—to commemorate an occasion or object.

Project 35 presents the principles of the critical response review. Project 36 is a double project in that it presents the principles of both presenting and accepting a gift or award. Project 37 is another double project. It presents the principles of the welcome and the response to a welcome. Project 38 is another double project that presents the nominating speech and the acceptance of a nomination. The final project—Project 39—presents the principles of radio and television speaking.

PROJECT **31**
Introducing a Speaker

Speaking generally, we may say that the rhetorical
function is the function of adjusting ideas to people and
people to ideas.
—Donald C. Bryant

One of the most frequent speaking situations is the introductory speech. Many untrained speakers are asked to give introduction speeches. Characteristically, people assume that there is nothing to introducing a speaker and that anyone can do it. However, too many introductions are haphazard and embarrassing. Aside from the criticism of the person making a poor introduction, the program usually also suffers in that the audience members feel the speaker is not worth their time.

A good introduction can be delightful to hear and set the mood for a pleasant experience. A good introduction establishes the credibility of the speaker and the importance of the topic the speaker has been given or chosen. By the time the speaker begins the audience members should be thinking, "This is going to be good! I'm really going to enjoy listening to this speaker." If your audience members don't, you have probably failed part of your task.

Principles of the Introduction Speech

Probably the best advice for the speaker introducing another speaker is to: "Stand up, speak up, shut up." The first principle of the introduction speech is that it *be brief.* There are any number of true stories told about long-winded introduction speeches. Lucas (1983) relates the following tale:

> During World War I, Lord Balfour, Britain's Foreign Secretary, was to be the main speaker at a rally in the United States. But the speaker who was supposed to introduce Lord Balfour gave a 45 minute oration on the causes of war. Then, almost as an afterthought, he said, "Now Lord Balfour

will give his address." Lord Balfour rose and said, "I'm supposed to give my address in the brief time remaining. Here it is: 10 Carleton Gardens, London, England."

Be certain your speeches of introduction do not take up any of the guest speaker's time. If you do, you insult your speaker, waste the time of your audience members, and risk the chance of losing a great speech.

A second principle of the introduction speech is to relate your speaker to your audience. Sometimes the speaker and the connection to the audience will be obvious, as in a convention speaker. However, most generally you must help your audience members answer the questions: Why should I listen to this speaker? How does this person qualify to speak on this topic? Why is this an important topic for me? In relating your speaker to your audience, you need to establish his or her credibility on the topic. This involves more than relating the person's pedigree, offices, occupation, degrees, and achievements. It means establishing a *person* with the credentials to speak on the topic or issue at hand. Not only is this a qualified person, he or she is also someone to whom we will all enjoy listening.

A third principle of the introduction speech is to be accurate. Accuracy includes checking the spelling and pronunciation of the speaker's name if you don't know the speaker personally. Imagine how embarrassed you would be if the speaker began his or her speech by correcting you. Probably the most well-known error of this kind was the introduction of President Herbert Hoover as "Hoobert Heever." While this is not exactly an error of mispronunciation, it is an error of accuracy—accurate pronunciation. Another story often told about an error in accuracy occurred when the governor of the Virgin Islands visited Washington, D.C. As he was being introduced to speak at one of his dinners, the toastmaster announced, "It's a great pleasure to present the virgin of Governor's Island." Being well prepared will prevent most errors in accuracy.

A fourth principle of the introduction speech is to adapt your introduction to your speaker, to your audience, and to the occasion. Just as you adapt any speech to yourself, your audience, and your situation, you also need to adapt introductions. In adapting to the speaker, try to be personal, but never get so personal that you embarrass or make your speaker feel uncomfortable. Use good taste! Likewise, set your audience members up for the speech and make them want to listen, but don't make them uncomfortable either. Finally, adapt to the formality of the occasion. Failing to adapt and suit the occasion may be an embarrassment to you. For example, don't try to be humorous in a serious situation. Trying to be funny on a solemn occasion may cause your speaker, your audience, and you to be uncomfortable.

The fifth principle of the introduction speech is don't give the speaker's speech. Sometimes you know what your speaker will say and get so involved that you want to tell the audience yourself. If you do this, there is nothing left for your speaker to say because you have already said it all. Your task in making the introduction is to set up the audience and present some credibility for your speaker—to introduce! Perform your role quickly and sit down. Let your speaker give the main address.

A sixth principle of the introduction is not to oversell your speaker. In your earnestness to make your audience members want to listen to a particular speaker, or to establish a speaker as credible, you may sometimes have a tendency to "lay it on a bit thick." If you announce your speaker as the world's best, funniest, most fantastic, and so on, speaker, you set up conditions that are nearly impossible for the speaker to live up to. It is best to avoid the supersell and let your speaker demonstrate his or her abilities to the audience.

A final principle of the introduction is to be prepared. Because the introduction is brief and you know what you need to accomplish, it is easy to underprepare and bungle the introduction. Lucas (1983) presents the following example of an unprepared introduction by a TV talk-show host. Consider how you would react if you were the guest or if you were an audience member listening to this introduction:

Okay, we're back. Thank you. You're a great audience tonight. Now, my first guest is a man who has made a name for himself . . . excuse me, a *woman* who has made a name for herself by teaching sign language to chimpanzees. Sign language to chimpanzees? That's what it says right here, folks! She's written a book called . . . What does it say? . . . *I Talk to the Animals.* (Aside) Where do you go after "I want a banana?" (Laughter) Will you please welcome . . . Jan Cunningham! (Applause. Host speaks over applause.) What? Oh, sorry, that's Joan Cunningham.

It is obvious that this host was not prepared to make a proper introduction that would set the audience up for the presentation—or establish the person's credibility for her presentation. In fact, few members of this audience are ready to hear the speaker and most can probably sense that the person doing the introducing is neither well prepared nor interested in the speaker.

Preparing an Introduction Speech

There are generally four sources of information from which you need to select your information for the introduction speech: (1) the speaker, (2) the subject, (3) the audience, and (4) the occasion. You may not use data collected from all four sources, but it is useful and necessary to consult or consider all four.

It doesn't matter whether you know the speaker personally; it is always in good taste to ask the speaker what he or she would like to have you tell your audience members. In some instances this may be your only source of biographical data on your speaker, such as preferred name and correct pronunciation, education, special training, travel experience, special honors or awards, memberships in organizations, important positions he or she has held, publications, and other notable achievements. If you can't talk directly to the person, you may need to research his or her background through other sources.

If the speaker is well known to your audience members, you may not have to say much more than the person's name. For example, the President of the United States is usually introduced in the following manner: "Ladies and Gentlemen, the President of the United States." Royalty are generally introduced in a similar manner. For example, "Ladies and Gentlemen, Her Majesty, the Queen of England." Lesser known royalty may need a bit more introduction so your audience members better understand who the person is. For example, dukes, duchesses, earls, lords, and dignitaries of third-world countries may need more introduction.

The second area you need to know about is the subject of the speaker's presentation. In some instances you will know because you ask a person to speak on a particular topic. In other instances you may have no idea what the speaker intends to say. By knowing the speaker's subject, you can relate the topic to the audience. Be cautious here! In no way do you want to "steal the speaker's thunder," but you do want to prepare your audience members for the speech about to be presented. For example, you might indicate the interest your audience will have in the topic. The following is an example of relating the subject to the audience: "Since the passage of the new tax structure last fall, all of us have wondered about the reasons behind the structure and how it would affect our incomes. We have read the reports in the paper, but the one most able to answer our questions is the author of the tax bill. So, today Senator Snort . . ." You get the picture.

The third area of concern is your audience. Obviously, if you are to relate the topic to your audience, you need to know who your audience members are. In some instances you will know the members of your audience because they will be members of your organization, work group, community, and so on. In that case your task is fairly simple in that you will need to do little more than recall persons you know personally and what motivates them. However, when you are introducing a speaker to a general audience of "community" members, you don't know the specific makeup of your audience until almost the moment of your speech, if even then. All you can do on such occasions is learn about the general community from which the audience members come, and think about the types of people most interested in hearing this speaker or type of speaker.

The fourth area of consideration is the occasion. You need to know what brings this speaker and audience together at this moment in time. Again, certain occasions, like the Fourth of July, Memorial Day, Labor Day, and other such holidays are obvious. Likewise, special events within your organization will also be obvious. A problem arises only when you can find no special occasion for the speech. However, most of the time, you will be very aware of the occasion for the gathering or event that is the impetus for the speech.

From these four sources, and yourself, construct your introduction speech. Although your speech is short, what you have to say is vital to the success of the entire program. Thus, you must plan, organize, and arrange your speech carefully, selecting those bits of information that will best unite your speaker and your audience. This is no time for an impromptu speech!

Before your ideas "set," you should confer, at least in imagination, with the person you are going to introduce and arrive at a definite understanding regarding what you plan to say in your introduction speech. After you decide this, rehearse aloud until you are confident you are thoroughly prepared to relate your speaker to his or her topic and your audience members.

Verderber (1988) presents the following format for the introduction speech. If you follow it, you should have little difficulty in properly structuring your introduction speech. Begin by relating your audience members to the occasion. You may need only a sentence or two to do this. In the body of your introduction speech establish your speaker and provide sufficient credibility to make the audience accept him or her as an authority on the topic of the speech. You should also be interested in creating a favorable atmosphere for your speaker. As you conclude, mention the title of the speech and repeat the speaker's name.

Presenting an Introduction Speech

When the moment arrives for you to introduce your speaker, rise calmly, take your place at the lectern, pause until your audience members get quiet, and then deliberately address your audience in your normal voice. Speak loudly enough for everyone to hear, but avoid straining your voice or using greater force than you need. You may use, "Ladies and gentlemen," or some other appropriate expression to gain the audience's attention and indicate that you are about to speak.

Your bodily actions and gestures should be limited; there will probably be no necessity for using either more than moderately. Your voice should be well modulated, your words spoken clearly, and your pronunciation correct—especially the pronunciation of the topic and the speaker's name.

Keep in mind your part in the total program. People did not come to hear you speak, they came to hear the guest. You are only a convenient, but necessary, link in the chain of events surrounding your speaker. Your poise and confidence and appropriate but brief remarks are all that are expected or wanted from you. You may greet your audience and mention the occasion, extend a welcome, and note that there is an exceptionally good audience (if there is). On the other hand, if there is a small audience, do not remark about it and do not make any apologies.

At the moment you present your speaker, announce his or her name and subject. For example, you might say, "I am happy to present Dr. Smith (use the person's name), who will speak to you on _____ (mention the subject). Then turn to the speaker and say, "Dr. Smith." You may welcome the speaker with a handshake at the lectern, bow slightly, or nod to the speaker. Then take your seat and focus your attention on the speaker. The remainder of your task is to pay undivided attention to your speaker.

At the conclusion of the speech it is appropriate for you or the chairperson to express appreciation publicly to the speaker. If you are not the chairperson, make sure you know who is handling that duty. If you are to make these closing remarks, wait until the applause has subsided, then stand and walk to the lectern to make your remarks. You should also be the person to lead the applause after your speaker has finished. Your audience members will likely wait for your cue to begin their applause. If a standing ovation is warranted, you also should lead this.

Introducing Yourself

Frequently, you will be asked to introduce yourself to a board of directors, officers of a club, or to an audience who has come to hear candidates seeking elective office. Usually, you will introduce yourself by presenting the same information you would if you were introducing someone else, but with somewhat less detail. Younger audiences ordinarily like more vigorous presentations and possibly more humor than older listeners, but both audiences demand honesty and sincerity.

Give a frank, friendly, modest account of your background, including your education, special training, experience, achievements, jobs held, honors received, your personality, personal goals, and ambitions. Sometimes you may want to express something about where you were born and have lived, or other information that will help fulfill the reasons you were asked to introduce yourself.

When telling your achievements, don't belittle yourself. Say, "I was fortunate enough to _____," or "I was elected to serve _____," or "I have held my current job five years," or "I believe I am qualified because of my experience and training in . . ." Remember, if you don't tell your listeners about yourself and include information they want to know, no one else is going to do it for you. If you do not present yourself as credible, you are not likely to be perceived as competent by many of your audience members. If you have forewarning, plan your remarks in advance. Also, rehearse three or four times.

SAMPLE INTRODUCTION

By Tracy Frederick

Introduction of Delma Hall to Pi Kappa Delta

Good Evening. I would like to welcome you to our annual Pi Kappa Delta banquet. Our speaker for this evening is Mrs. Delma Hall. Mrs. Hall will speak to us about the importance of a Forensics program.

Mrs. Hall has been a Speech Teacher for fifteen years. She graduated from East Central Oklahoma State College in 1968 with a Bachelor of Arts in Speech Education. She continued her studies after graduation and received a masters degree from the University of Oklahoma in 1983. She has had numerous teaching experiences. She taught in a public school in Germany for three years and then on an Indian Reservation for two years. Mrs. Hall has been on staff at East Central University for three years. She has been a valuable asset to East Central and especially to the students who need her help. She has helped students in many ways. She has helped coach students so they will be prepared for forensics events. She has also helped students who have high anxiety about speaking situations. We have also greatly appreciated her guidance in costume construction and design as she has helped us prepare for Theatre productions. Most of all, we have appreciated her guidance and assistance with personal problems and concerns of the day. The Speech and Theatre students feel that she is a vital part of the university. We have all needed her at times and she was always willing to help. Many times a student will have problems with characterization, enunciation or just an opinion about a speech. With her help, the problem is always quickly resolved. She is a vital force in our Speech-Theatre-Communications program. Much credit for our successes goes to Mrs. Hall.

And now, here to speak on the importance of the Forensics Program, Mrs. Delma Hall.

Project Assignment

Prepare and present a two- to three-minute introduction speech. You may present an introduction for a real guest on a real occasion or you may create a speaker and occasion. As an alternative, your instructor may assign you to introduce a classmate before a specific speaking assignment. In the latter instance be sure you prepare your introduction as carefully as you would any of the other speeches in your class.

In preparing for this assignment, be sure you collect data from the four sources introduced earlier, the speaker, your audience, the occasion, and yourself. Don't forget to find out about the speaker's topic and how it relates to your audience.

Organize your remarks into three main parts: Your remarks about the speaker and his or her qualifications, the speaker' topic, and relating the topic to your audience. As you establish your speaker's credentials, be thorough, but do not overdo it. Your final remarks should be a repetition of your speaker's name and topic.

Deliver your introduction enthusiastically and interestingly. Remember to be brief, as your audience members came to hear the speaker, not you. Use a conversational tone, not a dramatic, word-for-word reading of a composition. Above all, be friendly.

References

Ayres, J. & Miller, J. (1990). *Effective Public Speaking* (3rd ed.). Dubuque, Iowa: Wm. C. Brown Company, Publishers.

Bostrom, R. N. (1988). *Communicating in Public.* Edina, Minnesota: Burgess Publishing.

Bradley, B. E. (1988). *Fundamentals of Speech Communication* (5th ed.). Dubuque, Iowa: Wm. C. Brown Company, Publishers.

DeVito, J. A. (1990). *The Elements of Public Speaking* (4th ed.). New York: Harper & Row, Publishers.

Fletcher, L. (1988). *Speaking to Succeed in Business, Industry, Professions.* New York: Harper & Row, Publishers.

Gregory, H. (1990). *Public Speaking for College and Career* (2nd ed.). New York: McGraw-Hill Book Company.

Gronbeck, B. E., Ehninger, D., & Monroe, A. H. (1988). *Principles of Speech Communication* (10th brief ed.). Glenview, Illinois: Scott, Foresman and Company.

Heun, R. & Heun, L. (1986). *Public Speaking* (2nd ed.). St. Paul, Minnesota: West Publishing Company.

Hunt, G. T. (1987). *Public Speaking* (2nd ed.). Englewood Cliffs, New Jersey: Prentice-Hall, Inc.

Lucas, S. E. (1989). *The Art of Public Speaking* (3rd ed.). New York: Random House. See also first edition (1983).

Minnick, W. C. (1983). *Public Speaking* (2nd ed.). Boston: Houghton Mifflin Company.

Osborn, M. & Osborn, S. (1988). *Public Speaking.* Boston: Houghton Mifflin Company.

Samovar, L. A. & Mills, J. (1989). *Oral Communication* (7th ed.). Dubuque, Iowa: Wm. C. Brown Company, Publishers.

Sprague, J. & Stuart, D. (1988). *The Speaker's Handbook* (2nd ed.). San Diego: Harcourt Brace Jovanovich.

Verderber, R. F. (1988). *The Challenge of Effective Speaking* (7th ed.). Belmont, California: Wadsworth Publishing Company.

Wood. J. (1988). *Speaking Effectively.* New York: Random House.

PROJECT 32

The Farewell Speech

> There is only one way in the world to be distinguished.
> Follow your instinct! Be yourself, and you'll be
> somebody. Be one more blind follower of the blind, and
> you will have the oblivion you desire.
> —Bliss Carman

Whenever someone leaves for a new job, a promotion, or retires, there is an occasion for a farewell speech. The farewell speech has become more important in recent years because we have become a more mobile society. People are finding it easier to move, take new jobs, and change careers. When people have been active in a profession or community, it is common that they be honored before they leave.

The farewell speech is a special form of the speech of tribute. It pays a tribute to the person leaving, regardless of reason, by honoring the person and the person's accomplishments or contributions to the group or organization.

This project will acquaint you with the principles of the farewell speech, as well as tell you how to prepare and present the farewell speech so your farewell speeches will be more than a mumble of incoherent remarks.

Principles of the Farewell Speech

There are two types of farewell speeches. The first type of farewell is the speech a person gives upon leaving a group or organization to say goodbye to friends and co-workers. Presidents often give this type of farewell speech to the members of their staff before leaving the White House. The second type of farewell speech is one in which you speak for your group or organization to say goodbye to a departing member. This is the type of farewell speech often given for a person retiring or moving.

If you are the person leaving, you should express appreciation for the people present and their contributions to your accomplishments and happiness. Avoid praising yourself and your accomplishments, but rather concentrate on sincerely expressing your delight in having known the people present. You may mention sadness in departing, but don't dwell on the issue. Sadness can become contagious. If you can, comment on what your future holds for you. If it's a move to a new location or a new career, talk about the advantages and the new experiences you expect. If you are retiring, talk about what you want to do with your new-found time—how you expect to enjoy your retirement. Are you planning to travel, visit distant relatives, spend time with your children or grandchildren? Or are you going to become involved with some type of community work? Maybe this will be your time to spend catching up on years of lost time reading, fishing, and enjoying your hobbies.

If you are saying goodbye to a group member, you need to express appreciation for the contributions of the departing member and the happiness that member has brought to other members of your group. It is common to praise the departing member. This doesn't mean to heap undue praise on the person, but it does mean to avoid any negative elements in the relationship and concentrate on the positive elements without magnifying or diminishing the person and his or her accomplishments.

The occasion for the farewell speech may be formal or informal, depending on the person involved and the length of the relationship. Generally, you will want to have a formal dinner or "farewell" for a person retiring from a job or for a person who has been with your group for many years. If the person moving has not been with the group for a long time, the more informal gathering is generally more appropriate.

Regardless of the type of farewell or the degree of formality, avoid excessive sentimentality. Instead, present the accomplishments and strengthen the relationships with the group by showing sincerity about the person and optimism about the future. Do not treat the occasion with too much sadness. Feelings of deep emotion should be expressed in a manner in keeping with the occasion and everyone present.

Some occasions suitable for farewell speeches include:

1. Leaving on a two-year tour with the Peace Corps
2. Leaving on a two-year tour of the world
3. Leaving a community after 20 years
4. Leaving for South America to hunt oil
5. Moving to a new location for promotion
6. Joining the armed services
7. Going to the Middle East on a two-year archaeological excavation
8. Going to Washington to take a government job
9. Retiring from employment after 20 years
10. Retiring from a church or civic position

Preparing a Farewell Speech

If you are leaving, remember this is a special occasion and old friends are honoring you; if you are honoring an old friend, remember this is a special occasion and you are honoring an old friend. The farewell may create an atmosphere of considerable sentiment and emotion or mere friendliness. This means you must carefully analyze your audience, their probable mood, and the general atmosphere. If a gift is to be presented, review the instructions for presenting or accepting gifts (Project 36), depending on your position, so you can handle the task with ease and comfort if the task falls on you.

Farewell speeches usually follow a well-defined pattern with appropriate variations as you deem necessary. You may also need to adjust depending on whether you are honoring someone who is leaving or you are the one being honored upon leaving.

It is advisable to begin by referring to the time the honoree arrived on the job or the reasons behind the hiring of the person. A bit of humor or some interesting anecdotes may be in good taste. If you are leaving, you might relate how you were welcomed or made to feel at home.

The body of the farewell speech should point out how the ideals of the honoree and the co-workers, although not completely attained, inspired people to work together. You might express appreciation for the support of the honoree (or your co-workers) that made certain achievements possible. Commend the harmony and cooperation that prevailed. If you are leaving, it is good to say that you will always remember your associations with this group as one of the outstanding events in your life.

As the person leaving, it is always good to speak of your future work or retirement plans briefly. You may need to explain why you are leaving or what compelled you to go into a new field or move to a new location. On some occasions this will be clear, thus there will be no need to explain. Show that the work just completed will be background and inspiration for what is ahead. Continue by encouraging those who remain, predicting greater achievements for them and your successor.

Conclude with a genuine expression of your appreciation for the honoree (or your associates). Express a continued interest in the future of the honoree (or your co-workers). If you are speaking in honor of someone, this is a good place to present a gift. If you have received a gift, express thanks for the gift and mention what the gift means to you as a reminder of this group.

Regardless of the type of farewell speech, omit all references to any unpleasant situations or friction that may have existed. Do not make the occasion bitter or sad. Be happy and leave others with the same feeling. Smile. Make sure a good impression follows you.

Presenting a Farewell Speech

In this speech fit your manner to the mood of your audience members. Do not go overboard in solemnity, emotion, or enthusiasm. Be appropriate! Use a friendly and sincere approach throughout. Adjust your introductory remarks to the prevailing mood; then move into your speech. Be sure your language is appropriate to the requirements just listed. Avoid ponderous phrases, overemotionalized words and tones, redundancy, and flowery attempts at oratory. Cast your remarks in a positive tone. Let everything you do and say, coupled with good appearance and alert posture, bear evidence that you are genuinely and sincerely mindful of your listener's appreciation of you on your departure (or that you do truly honor the departing person.)

SAMPLE FAREWELL SPEECH

By Kelli Pizzino

Good afternoon, ladies. Thank you for the warm reception. For the past two years I have been President of the Ladies Golf Association. Although it has not been an easy job, it has been a very rewarding experience.

In the first few months of my presidency, we established goals we wanted our association to accomplish. Our first goal was to have more tournaments during the year. Our second goal was to raise more money through our fund raisers. But the most important goal we wanted to accomplish was to add new members to our association.

I am very pleased with the success we had reaching our goals. First, we added two tournaments to our schedule; both have had excellent turn-outs. We doubled our participation in tournaments the first year and almost tripled it this year. We raised more money this year than ever before. In fact, Sandra told me earlier that we have now doubled what we raised two years ago. But the most exciting goal we reached was increasing our membership by twelve. We have never had this many members since I have been a member of the Ladies Golf Association. In fact, I think our membership is the strongest that it has ever been.

None of these goals could have been accomplished without the hard work of many of you, the members of this Association. The President doesn't do all of the work in the association, the individuals who make up the organization do the work. I could not have asked for a more enthusiastic, more motivated group. You were quick to volunteer your time, your effort, and even your money whenever it was needed. I hope you will continue your efforts under the guidance of your new President. Marilyn will be a good leader, but she will also need your help as you gave it to me. I will be happy to give my assistance anytime it is needed. I hope Marilyn can call on all of you also.

Over the last two years, I have gotten to know most of you very well. I am truly grateful for all of your help and kindness. Thank you for making my Presidency of the Ladies Golf Association an enjoyable experience. I wish all the best to our new President.

Even though my term of office is finished, the friends and memories I have made will last me a lifetime. Thank you.

Project Assignment

Prepare and present a brief (two- to four-minute) farewell speech. You may be asked to be the honoree or the one to honor someone else. Keep your remarks positive without showing too much emotion.

As you prepare for this assignment, think of the honor you are bestowing, or is being bestowed upon you. This should be the focus of your presentation. Collect the pertinent information from all knowledgeable sources. Be sure you have the dates, events, and facts correct. Be straightforward in telling people about the reasons for change, but avoid emotional displays.

Deliver the speech extemporaneously, and without great fanfare. Avoid going overboard in praising others; also avoid being negative. Be friendly, polite, and congenial in your presentation.

References

Allen, R. R. & McKerrow, R. E. (1985). *The Pragmatics of Public Communication* (3rd ed.). Dubuque, Iowa: Kendall/Hunt Publishing Company.

Berko, R. M., Wolvin, A. D., & Wolvin, D. R. (1988). *Communicating: A Social and Career Focus* (4th ed.). Boston: Houghton Mifflin Company.

DeVito, J. A. (1990). *The Elements of Public Speaking* (4th ed.). New York: Harper & Row, Publishers.

Heun, R. & Heun, L. (1986). *Public Speaking* (2nd ed.). St. Paul, Minnesota: West Publishing Company.

PROJECT **33**
The Eulogy

. . . we have gathered here not merely to pay tribute, but
to refresh our spirits and stir our hearts for the tasks
which lie ahead.

—John F. Kennedy

When someone does an outstanding deed, she or he needs praise. When a person dies, someone should present the eulogy. Preachers aren't the only people who are called upon to eulogize or praise someone else; often a family member is asked to say some words of praise about a loved one. There are several ways to eulogize a person. The type of eulogy you may be asked to present will, of course, depend on different aspects of the speech situation. Whatever the requirements may be, you will be better prepared if you have had previous experience. This project presents the principles of the eulogy, preparing a eulogy, presenting a eulogy, a sample eulogy, and provides you the opportunity to practice eulogizing.

Principles of the Eulogy

The eulogy is a special form of the speech of tribute or praise. In general, a eulogy is a ceremonial speech of praise in honor of someone living or dead. Some people think of the eulogy only as the speech given at a person's death. However, the eulogy may be presented in memorial services to honor a person, or group of persons, long after the person's death. Eulogies have been presented at various times for Martin Luther King and John F. Kennedy, for example. Other eulogies are presented for all the soldiers who died in war, as in Memorial Day or Veteran's Day services. Sometimes eulogies are even presented for animals, particularly dogs and horses. Technically, a eulogy could be presented upon one's receiving an award or honor, upon the retirement of a person or animal, or upon a person or animal's death (e.g., Lassie or Trigger). A more imaginative eulogy would be for an inanimate object, such as the sea or the mountains or for trees and flowers. These are not as unusual as the former types, however.

Because your most usual occasions for the presentation of a eulogy will be for people, let us concentrate on the eulogy in praise of human beings. The general purpose of the eulogy is for you to praise and evaluate the honored person favorably. The eulogy commends the finer qualities and characteristics of the person concerned and tells of the person's greatness and achievements, his or her benefit to society, and his or her influence on society. The eulogy is not merely a simple biographical sketch of someone, though.

Since the eulogy is not a biography of the person, it must emphasize the person's accomplishments and virtues. Your audience members should recognize that the person is being honored and should know of the attributes the person possessed that deserved honoring. If the person is living, the audience should recognize (1) the honor conferred and (2) the personal traits of the individual that led to the honor. If the person is deceased, then you should emphasize the virtues for which the person should be remembered. Also, remind audience members that not only will the good continue to live with them and be a part of them for a long time, but that the person's virtues are to be admired and emulated in their own lives.

Wood (1988) lists a number of virtues you might consider: for example, did the person display a sense of fairness, courage, honesty, compassion, generosity, or wisdom? Other virtues include wit, intelligence, talent, leadership, friendliness, and self-control. Your task is to select the virtues of the person that best honor him or her and are exemplified in his or her life.

Occasions for eulogies are many. For living persons such a speech might be given on a significant birthday, at a dinner honoring the person's accomplishments, at the dedication of a project someone has created and/or donated, or upon the reception of an honor. Eulogies are often given on the formal announcement of a political candidate or at an inauguration.

For persons who are dead, eulogies are offered at funerals, on birthday anniversaries, or in connection with notable events or achievements in their lives. Two important examples of this latter form of eulogy mentioned earlier are those presented recently for Martin Luther King and John F. Kennedy on the anniversaries of their deaths. Sometimes eulogies in the form of character studies are presented as an evidence of good living; these become lessons of life. To see some of these principles in practice, read the eulogy by Edward Kennedy for his brother Robert, which can be found in *Vital Speeches of the Day*, July 1, 1968, pp. 546–547.

Some people suitable for presenting eulogies about include:

1. A family member
2. A close friend
3. A co-worker or superior
4. An employee
5. Any famous American (Eleanor Roosevelt, Martin Luther King, Jr., John F. Kennedy, Susan B. Anthony, Helen Keller, Abraham Lincoln)
6. A contemporary American [a former president, the president (current), a legislator, educator, or civic leader]
7. Any famous humanitarian or leader (General de Gaulle, Mahatma Gandhi, Golda Meir)
8. A contemporary leader, not American (Margaret Thatcher, Prince Charles, Princess Di, Queen Elizabeth, Sakharov)
9. A pet (a dog, cat, horse, etc.)
10. Some valuable inanimate object

Preparing a Eulogy

The purpose of a eulogy is set, regardless of the time, place, or occasion, because eulogies are intended to stimulate your audience members favorably toward the subject and to inspire them to nobler heights by virtue of the examples set by the person being praised. If you do not know the person, you need to study that person's life work to be able to make specific references to the person's accomplishments. Generalizing about the person as having been a "good person," will not establish good rapport with your audience members. Look for unusual or outstanding accomplishments of the person, the human side of the person, as well as the incidents we will remember about him or her.

Your first decision is to select a method for organizing your eulogy. Your method of organization and whether the individual is living or dead will substantially determine the material you will need to include in your eulogy. Let us examine two specific methods of constructing a eulogy.

First, you may follow a *chronological* order, taking up events in the order of their occurrence or development. This will permit a study of the growth and orderly evaluation of character in your subject. As you touch upon these broad and influential events in the person's life, point to them as evidences of (1) what the person accomplished, (2) what the person stood for, (3) the nature of the person's influence on society, and (4) the person's probable place in history. You might also want to point out that the person achieved much with few resources or against great odds. It is also possible for you to point out the extraordinary difficulties the person faced, and what was above the normal expectations for such a person. Obviously, you can't cover every event in the person's life, but rather you need to focus on several significant virtues and accomplishments in the person's life.

In preparing this aspect of your speech, make your events in the person's life pertinent to your audience members. If this is a funeral, tell your audience members what the person's life has meant to them—how they have been affected; if the person is an historical figure, tell how the person's life still affects us today.

In building your speech chronologically, be certain you do not compose a simple biographical sketch of the person. If you do, you will have an informative speech about the person's life—not a eulogy. This is the reason for showing how the person reacted to the events in his or her life and what happened as a result. In some instances you may have to interpret the events in a person's life by assigning good motives to his or her deeds.

For example, if you were eulogizing Franklin D. Roosevelt chronologically, you might recount as one event how he was stricken with infantile paralysis when a grown man, by not merely making a statement regarding that tragedy, but rather telling how his illness became a challenge to him, how he resolved to live a great life despite a pair of useless legs, how he overcame his handicap. You could show that, as a result of his illness, he became more resolute, more determined, more kindly, and that today the nation honors him on his birthday and contributes millions of dollars to the fund to aid children afflicted with infantile paralysis and birth defects. Other incidents should be given similar treatment. Your audience members should see the effect he has had on our lives today from the development of this point.

A second method of developing a eulogy is one called the *period method*. This method covers the individual's growth by looking at different periods in the person's life. It is very broad and makes no attempt to enumerate the many events of the person's life and their significance. Instead, you point out the significance of the periods to the person's overall growth or achievement.

Using John F. Kennedy as an example, you could speak of him as he went through (1) boyhood, (2) college life, (3) military life, (4) early political life, and (5) late political life. In following this method, you attempt to bring out the same points as in the chronological order in that you (1) point out what the person accomplished, (2) what the person stood for, (3) the nature of the person's influence on society, and (4) the person's probable place in history. Although this treatment is broad, it can be quite effective.

Regardless of the method you use, there are certain necessary points you should observe. First, omit the unimportant events, the small deeds, and the insignificant details. Second, point out the struggles the person made in order to achieve his or her aims, but avoid overemphasis and exaggeration. Third, show the development of the person's ideas and ideals. You should point out the education and influences that helped the person mature and aim for success. Fourth, describe the person's relations and services to other people and indicate their significance.

It is not necessary to cover up the faults of an individual. Just remember that no one is perfect. Admit the human element in the person or allude to the fact that the person had faults, neither dwelling on nor apologizing for them. Show that despite weaknesses or shortcomings, the person was a great human being. Generally, it is safer to understate one's accomplishments than to set the person up as perfect. Whatever the qualities of your subject, be honest in your treatment of that person. It is only fair to assume that the good outweighed the bad by far, or you would not have selected to eulogize the person.

A typical outline for a eulogy might look like this:

I. INTRODUCTION
    A. An attention-getting incident about the person
    B. An incident that illustrates a basic trait of the person's character
II. BODY
    A, B, C, and so on = focus on one or more of the following themes: (1) other events in the person's life that establish the person's character, (2) the significance of the person to society in general, or a specific segment of society (family), (3) humanize the person.
III. CONCLUSION
    A. Review the important aspects from the body.
    B. A statement by the person or you can tell of another event in the person's life that exemplifies the person's best qualities.

Presenting a Eulogy

The eulogy is a formal, ceremonial speech. Although some eulogies are long, as in ceremonies to eulogize a hero from the past, most eulogies are short and to the point. Do not go overboard in praising. Because it is ceremonial, the eulogy is often written out as a manuscript and either memorized and recited or read from the script. No matter which method of delivery you use, try to be personable with your audience members. Do not sound as if you are reciting a script or reading to your audience.

Your overall attitude must be one of undoubted sincerity. You must truly believe in the person about whom you speak. Aside from your attitude, you will, of course, observe all the requirements of good speaking. There should be no showiness or gaudiness in your presentation that will call attention to you instead of your ideas about the person you are eulogizing.

You need to be fully aware of the occasion and atmosphere when you deliver the eulogy. It is your responsibility to know what is required of you in the way of carrying out rituals or ceremonies if they are part of the program. Since you will be in the limelight, you should fit easily into the situation without awkwardness. Naturally, you must adjust your bodily actions and gestures to your environment and your audience. If you are sincere and well prepared, and mean what you say, the eulogy you present should be inspirational to all who hear it.

SAMPLE EULOGY

By Dr. Arlie Daniel

A Eulogy to Georgia Lizzie (Miles) Grover

Eighty-six years ago a small child entered the world and made a great impact upon the lives of each of us. If it were not for her life, we wouldn't be here today. Most of us knew her as Grandma or Mom. The full impact her life has had on the world will never be known, but that impact will follow us the rest of our days. She made us what we are today. Though some of her impact was indirect, it was still very powerful. Recall a day when you had a problem that needed a solution, or one when you needed a little love and attention and she was there. No matter how large or small the problem, Grandma was always willing to help—ready to make an impact on your life.

She gave us strength in times of trouble, wisdom in times of uncertainty, and inspiration in times of doubt. She shared in our sorrows and rejoiced in our happiness. She provided us the joy and love we needed to nourish our souls, the knowledge to cope with life's daily trials, and the wisdom to reach higher than we ever dreamed.

Love is not an easy feeling to put into words. Nor is loyalty, trust, or joy. But she was all of these and more. Much more. She loved life completely and lived it intensely. Thus she lived a complete and fulfilled life. Her life was complete in that she did not make mountains out of mole hills, nor did she avoid the difficult tasks in her life or try to make the significant elements seem unimportant. Her life was fulfilled in that she shared herself and her love with each of us. Indeed, she gave her all so that we might all have more.

What that adds up to is love. Not love as we sometimes hear about in books and the movies, but the kind of love that is affection and respect, order and encouragement, and support. Our awareness of this was an incalculable source of strength. Who among us has not felt that strength—that love? Who among us has not felt that awareness?

And because real love is something unselfish and involves sacrifice and giving, we could not help but profit from it. Beneath it all she was doing what was right in her heart. There were wrongs that needed attention, there were people who needed help. Out of the goodness of her heart those wrongs were righted and the people were helped.

Through no virtues, accomplishments, or desires of our own, we were born as descendants of that love. We, therefore, have a responsibility to pass that love and understanding on not only to our descendants, but also to our friends and acquaintances. That love is our greatest legacy. If we had not a cent more than that legacy, we would still be very rich people! Some of the richest in the world. Indeed, she has made us the richest family in the world today.

We are often told at times as these that "For those who have been faithful, life is not ended, but merely changed. And when this earthly abode dissolves, an eternal dwelling place awaits in heaven." It is with this assurance that we can let go. We shall miss her, but we know that she waits for us in another place. She has run the good race, won the prize. Now she goes to her reward.

Cervantes once said, "There is a remedy for everything but death." What he failed to note was that there is no need for a remedy. "Destiny calls and we go."

Yet, the end is not as abrupt as that. "Your name is still spoken. Your face is still remembered, and what you said, and what you failed to do—these are still remembered. Remembered, too, are the manner of your glance, the ring of your voice, the clasp of your hand and how your step sounded—as long as one is left who remembers you, so long is the matter unended." (quoted from "Carousel" by Rodgers and Hammerstein)

So it is with Grandma. We will long speak of her, as we have of our other ancestors. We shall long remember her face—her flashing smile, her gleaming eyes, and the way she gestured as she told a story. We'll not soon forget the ring of her voice as she related a tale of days long passed, or the clasp of her hand or the sound of her step. Indeed, this matter is not ended. Can anyone who lives in the hearts and minds of so many people be dead?

Grandma need not be idealized nor enlarged in death beyond what she was in life. She should be remembered simply as a good and decent person who saw wrong and tried to right it; saw suffering and tried to heal it; saw people and tried to love them.

Those of us who loved her and take her to rest today, pray that what she was to us we can become to others; that what she felt for others we can come to feel; that what she did for others, we can carry on for her.

May her soul rest in peace. May her memory be perpetuated in our hearts as a symbol of eternal love.

Project Assignment

Prepare and present a four- to six-minute eulogy in which you praise a person living or dead. Be sure you emphasize the person's accomplishments and his or her contribution to society. Avoid merely presenting a biography of the person.

In preparing for this assignment, be sure you know the facts about the person you will be eulogizing. If the person is someone you do not know personally, be sure you read and talk about the person with people who did know the person. Plan to prepare this speech as a manuscript you present by either reading or reciting to your audience.

As you prepare your manuscript, avoid using phrases that are too flowery or too sentimental. People have faults, so avoid going overboard in praising the person you are eulogizing. Neither should you elaborate on those faults. Your audience members will likely know of the person's faults and accept them as a part of the person. Concentrate on the good qualities, deeds, and accomplishments of the person.

References

Allen, R. R. & McKerrow, R. E. (1985). *The Pragmatics of Public Communication* (3rd ed.). Dubuque, Iowa: Kendall/Hunt Publishing Company.

Capp, G. R., Capp, C. C., & Capp, G. R., Jr. (1990). *Basic Oral Communication* (5th ed.). Englewood Cliffs, New Jersey: Prentice-Hall, Inc.

Dance, F. E. X. & Zak-Dance, C. C. (1986). *Public Speaking.* New York: Harper & Row, Publishers.

DeVito, J. A. (1990). *The Elements of Public Speaking* (4th ed.). New York: Harper & Row, Publishers.

Gregory, H. (1990). *Public Speaking for College and Career* (2nd ed.). New York: McGraw-Hill Book Company.

Hanna, M. S. & Gibson, J. W. (1989). *Public Speaking for Personal Success* (2nd ed.). Dubuque, Iowa: Wm. C. Brown Company, Publishers.

Lucas, S. E. (1989). *The Art of Public Speaking* (3rd ed.). New York: Random House.

Minnick, W. C. (1983). *Public Speaking* (2nd ed.). Boston: Houghton Mifflin Company.

Verderber, R. F. (1988). *The Challenge of Effective Speaking* (7th ed.). Belmont, California: Wadsworth Publishing Company.

Wood, J. (1988). *Speaking Effectively.* New York: Random House.

PROJECT **34**

The Dedication or Commemorative Speech

Be quick to praise. People like to praise those who
praise them.
—Bernard Baruch

You may not speak at a dedication ceremony for a long time, if ever; then again the
occasion for a speech of this kind may arise sooner than you had thought possible.
Regardless of when you are called on, you need to know the requirements for the
dedication or commemorative speech. The dedication speech is given on an occasion and
in an atmosphere that require strict observance of ceremonial aspects of speech making.
This project provides the principles of the dedication speech, preparing a dedication
speech, presenting a dedication speech, and a sample dedication speech, and includes a
practical exercise for you to practice the dedication speech.

Principles of the Dedication Speech

The commemorative speech is a broad classification of speeches of praise or celebration. The
dedication speech is a specific classification of the commemorative speech. As such it is basically
a ritual in which the speaker ceremoniously recites and extols the virtues of a place or event.
The dedication speech is presented on commemorative occasions. It is generally brief and has
a serious tone.

The objective of the speaker in a dedication speech should be to commemorate, that is,
to honor and praise the spirit of endeavor and progress that the dedication symbolizes. Although you may need to inform some audiences about your subject, your basic purpose is to
inspire them to admire or otherwise appreciate the honor and essence of the object of your
dedication. Because the dedication speech is ceremonial in nature, audiences tend to have
expectations for the speech, based on tradition and past experience. It is in your best interests
to fulfill your audience's expectations when you are dedicating or commemorating any achievement.

201

A part of dedicatory tradition says that the speech should fill the audience with pride regarding the object of dedication whether it is a statue, a building, a monument, or a person, as well as the community, ideals, and progress. In fact, Gronbeck (1983) says the thing being dedicated is only an "excuse" for praising the audience in that it *represents* the aspirations and accomplishments of the people.

The ultimate purpose, then, of the dedication speech is to (1) indicate what the object of dedication stands for and (2) celebrate the audience's accomplishments and ideas. If you are dedicating a monument, building, or other edifice, for example, you need to discuss how the symbol represents the person or event for which it is dedicated. For example, the monument to the missing Vietnam veterans was dedicated to honor the people who are still missing as well as the sacrifices made by them and their families during the Vietnam War. A second purpose was to relate the monument to the accomplishments and ideals of all Americans in the pursuit of freedom for other freedom seekers around the world and to relate to the sacrifices of all those who gave for the cause during the Vietnam War.

Occasions for the dedication speech usually involve group enterprises. Common among them are such occasions as erecting monuments, completing buildings, laying cornerstones, or opening institutions. Lincoln's *Gettysburg Address* at the dedication of the Gettysburg Cemetery is still one of the best examples of a dedication speech available today. Another example of a dedication speech was John Kennedy's speech at the Berlin Wall in 1963.

Some topics suitable for dedicatory speeches include:

1. Laying a cornerstone for a new building (church, lodge, campus building, community project)
2. Dedicating a monument to a leader or as a historical marker (local, state, or national hero, Vietnam War)
3. Opening a new building (campus building, church, hospital, library)
4. Renaming or dedicating an existing building
5. Opening a park, stadium, gym, building, and so on
6. Commemorating an event in history (end of a war, anniversary of freedom, and so on)
7. Honoring a person in history for his or her accomplishments (Martin Luther King, Jr., Joan of Arc, Winston Churchill, Eleanor Roosevelt)
8. Dedicating a landmark (a president's home, a local historical building, the site of an historical building)
9. Dedicating the site of an historical event (Lewis and Clark trail, first state capitol, battlefield)
10. Commemorating the birth of an idea (electricity, telephone)

Although it may appear that your options are limited, each of the preceding situations allows for endless numbers of opportunities for dedications on college campuses, in your local school districts, and in local, state, and national civic projects.

Preparing the Dedication Speech

Because the dedication speech is ceremonial, it takes much careful planning and preparation. It employs excellent use of language and demands careful construction, fine wording, and polished delivery.

As you begin your preparation, focus on the purpose of the dedication. Focus on the object and what it symbolizes as well as the accomplishments and ideals of the people for whom the dedication is presented. These are the points to cover in your speech: First, give a description of the object being dedicated or a history of the events leading up to the dedication. Sometimes you may want to do both. Make sure your audience members know what the object symbolizes. Second, mention the sacrifices, the hard work, the ideals and the service that lie behind the project. Third, explain specific accomplishments or ideals (qualities) that your audience members should emulate. Explain what the future holds for the symbol and your audience—the future use, the influence and/or the significance that will be associated with the dedicated object. Fourth, return to the concept of the object and what it symbolizes. Urge your audience members to continue their good works, their sacrifices and/or their values. Be sure you focus on the ideals the object symbolizes rather than on the object itself.

Organize your speech very carefully. First, outline it, then begin the wording of your speech. Do your wording meticulously. Do not be pretentious or ostentatious with your language, but rather be understandable and simple in your selection of words. Avoid using clichés and trite expressions that have no real meaning. Be imaginative and creative, but most of all be understandable and appropriately emotional. Since this is a special occasion speech, you might organize it in the following manner:

I. INTRODUCTION
    A. Description of object being dedicated or history of the events leading up to the dedication
    B. What the object symbolizes
    C. Sacrifices that lie behind the object

II. BODY
    A, B, C, and so on   An explanation of the future use, influence, and/or significance associated with the object
    A, B, C, and so on   Supreme qualities associated with the object and to be emulated by audience members

III. CONCLUSION
    A. Emphasize what the object symbolizes
    B. Urge audience members to continue their good works, sacrifices, and values

Presenting the Dedication Speech

Because of the ceremonial nature of this speech, you must be more formal in presenting it than in most of the other speeches you will present. Therefore, read your speech as a script or commit it to memory and deliver it in that manner, depending on the circumstances surrounding your speaking situation. This is a serious speech, so your attitude should be one of appropriate dignity. Since you are not merely telling your audience members about this object of dedication, you must stir their emotions and inspire them to emulate the virtues of the commemoration. Your emotion and dignity should be properly blended to fit the noble sentiments that will be present at the event. Your poise should be obvious from your appearance, your bearing, and your self-confidence.

As you speak, your bodily actions must be keyed to the tone of your speech. The environment of the occasion may permit much bodily action and movement or limit it severely. However, you can and should use appropriate gestures to help convey your message as completely and honestly as you can.

Whether speaking with the aid of a microphone or without, your voice should be full and resonant and easily heard. If your audience is large, a slower speaking rate is usually better. Your articulation must be careful, yet not so much that it becomes ponderous and labored. To sound as if you are enunciating every sound in every word too carefully, you may put your audience members to sleep instead of inspiring them. Your voice and actions must be in tune, neither one overbalancing the other. Be animated, alive to your purpose, desirous of communicating, and capable of presenting a polished speech. A recent commencement speaker violated several of these points and was the brunt of jokes around campus for several years. Make your presentation as dignified and important as the occasion for the ceremony.

SAMPLE DEDICATION SPEECH

By Donna L. Gough

Community Youth Center Dedication

Mr. Mayor, Distinguished Guests, Ladies and Gentlemen:
We began this project with only one thing in mind: providing a place for our children to go without fear of attack or abuse. Now, three years later, we are able to dedicate the first Youth Center ever built in our community.

All of us, parents, teachers, and public officials, agreed two years ago that one of the most urgent needs facing our community was a place set aside for the children of our community. We wanted a place reserved especially for children for times after school and on the weekends. We wanted a place where the children of this community would not only be able to meet with their friends but also a place that would provide alternate learning experiences to the regular school system.

In order to meet our goal, we held meetings, we took donations, and last year we finally began constructing a facility which would serve the community's needs. We have built a facility that meets the standards we set for our community as a group. We have built a facility we can all take pride in because we had a part in designing it and we invested our own money in it.

Today, we are gathered here to celebrate our past achievements. Not only does this facility provide space for our children to play and to interact with one another but the Youth Center will also provide supervision and counseling for those in need. Classes and special events will be held at the center for everyone. Each of us can see that the time and the effort that we have made to insure the Youth Center would become a reality has been worth the trouble. This facility will soon become the heartbeat of this community and will provide encouragement and assistance for everyone.

Today, this facility stands empty; tomorrow, it will open its doors to the leaders of the future. As we watch the children of the community grow and mature with the help of the Youth Center, we know in our hearts that the future will be left in good hands. May it become one of the few shelters of hope in a world filled with darkness.

Project Assignment

Prepare and present a three- to four-minute dedication speech in which you commemorate an object or event. Make sure that you emphasize what the object of dedication stands for and that you celebrate the group's accomplishments and ideals. Your instructor may have additional requirements for you. Be alert to these special instructions.

In preparing this assignment, make sure you relate the object of dedication to your audience members. If the reasons for the dedication are not clear, make sure you tell your audience members why you are making this tribute at this time. Keep this reason for the honor in mind throughout your preparation and presentation. This is your focus.

Deliver your speech from a manuscript, or commit it to memory and deliver it from your composed remarks. Since this is a ceremonial speech, it should be prepared and delivered in a very formal fashion. Your words need to be carefully chosen to convey a specific message. There should be no hesitancy in your presentation, nor in your conviction toward the honor.

References

Allen, R. R. & McKerrow, R. E. (1985). *The Pragmatics of Public Communication* (3rd ed.). Dubuque, Iowa: Kendall/Hunt Publishing Company.

Ayres, J. & Miller, J. (1990). *Effective Public Speaking* (3rd ed.). Dubuque, Iowa: Wm. C. Brown Company, Publishers.

Bradley, B. E. (1988). *Fundamentals of Speech Communication* (5th ed.). Dubuque, Iowa: Wm. C. Brown Company, Publishers.

DeVito, J. A. (1990). *The Elements of Public Speaking* (4th ed.). New York: Harper & Row, Publishers.

Gregory, H. (1990). *Public Speaking for College and Career* (2nd ed.). New York: McGraw-Hill Book Company.

Gronbeck, B. E. (1983). *The Articulate Person* (2nd ed.). Glenview, Illinois: Scott, Foresman and Company.

Lucas, S. E. (1989). *The Art of Public Speaking* (3rd ed.). New York: Random House.

Osborn, M. & Osborn, S. (1988). *Public Speaking*. Boston: Houghton Mifflin Company.

Rodman, G. (1986). *Public Speaking* (3rd ed.). New York: Holt, Rinehart and Winston, Inc.

Sprague, J. & Stuart, D. (1988). *The Speaker's Handbook* (2nd ed.). San Diego: Harcourt Brace Jovanovich.

Thompson, W. N. (1978). *Responsible and Effective Communication*. Boston: Houghton Mifflin Company.

Wood, J. (1988). *Speaking Effectively*. New York: Random House.

Zimmerman, G. I., Owen, J. L., & Seibert, D. R. (1986). *Speech Communication: A Contemporary Introduction* (3rd ed.). St. Paul, Minnesota: West Publishing Company.

PROJECT **35**

The Critical Response Review

Speech is the mirror of the soul; as a man speaks,
so is he.
—Syrus

When you read a book, see a movie or play, or attend a concert, you have a natural tendency to "review" it for those who have not yet experienced it. Not only do you want to let others know what you enjoyed, but you also want to interest the others in reading the book, seeing the movie or play, or attending the concert.

A well-prepared and presented review can be satisfying to both the presenter and the audience. Reviews are most effective before small social, educational, and religious groups. It is also a successful method used to present yourself favorably to people. This project presents the principles of preparing, organizing, and presenting critical response reviews, and presents several samples.

Principles of Critical Response Reviews

The critical response review is placed in the unit with other "special occasion speeches" because the general purpose at any moment may be to inform, to persuade, or to entertain, or some combination of all three purposes. For example, it may be your purpose to inform your audience of the content of a newly released book, play, movie, and so on (it could be a "classic" or a well-known object as well). At the same time, you may have the purpose of entertaining your audience members and/or persuading them to read the book, see the play or movie, or attend any other form of entertainment. Since the presentation does not clearly fit any *one* of the general purposes, it has been placed in this unit.

No matter which form of art you are reviewing, you need to approach your review with two questions in mind: (1) What is the entertainment value of the object? and (2) What comment does the source have on society? That is, what is its contribution to society?

Since reviews are *informed* judgments about the content and quality of the object presented for public consumption, it is essential that you, as the reviewer, be well informed. Your prime responsibility is to be informed enough to report all significant aspects of the event and to evaluate their worth to society. In fact, according to William Zinsser (1980), the reviewer is "the deputy for the average man or woman who wants to know: "What is the new TV series about?" "Is the movie too dirty for the kids?" "Will the book really improve my sex life or tell me how to make a chocolate mousse?"

When you perform the task of reviewer, simply ask yourself what you would want to know if you were going to spend money to buy the book, see the movie, and so on. Be cautious, however, that you do not become a critic instead of a reviewer. Critics differ from reviewers in that the former *present detailed analyses* of the art form and the artists as well as *criticize* the event (drama, art, music) according to rigid standards of performance. The critical response review includes elements of both a review (a report of what happened) and a critical response (an evaluation of the performance). When people hear a review, they are generally interested in two things: (1) What happened? and (2) Is it worth my time and money?

Preparing Critical Response Reviews

A critical response reviewer is expected to be well informed regarding the methods of giving a review, be able to present information in an organized and interesting manner, and to do this, must know the subject matter well. To know your subject well, you need to research your topic. For example, if you are reviewing a book or a play, find out what else the author has written and some facts about the author. Make comparisons and contrasts with previous works or parallels in the author's life. How were the author's other works received by reviews and the public? Is there any special training or skills the author possesses that lend credibility to the selection? In reviewing a movie, you may dwell more on the director than the author, but you will make the same kinds of probes. In reviewing a concert or other group performance, you must deal with the relationship of the artists and their relationship to the event. In some cases you may even need to interview the artists before you can complete your review.

Have enough experience in the area of your review to make judgments and comparisons. Read other books, plays, and movie scripts and attend other movies, plays, or concerts, so you have a basis for making your judgments and comparisons and contrasts. You may even benefit from having taken courses in literature, theatre history, music appreciation, and so on, which provide a broad background in the area of your review.

As you begin to make specific decisions about your presentation, rely on your basic speech preparation background. First, decide your general purpose—to inform, to persuade, to entertain, or some combination of these three. Second, you must decide which of the materials that you have researched and collected will help you achieve your purpose. Third, you must organize the material into a speech format with a beginning, a middle, and an end.

Because step two is so important, let us look independently at the areas of concern: (1) the book review, (2) the play review, (3) the music review, and (4) the film review.

The Book Review   Begin the book review process by trying to determine what the author intended the readers to feel or comprehend. Then determine how well the author did this, and finally, respond to the worth of the book.

In order to determine answers to the preceding, you need to refer to information collected earlier. For example, who is the author? What do we need to know about the author? Does the author do more than just write? What other books has the author written? Where does (did) the author live? Include other pertinent data of a similar nature. Opinions vary regarding how much should be told *about* the author. Probably the best criteria are whether the book is fiction or nonfiction, who makes up your audience (how much they know), and how much relates directly to the work under review. Generally, be brief about the author.

In reporting on the book itself, you need to tell the title (and maybe its significance), why you have selected this book to review, and when and by whom the book is published. You may even report on the circumstances surrounding the writing of the book if they are known. It is always advisable to know what other reviewers have said about the book also. Good book reviews are generally found in the *New York Times, Christian Century, Saturday Review, New Republic, The New Yorker, The Nation, The Atlantic Monthly,* and other similar publications. Don't forget to formulate your own opinions. Do not plagiarize someone else's evaluation of the book. Formulate your own opinions, but read other reviews to find out what others thought of the book so you can make comparisons.

For fiction, after you have presented background information about the author and the book, tell what the book is about. Mention the period in which it is set. Describe the leading characters and important subordinate characters, telling briefly of their relationships and interplay in the story. Indicate the plot briefly by citing various incidents and events that reflect its development. Usually, not much is disclosed concerning the outcome of the plot in order to stimulate reader interest. Some reviews, however, go into considerable detail for the express purpose of telling enough about the contents so it is unnecessary for the listener to read the books.

When reviewing nonfiction and textbooks, the reviewer usually gives the author's and book's background in more detail than for fiction. This assists in evaluating the book's validity. For nonfiction, the reviewer attempts to ascertain what the author was trying to tell, how valid the material is, how well the author develops ideas, and the extent to which he or she was able to accomplish his or her goals. In covering these points, the reviewer generally notes organization, use of illustration and example, consistency of ideas, and conclusions drawn. An evaluation is made of these.

In reviewing, you may cite paragraphs or passages from the book as examples of what you are talking about and in showing what the author thinks. Avoid a dull recitation of just the contents and also avoid presenting the contents as though they were your ideas. Evaluate the book as you present your review. This means discussing briefly the pro or con, the trite or unique, the doubtful or certain, the uselessness or usefulness, the practical or the impractical, among other points. Discuss these matters in relation to the material and state your point of view frequently as you proceed. Be sure to say whether you recommend the book and give the restrictions or reservations with which you recommend it. Tell your audience members where the book may be bought, rented, or borrowed.

One of the best ways to secure the preceding information is to read the book you are preparing to review several times. First, read it for enjoyment. The second and third times read for information you plan to use in your review. If time does not permit several readings, read it once carefully. As for getting your material in mind, use your own method. It is advisable either to write the speech out in full or to make a careful and detailed outline; then rehearse aloud until your sequence of thoughts is firmly fixed in your mind. If you use quotations, make them brief.

The Play Review   The play is both a literary form and a performance; therefore, the play review needs to begin as a review of the literature, performed much as you would a book review. The second segment of the review reports on the performance.

First, find out about the author and other plays the author has written. Find the same information that you require if you were reporting on a book. Since this aspect of the review has been covered, let's turn to the second aspect of the review—the performance. In this segment of your review report what happened. Record a glimpse of the play as you saw it. Then you respond to your feelings about the actions you witnessed. Respond to the quality of the performance also. If you thought it was good, why? If you thought the performance was a poor one, why? People hearing your review want to know if it's worth the price of admission and their time to watch it.

An important aspect of the play review is the players. Which character stood out? Why? How well did the company of players work together to produce harmony and unity in the play? Were the characters believable? Why or why not? By all means, review the technical aspects of the production too. How well did the set and scenery add to the portrayal of the characters without calling attention to themselves? Are there other technical aspects that enhance or detract from the overall production? Make sure the standards of performance you apply to the play are appropriate to the performance. You certainly would not expect the same quality of performance from a high school cast, a college cast, a community theatre group, and a professional theatre company. Apply the appropriate standards for the performance being reviewed.

The Music Review   Reviewing musical events is very different from literary events. First, you must have a good background in music and a great appreciation for the specific musical form you are reviewing. If the review is of an opera or a musical, you must prepare much as you did for the play review. Know the "story" and the music. Review the production in its entirety. Were the characters believable? How well did they sing? How well did the orchestra combine with the singers to produce a pleasing effect?

Other musical reviews concern themselves solely with the music. For example, any concert, whether of classical music or of rock music, should let the audience members know what you thought of the concert and whether they want to attend the concert. Sometimes, you may need to review the entertainer's career or part of his or her life so your audience can more fully comprehend the music and its significance to the musician.

The Film Review   As with other reviews, you must gain a great deal of experience and knowledge about the art itself before reviewing. If you don't understand the art form, it is very difficult to tell when something is done well.

Many films are based on novels, plays, or other literary forms. When they are, it is important for the reviewer to be familiar with the original form so comparisons and contrasts can be made between the two forms. The ideal film review will be a combination of the book review, the play review, and the music review, as there are elements of all involved in the typical film. Although you may not have enough time to cover all elements in detail, you need to consider all elements so you can give your review the most important aspect of the total product.

For instance, in a film based on a novel, you may want to study the author as completely as you would in a book review. In other film reviews you may be more concerned with comparing the director's works because they are more pertinent than the author of the movie script. In making comparisons, don't forget to compare a film with other films of its genre (documentary, science fiction, and so on).

As in reviewing plays, you need to take note of the acting and its contribution to the total impact on your audience. Just because a film has a well-known "star" does not mean that the acting will be well done. Nor does the absence of a star in a film guarantee a poor performance. Determine the ability of the actors and actresses to carry out their roles as believable characters. If you can believe them, they are probably doing a credible job; if you can't accept them as "real," then they are probably not doing well.

One aspect of the film review that is different from the other forms is cinematography. This is not exactly the same as critiquing the scenery and technical aspects of a play. Cinematography includes all aspects of filmmaking, including such areas as camera angles, movements, scenes, costuming, and special effects.

To present only a summary of what goes on in the movie is to be incomplete. Review the entire film art, just as you would review the entire literary art, dramatic art, or musical art. Look for the meaning in the film, but do not divorce it from the technique of the art form also.

Organizing Critical Response Reviews

There is only one general form for organizing a review. Prepare an introduction, a body, and a conclusion. In the introduction you should concentrate on using some attention-getting materials about either the author or the specific performance. To state that a publisher has a new book or that a play has opened is not very attention-getting. To proclaim that Star X's new film is "smashing" or "a total disappointment" would do more to arouse audience interest, for example. Second, let your audience members know the specific nature of the event being reviewed—a comedy play, a rock concert, an adventure novel, a science fiction movie, and so on. Third, relate the topic to your audience by referring to the social importance of the play, novel, film, and so on.

The body of your presentation should include your summary of the book, play, film, or musical event. Often the summary includes quotations for support when dealing with books, plays, and movies. The body is also the section of your review where you include your judgments about the quality of the book, concert, and so on. Be sure your opinions are supported. In order to support your opinions on the quality of a novel, you may point out problems or show progress in the development of the plot, developments, or shortcomings of characters, the writing style, and so on. For plays, films, and musical reviews, discuss the strengths and weaknesses of the various aspects of the performance. Always be specific about what you liked or disliked and why. Finally, you should comment on the impact of the art form on society or the art field, if pertinent.

In some instances, a concert, for example, you may not need to comment on the value to society. However, most books, plays, and films should respond to some social problem or issue. You need to respond to the author/director's understanding of the issue and how the product responds to that problem or issue. For example, Michael Christofer's play *The Shadow Box* deals with impending death. How adequately do the play, the art, and the director deal with this subject? What is the ultimate message the book, play, or film leaves with the audience? Is this what was intended? Is it appropriate?

The conclusion should be a brief summary of the message you intended. You may also end with a final quotation that summarizes the message of the event. It might also be appropriate to make a final statement regarding the worth of the event. You can suggest that audience members read the book, see the play or movie, or attend the concert. You can also recommend that they save their money if you feel the book, play, film, or concert is so poor that the specific people in your audience would not enjoy themselves.

Presenting Critical Response Reviews

Generally, you can follow the rules for presenting an informative, persuasive, or entertaining speech, depending on your purpose. There are certain expressions and phrases you would be best to avoid since they are usually trite and overused. For example, avoid "inspiring," "well-conceived," "best ever," "outstanding," "never before . . ." and any of the other common statements used to advertise books, plays, and films. Audiences will tend to react more favorably to a review that presents points worth praising and also notes areas of inadequacy without making gross overstatements about the good or bad aspects.

Present your review extemporaneously. This is important to help establish your credibility. If you are going to recommend that your audience members either read a book or attend a play, film, or concert, you need to project the image of one who has read the book or seen the play, movie, or concert. If you stand before your audience with the book, play script, or too many notes clutched in your hands as a crutch, for example, or occupy time by merely reading previously marked pages, you will not be reviewing, and you will not be presenting a speech to your audience. It is permissible to carry the book, and even to read quotations from it, but you must use it sparingly if you are to make a good oral presentation.

SAMPLE CRITICAL RESPONSE REVIEWS

SAMPLE MOVIE REVIEW

By Keith Ward

"Roger Rabbit" Critical Review

Just when you thought original films were a thing of the past, a masterpiece graces the theaters with a magic all its own. Dazzling production by Steven Spielberg (yes, once again); a solid, intricate plot; and a combination of performances by human, as well as animated actors and actresses, make "Who Framed Roger Rabbit?" a one in a million creation. Walt Disney had toyed with human-animation mixtures in films like "Pete's Dragon," but his work was nothing of the magnitude of "Roger Rabbit."

In this film, cartoons, or simply "toons" as they are referred to, are commonplace in society, and are as tangible as the next person. Spielberg's effect is realistic in that he has toons utilizing items of a human society, as well as humans using those of a toon society. This is where the magic of this picture comes alive. Toons are made to look as if they are using everyday human items. For example, in one scene the viewer sees a human get thrown out of a bar by a toon. The man was strapped in a harness and swung across the alley on a rope until he crashed into a pile of trash cans, giving the effect that the toon had actually thrown the man out. The audience doesn't see the harness or the rope, of course. Endless hours must have gone into producing the effect that toons were actually alive and a part of everyday life. The role for humans was to pretend that they had a toon item and act accordingly. For instance, one person used a cartoon gun while chasing his enemy. The actor had to pretend that he was holding a gun and firing a gun when he actually had nothing in his hand. The film was centered around this most complicated method of cinematography and the time spent to create such a realistic effect must have been enormous.

The centralized plot of the movie focuses on the murder of a certain Mr. Acme, copyrighted prankster and owner of the community where all the toons live, more simply, Toontown.

Roger Rabbit, an animated rabbit whose antics make Bugs Bunny look like a Harvard graduate, is the central character of the movie. Roger's wife, Jessica, a saucy, animated redhead, was caught playing "pattycake" with Mr. Acme. Someone subsequently dropped a safe on Mr. Acme's head (a classic toon trick) and killed him. Roger, the prime suspect, turns to Eddie Valiant, a famous toon detective and protector, for help.

The element making the initial plot work so well is the evolution of countless subplots. For example, one subplot follows the detection and apprehension of the villain (played brilliantly by Christopher Lloyd) and his scheme to destroy Toontown. Another subplot traces the mysterious death of Valiant's brother, while another has Eddie and Roger eluding the toon patrol (Lloyd's henchmen). All of these effects combine ingeniously with additional but less substantial subplots to form an intricate mesh which nets the viewer.

The film also reincarnates a number of Disney's and Looney Tunes' characters from Donald Duck and Mickey Mouse to Bugs Bunny and Woody Woodpecker. Many more recognizable characters make guest appearances but audience members must have very sharp eyes to catch them all.

The greatest misconception, and perhaps the film's only major drawback, is the myth that this movie is a kid's show. I'll agree that there are many toons in the picture and that, therefore, it will hold a child's attention. However, the film is primarily oriented to an adult audience in plot, language, and content. Baby Herman, for example, is a cigar-smoking, obscenity-throwing, animated baby with a taste for adult women. Elements ranging from a character being run over, in graphic detail, by a steamroller, to the melting of a toon in an acidic solution, typify part of the adult oriented content of the film.

Regardless of your age or tastes, "Roger Rabbit" offers something for every viewer. Its originality and entertainment value merit this picture a **** rating.

SAMPLE PLAY REVIEW

By Karen Piercy

The Shadow Box

"A very moving performance" seems to be the general consensus about East Central University Theatre's opening performance of *The Shadow Box* last night. This 1977 Pulitzer Prize-winning drama by Michael Christofer covers the emotions felt by three terminally ill patients and their families when coping with death. Set in "cottages" similar to a hospice, Christofer uses as a base for his play the research of Dr. Elisabeth Kubler-Ross who has been in close contact with terminally ill patients living in a California hospice. From her research, Elisabeth Kubler-Ross concurs that people will experience five states when dying: anger, denial, depression, bargaining, and acceptance. Michael Christofer thoroughly depicts his characters to be experiencing, at one time, four of these stages. But the first stage, anger, Christofer seems to have some trouble with. All the characters show anger sometime throughout the play, but the way in which they show it is through the use of profanity. Christofer has even gone to the extent of allowing the character of Steven, a fourteen year old—in East Central's production this part is played by Jim Spencer—to use four letter words continuously. The language of the play does not necessarily take away from the intensity of the drama, but it does limit the audience in that the director of East Central's production, John Galyean, is promoting this play "for mature audiences only."

Although the playwright and director may have made a mistake in the use of the profane language—Christofer for his choice of words and Dr. Galyean for keeping the language in his production at ECU—both were right on target with their character choices. Christofer makes his characters believable and extremely interesting, and Galyean keeps with the playwright's intent by choosing very competent actors/actresses to capture the range of emotions the playwright invented.

There is not a weak member in this cast. Each character is fully believable. At one time, each of the three cottages steals the play. Cottage Three captures the audience's attention toward the beginning of the play with Felicity's rendition of the popular song, "Every Breath You Take." Felicity is portrayed by Holly Lamb. Cottage Three again has the audience on the edge of their seats when Agnes, played by Rose Mary Martinez, relates the missing pieces to the lives of the characters in this cottage. Cottage Two spellbinds the audience also from the beginning because of the nature of the relationship between Mark, played by Jerry Bryant, and Brian, played by John S. Murray. The intrigue of this cottage is enhanced by the promiscuous lifestyle of Brian's ex-wife Beverly, played by Ranae Wade. Cottage One waits until near the end of the play to captivate the audience. Mike Langley playing Joe and Elizabeth Kenley portraying Maggie capture all the poignancy Christofer intended in a moving scene that touches the audience to the point of tears. Throughout the play, the cast acts not as individual players but as a moving, workable ensemble.

The set designed by ECU Technical Director David Schallhorn is as subtle as the actors' interpretation. Because of the platforms of each cottage, a distance is set between the families in each cottage. But because the actors conjunctively use an extended lip of the stage as an interview area, a sense of unity between cottages is developed.

From the moment the fitting overture, "The Twelfth of Never," begins to the ending black-out, the audience is drawn into a sense of wonderment. All in all, ECU's production of *The Shadow Box* is considered to be a very thought-provoking play done with extreme skill. This production is highly recommended "for mature audiences only."

SAMPLE BOOK REVIEW

By Veronica McCabe Deschambault

Breathing Lessons

In 1985, Pulitzer-Prize winning author Larry McMurtry wrote in a review of Anne Tyler's novel *The Accidental Tourist* that "She is steadily raising a body of fiction of major dimensions."

Tyler's eleventh novel, *Breathing Lessons* (Alfred A. Knopf: New York, 1988), was favorably received by critics. Those who considered it her best work to date were not surprised when it received the Pulitzer Prize for fiction in 1989. *Breathing Lessons* is a bittersweet story focusing on forty-eight-year-old Maggie Moran coming to terms with life and marriage.

The entire novel takes place in a single day. It's not a "day-in-the-life" story but rather a "life-in-the-day" kind of work. In this book we follow Maggie Moran through a single Saturday and see her whole life through flashbacks.

Maggie is "not a straight line kind of person," as one character describes her. She's easily distracted by incidental people and events. Her life is dominated by tangents. The novel reveals that neither is life a straight line kind of progression. It twists and turns and knots as it passes.

The story line of *Breathing Lessons* "twists and turns and knots" as it entertains you in the process. It is full of unexpected twists, turns of events, as well as knots that create suspense. You are never quite sure how the novel will end.

Breathing Lessons is set in Baltimore, the setting for most of Tyler's novels. Maggie Moran and her husband, Ira, leave early one morning to attend the funeral of Max Gill, the husband of Maggie's best friend from high school, Serena. The funeral is central to the plot, and Tyler skillfully interweaves the past with the present, death with life, as well as life with marriage. Serena chooses to invite all her old high school friends to Max's memorial service and arranges to have them reenact key parts of the wedding ceremony that united she and Max 30 years before.

The wedding had been a 1960s affair, full of popular music performed by their friends and readings from *The Prophet* by Kahlil Gibran. Serena's wedding had a special significance for Ira and Maggie. They had sung "Love Is a Many Splendored Thing" that day and had become informally engaged. Thirty years later, Ira refuses to sing with Maggie at Max's funeral. Maggie's mind races back across the years and traces the changes her marriage has seen.

All the marriages in the book are less than perfect, although Maggie tries to gloss this over. Maggie's tendency is to romanticize her circumstances and deny the shortcomings of her own life and the people she loves. Her indomitable optimism makes her a meddler as she attempts to orchestrate the lives of those around her to meet her need for a perfect world inhabited by loving, kindhearted people.

So it is that after the funeral in Deer Lick, Pa., Maggie coaxes Ira to take a detour to Cartwheel, Pa., where their granddaughter and former daughter-in-law, Fiona, live. Maggie is convinced that she heard Fiona on a radio talk show earlier that morning saying she had married the first time for love but would marry the second time for security.

Fiona had married the Moran's son, Jesse, when she was 17 and pregnant with his child. Jesse, a high school dropout with illusions of making it as a rock and roll singer, drifted from job to job, purposeless and listless. His marriage to Fiona had been a fiasco that lasted less than two years, during which time he and Fiona had lived with his parents.

Ira, ever practical, sees his son, then and now, as a failure. Maggie, ever a romantic, sees Jesse as a talented, good-hearted boy, lacking confidence. In her memory, Jesse and Fiona's marriage had been magical and special, and she clumsily tries to affect a reconciliation between the two despite the fact that they've been divorced for six years. The last third of the book is devoted to her efforts to reconcile the marriage.

In *Breathing Lessons,* Tyler renders Maggie's character with a certain tenderness. We forgive Maggie's lack of logic, her meddling, and her white lies because her goal is to bring her family together and to make the world a more loving, compassionate place than it is. Ira is a good foil for Maggie. His grim determination to accept his lot in life contrasts with Maggie's optimism.

Serena also functions to dispel Maggie's romantic notions. It is Serena who tells Maggie that marriage isn't a Doris Day–Rock Hudson movie, that people don't get married because they love one person more than anyone else, but because they love someone and are tired of being single. Serena is the first to say that parenthood may not be worth the effort, and grandchildren are hardly a comfort.

Through Ira and Serena's observations, Tyler seems to be saying that modern family units are fraught with frailties, and we shouldn't expect too much from the people we love and life in general. Her characters fumble through life, are frequently detoured, and don't quite know what they want. In the book's title, Tyler seems to indicate that when it comes to living, there are no experts, that even something as simple as breathing doesn't always come naturally.

The title is drawn from a passage where Maggie tells the young bride Fiona how lucky she is to be taking Lamaze classes and getting breathing lessons:

"My first pregnancy, there wasn't a course to be found, and I was scared to death. I'd have loved to take lessons! And afterward: I remember leaving the hospital with Jesse and thinking, 'Wait. Are they going to let me just walk off with him? I don't know beans about babies! I don't have a license to do this. Ira and I are just amateurs.' I mean you're given all these lessons for the unimportant things—piano-playing, typing. You're given years and years of lessons in how to balance equations, which Lord knows you will never have to do in normal life. But how about parenthood? Or marriage, either, come to think of it. Before you can drive a car you need a state-approved course of instruction, but driving a car is nothing, nothing, compared to living day in and day out with a husband and raising up a new human being."

Yet Maggie and Ira, Jesse and Fiona, Max and Serena and all the other characters of this novel manage to make it through. The novel is both funny and sad, and in the end, hopeful. Maggie ponders in the final chapter what she and Ira are going to do for the rest of their lives.

Tyler provides the answer by describing Ira's solitaire game. He is past the part where any number of moves are possible. Now he faces the most interesting part of the game, where the choices are narrower and require real skill and judgment.

As you read *Breathing Lessons,* you will be reminded through Tyler's understated prose and deftly drawn characters that though life isn't always what you expect it to be, it's always interesting and sometimes fun.

Tyler's novel is a sure hit with those readers who like to explore the subtleties of family relationships. Her characters are believable and unforgettable. Her crisp writing style makes for easy reading. Spending a weekend reading *Breathing Lessons* is a lesson in itself: the finer things in life are often deceptively simple and ordinary.

SAMPLE MUSIC REVIEW

By Jim Miller

"Chicago/19"

The band that will never say die. No matter how old the members are, and no matter how many times the faces in the group change, they continue to produce good music. This seemingly ageless band is Chicago; and their latest album is "Chicago/19."

The album is so titled because it is the nineteenth LP release for the group. It is also their second album since former lead singer Peter Cetera left the group to pursue a solo career.

Even without the silky tenor vocals of Cetera at the lead, Chicago continues to produce ballads and love songs that grip the heart. The first single release from the album, "I Don't Wanna Live Without Your Love," and the number one smash "Look Away" are living proof that lead vocalist and keyboard player Bill Champlin can handle the job.

Chicago throws in their usual taste of positive, up-tempo cuts with "Heart in Pieces" (by far the best cut of the non-ballads), "I Stand Up," and "You're Not Alone," another top ten smash.

The newest member of Chicago, bassist Jason Scheff, also adds his talents with his vocals, contributing to the very Cetera-sounding "We Can Last Forever."

The brass section sounds as fresh as ever. Lee Loughnane on the trumpet, James Pankow on trombone, and saxophonist Walt Parazaider are three long-time members of Chicago who continue to add the "class of the brass" in songs like "I Stand Up" and "Come In From The Night."

Lead singer and keyboardist Robert Lamm co-writes most of the material along with Champlin. Lamm is one of the original members of the group, as well as drummer Danny Seraphine.

If you like Chicago's ballads, the good music doesn't stop with the cuts released for radio airplay. "Victorious" and "What Kind Of Man Would I Be?" are also enjoyable.

If you are a Chicago fan, you will love "Chicago/19." If you are not a Chicago fan, you might still like the brassy rock style of "the band that will never die."

Project Assignment

To gain the most from this project, your instructor will either assign or allow you to sign up for specific books or events to review. Some people will review books, some will review plays, some will review concerts, and some will review films. Review the essentials for all critical response reviews and your specific type of review. Study the art form so that you have a broad background for creating your review. Then read your book or attend your play, concert, or film. Make notes as soon as possible following completion of the second phase. Finally, prepare and present your critical response review to the class.

Your instructor may add requirements to the assignment, such as try to get your audience members to see the play, concert, or film, or to read the book. Make sure you check all requirements before beginning.

References

Ayres, J. & Miller, J. (1990). *Effective Public Speaking.* (3rd ed.). Dubuque, Iowa: Wm. C. Brown Company, Publisher.

Minnick, W. C. (1983). *Public Speaking.* (2nd ed.). Boston: Houghton Mifflin Company.

Newsom, D. & Wollert, J. A. (1985). *Media Writing: News for the Mass Media.* Belmont, California: Wadsworth Publishing Company.

Ward, H. H. (1985). *Professional Newswriting.* San Diego, California: Harcourt Brace Jovanovich.

Zinsser, W. (1980). *On Writing Well* (2nd ed.). New York: Harper & Row, Publishers.

PROJECT 36

Presenting and Accepting a Gift or Award

Nothing places one ahead of other men so quickly or surely as the ability to address an audience effectively.
—Lowell Thomas

Whenever someone receives an award or gift, someone must make the presentation; whenever you receive an award or gift, you must respond. In public situations the presenter needs to say more than "here's your award (gift)." When you receive an award or gift publicly, the situation demands that you say more than a "thank-you." Both the presenter and the recipient of a gift or award should concentrate on communicating sincerity. The person or group of persons making the presentation should communicate the message of honor and appreciation to the recipient. The recipient should communicate heart-felt honor at receiving the recognition and honor bestowed upon him or her.

It is not easy to make a public presentation graciously and utter thoughts that symbolize the spirit of the event. Neither is it easy to accept an honor graciously when you are surprised. This project presents the principles of presenting and accepting a gift or award so you can be prepared and thus avoid embarrassment when you are called upon to be either a presenter or a recipient of a gift or award.

Principles of the Presentation Speech

Generally, the presentation speech is a short, sincere, commendatory speech. In this type of speech audience analysis is very important, especially if there has been competition or rivalry in seeking the award. Your task is to understand the feelings of audience members, avoid embarrassing anyone, and at the same time make the audience feel good about the award and the recipient.

The first principle of presenting a gift or an award is that the presenter talk about the recipient and the recipient's accomplishments that have earned him or her the honor being bestowed. Be as factual as you can, without boring your audience members. Obviously, you can't tell everything the person has ever done, so you focus on the person's achievements related to the honor of the moment. Make your audience members feel that the person is a recipient because he or she deserves the honor, but don't overdo it. Let the deeds of the recipient speak for the recipient without undue embellishment or without slighting any significant accomplishments.

Second, the award or gift needs to be presented within some context. In some situations your audience members will not understand the occasion or significance of an award or gift. As the presenter, you are responsible for providing the appropriate context for the presentation. In other instances people may have lost track of the reasons or the real *honor* behind an award. For example, student organizations may have awards named in honor of people who have retired, are deceased, or have moved away from the school. When the significance of the name and award are not immediately apparent to your audience members or the recipient, you must explain the significance, the status, previous honorees (if they are well known), and so on.

You may even need to honor the donor of an award. Sometimes a person, a family, or a corporation sponsors a competition for an award. Or the award is named in honor of a person or group. In either case a part of the presentation should be devoted to recognizing the donor of the award and the significance of the donor to the community, your program, and so on.

Occasions for the presentation speech vary. A prize may have been won in a contest. In this instance the prize, and perhaps the winner, is known beforehand. For this reason, there is no surprise element involved. On other occasions there will be expectancy, uncertainty, and even divided opinions among the judges regarding the winner. For example, we sometimes make awards for superior accomplishments, scholarships, and other contests. This poses a delicate problem for you as the presenter. To help your audience members and those who may have competed for these awards accept the decision gracefully, you should emphasize and stress the careful consideration given by the judges and their difficult position. Sometimes multiple awards can be bestowed to symbolize the merits of several recipients without diminishing the value of the award.

Another occasion for a presentation is the giving of an object to a person or to an organization such as a school, church, city, society, or other group. On such an occasion the whole atmosphere is formal. An example of one such occasion is the presentation of a memorial to a church. The ceremony is ritualistic; the procedures, plans, and persons who are to participate are known long before the actual donation takes place. There is no surprise and the speech itself serves to emphasize the symbolism or the utility of the gift.

Still another occasion involves awarding a medal or other recognition for service. An example of this type of award is "student of the year" or "teacher of the year" in a particular school or state, or within an organization. Business organizations sometimes honor an employee's record of achievement with an "employee of the month/year" award or recognize an employee's years of service to the organization. On these occasions there may or may not be a surprise element. Depending on the occasion and the type of recognition, there may be much emotion. The ceremony and the speech itself should not make it difficult for the recipient. Don't let the sentiment involved obscure the gift or award.

A final occasion of a presentation combines an award for services with a farewell. Surprise is often present on these occasions. There is no rivalry, but rather good fellowship and possibly a little sadness. Occasions for this kind of presentation are the retirement of a long-time member from a society, a school, or a civic organization, the leave-taking of a pastor, and the departure of any prominent citizen from a community or a group service. On this occasion place emphasis on the happy side of joyous fellowship. Express some regret for the departure of the person, but also express hope for the future either in retirement joy or for success in a new location.

Preparing the Presentation Speech

First, prepare yourself concerning the occasion and the circumstances surrounding or governing the presentation. If the occasion is formal and ritualistic, be sure you know the ritual and your part in the ritual; if it is to be informal and personal, personalize your presentation. Remember: It is an *honor* to present a gift or award. Do your homework well, and you will probably be invited to make other presentations; do your job poorly, and it may be your last such honor. By all means, observe proper speech construction rules and *never* attempt to make a speech regarding your pet peeve or favorite topic. This is someone else's time of honor— honor the other person.

Second, in preparing your speech, keep in mind the award and what it means as well as the recipient and why he or she deserves the award. Do not overpraise the individual but pay *deserving* tribute to the recipient. Be careful not to overemphasize the award or its value. Stress instead the work or honor the award signifies. Let glory abide in *achievement,* not in the *material object.*

Briefly, your specific organization of ideas may fall into the following sequence. First, make appropriate remarks to your audience; let these remarks refer to the occasion that brought the group together and the significance of the occasion. Next, give a short history of the event or award and its origin and standards. The body of your presentation should emphasize the virtues or accomplishments of the recipient of the award, show appreciation to any donor(s) for the gift or award, and describe or show the gift or award. Then state the immediate reasons for the award and show that, regardless of its value, it is only a *token* of the real appreciation of the service rendered or the esteem felt for the recipient. As for the recipient, recount his or her personal worth and tell how it was recognized or discovered. If you know him or her personally, mention the fact that you are intimately aware of his or her service or merit.

Finally, explain the character and purpose of the gift or award. Should it be a picture or statue, the custom is to have it veiled until the speech is concluded and then at the proper moment withdraw the veil. If the gift or award is to be presented to an organization, be sure someone is informed ahead of time that he or she is to represent the organization in receiving the gift. Then call the recipient forward with words of congratulations for his or her achievements.

Delivering the Presentation Speech

Be sure the award or gift is available and ready to be presented. When the moment arrives for you to make the presentation, call the recipient to the platform, if it is not to be a surprise announcement. If the award is to be a surprise announcement, wait to call the recipient forward until the conclusion of your presentation speech. If the competition for the award has been a rivalry, begin by talking about the award and its significance, then make the announcement of the winner. When the recipient is standing at the speaker's stand, present the gift in a few well-chosen words, summarizing the reasons that this person is the recipient of the award. No one wants to hear a long speech of presentation, so be brief. Mention the appropriateness of the award and offer the recipient good wishes for the future. As soon as the presentation is completed, give the recipient time to respond to the award or make other remarks concerning the occasion. It is best to step upstage and then sit down while the recipient responds.

Observe the following technicalities: (1) Be sure you stand so the audience can see and hear you—front and center is the best position. (2) Do not stand in front of the gift or award. Your audience members came to see, let them see the presentation and the award. (3) Near the end of your speech, when you are ready to make the presentation, pick up the award, and carefully hold it so that it is clearly visible to everyone. (4) Stand with your side turned slightly toward the audience. Without presenting a total profile to your audience members, you need to direct yourself toward the recipient. (5) In giving the award to the recipient, use the hand nearest the recipient (the upstage hand). You don't want to "cover" the recipient with your hand. This also allows the recipient to accept the gift with the upstage hand. If the award is a medal you are to pin on a coat or dress, stand with your side turned to the audience while pinning it on. Never turn your back to your audience members as that will totally block most of them from seeing the "pinning." If the award is a picture, statue, or other object that cannot be transferred from hand to hand, show it or unveil it at the moment of presentation. Be sure you are standing to the side again, so your audience members can see the object you are presenting.

SAMPLE PRESENTATION SPEECH

By Krista Williams

Best Technician Award

Fellow students and faculty:

Each year at this time we give an award to someone for being a technician on our plays. Being the best technician means using your creativity to design sets, design lighting schemes, and to set the sound cues. At East Central University, that involves five to six productions per year.

This year's recipient has done all of these tasks for all five productions during the 1988–89 production season. In addition, he helped construct most of the sets (not one of his regular duties). He also set the lights for all five of our productions, in addition to designing the lighting schemes, and he helped produce the sound tracks for most of the productions.

Using his own creativity and the directors' instructions (and this year we had four different directors) he prepared all of the designs. In addition, this year's Best Technician winner also performed in two of the productions.

It should come as no surprise to most of you that this year's Best Technician Award goes to George Enfield. George, this plaque is but a small token of our appreciation for the work you have done all year. I know the plaque and this award can never compensate you for the many hours you have put into our theatre season. But without you and your dedication to these tasks, we could never have had the successful season that we did. Thanks for your creativity and your hard, dedicated work.

Principles of the Acceptance Speech

When you receive a gift or award, the group bestowing the honor want to hear more than a mere "thank-you." If your response is too brief it will sound as if you are saying, "I *deserve* this award and I'm glad you finally realized it." On the other hand, a lengthy acceptance speech will sound as if you are trying to *justify* being the recipient of the award.

Your acceptance speech must be a sincere expression of your appreciation of the honor bestowed on you. Your speech should establish you as a friendly, modest, and worthwhile individual to whom the people bestowing the honor may rightfully pay tribute for merit and achievement. The primary purpose should be to impress the donors with your worthiness and to make them happy in their choice. You do this by speaking from your heart. This is no time for artificial or hollow remarks uttered only because you think your audience members expect something.

There are three distinct aspects of the acceptance speech that are essential to include. First, you must thank the person or group of persons who have decided to honor you. It doesn't matter if you have been chosen by a single judge, a panel, or an entire organization, you need to respond to those who had a hand in the honor. Sometimes you may need to thank a donor organization and a selection committee in addition to the person or group who make the presentation.

Second, you need to acknowledge others who have helped you earn the award. No one ever is solely responsible for any achievement. There are always people who have helped and supported you as you worked toward a goal. In thanking these people, be cautious that you thank only those people who are most responsible or you can sound like the Academy Award recipient who thanked her mother, her father, her grandparents, her teachers, her fellow actors and actresses, her directors, producer, makeup person, hairdresser, her husband, and her children. While all these people may be important and significant in her life, they were not all equally responsible for her winning the Academy Award. Select only the most significant people who contributed to your success. Likewise, it is not necessary to point out the specific contributions of each person, but sometimes it is nice for your audience members to know that a particular person they know has made a significant contribution to your achievement.

Finally, put the award on a personal basis. You will want to tell your audience members what it means to you to receive the honor, both now and in the future. Be sincere! Do not pretend that the award is much more important or significant than it really is. Likewise, do not try to minimize its importance. Let your audience members know how you genuinely feel about your honor.

Preparing an Acceptance Speech

On some occasions you will deliver the acceptance speech impromptu. On those occasions when you do not know that you will receive the award, you cannot prepare and must speak from your knowledge of acceptance speeches. If you know in advance, or even suspect that you will receive a gift or award, or when you have been in competition for an honor, you need to prepare a speech of acceptance. Be assured that every nominee for an Academy Award has prepared an acceptance speech, but only one person in each category gets to present the speech. The important point here is that you be prepared to speak on those occasions when you are aware that you may receive an award or an honor. To plan to speak impromptu invites a hasty, ill-prepared speech that may do you more harm than good.

When you prepare your acceptance speech, follow all the principles of good speech construction and organization. In addition, follow these suggestions:

1. *Use simple language.* Elaborate and flowery language will make you sound pretentious.
2. *Avoid trite language and clichés.* Clichés suggest that you either have a "canned" speech or you can't do any original thinking. In this speech you need to make your audience members feel that you are genuine and sincere about the honor.
3. *Express a true sense of gratitude and appreciation for the gift or award.* If you are truly surprised you may say so; however, your surprise must be genuine. If you are not surprised, omit any reference to your feeling because the audience will likely not be moved by an attempt at naiveté.
4. *Modestly disclaim all the credit for winning the award.* Give credit to those most instrumental in assisting you, for without them you could not have achieved your success. Praise their cooperation and support.
5. *Never apologize for winning or disclaim your worthiness for the award.* Inasmuch as you were selected to receive the tribute, be big enough to accept it modestly and graciously, but do not grovel.
6. *Remember to express your appreciation for the beauty and the significance of the gift.* It's nature will naturally determine what you say. Do not overpraise or overvalue it, just observe suitable restraint.
7. *Never express disappointment.* It should never be disappointing to receive a gift or award. Even if you think the award or gift should have been bigger, better, or more, you should accept it in the spirit in which it is presented.
8. *Conclude your remarks by speaking of your plans or intentions for the future.* It is especially important to mention your plans as they are connected with the award or gift. In a final word, you may repeat your thanks for the object or recognition.

Delivering an Acceptance Speech

The first principle of the acceptance speech is to be brief. Just as the presentation needs to be brief, so, too, must be the acceptance speech. If you carry on too long, you may be considered conceited and egotistical. Your attitude at this moment must be one of sincerity, friendliness, appreciation, modesty, and warm enthusiasm. Just don't let your enthusiasm consume you and let you make a fool of yourself. Be personal if the award is for you. If you represent a group of people, use the pronoun "we" instead of "I."

When the donor calls your name, either go to the platform or stand and move toward the speaker if you are already on the platform. If you approach from the audience, move alertly, neither rushing nor loitering to speak with people on the way. Let your bearing be one of appreciation for what is to come. On the platform, stand near the donor but avoid viewing the award anxiously or reaching for it before it is extended to you. Do not stand in front of it. Remember, your audience members have come to see the award as much as they have come to see you receive the award. Don't block their opportunity to see what they have come for.

In accepting the award, stand slightly sideways toward the audience, reach for and take the award with the hand nearest the donor (the upstage hand); in this way you will avoid reaching across yourself or turning away from your audience members. Remember, they came to see the presentation—let them have their moment also. After receiving your award, hold it so it remains in full view of your audience members. If it is too large to hold, place it in an appropriate spot on the stage and step to one side and begin your speech. Be sure you face your audience members while you speak; you may glance or nod to the object, but focus your attention on your audience members as they should be the object of your attention at the moment. To do otherwise may convey a lack of sincerity.

Carry your award in your hand as you return to your seat. Keep your award available for others to see after the ceremony is finished. There are likely to be several members of the donor group who have not had the opportunity to see your award. Be pleased to show the award and share your joy with members of the donor organization.

As to the speech itself, observe all the principles of acceptable stage presence. Be dressed appropriately, maintain an alert posture, and speak clearly, distinctly, and loudly enough to be heard by all. If your speech is impromptu, you will not be expected to have the fluency of one who has been forewarned. If you have been forewarned, make sure you are able to speak fluently about the award and its meaning for you. Let your manner express undeniable friendliness and appreciation for the honor accorded you.

Sincerity is the most important quality of your speech. It must be evident in your voice, your bodily actions, your gestures, the expression on your face, everything about you. Do not be afraid of a little emotion, especially if the honor is a surprise; just control it so you can maintain your dignity and not be overcome by emotion. Make no apologies for your speaking. Avoid awkward positions that are indicative of too much self-consciousness. Follow these guidelines, and your acceptance speech will be genuine and applauded by all who see and hear you.

SAMPLE ACCEPTANCE SPEECH

By Krista Williams

Summers Scholarship

Although I haven't been a student in this department very long, I have come to know the significance of the various awards that are given every year. I know that the Dorothy I. Summers Scholarship is one of the top awards given for students involved in teacher education and/or theatre. It means to me that you liked what I have done and want me to continue. But receiving the Summers Scholarship means more to me than just receiving a scholarship. The Summers Scholarship represents a personal achievement for me.

Dr. Summers' reputation as an excellent teacher and Director of Theatre has been a major inspiration for many of us. It is especially inspiring for me because we basically come from the same roots. Some of you may know that I went to Wewoka High School. I recently learned that Dr. Summers began her teaching career in Wewoka many years ago. In fact, some friends of my parents remember when Dr. Summers was there and the reputation she began for good theatre in Wewoka.

In receiving this scholarship, I hope I can live up to the high standards set and demanded by Dr. Summers, so she will be proud of my efforts and our common roots. Thank you Dr. Summers for setting an example for us to follow, and thank you also to all of you who voted to bestow this honor on me. I promise I won't let you down. Next year will be a banner year for me!

Project Assignment

This is a two-part assignment. First, prepare a speech of presentation for an award or honor for one of your classmates. Your instructor may wish to pair you so you know of the presentation ahead of time, or you may not be told of the presentation ahead of time. You may not know until the moment your name is called that you will be the recipient of a gift or award, in which case you may practice impromptu speaking. As your name is called for the award, rise and present a speech of acceptance. All speeches should be brief, but should be between two and five minutes.

References

Capp, G. R., Capp, C. C., & Capp, G. R., Jr. (1990). *Basic Oral Communication* (5th ed.). Englewood Cliffs, New Jersey: Prentice-Hall, Inc.

DeVito, J. A. (1990). *The Elements of Public Speaking.* (4th ed.). New York: Harper & Row, Publishers.

Hunt, G. T. (1981). *Public Speaking.* Englewood Cliffs, New Jersey: Prentice-Hall, Inc.

Lucas, S. E. (1989). *The Art of Public Speaking* (3rd ed.). New York: Random House.

Myers, G. E. & Myers, M. T. (1978). *Communicating When We Speak* (2nd ed.). New York: McGraw-Hill Book Company.

Stone, J. & Bachner, J. (1977). *Speaking Up, A Book for Every Woman Who Wants to Speak Effectively.* New York: McGraw-Hill Book Company.

Thompson, W. N. (1978). *Responsible and Effective Communication.* Boston: Houghton Mifflin Company.

Verderber, R. F. (1988). *The Challenge of Effective Speaking* (7th ed.). Belmont, California: Wadsworth Publishing Company.

PROJECT **37**

The Welcome Speech and Response

The way to gain a good reputation is to try to be what you desire to appear.
—Socrates

The speech of welcome is one of the most common and most used special occasion speeches. You will use it whenever you want to greet guests or welcome a group of your organization's members to an official function. You will generally want to comment on the importance of this gathering and the benefits for all present. A second occasion for such a speech is to welcome new members to your group. On these occasions, you are more concerned with one or a few new members than you are in the one special guest or the entire group present.

When you are welcomed publicly, it is usually expected that you make some sort of response appropriate to the occasion. Both the welcome and the response are goodwill or public relations speeches that may have great bearing on the success or failure of a venture. This project presents the principles of the welcome and response, how to prepare and present each speech, as well as sample welcome and response speeches.

Principles of the Welcome Speech

The basic purpose of the welcome speech is to make a public acknowledgment of the presence of a guest, or guests, or to make people feel welcome at a particular gathering. It has the double purpose of making people known to each other and putting people at ease with one another. If you have never attended a public event to which you were not "welcomed," you may know the uneasiness of not knowing whether you were welcome. On the other hand, in those situations where you have been welcomed publicly, you know your presence is wanted and appreciated. This special speech is partly informative and partly persuasive. You are informing your guests that you want them to be present, and at the same time you are persuading them that they are welcome.

Your speech should make your guests feel that they are sincerely wanted and that the host or hosts are delighted in their presence. The warmest kind of hospitality should be expressed. You need to be sincere and reflect in your speech a spirit of gladness because your guests are present. This speech is characterized by brevity, simplicity, geniality, and sincerity. To violate these expectations invites criticism and possible chastisement from others involved in your organization or in the planning for the day's events. You could even invoke the wrath of those you intend to make feel welcome.

As the presenter of a welcome speech, it is important for you to remember that you *represent* a group of people and are speaking on their behalf. Because you do not speak for yourself only, you must make clear for whom you speak and acknowledge that the welcome comes on behalf of all your group's members. It is easy to get caught up in the spirit of the occasion and think you are more important than you really are. On the occasion of the welcome speech, you are simply speaking for everyone and creating a feeling of welcome for all persons present. Above all, you must show your friendliness and hospitality toward your guests.

As a part of your welcome, you need to relate your guests to your audience members, and vice versa. To do this, tell a little about your guests and the occasion and/or organization to which they are being welcomed. You don't need a complete biographical sketch, but the major qualities or accomplishments that have brought the two entities together should be related. If your guest is to be a speaker later, don't steal the introduction speech as a welcome speech—your purpose is to welcome all parties to the event, not present a guest to be a speaker. Note the differences in the purposes of these two distinctly different tasks and review Project 31 to avoid overstepping your boundaries.

A common element of welcome speeches is a statement of expected outcomes from the meeting. Generally, both the guests and the hosts at a major function will benefit in some way from joining together. It is a part of the welcome to express hope for mutual benefit. If the benefit is not generally known, or is not readily understood by your audience members, you may have to suggest the mutual benefit you hope to accomplish.

Occasions for the welcome speech may be extremely varied. It may be a reception for a distinguished visitor, a returning native son or daughter, a total stranger, or a new citizen or group member. If an organization is honored, the welcome may be to a delegation such as a booster club or a group of community representatives. Often a welcome is extended to members of a conference or convention, and to participants in tournaments, meets, and contests.

Some topics suitable for welcome speeches include:

1. A government official visiting your city
2. A booster club visiting your city
3. A new minister's arrival in town
4. A diplomat visiting your city
5. A well-known person joining your organization
6. A conference meeting in your city
7. A nearby city sends a delegation to visit your town
8. A native son or daughter returning home
9. A scholastic meet being held on your campus
10. A stranger visiting your organization

Preparing a Welcome Speech

First, determine your specific purpose—that is, who is being welcomed to what. Your task is to make your guests glad to be where they are and to make all the hosts know you have spoken on their behalf in making your guests feel welcome. You should make everyone admire your hospitality. Second, collect your information and organize your speech. If necessary, explain what your organization represents and mention its character and the work it is doing. You may also relate points of interest about your organization and its future plans.

The body of your speech should be a tribute to your guests for their work. Be sure you tell of the advantages gained by your organization because your guests are visiting you. Note who the guests are, where they come from, and whom they represent. Explain briefly what the presence of your guests means and comment on the common interests between your guests and your organization. Sometimes you may want to mention special events that will be held for your guests, special accommodations such as lounges, lunches, cars, rooms or equipment available, and objects or sites to see and visit in your community.

As you conclude your welcome, speak of the occasion, its present enjoyment, and its future importance. You may want to mention the mutual benefit of both your guests and the hosts here and present a hope for great success. Invite your guests to feel fully at home in your community. Note that not all of the material included here will be presented in every welcome speech. Use only what is appropriate for your specific occasion, and adjust it to meet your situation. Make your remarks brief and pertinent. No one wants to sit very long to be welcomed. The main events that are to proceed should not be held up while you express your feelings about the event. Under no circumstances should you steal the thunder of the main attraction.

Presenting a Welcome Speech

Let the occasion govern your presentation. If the occasion is formal, act and speak appropriately; if it is informal, adjust yourself and your remarks accordingly. In either case be sincere and genuine. Feel what you say and say it enthusiastically! Give to your guests the same friendliness you express when you open the door of your home to a friend. Your language should be simple, vivid, and without slang and redundancy.

You should be prepared to make your welcome extemporaneously. You could ruin a perfectly good welcome speech by reading it or referring to notes. If you are genuine and sincere in your feelings of welcome, you will know the person by name, rank, title, position, and so on, and be able to pronounce all the words correctly. You will also know how this person and his or her visit relates to your audience members. If these are not common knowledge to you as a member of the welcoming group, you probably are not the right person to be making the welcome.

SAMPLE WELCOME SPEECH

By Robbin Gilbreath

Welcome

Good evening, ladies.

Tonight we welcome a very important guest to our Ladies Acting Association Club. As you know, we have been working for several years to bring a well-known actress to our club for a special meeting. We could have acquired any number of actresses over this period of time, but we were looking for someone special, someone who had credentials like tonight's guest. And if you want something good, you sometimes have to wait a little while for it.

I'm very glad we were patient enough and had the insight to seek tonight's guest beginning several years ago. Can you imagine having your calender filled for the next three years? Tonight's guest has had her calender filled for at least three years, and will not be available again until 1993. Some of us think we are busy, but I know my schedule is not filled for that long. So, you can imagine our extreme pleasure that we were fortunate enough to have the opportunity to get our guest to appear in Ada, Oklahoma at all.

Not only is our guest busy working on films of the caliber of her two Academy Award winners, "The French Lieutenant's Woman" and "Sophie's Choice," but she is also busy working on her favorite charities, and speaking and conducting workshops around the country and around the world. Tonight's session is only one of a series of such sessions she is conducting over the next several months. We are truly the beneficiaries of this woman's great talent. We will be learning not only about our common interest in quality theater for this area, but we will also be working on expanding our horizons with our common charity.

As we welcome you to our club tonight, Miss Streep, we are pleased to make you an honorary member of our small and humble group. And so that you can feel totally at home here, we invite you to stop in and attend any of our meetings. If you let us know a few minutes ahead of time, we can even arrange to bake a cake or a few cookies and put the coffee pot on.

Ladies, join with me in welcoming to our club, the very talented and gracious actress, Miss Meryl Streep.

Principles of the Response to a Welcome

Occasions for the speech in response to a welcome may arise any time a welcome is given, although a speech in response is not always necessary. The speech in response is simply a reply to the greeting expressed by your host. Its purpose is to cement goodwill and friendship and to express the good feelings that exist between the guest and the hosts. Briefly, respond to the welcome, express your gratitude at being at the meeting, conference, or other event, and express your hope for the same mutual benefits expressed in the welcome.

The response to a welcome is brief, courteous, and friendly. Often the response is presented impromptu because you do not know exactly how your hosts will handle the welcoming situation. The impromptu aspect of this speech places a burden of fast thinking and logical talking on the person who presents it. Sincerity and cordiality are also demands of the response. You want your audience members to know you are truly honored and that you are genuinely glad to be joining this specific group of people at this time, whether it is for a single meeting or for a longer period of time. This implies ability and art in the speaking process. You can't simply stand up and say "thank you" and sit down, you must respond to the situation and the specific statements made in your welcome and acknowledge that you have something to offer this group.

As you respond to the welcome of your hosts, be sure you mention the kindnesses you have been shown, the warmth and hospitality you have felt, and any specific events that have been organized to make you feel welcome and a part of the group. Here you can note special sessions, luncheons, both formal and informal associations you have had, and generally let your audience members know that you appreciate all the special considerations that have been made on your behalf.

Preparing a Speech of Response

First, keep in mind the purpose of your talk—to express your appreciation of the hospitality extended to you and to strengthen mutual feelings of friendship. Second, follow the principles of good speech construction and include an introduction, a body, and a conclusion. Make your speech brief. As in welcoming speeches, this speech is not the major attraction. Save any comments other than those referring to your hosts and their hospitality for another time and place.

In general, compliments directed to you may be redirected to the occasion. More specifically, your remarks may be developed in the following manner. Address your host and other members of the hosting organization, acknowledge their welcome and the hospitality of their organization. Express your sincere thanks for their courtesies. In some situations you may need to extend greetings from your organization and show how the occasion is mutually advantageous to your host and your own group.

Explain briefly what this meeting means to you and what it symbolizes, if this is pertinent. Mention the benefits to be derived from the attitudes of mutual helpfulness and enjoyment that are evident at this meeting. Predict future pleasant associations with your host's organization and show that this acquaintance is only the beginning of long-lasting cooperation and friendship. Mention in conclusion that you have been made to feel most welcome and at home. Thank your hosts again for their hospitality and any special considerations they have made for you, and extend your best wishes.

Presenting a Speech of Response

Your attitude must be a happy combination of appreciation and friendliness. Your remarks must have the qualities of sincerity and gratitude. When you are presented by your host, rise politely, smile pleasantly, and begin to speak. Accept your responsibility and meet it head on by having something worthwhile to say. Be enthusiastic in your presentation, sincere in your gratitude, and friendly in your attitude. If you truly wish for this meeting to be productive, nothing will establish goodwill with your hosts more than a well-presented response to their welcome.

Avoid any negative comments about accommodations, travel arrangements, and so forth unless their is a humorous side that will show your good sense of humor and establish good rapport with your hosting organization. Never let your audience know that you are anything but appreciative of their kind gestures toward you and their efforts on your behalf to make you feel welcome. If you can't be genuinely appreciative, at least acknowledge the work and efforts of your hosts.

SAMPLE RESPONSE SPEECH

By Jill Reynolds

Welcome Response

Superintendent Kirtley, members of the School Board, Faculty and Student body:

Let me begin by thanking all of your for the warm hospitality my husband and I have received upon our visit to your city and the school campus. As the citizens of your community offered a warm welcome and encouraging smiles, our anxieties about moving and accepting this new assignment were swept away.

My goal as the new Principal of Horace Mann Schools is to provide open communication with all members of the school and the community. Horace Mann is a vital part of this community, and I want the community to play a vital part in the school. I have not taken this position to make drastic changes in your school. My greatest desire is to become an effective member of the school staff and a leader in your community.

My experiences include nine years teaching high school mathematics and five years as a Principal in that school. This change will be a new experience for me. My old school provided me with knowledge, experience, and stability in school administration. I feel that this move will expand my horizons as I join your team and learn about this new system. Not only will I grow as an educator, but I will also grow as a person, and in the process I plan to help Horace Mann continue to be a top educational center in this state.

For the past week, I have attended local functions, settled in my new home, and met some of the finest people in this state. I extend my appreciation to all of you for this opportunity to join your staff. Thank you again for the wonderful welcome to my new home.

Project Assignment

Prepare and present a two- to three-minute speech in which you welcome an individual or a group to your city or campus. You may be asked to present impromptu responses to the speeches of welcome. Your instructor may give you other requirements.

References

Allen, R. R. & McKerrow, R. E. (1985). *The Pragmatics of Public Communication* (3rd ed.) Dubuque, Iowa: Kendall/Hunt Publishing Company.

Ayres, J. & Miller, J. (1990). *Effective Public Speaking* (3rd ed.). Dubuque, Iowa: Wm. C. Brown Company, Publishers.

Bostrom, R. N. (1988). *Communicating in Public.* Santa Rosa, California: Burgess Publishing.

Capp, G. R., Capp, C. C., & Capp, G. R., Jr. (1990). *Basic Oral Communication* (5th ed.). Englewood Cliffs, New Jersey: Prentice-Hall, Inc.

Dance, F. E. X. & Zak-Dance, C. C. (1986). *Public Speaking.* New York: Harper & Row, Publishers.

DeVito, J. A. (1990). *The Elements of Public Speaking* (4th ed.). New York: Harper & Row, Publishers.

Gronbeck, B. E., Ehninger, D., & Monroe, A. H. (1988). *Principles of Speech Communication* (10th brief edition). Glenview, Illinois: Scott, Foresman and Company.

Verderber, R. F. (1988). *The Challenge of Effective Speaking* (7th ed.). Belmont, California: Wadsworth Publishing Company.

PROJECT 38

The Nominating Speech and Acceptance

Sincerity and truth are the basis of all virtue.
—Confucius

All organizations to which you will belong hold elections. When an election is held, people need to be nominated for particular offices. The American political system is predicated on the premise that people will want to fulfill the duties of necessary offices. Because everyone cannot be elected and we generally need to select people to "run" for offices, we need to know the method of placing someone's name in nomination by means of a speech. This project presents the principles of the nomination speech and the acceptance of a nomination, how to prepare and present each of the speeches, and sample speeches.

Principles of the Nominating Speech

A nominating speech is a persuasive effort to place the name of another person before an assembly as a candidate for office. The nominating speech is usually brief, often lasting only a few minutes. In presenting your candidate to your audience members, you should tell them what the qualifications for the office are, and why your candidate is especially fitted for the office in question. All your remarks should set forth, in an orderly manner, the reasons your candidate should be elected. For example, a candidate for president (or other equal title) should be well skilled in leadership and able to lead the group. A nomination speech for this individual should praise the qualities that would enable the nominated person to lead and present his or her general commitment to the goals and objectives of the group.

The nominating speech fulfills the requirements for both informative and persuasive purposes. In your nominating speech your duty (and your objective), is to inform your audience members of the qualities of your candidate that make him or her suitable to fill the office. Your purpose should also be to persuade your audience members to vote for your candidate.

Generally, before a speaker can make a nomination, the chairperson of the assembly must announce that nominations for the office are in order. The speaker must then be recognized by the chairperson. Only after the chairperson has called on you to speak is the nominating speech in order.

Besides the nominations for office, people can also be nominated for awards, tributes, and other recognitions. The procedure for placing a name in nomination are the same as those for nominating someone for an office in an organization. Relate to your audience members what the qualifications for the award, or recognition are, and then present the qualifications of your candidate. For examples of good nominating speeches, look in *Vital Speeches of the Day* for sample speeches for nominating people to be President of the United States. Most of them will follow all the guidelines provided here.

Preparing the Nominating Speech

Because your purpose in presenting the nominating speech is to establish your candidate as the one best suited for the position to be filled, you must set forth the requirements for the office and show that your candidate is the best qualified person for the job. Be specific. Mention such qualifications as training, experience, education, abilities (especially leadership and cooperation with people), and outstanding qualities of personality and character. Make sure the traits you stress are relevant to the office for which you are nominating the person. If your candidate has training and experience in journalism, for example, you would stress those in nominating a person as a reporter for your organization. However, those skills would do little to enhance your candidate's position for treasurer. As the nominator, you are obligated to present your candidate as well qualified to carry out the functions of the office, or as worthy of the honor in the case of an award. Do not place a person's name in nomination if you do not wholeheartedly believe that your candidate is the best qualified for the position.

As you organize your speech, you might use the information about the office and its requirements in your introduction. The body of your speech should consist of your candidate's commitment to your party, to its platform, or to the effectiveness of your organization. Use examples to demonstrate past performances also. Any time you can show that your candidate has had past experience that has been exemplary, or that would qualify him or her for this new position, you should stress it. Conclude your nomination with a statement to the effect that your candidate is undoubtedly the best person for the office. If your candidate is well known, you may present his or her name at the conclusion of your speech. If he or she is not well known, you should present the name early in your speech and mention it again once or twice at appropriate times, and conclude with it. Be cautious that you don't overdo the mentioning of your candidate's name or you could alienate some potential supporters who think you are pushing too much because your candidate is not well qualified.

Presenting the Nominating Speech

Have confidence in yourself and in your candidate. Your audience members can and will sense this. Using appropriate bodily actions, gestures, and posture, give evidence of your poise and confidence. By your fluency and the readiness of your speech, you can tell your audience members that you *know* what you are talking about and that you want them to understand how important it is for the right person (your candidate) to be elected to office. Avoid giving the appearance of overconfidence, overbearance, or conceit.

Have a lively, energetic, unhesitant manner, as well as a pleasant, confident voice, an appropriate appearance, and a sincere desire to communicate. To be most effective, deliver your speech extemporaneously. Your use of notes or a manuscript might suggest that you don't know your candidate well enough or that your candidate needs more support than you have available. Only on special occasions, as in the nomination of a person for the President of the United States, should you use a manuscript delivery.

SAMPLE NOMINATING SPEECH

By Dina Louise Kemper

PTSA President

We are gathered here today with the common purpose of improving the education of our children. There are many problems in our school district. It is disheartening that we cannot afford to keep some of this city's great educators teaching in our schools. Did you know that last year alone we lost ten of our best teachers to larger, more well-funded school districts?

Moreover, this school district cannot afford adequate supplies and textbooks. Every year we are told another story about a class that has to use outdated textbooks (this year it is the second grade readers) or we hear about a class that cannot do a specific lesson because the school does not have the funds for the project. Last spring, my son's class could not have art classes after the middle of March because of the lack of supplies for the entire year.

A leader is needed to orchestrate necessitated changes in our public school system. Therefore, I nominate Mr. Paul Edwards for the Huntsville Chapter of PTSA.

Mr. Edwards has a direct interest in improving our school district because he has three children enrolled in the Huntsville schools. He has also been a lobbyist for fifteen years. His experience should prove beneficial in organizing effective lobbying campaigns for additional school district funds. Moreover, since I have known him, Mr. Edwards has consistently displayed an active concern for the education of our children. It is because of this active concern for improving the quality of our school system that I nominate Mr. Paul Edwards for this presidency of the Huntsville Chapter of the Parent-Teacher-Student Association.

Accepting a Nomination

It is customary that once your name has been placed in nomination for an office, that you present an acceptance speech, acknowledging that you will accept the responsibilities and dutifully carry out the functions of the office for which you have been nominated. Although you many not believe today that you will ever be nominated for an office, or elected to one, you may someday be asked to perform public service. Some of you may even seek nomination for public office. When you do, you will likely be expected to present a speech of acceptance.

If you are nominated for an award, you may not be expected to present a speech of acceptance until you receive the award. For information regarding that speech, see Project 36 on accepting an award. On the other hand, you may be asked to accept the nomination to an office, so you should be prepared to make that type of speech.

Principles of the Acceptance Speech

Briefly, this speech is one in which you publicly accept your nomination to an office. Your speech should firmly establish you as a person of ability, courage, and modesty. It should create confidence in you in the minds of your audience members. Your purpose is to establish this confidence so people will vote for you at the time of the election. Imagine your response to a person who says, "I really don't know why I was nominated for this office. I'm really new here and don't know much about this group. I hope you vote for me." Very few people would vote for a candidate who doesn't seem to inspire self-confidence. Remember, everything you say may be used, *for* you or *against* you.

If you want to be elected to the office for which you have been nominated, inspire people to have confidence in your skills and abilities to perform the duties of the office better than any other candidate. If you do not feel qualified, do not have the time to fulfill the duties of the office, or otherwise feel uncomfortable with your nomination, it is your obligation to tell your audience members that you decline the nomination, and thank your nominator. In some instances you may be nominated for a position for which you do not feel qualified. Do not demean yourself or make apologies. Simply state that you are not prepared at this time to assume the responsibilities of the office for which you have been nominated.

Preparing an Acceptance Speech

Consider the purpose of your speech: *to establish yourself as a leader and to impress people with your capability so they will vote for you.* To accomplish this, you should speak somewhat as follows. Express your appreciation and thanks for the honor conferred upon you. (Never talk about *yourself.*) Speak about the organization, or the position, and its importance. Commend its history, its achievements, and its principles. Explain how these have made it grow and how they will continue to do so in the future. Pay tribute to past great people in the organization. Promise to uphold their ideals. Pledge your loyalty and support to the principles of the organization. Say frankly that you accept the nomination or office with complete realization of its responsibilities and that you intend to carry them out to the best of your abilities. As your final remark, express again your appreciation of the honor conferred upon you.

Here are a few points to keep in mind. Do not belittle yourself or express doubt regarding your fitness. Do not express surprise at your nomination or election. In no way should you let your supporters down by causing them to feel that they have made a mistake. Use simple and sincere language. *Vital Speeches of the Day* will present the acceptance speeches for both candidates for President of the United States. While these examples are for the top elected office in our country, you can see the principles of the acceptance speech in each of them.

Presenting an Acceptance Speech

Your attitude in presenting the acceptance speech should be one of dignity, friendliness, sincerity, and enthusiasm. Be sure your attire is appropriate to the occasion, your audience, and yourself. Talk loudly enough to be heard by all, speak clearly and distinctly, and talk neither too fast nor too slowly. If your voice echoes because of the size of the room, or the presence of a speaker system, slow down. You may even want to read Project 39 for some tips on using the media if that becomes part of your presentation.

Never present yourself in a boastful or bragging manner. Although you will want to present yourself as confident in your abilities and capable of handling the duties of the office for which you have been nominated, you should never set yourself above your audience members. Aloofness may well do you more harm than good in presenting this speech. Humbly accept your nomination, promising to fulfill the duties of the office, as best you can.

SAMPLE ACCEPTANCE SPEECH

By Eddie Paul Hunter

Presidential Acceptance

Mr. Dean and fellow members of the Association:

We have all been a part of this outstanding community for many years. I can remember being a young boy growing up on Green Street with not a care in the world. Some of you grew up with me. Some of the rest of you grew up before I did, and I see a few of you who were somewhat younger than I was. What we all have in common is our concern for the welfare and self-preservation of this community.

I never appreciated school very much until a teacher told me about a man call Plato. He told me that Plato had said, "The direction in which education starts a man will determine his future life." Plato's philosophy really stuck with me then. Later, as a Law Student, I learned of another man, Aristotle. Appropriately enough, he was a student of Plato's. Aristotle said, "Education is the best provision for old age." After studying these philosophies from two of the world's greatest scholars, I started to appreciate education. I also started to look at my education and what we are doing here to educate the students of this community.

Today, I have come up with my own ideas about education and what it means to all of us. To me, good education is essential in both the beginning and the end, which led me to join the cause of fighting for better education. If our students are to compete with the rest of the world of the future, we must offer the best elementary schools in this state, and in this country. At the same time, we must not neglect our secondary schools and colleges and universities. We must offer the best education from beginning to end.

It is this philosophy that led me to join this distinguished group of people interested in improving education standards. It is now both an honor and a privilege to accept the nomination to lead this group during the last decade of this century. What we begin now, will be the ending that our children will have as they begin the next century.

If elected, I will work to continue the efforts begun by Dr. Brooks, our former president. I will continue to work toward improving our educational system so this generation of students will not have the problems that we have seen during our generation. In addition, I will work with other groups of interested individuals who want to improve our educational system so we can be proud of the schools we have as we enter the twenty-first century.

Project Assignment

Prepare and present a brief three- to five-minute nominating speech for one of your classmates. You may use real or imaginary organizations. Your classmate should be selected in advance and prepare an acceptance speech in response to your nomination. Your instructor may establish other requirements for this assignment. Be alert to all your obligations.

References

Bostrom, R. N. (1988). *Communicating in Public.* Santa Rosa, California: Burgess Publishing.

Bradley, B. E. (1988). *Fundamentals of Speech Communication* (5th ed.). Dubuque, Iowa: Wm. C. Brown Company, Publishers.

Dance, F. E. X. & Zak-Dance, C. C. (1986). *Public Speaking.* New York: Harper & Row, Publishers.

Hunt, G. T. (1987). *Public Speaking* (2nd ed.). Englewood Cliffs, New Jersey: Prentice-Hall, Inc.

PROJECT **39**

Radio and Television Speaking

> The most valuable contribution you can give the world is
> a good example.
> —Anonymous

We have all become consumers of the mass media, especially radio and television. In fact, it is difficult for most Americans today to recall a time when there was no radio or television. Today's youth accept radio and television as a way of life, not as a new technology to be marveled or wondered at. Because of its omnipresence in present-day society, the likelihood that you will be interviewed for a radio or television program is great.

One of the greatest uses of radio and television is by businesspeople. Increasing numbers of businesspeople, especially in small towns, are appearing in their own commercials, creating radio jingles, and even appearing on local access cable channels to explain their products, businesses, and organizations. In addition, television cameras have found their way into courtrooms, classrooms, and the pulpits of our churches on a regular basis.

Despite the prevalence of radio and television in all aspects of society, one of the most horrifying experiences for many people is to have a microphone put in front of them or to have a television camera rolling while they talk. Since the opportunities for speaking on radio and television increase daily, and the likelihood that you will be asked to perform in some manner become more pronounced every day, it is advisable that you learn the principles of speaking on radio and television as well as how to prepare and present a radio or television speech.

Principles of Radio and Television Speaking

One of the first principles you must realize as you think about a mass media presentation is that your audience members have much more control over the communication situation than you do. Unlike most other speaking situations, your audience is not a captive one. In face-to-face communication it is unlikely that your audience members will get up to get a drink, get something to eat, or perform other chores while you speak. People rarely sit and focus their undivided attention on radio or television presentations.

In this respect the mass media audience differs significantly from the face-to-face audience. Because your audience members can turn you off (change stations or shut off their sets) if they don't become interested immediately, it is doubly important in this presentation that you *gain* and *maintain* your audience's attention.

Timing is also more important in the media presentation than in a face-to-face encounter. Most radio and television stations have their programs scheduled to the minute, so you cannot be several minutes long or short of your time limits and satisfy the program producers. If you have been allotted ten minutes, that is what the producer has scheduled and if your pacing is off, you may be told to speed up as you speak or to ad-lib remarks if you end too abruptly and need to fill more time.

Another aspect of the media presentation that makes it more difficult than the face-to-face presentation is the lack of feedback. You have no one to cue you in when your ideas are not clear, and usually you hear no laughs or other responses to your attempts at humor, and so on. Generally, during your speeches you have come to expect audience members to respond to these aspects of the speaking situation, and when they are absent, you may pause or become doubtful of the outcomes and waver or change your plan. Be aware that your audience members will not be present to provide immediate feedback for you to adapt to.

In both radio and television speaking you must adjust to using a microphone. In most radio stations you will likely have a microphone that is visible and sits on a desk in front of you. Television stations generally use clip-on microphones that are practically invisible to your audience members. In either case the microphones are very sensitive and should not be shouted into. Be especially cautious while you are wearing the microphone that you don't scratch yourself or brush against the microphone. If you do, it may cause a loud buzzing sound to travel through the studio. It is best to use your normal speaking voice and a conversational tone. Don't mumble, yell, whisper, or try to sound like something you are not. Let the real you show through. A caution worth noting is that when your producer asks for a test for your microphone, don't say, "Testing, one, two, three." That's artificial. You will be much better off to recite a part of what you intend to say—that is real and will more adequately reflect what your voice will sound like. This latter test will also give the engineer a much more accurate reading of your microphone level.

Radio and television presentations should follow the general guidelines for good speaking that you have already learned. That is, you need an introduction, a body, and a conclusion to your presentation. No matter what presentation your audience members hear, they expect to hear a beginning, a middle, and an end. After all, a speech is still a speech, regardless of where it is presented.

The beginning of the radio or television presentation should gain the attention of your audience members, establish you as credible to speak on your topic, establish the importance of your topic, and relate your purpose to your audience, as a minimum. The body of your presentation should develop the details and fulfill the purpose you set forth in your introduction. As in any other speech, you must structure the body of your speech so it is easy to follow and understand. Your conclusion should be a review of the highlights of your speech plus an opportunity for you to leave a lasting impression on your audience members. Notice that the segments do not differ from any other speech—nor does the purpose of any segment of your speech differ. The possible differences are really only matters of degree. It is important for you to gain the immediate attention of your audience members, and your final remarks should make the audience members remember what you have said long after you have finished.

Topics suitable for radio and television speeches include:

1. Educational problems, changes, or advancements
2. Safety
3. Business opportunities

4. Recreational advantages, problems, or changes
5. Public utilities
6. Taxes
7. Services performed by any local group
8. Government spending, new legislation, and so on
9. Health problems and/or senior citizens
10. Any issue that has become locally prominent

Preparing a Radio or Television Speech

The principles that govern the type of speech and your intended delivery mode govern how you prepare. Generally speaking, the rigidity of the time requirements suggests that you use a manuscript delivery. However, this is not always the case as in talk shows where you participate in a discussion with other people or take part in an interview. In all instances being thoroughly prepared will greatly benefit your presentation.

A special problem in preparing for a radio or television presentation is that you never know exactly who your audience members will be. Because of this, you must select examples and language that will appeal to a wide variety of people. You must speak so you will be understood by almost everyone in your audience. Give special attention to details and correctness of expression. If you have a copy of your script in front of you, there is no excuse for errors, but if you are conducting an interview or are being interviewed, you need to monitor your language usage so you speak correctly. Otherwise you run the risk of sounding more uneducated than you are. If you must read a script, use a portion of your preparation time to rehearse so you sound as if you are speaking, not reading.

Language in a broadcast speech should be simple, understandable, and conversational in style, so it will build word pictures in the minds of your listeners. Your sentences should ordinarily average not over 15 or 20 words each. Avoid trite and overworked words and phrases. Strive for language that makes your listeners feel you are having a lively and interesting conversation with them.

Probably the most important aspect of your preparation is your rehearsal. Although we have mentioned this already, rehearsal is so important that it bears repetition. Unless you have substantial experience with radio and television presentations, you should familiarize yourself with the techniques of the medium as well as with your speech content.

If your presentation is to be on radio, visit the station and observe the studio from which you will be speaking. Ask to rehearse with the microphone. You may use a desk microphone or a clip-on that is not visible. *Always rehearse aloud!* Just going over the words of your speech in your mind is not the same as speaking. You must get your tongue, your lips, and your entire vocal mechanism working together. Listen to your recorded message to see if it sounds like the message you intend. Don't listen to determine if your voice sounds like you (it will not), but rather, listen to your message to determine if that is what you mean to say.

If your presentation is to be on television, you need to rehearse in much the same way, except that you must also concern yourself with the visual image you project. This includes finding out if you come across better while seated or standing; if you should be behind a set or speaker's stand, or without one; if you need makeup, and how much; if you are to look at the camera or (as in the case of the interview) at the interviewer; whether the colors of your clothing blend or contrast with the background. All these are problems that can affect your total visual image. If you don't rehearse, you don't get to see the possible problems your visual image might create for your total message. In all cases you will want to make sure your visual message does not contradict or destroy your verbal message.

If a studio is not available for rehearsal, do the next best thing—use a tape recorder for a radio presentation and a video recorder for a television presentation. Most schools have equipment available for student use. In some instances, your instructor may need to arrange for the use of this equipment. No matter what it takes, find the equipment, find out how to use it properly, and prepare yourself for your presentation.

Presenting a Radio or Television Speech

If you have prepared your speech properly, your presentation should be easy and effective. Remember, on radio you need to be concerned with the sound only, but on television you must be concerned with both your visual and oral message. Both are presented for people who may be scattered throughout your broadcast region. They may be congregated in groups or alone, sitting at home, working, or driving in their cars. Your presentation should attempt to reach people in all these situations.

Since the sound of your voice is all your radio audience members have to judge the meaning of your message, you must use an energetic delivery to maintain their interest. Your voice also needs to be clear, distinct, and forceful. A good general rate of delivery is 125 to 150 words per minute. You don't want to speak so slowly that you lose your audience members' interest. On the other hand, speaking too rapidly may cause some of your audience members to miss some of your message. You will also want to use vocal variation to maintain interest. Be cautious that you don't overmodulate your voice in trying to add variation. Overmodulation sounds as bad as undermodulation. Generally, sound as if you are interested in your topic and excited about presenting your materials, and your audience members will hear the modulation in your voice.

In giving a radio speech, you should hold your script in your hands or read from the pages on the desk. Avoid rustling your papers. If you think they will rustle, leave them on the desk and just slide them when reading. Do not cough, sneeze, clear your throat, or shout into the microphone. Keep a uniform distance of about ten inches from the microphone while you are speaking. This will prevent sudden increases or decreases in volume and will help keep down some of the hisses. If you feel like gesturing, go ahead. It will give life to your presentation. Just be sure to talk *into the microphone* all the time. If you try to look from side to side or look somewhere other than straight ahead, you may muffle or lose the sound.

In giving a television speech, be just as concerned with your visual image as you are with your vocal presentation. Television directors generally use a number of close-up shots of the face of a speaker. The best advice is to be yourself! Be expressive, smile, and try to appear natural. Of course, you will want to avoid a "dead pan" expression. All other movements on camera should be somewhat controlled. By moving too much, you may move out of the camera operator's frame or be somewhat out of focus. Gesturing toward the camera can cause a distortion in the picture. This is the reason for rehearsing your presentation before going on television. You have the opportunity to look back at your tape and gauge how your movements look and how they will affect your presentation. Also, you will have time to correct any problems you may have in making your presentation before the camera if you do so far enough in advance of your live broadcast.

In the television presentation you should know your script well enough to be able to look into the cameras most of the time. However, if your presentation is an interview, look at the interviewer, not the cameras. To avoid profile views by the camera, keep your eyes on the camera that is operating at the moment. Usually, a special light on the camera or a director will indicate which camera is operating. If you are to use a teleprompter (or other mechanical means for reading), rehearse with it sufficiently to use it skillfully.

Project Assignment

Prepare and present a five-minute radio or television speech. Prepare a manuscript that you can use on the air. Remember to make your manuscript sound like you (review Project 9). Your instructor will inform you as to whether you can use a campus station, local radio, or television station, or whether you will use some other means to simulate radio or television.

Record your speech and replay the recording to evaluate your effectiveness for either radio or television. As you prepare and present this speech, simulate the real conditions of radio or television so you can get the real effect. Have a director who keeps track of times and signals when you start and stop the presentation. Audience members should not be physically present but should be assembled around "radios" and "televisions" to hear and watch this speech.

References

Blythin, E. & Samovar, L. A. (1985). *Communicating Effectively on Television.* Belmont, California: Wadsworth Publishing Company.

Heun, R. & Heun, L. (1986). *Public Speaking* (2nd ed.). St. Paul, Minnesota: West Publishing Company.

Minnick, W. C. (1983). *Public Speaking* (2nd ed.). Boston: Houghton Mifflin Company.

Rodman, G. (1986). *Public Speaking* (3rd ed.). New York: Holt, Rinehart and Winston, Inc.

Samovar, L. A. & Mills, J. (1989). *Oral Communication* (7th ed.). Dubuque, Iowa: Wm. C. Brown Company, Publishers.

Sprague, J. & Stuart, D. (1988). *The Speaker's Handbook* (2nd ed.). San Diego: Harcourt Brace Jovanovich.

UNIT VIII
AUDIENCE PARTICIPATION

The young become good communicators if they have parents or relatives or teachers who are good listeners. A parent, therefore, is never wasting time when patiently listening to a child try to explain something. Listening helps the child become an articulate—perhaps even an eloquent—adult.

S. I. Hayakawa

Project 40: Listening to Speeches

Project 41: The Forum

Project 42: The Heckling Speech

Unit VIII consists of three projects designed for aiding audiences and speakers. Project 40, "Listening to Speeches," presents the principles of effective listening and for evaluating speeches. Project 41 presents the principles of the forum, a method of speaker–audience interaction. The final project in the book, Project 42, presents the principles of the heckling speech and how speakers should deal with audience members who heckle them while they are trying to speak.

PROJECT 40

Listening to Speeches

A wise skepticism is the first attribute of a good critic.
—James Russell Lowell

When someone speaks, presumably someone else is listening. Listening is the counterpart of speaking. In public speaking there is no speech without listeners; for the speech act to be complete, there must be an audience. The listener, then, is a key component in the communication process.

As you go through the other projects in this text, you will see numerous references to your audience members and the concern you as a speaker must have for them. Many choices you make, such as your topic choice, wording, delivery style, supporting materials, and so on, are based on what your audience analysis tells you about your listeners. Your listeners, then, influence a major portion of your speech from the topics you select to the manner in which you deliver your speeches. However, the listener must also assume certain responsibilities for the completion of the communication process. Both the listener and the speaker must share responsibility for completing the communication process.

Because the listener is half of the communication process, this project will explain the listening process, discuss how to listen effectively, and present a method for evaluating speeches.

The Listening Process

Listening is not hearing. In fact, George Burns as God in the movie *Oh God,* when he was asked if he listened to everyone's prayers said "I can't help hearing, but I don't always listen." So it is with most of us at various times. We hear because we can't turn our ears off, but we don't always listen. The hearing and listening processes are distinct but related processes.

Hearing is the physical process of receiving sound waves and transmitting them to the brain. The process of hearing is a complicated set of actions that begins with the sound waves hitting the ear drum. The ear drum then vibrates and sets the ossicular chain into vibration. This in turn affects the oval window that transmits the sound to the cochlea where the sound is converted to electrical impulses, which are then sent to the brain. This oversimplification of that complex process of hearing explains the physical process.

Listening, on the other hand, is a mental process of "receiving, attending to, and assigning meaning to aural stimuli" (Wolvin & Coakley, 1988). Obviously, you can't listen to sounds you do not hear or receive, so the first essential component in the listening process is the reception of the sound. Second, you must focus attention on the sound stimuli. You may receive several stimuli at one time, so you need to focus on a stimulus to listen to it. For example, someone may be talking to you on the phone while you try to listen to your favorite TV program. Unless you focus on one or the other, you will likely not be "listening" to either, but rather you will catch glimpses of both.

The third essential component of listening is assigning meaning to aural stimuli. If you can hear a sound and concentrate on it, you still may not be able to identify what it is. Sometimes this happens to us when we are inside the house and hear an unfamiliar noise outside. If you can't make sense of the sound, you go outside to identify the sound so you can make sense of it and assign meaning to it. Only when you assign a meaning to a sound is the listening process complete. This process explains what happens in the mental process of collecting sounds and interpreting them.

Listening Effectively

Simply completing the listening process does not make you an *effective* listener. So what, you ask? Is ineffective listening a problem? For most of us ineffective listening causes us tremendous problems in our personal lives as well as in our work relationships. Every time we are not listening when we should be, it costs us something.

In our personal lives the costs of ineffective listening can be a major problem in our relationships with our family and friends. When was the last time someone said to you, "You're not listening to me."? Can you recall the relationship? How much harm did you cause the relationship? It probably can't be measured in dollars and cents, but ineffective listening can cause irreparable damage to a relationship, which may lead to divorce, strained relations with a friend, or the end of a relationship. It also causes hurt feelings when you forget important events in the lives of your friends and family. Hurt feelings cause emotional pain and suffering that often strain a relationship. In short, ineffective listening may be the cause of such occurrences as the "generation gap," poor grades in school, missing important information, missing important dates, ruined friendships, divorce, and many other similar events. Inefficient listening can be costly in our personal lives!

Ineffective listening can also cause problems in our business relations. How many times have you had to redo a task or failed to perform a task correctly because of ineffective listening? Probably more times than you are willing to admit. Lost time and deteriorating relationships are costs most of us are not willing to pay, but they are the results of ineffective listening in business. Every time you have to complete a task a second time, rewrite your report, or your work is late, it costs your business money. When the company loses money, you also lose because your raise (or potential for a raise) has been diminished. Employers can't give raises if they don't make a substantial profit. Ineffective listening can also be costly in business!

What, then, is *effective* listening? Steil, Barker, and Watson (1983) list the following descriptors for effective listeners:

alert	caring	noninterrupting
attending	patient	other-centered
curious	empathic	effective-evaluator
responsive	interested	nonemotional
understanding	nondistracted	

Ineffective listeners, on the other hand, can be called:

inattentive	defensive	self-centered
uncaring	impatient	quick to judge
interrupting	distracted	disinterested
apathetic	insensitive	emotional

While these descriptors do not capture the entirety of effective and ineffective listeners, they do provide a basis for the beginning of a determination.

In his presentation "Listening Is Good Business," Dr. Ralph Nichols identifies our ten worst listening habits and suggests how we might improve. Here is what Dr. Nichols reports:

Bad listening habit number one is *calling the subject uninteresting.* Whenever we find ourselves in a listening situation, we determine almost immediately whether the subject is one we want to hear about or tune out. When we call a subject dull or boring, we set ourselves up for an ineffective listening situation. Good listeners look for something they can *use* from a presentation. To be effective listeners, we should look for something which will benefit us rather than dismissing the subject.

Bad listening habit number two is *criticizing the speaker's delivery.* Ineffective listeners concentrate their attention on the delivery aspects of the speaker and criticize what she/he is doing rather than listening to the message of the speaker. Effective listeners, on the other hand, concentrate on the message of the speaker and try to overlook or block out the ineffectiveness of the speaker's delivery.

Bad listening habit number three is *getting overstimulated by some point in the speech.* The ineffective listeners let their emotions get in the way. When they disagree with a speaker, they begin thinking about how to voice their objections. Effective listeners hear the entire message before they make judgments about the speech.

Bad listening habit number four is *listening only for facts.* Ineffective listeners condition themselves to be fact listeners, dismissing everything else. Most of the time, they forget the facts within a couple of days. Effective listeners, on the other hand, are *idea* listeners. They have ideas which still make sense when they add the facts to the ideas.

Bad listening habit number five is *trying to outline everything.* Ineffective listeners try to force all of their notes into an outline format. This is okay if all of your speakers have outlined their materials. Effective listeners try to determine the organizational scheme of the speaker and then concentrate on listening for and writing down the key concepts. They adapt to the speaker and the organizational scheme of the speaker.

Bad listening habit number six is *faking attention to the speaker.* Ineffective listeners pretend that they are listening by looking at the speaker and fake attending to the message. Effective listeners do not fake their eye contact, head nods, and facial expressions. They focus their skills on attending to the speaker's message.

Bad listening habit number seven is *tolerating or creating distractions.* Ineffective listeners try listening to more than one thing at a time. For example, trying to study and listen to music at the same time. Effective listeners adjust to distractions or control conditions so distractions are reduced to a minimum.

Bad listening habit number eight is *avoiding difficult materials.* Ineffective listeners spend their time listening only to relaxing materials such as comedy routines, music, and relaxing television programs. Effective listeners listen to relaxing materials, but can also motivate themselves to listen to difficult materials when they need to.

Bad listening habit number nine is *letting emotion laden words throw us out of tune with the speaker.* Ineffective listeners overreact to words the speaker uses rather than listening to the message of the speaker. Most of the time, the ineffective listeners aren't even aware that it was a word which upset them. Effective listeners overcome the impulse to react to the words a speaker uses. They respond instead to the total message of the speaker.

Bad listening habit number ten is *wasting the differential between speech speed and thought speed.* Most listeners can think at a rate between 400 and 800 words per minute. Most speakers talk at a rate between 125 and 150 words per minute. Ineffective listeners waste the difference between the two by day-dreaming and thinking about things other than the speaker's topic. Effective listeners use the time differential to evaluate the speech, anticipate the speaker's next point, and summarize what the speaker has just said.

These are not the only bad habits of ineffective listeners. If you find that you have other bad listening habits, work to eliminate them. Work hard to listen so you can get more out of the speaker's message. Commit yourself to becoming a more effective listener.

Evaluating Speeches

It does little good to just listen to a speech. As you listen, you make evaluations and judgments about the speech and about the delivery of the speech. This section of the project is designed to help you prepare to listen better and evaluate the speeches you hear. It presents ideas to help you know what to listen for as well as presents some ideas on what to do with your evaluation once it has been made. This whole process is called "critical listening."

Critical listening does not mean that you try to find only the negative aspects of a speech. Rather, it means using your listening skills to determine better what a speaker means and when a speaker is trying to slip something past you. In critically evaluating speeches, you need to listen to basically four areas of the speech: the content of the message, the organization of the message, the language of the message, and the delivery of the message.

Content   One of the major concerns in evaluating any speech is that the speaker say something significant. In addition to reviewing Project 4, you can review the "preparing" section of each project for specific items that ought to be included in the specific assignment.

What you should listen for specifically is to determine that the speaker has knowledge of the subject area. You might begin by asking yourself if the speaker has identified a specific area of the topic to speak about. Remember, you can't speak "about war" and do a credible job—you must have a specific goal.

Next, you might determine how well prepared the speaker was by listening for references you know about. Note also the use of credentials for unfamiliar references. Ask yourself if the speaker has developed the content with more than his or her opinions on the topic. Is there support for opinions? Do the materials used for support seem appropriate for this topic? Is there sufficient support and a good variety of supporting materials? These are some basic content concerns that will be important for you to listen for and evaluate as you attempt to determine the overall effectiveness of the speech.

Organization   A second area of concern is the organization of the materials. One primary responsibility of all speakers is to be organized. If audience members are expected to make any sense of a speech, it is important that materials fit into a sensible sequence. Listen for a distinct introduction, body, and conclusion, in that order.

Next, listen to the divisions and subdivisions in the body of the speech. Are these the most appropriate divisions for this topic? Do they follow in a logical sequence? Did the main points develop the thesis? Do the subdivisions develop the main divisions? Is the order clear? These are some basic organizational concerns that will be important for you to listen for and evaluate.

Language   A third area of concern is the use of language in the speech. A review of Project 12 is important, but there are other considerations as well. First, you will want to determine that the language used was appropriate for the speech, the speaker, and the audience. Of primary importance here is that the audience members be able to understand and share a common meaning with the speaker. If the speaker uses words and concepts with which the audience members are not familiar, the terms must be explained or defined so the audience members do understand.

Next, you might ask whether the language was appropriate in that it was grammatically correct and devoid of slang. It is true that audiences may understand language that has grammatical errors (e.g., ain't) or makes use of slang expressions like "real rad," but it is more important that a speaker sound educated.

Additionally, you may listen for offensive language—vulgarities, derogatory terms, inflammatory expressions. Any of these can serve to offend audience members and lessen the total impact of the speech. These are some of the basic language concerns that you should listen for and evaluate.

Delivery   The fourth area of concern is the delivery techniques of the speaker. We have reserved this for discussion last because it sometimes becomes the focus for the entire evaluation of a speaker. Notice that it is only one of four basic concerns in evaluating a speech. Focusing on the delivery techniques of the speech because they are the most obvious suggests that the delivery is more important than the message of the speaker. Nothing could be more untrue. Before you can worry about how to say something, you have to have something to say. As you consider critiquing the delivery of a speech, review the appropriate projects from Unit II, plus the specific suggestions for the "presenting" sections of the appropriate projects.

In evaluating a speaker's delivery, listen to and observe both the verbal and nonverbal aspects of delivery. One of the most significant aspects of delivery is eye contact. Does the speaker appear to be looking at members of the audience? In addition, does the speaker show enthusiasm for the topic both vocally and in body movements? Eye contact with your audience members shows how you feel about yourself and your audience members.

Listen to the voice to note vocal variations, sufficient volume, correct articulation and pronunciation, as well as rate and vocal quality. All these characteristics should show that the speaker is poised and confident about his or her topic. Only when it detracts from the *total* impression of the speech, does it become a problem. These are some of the basic delivery concerns that you will want to note for evaluation.

Expressing Speech Evaluation

Feedback is the primary means by which we learn to improve, especially in the classroom situation. By both receiving and presenting feedback on speeches, you learn better the impact of the various speech techniques. Look at criticism as a means of helping you improve your effectiveness rather than a series of personal attacks on you and your presentation. On the other hand, criticism needs to be constructive, not destructive, if it is to be useful for a speaker.

DeVito (1990) makes the following suggestions for providing constructive criticism:

1. *Say something positive.* If all you can do is recognize the negative, you haven't heard the entire speech. Without overdoing it, publicly praise the speaker for doing well. Any negative aspects should be done in writing and not dealt with publicly for beginning speakers.
2. *Be specific.* The purpose of all criticism should be to help a speaker improve. Vague generalizations don't help; specific references to what a speaker might have said or done, do help.
3. *Be objective.* Try to look beyond your own biases and prejudices. Just because you do not agree with a speaker's point or a source, does not necessarily make the reference bad. Listen to the speaker's point and judge it on its own merits.
4. *Be constructive.* Your objective in expressing evaluation should always be to help the speaker improve. Never try to destroy a speaker's self-image.
5. *Remember the irreversibility of communication.* Once you say something, you can't take it back. Be kind and generous in your remarks. It is better to offer too much praise than to be too negative.

In addition, here are two other suggestions that will help you in offering constructive evaluation of a speech to someone else:

Limit your criticism.   If you find many minor elements that the speaker can improve but only one major area, it is better to recommend one change rather than ten minor ones. Consider the value of your comments in helping the speaker improve. Most of us would have difficulty dealing with more than two or three ideas at a time. Remember, we limit most of our speeches to two or three points because it is difficult for audience members to remember more points. This applies to elements of evaluation also.

Support the speaker during the speech.   Being an attentive listener and showing your interest in the speech will help considerably when you make a comment in evaluating the speech. If the speaker gets feedback from you during the speech, she or he will know that you have been listening, and know that you have valid comments to make. If you act disinterested, you probably will give meaningless feedback.

Don't be afraid of offending people by telling them they are not perfect. All speeches, no matter who the speaker is, can be improved. Even presidents, teachers, and others who speak publicly for a living can improve their speeches and speaking skills. The purpose of critiquing speeches is to suggest the manner in which those speeches and skills can be improved. This should never be considered a "payback" or "get even" time for speakers and listeners. If you view speech evaluation in this manner, you will fail miserably in your task.

Project Assignment

Your instructor will give you specific guidance in what you will be expected to do and say in regard to listening and evaluating speeches during your class. Appendix A provides a specific format for providing elements of feedback on the effectiveness of your speeches. In addition, you may be asked to provide oral evaluations of speeches in any of several formats.

One effective means is to have oral comments of the good points of a speech immediately following every speech. Another method is for several speakers to speak and then break the class into several small groups and have group feedback on the good qualities of the speakers in your group. A third method is to combine a comment about "most needs to improve" with the other methods. Some instructors may wish to have students periodically both write and orally critique other speakers. Be prepared to adapt to your instructor's method of critiquing speeches.

References

Berko, R. M., Wolvin, A. D., & Wolvin, D. R. (1988). *Communicating: A Social and Career Focus* (4th ed.). Boston: Houghton Mifflin Company.

Bradley, B. E. (1988). *Fundamentals of Speech Communication* (5th ed.). Dubuque, Iowa: Wm. C. Brown Company, Publishers.

DeVito, J. A. (1990). *The Elements of Public Speaking* (4th ed.). New York: Harper & Row, Publishers.

Fetzer, R. C. & Vogel, R. A. (1982). *Designing Messages: A Guide for Creative Speakers.* Chicago: Science Research Associates, Inc.

Heun, R. & Heun, L. (1986). *Public Speaking* (2nd ed.). St. Paul, Minnesota: West Publishing Company.

Hunt, G. T. (1987). *Public Speaking* (2nd ed.). Englewood Cliffs, New Jersey: Prentice-Hall, Inc.

Lucas, S. E. (1989). *The Art of Public Speaking* (3rd ed.). New York: Random House.

Nelson, P. E. & Pearson, J. C. (1990). *Confidence in Public Speaking* (4th ed.). Dubuque, Iowa: Wm. C. Brown Company, Publishers.

Nichols, R. G. (1960). *Listening Is Good Business* (a recording). Grand Rapids, Michigan: Edward M. Miller and Associates, Inc.

Ochs, D. J. & Winkler, A. C. (1983). *A Brief Introduction to Speech* (2nd ed.). New York: Harcourt Brace Jovanovich.

Osborn, M. & Osborn, S. (1988). *Public Speaking.* Boston: Houghton Mifflin Company

Roach, C. A. & Wyatt, N. J. (1988). *Successful Listening.* New York: Harper & Row, Publishers.

Samovar, L. A. & Mills, J. (1989). *Oral Communication* (7th ed.). Dubuque, Iowa: Wm. C. Brown Company, Publishers.

Steil, L. K., Barker, L. L., & Watson, K. W. (1983). *Effective Listening: Key to Your Success.* New York: Random House.

Verderber, R. F. (1988). *The Challenge of Effective Speaking* (7th ed.). Belmont, California: Wadsworth Publishing Company.

Walter, O. M. & Scott, R. L. (1984). *Thinking and Speaking* (5th ed.). New York: Macmillan Publishing Company.

Wilson, J. F. & Arnold, C. C. (1983). *Public Speaking as a Liberal Art* (5th ed.). Boston: Allyn & Bacon, Inc.

Wolff, F. I., Marsnik, N. C., Tacey, W. S., & Nichols, R. G. (1983). *Perceptive Listening.* New York: Holt, Rinehart and Winston, Inc.

Wolvin, A. D. & Coakley, C. D. (1988). *Listening* (3rd ed.). Dubuque, Iowa: Wm. C. Brown Company, Publishers.

PROJECT **41**

The Forum

It is useless to attempt to reason a man out of a thing he
was never reasoned into.

—Jonathan Swift

Frequently, after a speaker finishes speaking, audience members want to ask the speaker questions about his or her topic. In general, any public discussion that follows a presentation is called a forum. The customary procedure for the forum is for the audience to ask questions and for the speaker to provide answers, with a moderator serving as an intermediary.

Speakers seldom know how many questions their listeners have because there is no chance for a question-and-answer session. Speakers can be more sure that their audience members have clearly understood their messages if they exchange questions and answers after the speech.

This project focuses on the skills involved in answering questions in a forum. Since this is a public speaking text, we will concentrate on the lecture-forum, but the skills involved would be appropriate for any forum. Included in this project are the principles of the forum, preparing for a forum, presenting a forum, and responding in a forum.

Principles of the Forum

The forum is simply a public question-and-answer session that follows a presentation. Cragan and Wright (1986) list five specific public discussion types: (1) the lecture-forum, (2) the debate-forum, (3) the dialogue-forum, (4) the panel-forum, and (5) the symposium-forum. In each instance the presentation is a two-part presentation with the second part a public discussion of the issues.

The purpose of the forum is for your audience members to clarify any issues that may not be clear to them from your speech or for them to find out why you feel as you do about some aspects of your speech. During a speaker's presentation it is usually not appropriate to interrupt and ask questions or to comment on statements by the speaker. The forum allows the audience to do this after the presentation.

The forum can help to present new information to the audience, clarify an obscure point, and motivate the audience about a topic. It also allows the audience members to share their opinions on a topic. Often the audience members don't get the opportunity to interact with a speaker, especially if the speaker is an "expert" in a particular area. Politicians sometimes use the forum to obtain the views of their constituents on an important and controversial issue coming up for a vote. This is the best method for a legislator to explain a proposed change and clarify for people how they would be affected.

The use of a forum requires that you be better informed than any member of your audience. If you are to answer questions, you must know more than you can put into your presentation. A second requirement of the forum is that you be capable of handling questions from an audience. It does little good for you to have tremendous stores of knowledge if you are unable to use that knowledge in responding to your audience's questions.

Occasions for the forum are many. Any time it is advantageous for the speaker and audience to share information or to clarify doubts, you have an occasion for a forum. Forums are often used with committee reports, before business groups, church organizations, civic audiences, educational meetings, political rallies, fraternal orders, and the like. There is almost no limit to occasions for a forum.

Preparing for a Forum

Because presentations that make use of the forum are largely informative in nature, prepare your presentation much as you would a speech to inform (Project 13). One distinct difference between Project 13 and this assignment is that you will need also to prepare to answer questions, some of which will call for persuasion instead of information. Begin this preparation by trying to decide who your audience members are likely to be and what will be their primary concerns. You should begin by thinking of specific questions audience members might ask.

In your presentation you should address the major issues, but be prepared with additional support for what you say. You will not have time to cite all the references or give all the examples you wish, so use these to supplement your speech as you answer questions. Instead of repeating what you have said in your speech, add materials that you didn't have room for in the speech. Extend your speech time, actually. There are probably also materials or subissues that you will not include in your presentation that you should prepare yourself to respond to during the forum.

A typical presentation may range from 5 to 30 minutes in length with a forum that may last up to an hour. Be sure you know your time limits and work within those limits for both your presentation and the forum. Audiences can become more volatile if you violate their expectations.

Participating in a Forum

Project 13 tells you how to present the first part of the forum. Since you are generally presenting an informative speech, conduct yourself accordingly. Review the materials of the informative speech presentation, and then prepare to provide more information during the forum. If you must defend an answer, which would be persuasive, give your audience members reasons for your position.

Whenever a forum is involved, a chairperson or moderator usually makes introductions and controls the forum. If there is no moderator, you must control your own forum. It is best to announce to the audience before your presentation that a forum, or question-and-answer period, will follow your presentation. This gives your audience members time to prepare questions they want clarified or issues they want discussed. It should also be clarified at that time whether questions only or questions and comments will be permitted, and whether questions should be confined to materials presented in the speech only. This allows your audience members preparation time and a guide for their preparation.

Responding in a Forum

Immediately following your presentation, the moderator should indicate that audience members may ask questions. If you are serving as your own moderator, announce at the conclusion of your speech that you are "open for questions." In making this announcement, you or the moderator should spell out all "rules" your audience members are to follow. For example, people may be asked to raise hands or stand to be recognized; generally, questioners are to ask one question at a time; if it is a panel presentation, questions should be addressed to a specific member; responses should be limited to one or two minutes. While this may seem petty (and in small groups may be), it is best to limit everyone so no one audience member uses most of the forum time for a rebuttal speech.

The moderator should also announce the total amount of time allowed for questioning. Do not make the forum too long. You can generally agree to extend it if questions still prevail when time expires, or the issue is one of such significance that it warrants further discussion. On the other hand, do not hold your audience members the full time allotted for the forum by adding to your speech if it is obvious that no one has any more questions. Flexibility is the key to a successful forum. Keep things moving briskly, but allow all who want to ask pertinent questions to do so.

Asking Questions   If you are an audience member of a forum, how do you ask questions? How do you know what to ask? First, questions need to be ones to which you do not have answers, and ones germane to the rules established by the moderator. If questions regarding topics other than the presentation are not allowed, don't wander off the topic or work a question regarding another subject around so it comes slightly close to the topic. Also, don't make flagrant violations of the rules by asking embarrassing questions that have nothing to do with the speech topic.

Most questions should be of the variety that ask for clarification rather than a short "yes-no" response. For example, instead of asking a speaker if a proposal is good or bad, ask for the merits (or demerits) of a proposal. Ask for explanations or reasons if the speaker has already made a stand on an issue. In cases where you think the speaker needs support from other sources, ask for that or further substantiation on an issue. It is generally not a good idea to ask a speaker to repeat a part of a presentation because that indicates you weren't listening. It might be acceptable, however, if a significant number of audience members were absent and missed a very important point. You must be the judge of this in each separate situation.

Responding to Questions   Answer questions completely, but be direct and to the point. Do not "beat around the bush." If a question is asked that you do not feel qualified to answer, state that you do not have the information necessary to give a reliable answer. But if you don't know the answer because you are poorly prepared, you will quickly lose the confidence and respect of your audience members—and you should.

If a question is asked that does not pertain to your subject, say politely that it is beyond the scope of your topic. Should you by chance have information that enables you to answer it, state briefly that the question is somewhat far afield of the topic but you can answer it, and then make a very brief reply. Do not let off-topic questions take you off your subject for more than a moment.

If a heckler troubles you, handle it courteously but firmly. Project 42 will help you deal with hecklers. You should plan to read that project prior to this presentation, just in case you need to deal with someone who feels like heckling, or insists on asking questions that are not pertinent to your topic.

If questions are obscure and long or drawn out, rephrase them, but ask the questioner if your rewarding expresses the intent of the question. At other times it may be necessary for you to ask for a restatement of an inquiry. Always do this when you do not hear or understand the question clearly. If a questioner seems to be asking several questions at one time, try to get him or her to ask one question at a time.

Observe acceptable speaking practices throughout the forum. Maintain an alert and friendly attitude. Do not become ruffled when you meet obvious disagreement or criticism. Simply explain your position firmly but courteously. Do not engage in a debate or exchange of unfriendly remarks and accusations. Dismiss the matter and go on to the next question. If some of the questions are "hot"—and they will be—keep your head, add a touch of humor to cool them off if it seems advisable, then reply as capably as you can.

Making Statements If the situation allows for audience members to make statements as well as to ask questions, remember the rules established by the moderator. All comments should be brief (one to two minutes maximum) and pertain directly to the topic. This is not a time for rebuttal speeches, nor is it a time for being obnoxious. If you want to support or oppose a position on an issue, state so and then briefly tell why you are taking your stand. If you have support for your position, present it also, but keep within the limits set for you. As an audience member making a statement, you should never poke fun at the speaker, nor should you embarrass the speaker by belittling his or her presentation.

The chairperson or moderator should close the forum. When time is up, or it appears that there are no more questions, the moderator should thank all participants, both the speakers and audience participants, for their interest in the subject and cooperation during the forum. If you also serve as your own moderator, then you need to close the forum by thanking your audience members for their cooperation with you. Keep the closing brief, as this is no time for speeches; it is a ceremonial closing to a program.

Project Assignment

Prepare and present an informative speech to an audience in either a lecture-forum or as a member of a panel-forum. Your instructor will inform you of the type of forum you are to prepare for. Be prepared to field questions on your topic for a brief period of time. Your instructor will also advise you on the length of speech and the forum.

References

Applebaum, R. L., Bodaken, E. M., Sereno, K. K., & Anatol, K. W. E. (1979). *The Process of Group Communication* (2nd ed.). Chicago: Science Research Associates, Inc.

Brilhart, J. K. & Galanes, G. J. (1988). *Effective Group Discussion* (6th ed.). Dubuque, Iowa: Wm. C. Brown Company, Publishers.

Cragan, J. F. & Wright, D. W. (1986). *Communication in Small Group Discussion: A Case Study Approach* (2nd ed.). St. Paul, Minnesota: West Publishing Company.

Gregory, H. (1990). *Public Speaking for College and Career* (2nd ed.). New York: McGraw-Hill Book Company.

Hanna, M. S. & Gibson, J. W. (1987). *Public Speaking for Personal Success* (2nd ed.). Dubuque, Iowa: Wm. C. Brown Company, Publishers.

Samovar, L. A. & Mills, J. (1989). *Oral Communication* (7th ed.). Dubuque, Iowa: Wm. C. Brown Company, Publishers.

Sprague, J. & Stuart, D. (1988). *The Speaker's Handbook* (2nd ed.). San Diego: Harcourt Brace Jovanovich.

PROJECT **42**

The Heckling Speech

I am in earnest—I will not equivocate—I will not excuse—I will not retreat a single inch—and I will be heard.

—William Lloyd Garrison

Although the heckler is rare in public communication except for occasional political rallies, you never know when you will be heckled by your audience. Generally, heckling occurs when you least expect it. When it does come, you should be ready to meet and deal with it. This project provides practice in speaking under the pressure of heckling from your audience members.

Another reason this assignment is given is that as a beginning speaker, you will probably become aroused when under fire from your audience members. If you can throw off your habitually meek speaking personality and face your tormentors with confidence and power, you can inspire confidence in yourself. This is a power you have inside, but not one you easily display. A secondary purpose of this project is to make you aware of your latent powers of expression so you can use them in forthcoming speeches.

Principles of the Heckling Speech

A heckling speech is one a speaker delivers while subjected to heckling from audience members. The heckling speech generally supports or opposes a definite proposition. Normally, the speaker's purpose is to convince; however, you could use an informative purpose or one to stimulate, but such speeches are not likely to draw natural heckling like one where you are trying to convince your audience members that yours is the best solution to a problem.

Select one side of a contention that you will support and then do your best to justify your views. Present arguments and evidence that strengthen your stand. While you are doing this, your audience is free to heckle you in any way it sees fit. Your problem is to control the volatile attention of your listeners, and at the same time successfully present your ideas. You should have positive control, retain your sense of humor, be fully prepared, and understand how to handle hecklers.

An important point for you to remember now is that as the speaker, you are generally regarded as the one who is in the right when a heckler interrupts you and the heckler is in the wrong. Because you are at the front and center of your audience, you also have a psychological advantage over a heckler who speaks out of anonymity in your audience. The rudeness of interrupting a speaker also places the rest of your audience members "on your side." Most people will consider the heckler's behavior as inappropriate, so your best bet will be to remain calm and polite. A rude remark in return may make your audience members believe you deserved to be heckled.

Comments such as, "If you will let me finish, uninterrupted, then I will give you an opportunity to make your point" do a great deal for your respect and cause audience members to help quiet the heckler. If the heckler persists, you might ask the heckler if he or she is trying to deny you your right to free speech? Even the most obnoxious or rude heckler probably will not agree to deny you your constitutional rights. To do so would be an admittance of foregoing the right for him-or herself.

Following are some topics that are suitable for a heckling speech. You are to take a side on your topic and uphold only that side of the argument.

1. All colleges should abolish ROTC units.
2. Third and fourth terms for presidents should be allowed by law.
3. National marriage laws with a minimum age limit, a standard physical examination, and a waiting period after applying for a license, should be established by Congress.
4. A national drinking age should be set at . . .
5. War should be declared only by a majority vote of the people.
6. Pollution violators should receive jail sentences and fines.
7. A national health plan should be instituted.
8. The student newspapers should have no faculty control.
9. Students should be allowed to take any courses they want.
10. Public servants should be tested for AIDS.

Remember, you may take either side of any of these issues, or any other issue about which you would like to speak.

Preparing for a Heckling Speech

Generally, prepare this speech as you would any speech to convince (see Project 19 for details). The purpose of this particular heckling speech is to convince your audience. Because you know in advance that you will be heckled, your secondary purpose will be to control your audience while you put your ideas across.

The organization of this speech should be modeled on that of any speech to convince. Reread Projects 3 and 19 for information on organization. You should know your sequence of ideas so thoroughly that you can't forget it. Under heckling pressure loss of memory may be so overwhelming that you may stand blankly before your audience. If your audience members can disturb you to this extent, they will be delighted. This speechlessness need not trouble you if you are prepared for many interruptions.

Presenting a Heckling Speech

Keep your head. Your attitude should be one of firmness and good humor, but not officiousness or haughtiness. Your good humor should not permit you to be so sensitive to its presence that you laugh or turn to histrionics every time someone shoots a question at you or puts you on the spot. Be sensitive to any situation that demands a witticism or similar response from you. Demonstrate enough flexibility in meeting your hecklers to display the basic qualities of poise and self-confidence.

Your audience members will be greatly pleased if they can disturb you or cause you to become so confused that you forget your speech or fly off on a tangent, leaving your speech somewhere behind you. How can you avoid losing your poise? First, know your speech and know it well. Do not have a memorized talk, but have a memorized sequence of points that comprise your main ideas. Refuse to answer irrelevant questions that are nothing but quips, popoffs, or teasers. Simply state that such remarks are irrelevant, do not pertain to your speech, and hence can't be answered. Whenever you are in doubt as to what your interrogator wants, ask him or her to repeat his or her question. Persistent hecklers can sometimes be silenced by a quick retort to some of their senseless chatter.

Expect all kinds of interruptions, but don't be disturbed by them. If the questions are legitimate, clear them up or tell the group that you will answer a certain question later in your speech after you discuss the point that has just been brought up. *Before you end your remarks, draw your thoughts together with a good conclusion.*

Throughout your speech, talk clearly, forcefully, and correctly. Accompany your words with effective bodily actions and gestures. Look and act confident.

Special Hints:

1. Be firm but flexible.
2. Retain a sense of humor but do not interpret everything as if you were a comedian.
3. Show no anger but do not be afraid to stand up and face your audience vigorously and forcefully.
4. Maintain self-control.
5. Take advantage of opportunities offered by events that occur while you speak.
6. Stay with your speech by refusing to be "jockeyed" out of position.
7. Do not ask questions or opinions of your hecklers when replying to them. They will only argue with you. Give short, direct, vigorous, and specific replies.
8. If a heckler is a constant irritant who just sits and makes noises that he or she thinks are questions, ask him or her directly to be quiet and give other people a chance.
9. When questions come fast and furious, point to one person to ask a question while signaling for the others to be quiet so you can answer. Try to direct your audience members' attention to the person who is questioning (and heckling). Audience members will usually be courteous to one of their own. This will give you a chance.
10. Whenever the opportunity comes to flatten a heckler verbally, give him or her both barrels with a triple charge of powder.
11. Do not answer more than two questions at a time from one person. Give others a chance to be heard.
12. Do not argue with a heckler; switch to someone who has a question.
13. If the session gets too rough, frankly ask your audience members to give you a chance—appeal to their sense of fair play.
14. When the heckling gets loud, stop completely, *wait calmly until quiet returns,* then quietly and definitely answer a question or resume your speech. Do not attempt to talk louder than your hecklers.

Heckling a Speaker

(Note: This section explains how to heckle a speaker during this speaking assignment. Since it is important that speakers be heckled to gain the experience of handling hecklers, this is what is recommended for the assignment. *It is not recommended, however, that you ever heckle a public speaker. This material is intended for use during this speaking assignment only, and only as an aid in learning to deal with hecklers.*)

Interrupt the speaker at will, either seated or standing up. Ask such questions as: How do you know? Who's your authority? Where did you read that? What do you mean? Will you please explain . . . ? What is your evidence? Members of the audience may argue with the speaker (if he or she is naïve enough to fall into such a trap). Clever remarks about the speaker, what he or she is saying or doing, are excellent heckling devices. Be a skillful heckler, not a boring one. "Getting the speaker's goat" is an effective method of heckling.

These practices should not be overdone. However, you as the audience members are obliged to see that each speaker knows, when he or she has finished his or her speech, that he or she has been through the fire; otherwise his or her experience will be weakened. Applaud each speaker generously when he or she concludes.

Project Assignment

Prepare and present a heckling speech. Prepare yourself to speak and control the situation. An added part of this assignment is that you should also prepare yourself to heckle other speakers so they can gain the valuable practice they need in knowing how to handle hecklers.

References

Gregory, H. (1990). *Public Speaking for College and Career* (2nd ed.). New York: McGraw-Hill Book Company.

Hart, R. P., Friedrich, G. W., & Brummett, B. (1987). *Public Communication* (2nd ed.). Lanham, Maryland: University Press of America.

Sprague, J. & Stuart, D. (1988). *The Speaker's Handbook* (2nd ed.). San Diego: Harcourt Brace Jovanovich.

Stone J. & Bachner J. (1977). *Speaking Up, A Book for Every Woman Who Wants to Speak Effectively.* New York: McGraw Hill Book Company.

Zimmerman, G. I., Owen, J. J., & Seibert, D. R. (1986). *Speech Communication: A Contemporary Introduction.* (3rd ed.). St. Paul, Minnesota: West Publishing Company.

APPENDICES

APPENDIX A

The First Speech

The only way to have a friend is to be one.
—Ralph Waldo Emerson

Everything must have a beginning. So it is in the speech class also. You must have a beginning place to start giving speeches. This first speech is designed to introduce you to the idea of giving speeches and to do so in a nonthreatening situation where you will not need a lot of preparation prior to giving your speech. Consider this a "free" assignment where you can get started without having to worry about your grade or what others will think of you.

Principles of the First Speech

Your first speech will be one of limited preparation. In this speech you will stand before your classmates and speak for one to two minutes about one of your classmates. You will be allowed a few minutes to interview one of your classmates and become acquainted with each other. Then you will introduce this new friend to your new classmates.

Getting to know your classmates is one of the essential tasks for this class. In order to help your classmates and for them to help you, you must get to know each other. It is difficult to speak to an audience about whom you know little or nothing. Likewise, it is difficult to know what and how to respond to others when you don't know them. Much of what you learn in a speech class comes from the evaluations and critiques of the instructor and your classmates. If you learn from their comments, you will have made a giant step toward the ultimate goal—self-improvement.

The basic purpose of this assignment is for class members to get to know each other. A second purpose is to give you an opportunity to experience the speaking situation. Once you have proven to yourself that you can do it, all you need do then is concentrate on learning to improve your skills. To avoid any embarrassment in speaking about yourself and your accomplishments and achievements, this assignment is designed so you can tell this information to a classmate, who should have no problem in talking about you to others.

As human beings we are naturally curious about the people around us. We like to know who they are, what they like, what they dislike, and so on, so we can establish relationships with them. You will also want to get to know the members of your class so you can speak to them as individuals rather than as a "group of people." The more you know about your audience members, the easier it will be to know their interests and thus be able to adapt your speech to them.

Even though this is the first speech you present in this class, and therefore probably the most emotional, it will also likely be the easiest. The speech may be emotional because it is your first speech in the class and you don't quite know what to expect, and you are also probably not familiar with most of your classmates yet. It may be the easiest because the amount of time between your research and your presentation is very short, and the atmosphere is very informal.

Preparing Your First Speech

A Student Information Survey has been placed at the end of this project. Complete the information on the survey form. Then using the survey form as a discussion starter, interview a classmate as directed by your instructor. Your teacher may assign a partner to you or ask you to select a partner or to "draw names" for partners for this part of the assignment. It will work best for both partners if neither one knows the other well. If you are allowed to select a partner, select the person you know the least about or the one you would like most to know better.

As you talk with your partner, make some notes that you think would interest others in your class. Remember, your classmates are similar to you in many ways, so what you find interesting is likely to be interesting to them also. Some interesting and important questions to ask are: (1) What name should we call you? (2) Where are you from? (3) What do you like? Dislike? (4) What are your hobbies? Skills? Favorite pastimes? (5) What sorts of activities do you enjoy? These are just conversation starters. Use your own imagination and interests to complete the information.

Presenting Your First Speech

Your first speech is a very informal presentation. Your teacher may ask you and the person you introduce to stand in front of the class, or you may be asked to stand beside your chair as you are introduced and as you introduce your partner. Relax, take a deep breath, and in a clear, distinct voice introduce your partner.

A good beginning for this presentation is to say, "Class, let me present _____ " and add the person's preferred name. After that you need only present the information you found of interest in interviewing the person. Try to make your partner sound as intriguing and interesting as she or he really is. If you need to refer to your notes, bring them up closer to your eyes rather than slumping down to the notes. Hold them lightly in your hand rather than rest them on a desk or speaker's stand.

When you are ready to end your remarks, conclude with a brief summarizing statement. Be sure you repeat the person's name. This will help your audience members to remember who this person is when you return to the next class session. In fact, try to mention the person's name several times during the speech, as that also helps others to remember the person's name. When you have finished, smile and sit down calmly. In no way indicate to your classmates that you are anxious to sit down.

Alternate Assignment

As an alternative to the first speech in this project you could be asked to provide your class with some background on yourself. Again, this project will allow you to stand in front of your classmates and get the feeling of an audience as you introduce yourself to your classmates. As in the previous materials, use the information you have put on the survey as a starter for ideas of what kinds of information to provide your audience members. Do not merely repeat the answers you have to the questions. Talk with your audience about who you are, where you are from, and what your likes and dislikes are.

Name _____ Age _____ Married _____

Address _____ Year in School _____

Major Field _____ Minor Field _____

Hometown _____

Parents' Names _____

Parents' Occupations _____

Brothers/Sisters _____

Schools Attended _____ Where _____ When _____

Speech Courses Taken _____

_____

Speeches Given _____

_____

Dramatic Activities Participated in _____

_____

Major Interests in High School _____

_____

Known Speech and/or Hearing Defects _____

_____

What I Want to Get from This Course _____

_____

_____

Write below additional information you think will be helpful to your instructor and classmates (travel experience, military service, hobbies, places you have lived, work experiences, recreational likes, favorite TV shows, musical groups, sports, personality traits, etc.). Use the back of the page if necessary.

APPENDIX B
Managing Speech Anxiety

> I believe that anyone can conquer fear by doing the
> things he fears to do, provided he keeps doing them until
> he gets a record of successful experiences behind him.
>
> Eleanor Roosevelt

You say you're afraid to speak in public. Well, who isn't? Or better yet, who hasn't had apprehensions about speaking in public? Of course, the answer is that there is probably no one who has not had some anxieties and apprehensions, or "fears," about public communication. Yes, even such politicians as Abraham Lincoln, William Jennings Bryan, and Geraldine Ferraro, and entertainers such as Mark Twain, Jack Benny, Carol Burnett, Johnny Carson, Debbie Reynolds, James Taylor, Lee Meriwether, and Jane Fonda have suffered from and have attested to a degree of "speech fright" at one time or another. Why, then, should you be any different? Why should you be anything but "normal?"

We use several terms to characterize the same general feelings about speaking in public. Although we often hear them used interchangeably, there are slight differences in the terms. For example, the term "stage fright" refers to the nervousness and anxiety before speaking. This term usually refers to a theatrical presentation, which does not characterize all speeches well, and it has a rather intimidating sound to it. A speech does not necessarily need to be viewed as a "stage" presentation. Likewise, if you are properly prepared, a speech need not be intimidating.

A few scholars have begun to use the term "communication apprehension" to refer to these same anxieties (see, for example, McCroskey, 1970). The problem with using this term is that McCroskey and the others refer to a much broader area of concern than we will discuss here. We do not intend to deal with the day-to-day anxieties or apprehensions of communication. That is, we are not talking about the anxieties of communicating on a one-to-one basis with others, the apprehensions of dealing with people in groups, and so forth. Therefore, we will use the more specific term "speech anxiety," which refers to the real anxieties, fears, or apprehensions that people feel in the public speaking situation.

With that focus, this article first identifies the symptoms of speech anxiety, then presents some of the causes of speech anxiety, and finally, suggests some means of managing speech anxiety.

Symptoms of Speech Anxiety

First, what are the symptoms of speech anxiety? Some authorities suggest that there is a fear response to the speaking situation. What happens is your body secretes hormones and adrenalin into the bloodstream when you are called upon to speak in front of an audience. The more excited you get, the more secretions you have. These chemical reactions are the same reactions you experience when you are suddenly startled by a huge dog or other large animal. Your heart begins to beat faster, your blood pressure rises, more sugar is pumped into your system, your stomach begins to churn, and your body adds several other secretions. All your glands begin operating at full speed. In fact, all your body systems are going full speed except your brain. Beginning speakers sometimes think the audience can even see and hear their hearts thump and see the trembling in their bodies. All this does is to compound your fear.

The visible signs of severe fear are laid out quite nicely by Ochs and Winkler (1979, p. 33). They indicate that the following symptoms may occur separately or in combination:

Voice:	1. Quivers
	2. Too fast
	3. Too slow
	4. Monotonous: unemphatic
Verbal Fluency:	5. Stammers; halting
	6. Awkward pauses
	7. Hunts for words; speech blocked
Mouth and Throat:	8. Swallows repeatedly
	9. Clears throat repeatedly
	10. Breathes heavily
Facial Expressions:	11. No eye contact; rolls eyes
	12. Tense face muscles; grimaces; twitches
	13. Deadpan expression
Arms and Hands:	14. Rigid or tense
	15. Fidgets; waves hands about
	16. Motionless; stiff
Gross Body Movements:	17. Sways; paces; shuffles feet

There are also a number of verbal symptoms that indicate a difficulty in oral communication. These verbal symptoms include excuses and apologies exemplified by self-belittling comments such as "I'm really no good at this," "I haven't had much time to prepare," "I haven't thought about this much," or "I'm probably not saying this right, but...." These verbal clues combined with the nonverbal cues to this lack of preparedness or feeling of inadequacy include actions such as a lack of eye contact; an unenthusiastic tone of voice; a facial expression showing resignation, confusion, or frustration; a slouched posture; and/or a croaking voice.

Another group of symptoms (nonpurposeful, nervous movements) are more visible. These include such movements as shuffling your feet, letting your body sway back and forth, swinging your arms, or holding your body stiff or rigid. An intensified version of movement is pacing back and forth. While not all pacing is a symptom of speech anxiety, or nervousness, speech anxiety might well surface as pacing.

Occasionally, you will exhibit your anxiety through uncontrolled bodily functions such as profuse sweating, dry lips, blushing, heavy breathing, and repeated swallowing and/or throat clearing. These symptoms are signs that your body is overfunctioning to compensate for your nervousness.

It may be helpful to distinguish between these "observed" symptoms that members of an audience may perceive and those "experienced" symptoms that you as a speaker may feel. Through experience we have found that most speakers tend to *overestimate* the degree to which they are affected by anxiety and the extreme to which audience members are aware of it. At the same time members of an audience tend to *underestimate* those same anxieties. It seems rather obvious that some of the symptoms of speech anxiety are not observable to your audience members. For example, listeners can't see apprehension, anxiety, embarrassment, or self-consciousness. Nor can they see how fast your heart is beating or how short of breath you are. They can only infer what you are feeling from your behaviors, which they do see. In fact, audiences often do not notice symptoms that may disturb you and magnify your problem—the slightly quavering voice, unnatural inflection, trembling hands and knees, flushed or pale face, rigid or uncomfortable posture, dry mouth, heavy breathing, rapid heart beat, or difficulty in finding the right word. The farther the audience is from you, the less obvious these symptoms become to them. Remember, light and sound waves get wider as the distance increases, so what you may notice up close, your audience members in the back of the room may not perceive at all.

Just as you seek the causes for an illness, you must also seek the causes of speech anxiety if you wish to deal with it. Understandably, a doctor would not treat the symptoms of an illness. Doctors treat the causes of your illnesses. So, too, you must treat the causes of speech anxiety and not the symptoms. Often the symptoms are confusing and you tend to react (and sometimes overreact) to the symptoms rather than try to determine their causes. The next section of this article deals with identifying the causes of speech anxiety in the hope that you will learn to diagnose the causes of your own specific fears and be able to work on lessening the level of your anxiety.

Causes of Speech Anxiety

Unfortunately, there is no test yielding an immediate, foolproof analysis of your systems. Nor is there a diagnostic examination like a computer inspection of your body's systems for what is causing your anxiety. Determining the causes of your anxiety is much like the physician and his or her diagnosis of your illnesses; there may be several causes for a single symptom, and some symptoms may be situation-specific. Furthermore, you may not be concerned with the cause of your anxiety; you may be concerned only about avoiding the uncomfortable feelings and nervousness that you associate with the speaking event. In this case the elimination of the speaking situation would solve all your problems. Be assured, ignoring the causes of speech anxiety will not make them go away, no matter how much you may wish it. If you are going to deal with the feelings you have concerning speech anxiety, you must deal with the causes of that anxiety.

Several authorities suggest that speech anxiety is a learned behavior. According to their theory, from the time we are small children we are taught to fear performing in public. Parents and teachers reassure us by saying, "you'll do fine, just don't be scared." Calling attention to public performance as a fearful thing (something to be avoided and dodged if possible) instills fear in us. It is something we have learned.

Likewise, in today's success-oriented society, winning becomes all-important. Perfection usually has been stressed since we were children. Anything that is not perfect (or at least successful in some measure) is spurned. You, no doubt, have been taught to fear failure. You have seen winners rewarded and losers punished. You have seen admiration for success and ridicule for failure, and the only way you can avoid punishment (ridicule) is to win (succeed). This drive for success has further reinforced within us the need to be perfect and not make any mistakes—especially in front of other people.

This "public fear" is compounded in the public speaking situation because so many people can witness and ridicule our mistakes. Thus, the public speaking situation is about the most fearful experience known to humans. Almost every year someone reports a new study claiming that the fear of public speaking is the number one fear of most Americans. In fact, most Americans report that the fear of public speaking is greater than the fears of snakes, heights, flying, and even death.

Ochs and Winkler (1979) explain that according to the theory of emotion (William James and Carl Lange) we react from an awareness of emotion. This is illustrated by the story of the man walking in the woods who suddenly encounters a bear:

Perceiving the bear as a danger, the man's brain immediately prepares the body for an emergency by putting the muscular, glandular, and vascular systems on the "red alert status." The heartbeat and pulse races; the bloodstream is flooded with adrenalin and thyroxin; in short, the man meeting the bear feels very much like a speaker mounting a dais to give a speech.

According to the theory, the man's bodily reaction to the bear is normal and useful. What frightens the man is not so much the bear as his body's sudden and urgent reactions to it.

The same is true of the speaker. What upsets you most is your awareness of your own uncomfortable feelings. It is unnerving to hear the frantic thumping in your heart and feel the blood racing through your veins, especially when you imagine that your audience members can see what you are feeling. As audience members most of us have little notion of the real suffering of a speaker.

It is common to hear that a certain amount of nervousness or anxiety is normal; or that most speakers suffer from speech anxiety. While this is probably somewhat true, it does little to diagnose the causes and helps even less in reducing the tension in public speaking situations. As speakers, we want actions, and we want them soon. We are not too interested in other people's fears, but rather, we want to know about our own fears and what we can do about them.

Buehler and Linkugel (1962) listed a number of potential sources of speech anxiety. While you should not view this list as exhaustive, it may help you in determining which factor or factors produce your anxiety:

Fear of physical unattractiveness. The speaker feels that she/he is not handsome, pretty, or is improperly dressed.

Fear of social inadequacy. The speaker fears that his/her behavior will be perceived as inappropriate or crude. This implies social inferiority.

Fear of criticism. The speaker fears and may be over-sensitive to negative feedback from the audience. It may be that this person has lived an entire lifetime of negative criticism.

Fear of failure. The speaker fears a social blunder (or possibility of blundering) or at least not meeting with success.

Fear of the unknown. The inexperienced speaker has not yet met with the situation and does not know what to expect. It may be that the speaker is merely inexperienced and has met with embarrassment in a previous speaking experience.

Fear of speech anxiety. The speaker is afraid of being afraid. The symptoms of speech anxiety may set in and prompt this fear.

Conflicting emotions. The speaker faces the simultaneous fear of failure and desire to succeed. This causes a turmoil that adds to the distress.

Excitement from anticipation. The speaker is so intoxicated and excited about the event itself that it prompts the same physical reactions as would fear.

Finally, Buehler and Linkugel (1962) speculated that character traits might play a large part in causing speech anxiety. If you have developed a full measure of courage, determination, patience, enthusiasm, and friendliness, you will cope better with speech anxiety than the speaker who is naturally timid, cowardly, lazy, indifferent, impatient, and unfriendly.

All of this is ultimately linked to your self-concept. It seems that being happy with who you are and what you stand for means a lot when it comes to coping with your anxieties. Having confidence in your abilities and pride in those characteristics that make you unique are also important. It is essential, then, to think and feel good about yourself in order to minimize your speech anxieties.

In analyzing yourself and trying to diagnose your particular communication anxieties, you need to ask yourself some questions about the potential causes for your personal anxieties. For example, am I expecting too much of myself? Am I afraid to fail? Am I willing to accept negative feedback? Am I willing to perceive of speaking in public as having positive outcomes? Am I willing to accept that the rewards for communicative success outweigh the penalties for failure? Am I willing to develop a positive attitude toward myself? Am I willing to work on improving? When you can answer "yes" to all these questions, then you are ready to begin managing your speech anxieties.

Managing Speech Anxiety

Anxiety is inevitable for most people and need not detract from your speech presentation. Instead, you need to learn to control or "manage" speech anxiety so it does not impede the effectiveness of your speeches. In fact, you can channel your tension into energy and involvement in your speech, which adds to the overall enthusiasm of your presentation. Learning how to channel your excess energy into positive rather than negative effects is difficult. A couple of shots of whiskey (or another drug) before your speech will probably serve to eliminate some of your fears; it will probably also make you inarticulate, comical, and pathetic. In addition, your speech will likely be a total waste of time for your audience members. When you experience speech anxiety, excess energy accumulates in your body and needs release. What you need to do is find a way of releasing your excess energy so it is a positive rather than a negative factor in your presentation.

To prevent losing your hard-earned credibility, here are some strategies for managing your speech anxiety. View these suggestions as tactics to be tried because they have worked for others, not as prescriptions to be taken to "cure" your anxiety. In the case of speech anxiety there are no known "cures"; there are only suggestions to help "manage" or control the anxiety so it does not interfere with the speaking situation and your presentation.

Know the Source of Your Anxiety   First, you must do some careful self-analyzing to find out what is causing you to be nervous or anxious in the speaking situation. Anxiety, to some degree, is natural in a risk-taking situation; and for most people a speech is a risk. Since it is natural to desire success, it is normal to be nervous over a speaking situation when you can't accurately predict the level or degree of success. If you don't have some anxiety, you either don't care or you don't understand the situation. If the cause of your anxiety is a desire to succeed, you should not let it bother you too much because your preparation will be sufficient to handle the situation. On the other hand, if your anxiety comes from another cause, you need to discover ways to reduce your anxiety.

In addition to the analysis of the cause of your anxiety, you can work on developing a positive attitude about yourself. By telling yourself that you can do it, you will soon begin to believe that you actually *can* do it. Telling yourself "you can do it" helps build your self-concept and allows you to accept negative feedback as a way to improve.

Then, in your public performance, project a positive image. If you as a public speaker look, act, and speak as if you expect to do well, your audience members will accept you and your ideas more readily. This in turn helps to build your self-confidence further. It is a never-ending cycle of building and growing. On the other hand, apologies and excuses for not doing well could further damage an already fragile self-concept. Develop and project a positive self-image.

Know Your Audience   Try to get to know as much as possible about your audience members ahead of time. You may want to know about the occasion, the rest of the program, the time limitations, the approximate ages of your audience members, their educational backgrounds, and so on. Such knowledge helps eliminate the element of surprise, makes you aware of the speaking situation, and assists your preparation so the materials you present are adapted as much as possible to your specific audience for maximum effectiveness.

Remember, also, your audience members are on your side. It is extremely rare to find audience members who enjoy watching a speaker fail. The classroom audience is particularly supportive in this manner, so just talk to them. After all, all of you have the same problems and all of you have to speak to each other.

Select a Topic You Like   A third suggestion for managing speech anxiety is to select something to talk about that interests you. It is very difficult to discuss something about which you know little, in which you have little interest, or about which you care little. On the other hand, you will soon forget that you are speaking to an audience and really get enthusiastic if your topic interests you. If you merely select the first topic that you hear or read or think about, you may have a topic that will itself increase your fears and anxieties. The pressures and jitters will always be compounded when you speak on a dull or uninteresting topic.

Be Prepared   For many speakers anxiety is caused by a fear of failure and/or ridicule. If this is the case with you, a well-prepared speech will increase your self-confidence, and thus help you reduce your anxiety. Self-confidence is taking command of the situation causing your anxiety. Just knowing that you are ready to speak will help you *feel* confident that you can cope with the situation.

Practice   Another closely related area is practice, which needs special attention. One of the most difficult tasks in speaking is to speak from a manuscript. No beginning speaker is ready to speak in this advanced form. So, do not write out your speech and try to "read" it. Likewise, do not write it out and try to memorize the words so they come out precisely as you have written them. This is also an advanced method of delivery. Manuscripts and memorization add undue pressure to the speaking situation by creating barriers and causing more worry (i.e., fear of forgetting) than the help they might offer. Instead, practice various phrasings, use different words each time you rehearse, and rearrange the order of minor supporting ideas and supporting references. What this actually does is give you several options when you are actually speaking. Ideas do not have to be presented in a "set" order. In this manner, you will not be searching for an exact word when you need it, but rather, you will need only the idea you want to express. This exercise will help develop and further build your self-confidence also.

Exercise   Now it may sound dumb to recommend that a speaker exercise just prior to a speech. But remember, as the public speaking event gets closer, you tend to secrete more sugar into your circulatory system, and thus have an excess of energy. Because of this, you need some way to rid yourself of that excess energy, and exercise is one of the best methods. The question is how?

It is rather obvious that a speaker can't do jumping jacks or pushups immediately prior to speaking, or run around a classroom in order to reduce tension. It is equally ridiculous to expect that students would run around the building until it was time to speak, then rush in and make a presentation. Here are some exercises, however, which you can perform easily to help reduce your tension and anxiety.

1. You could do some isometric exercises as you sit at your desk. For example, you could clench your fists very tightly, hold them for a few seconds, and then relax them. Likewise, you could push against the arm of the chair, or press your feet on the floor. In each case, if you repeat the exercise several times, you will feel some of the tension escaping.
2. Another exercise that works very well for some people is a breathing exercise. No matter how tense you might get, you never completely stop breathing, so work on controlling your intake and exhale of air. For example, take a slow, deep breath; hold it; then let it gush out. As you continue, keep your intake slow and deep, but as you exhale, control your breath more and more until you have a natural, slow, deep inhalation and exhalation. The advantage of such an exercise is that it helps control your pounding heart, takes your mind off other activities, and, of course, can be done without being noticed by other people.
3. Another exercise that is helpful for some people is a yawning exercise. If your voice has a tendency to crack when you speak, or has a high pitch to it, try yawning before you get up to speak. Yawning tends to relax your vocal cords, and also relaxes your tense facial muscles. These tightened muscles are what cause you to sound different.
4. A fourth exercise that can help is a mental exercise. Again, it can be done without others noticing and has the added advantage of making you forget about yourself. In

other words, it takes your concentration away from yourself and transposes it to another topic. As you sit in the classroom listening to other speeches, listen carefully. Ponder each point made by the speaker, question the speaker's evidence (or lack of evidence), note the content of the speech, what the speaker uses for support, and the organizational pattern. You can even analyze the speaker's delivery. By the time it is your turn to speak, you will be ready to show that you can do as well as that speaker or better.

5. Another group of exercises can be performed while you are speaking, and tend to give you something to do to release your excess energy during the speech. For example, even before you speak, if you pause and smile, it has a tendency not only to use some energy, but it also tends to disarm yourself and the audience. It relaxes both of you. As you speak, use gestures. These movements will again use up some of your excess energy. The use of visual aids also causes you to use up some more of your excess energy.

Be Conversational   Using a conversational style of delivery can also help you relax. If you mentally and physically prepare yourself to just "talk" with your audience members, you should have no problem in being conversational. The idea of "making a speech" or "preaching" at people in your audience may cause you to become less than conversational, plus it has a tendency to make you sound a little artificial.

Reward Yourself   A good technique for helping you reinforce yourself is to provide some system of self-reward for presenting a speech. Because feedback is not always immediate (especially in the classroom situation), this might provide another means of building self-confidence. All it really amounts to is giving yourself a treat, a small luxury (a dinner out, a new item of clothing, and so on) as a reward for doing well. Besides, you deserve it.

Get Involved with Your Speech   Get excited about what you are saying. Believe in it. The more you focus your energy on your speech itself, the less you focus on your own nervousness and yourself. Getting involved with your speech will make it much easier for you to forget your speaking situation.

Desensitization   A final suggestion for managing the fears of public speaking is through desensitization. This practice is recommended only for those people who, after *repeatedly* trying the previous suggestions (plus any others they can think of or someone else suggests), can't control or manage their anxieties. There are various methods and techniques for this, so see a speech teacher or counselor who can either provide the necessary training or recommend someone who can provide it.

Conclusion

Although managing your speech anxieties is not an easy task, it is not an impossible one. Remember, anything worth doing is worth doing well. Work on reducing your own anxieties through finding out what causes them, treating the causes of your anxiety rather than the symptoms, and building your own self-confidence. Give yourself time and as many public speaking experiences as possible, and you will inevitably have some very rewarding experiences. Look at the people listed earlier who had similar problems. These people learned to manage their speech anxieties before they became famous.

References

Bostrom, R. N. (1988). *Communicating in Public.* Edina, Minnesota: Burgess Publishing.

Buehler, E. C. & Linkugel, W. (1962). *Speech: A First Course.* New York: Harper & Row, Publishers.

McCabe, B.P., Jr. & Bender, C. G. (1981). *Speaking As a Practical Matter* (4th ed.). Boston: Allyn & Bacon, Inc.

McCroskey, J. C. (1970). Measures of Communication-Bound Anxiety. *Speech Monographs, 37,* 269–277.

Ochs, D. J. & Winkler, A. C. (1979). *A Brief Introduction to Speech.* Chicago: Harcourt Brace Jovanovich.

Samovar, L. A. & Mills, J (1989). *Oral Communication* (7th ed.). Dubuque, Iowa: Wm. C. Brown Company, Publishers.

Sprague, J. & Stuart, D. (1988). *The Speaker's Handbook* (2nd ed.). San Diego: Harcourt Brace Jovanovich.

Taylor, A. (1984). *Speaking in Public* (2nd ed.). Englewood Cliffs, New Jersey: Prentice-Hall, Inc.

Zimmerman, G. I. (1979). *Public Speaking Today.* St. Paul, Minnesota: West Publishing Company.

APPENDIX C

Articulation Exercises

In Project 11 we identified several problems in the vocal aspects of delivery, including such problems as articulation and pronunciation. The following exercises will help you identify your problems and provide practice in eliminating errors:

I. Articulation is the shaping of the sounds of words by the speaker's lips, teeth, tongue, and hard and soft palates. Common problems are nasality, indistinct articulation, and haste and indifference. Work on correcting the problems of laziness you have when you make "pen" become "pin"—remember, a pen you write with, but a pin is for holding pieces of cloth together. Following are some common sounds to watch out for:

flat *a* sound	man, fat, piano
i and *e* sounds	beg, get, big
ow sound	bow, brown
oi sound	boil, toil
ng sound	going, doing
th sound	with, that
wh sound	which, what, when, where
final *t* sound	west, best, jest
s sound	sister, salt, save

II. Articulation Errors

A. Addition: The problems with these words is that sounds have been added that do not belong in the words:

athalete	instead of	athlete
realator	instead of	realtor
idear	instead of	idea
filim	instead of	film
alblum	instead of	album
warsh	instead of	wash

B. Omission: The problems with these words is that sounds have been omitted from the words:

govment	instead of	government
reconize	instead of	recognize
varable	instead of	variable
histry	instead of	history
wanna	instead of	want to
runnin	instead of	running
biness	instead of	business
bub	instead of	bulb
favrit	instead of	favorite
wensdy	instead of	Wednesday

C. Substitution: The problems with these words is that incorrect sounds have been substituted for the correct ones:

jist or jess	instead of	just
git	instead of	get
wader	instead of	waiter
beder	instead of	better
ax	instead of	ask
vetrin	instead of	veteran
far	instead of	fire
pitcher	instead of	picture
grain	instead of	green
futher	instead of	farther
eye talian	instead of	Italian

III. Pronunciation problems: We generally have two problems in pronouncing words—we either accent the wrong syllable, or we pronounce silent letters.

A. Errors in accenting the wrong syllable:

in´surance	instead of	in sur´ ance
the a´ ter	instead of	the´ a ter
poe´ lese	instead of	police´
see´ ment	instead of	cement´
bat´tree	instead of	battery
re´tire	instead of	re tire´
ree´sent	instead of	re sent´
ree´ward	instead of	re ward´

B. Errors in pronouncing silent sounds:

off ten	instead of	offen	for often
herbs	instead of	erbs	for herbs
Illinois	instead of	Illinoi	for Illinois
Des Moines	instead of	De Moine	for Des Moines

IV. The following exercises are designed for you to practice both articulation and pronunciation problems. They should also help you enunciate more clearly.

A. To practice enunciating words clearly, try the following:

ESAW WOOD

Esaw Wood sawed wood. Esaw Wood would saw wood. All the wood Esaw Wood saw Esaw Wood would saw. In other words, all the wood Esaw saw to saw Esaw sought to saw. Oh the wood Wood would saw! And oh, the wood-saw with which Wood would saw wood. But one day Wood's wood-saw would saw no wood, and thus the wood Wood sawed was not the wood Wood would saw if Wood's wood-saw would saw wood. Now, Wood would saw if Wood's wood-saw would saw wood. Now, Wood would saw wood with a wood-saw that would saw wood, so Esaw sought a saw that would saw wood. One day Esaw saw a saw saw wood as no other wood-saw Wood saw would saw wood. In fact, of all the wood-saws Wood saw saw wood would saw wood, and I never saw a wood-saw that would saw as the wood-saw Wood saw would saw until I saw Esaw saw wood with the wood-saw Wood saw saw wood. Now Wood saws wood with the wood-saw Wood saw saw wood.

B. To practice your *t* sound words, try this:

Tit for tat	Tit for tat	Tit for tat
Tit tat toh	Tit tat toh	Tit tat toh

Oh East is East and West is West

A tutor who tooted the flute
Tried to tutor two tooter to toot;
Said the two to the tutor: "Is it harder to toot, or
to tutor two tooters to toot?"

Betty Botta bought some butter
"But," said she, "This butter's bitter,
If I put it in my batter
It will make my batter bitter;
But a bit of better butter
Will make by bitter batter better."
So she bought a bit of butter
Better than the bitter butter
And it made her bitter batter better.
So, 'twas better Betty Botta
Bought a bit of better butter.

C. To practice your *d* sound, try this:

Thud!   Thud!   Thud!

The rider was riding in the meadow.
The writer was writing a letter.
The rider was on his mettle.
The writer won a medal.

The writer's daughter started to go to a theatre party in the city.
An old motto of the United States is, "United we stand, divided we fall."
The city had a beautiful waterfront.
She visited a pretty little city in the middle west.

D. To practice articulating sounds, try these:

1. Bring me some ice, not some mice.
2. The sea ceaseth and sufficeth us.
3. Suddenly seaward swept the squall.
4. He sawed six long, slim, sleek, slender saplings.
5. Amos Ames, the amiable aeronaut, aided in the aerial enterprise at the age of eighty-eight.
6. She sells sea shells; shall Susan sell sea shells?
7. Six thick thistle sticks; six thick thistles stick.
8. A big black bug bit a big black bear.
9. Amidst the mists and coldest frosts
   With stoutest hearts and loudest boasts,
   He thrusts his fists against the posts,
   And still insists he sees the ghosts.
10. He rejoiceth, approacheth, accepteth, ceaseth.
11. A blue trip slip for an eight-cent fare.
    A buff trip slip for a six-cent fare.
    A pink trip slip for a three-cent fare.
12. Geese cackle, cattle low, crows caw, cocks crow.
13. An analogy of another art is as effective as is ours.
14. What whim led White Whitney to whittle, whistle, whisper, and whimper near the wharf, where a floundering whale might wheel and whirl?
15. See the pretty rubber buggy-bumpers.
16. And that government of the people, by the people, and for the people, shall not perish from the earth.

17. Round about them orchards sweep,
    Apple and peach tree fruited deep.
18. She left the web, she left the loom,
    She made three paces through the room,
    She saw the water lily bloom,
    She saw the helmet and the plume.
19. There was a rustling that seemed like a bustling
    Of merry crowds justling at pitching and hustling;
    Small feet were pattering, wooden shoes clattering,
    Little hands clapping, and little tongues chattering,
    Out came the children running.
20. Think before you speak; pronounce not imperfectly, nor bring out your
    words too hastily, but orderly and distinctly.

APPENDIX **D**

Special Forms

Outline Forms

Speech Criticism Forms

Report on a Speech Heard in Public

Name _____ *Date* _____ *Type of Speech* _____

Time Limits:
Type of Outline:
Number of sources required:

TITLE _____

    I. INTRODUCTION

        A. Attention getter:

        B. Credibility:

        C. Arouse Interest:

    II. THESIS and PREVIEW:

    III. BODY (main points and supporting materials)

    IV. CONCLUSION (summary or other suitable conclusion)

PRINTED SOURCES OF INFORMATION

Give complete information for each source. When the author's name, the title of the article, or the date is not listed, write "none listed."

1. Author's name _____

Title of article _____

Book or magazine containing article _____

_____ Date of publication _____

Chapters and/or pages containing material _____

2. Author's name _____

Title of article _____

Book or magazine containing article _____

_____ Date of publication _____

3. Title of pamphlet or folder _____

Published by _____ Date of publication _____

Chapters and/or pages containing material _____

INTERVIEW SOURCES OF INFORMATION

1. Name of person interviewed _____ Date of interview _____

Title, position, and occupation _____

_____

Why is this person an authority on the subject? Be specific _____

_____

2. Name of person interviewed _____ Date of interview _____

Title, position, and occupation _____

_____

Why is this person an authority on the subject? Be specific _____

_____

_____

PERSONAL SOURCE OF INFORMATION

1. Personal source—your name _____

Why are you an authority on this subject? Include dates, places, and circumstances under which you became an authority. Be specific.

_____

_____

_____

Time Limits:
Type of Outline:
Number of sources required:

TITLE _____

    I. INTRODUCTION

          A. Attention getter:

          B. Credibility:

          C. Arouse Interest:

    II. THESIS and PREVIEW:

    III. BODY (main points and supporting materials)

    IV. CONCLUSION (summary or other suitable conclusion)

PRINTED SOURCES OF INFORMATION

Give complete information for each source. When the author's name, the title of the article, or the date is not listed, write "none listed."

1. Author's name _____

   Title of article _____

   Book or magazine containing article _____

   _____ Date of publication _____

   Chapters and/or pages containing material _____

2. Author's name _____

   Title of article _____

   Book or magazine containing article _____

   _____ Date of publication _____

3. Title of pamphlet or folder _____

   Published by _____ Date of publication _____

   Chapters and/or pages containing material _____

INTERVIEW SOURCES OF INFORMATION

1. Name of person interviewed _____ Date of interview _____

   Title, position, and occupation _____

   _____

   Why is this person an authority on the subject? Be specific _____

   _____

2. Name of person interviewed _____ Date of interview _____

   Title, position, and occupation _____

   _____

   Why is this person an authority on the subject? Be specific _____

   _____

   _____

PERSONAL SOURCE OF INFORMATION

1. Personal source—your name _____

   Why are you an authority on this subject? Include dates, places, and circumstances under which you became an authority. Be specific.

   _____

   _____

   _____

Name _____ *Date* _____ *Type of Speech* _____

Time Limits:
Type of Outline:
Number of sources required:

TITLE _____

   I. INTRODUCTION

       A. Attention getter:

       B. Credibility:

       C. Arouse Interest:

  II. THESIS and PREVIEW:

  III. BODY (main points and supporting materials)

  IV. CONCLUSION (summary or other suitable conclusion)

PRINTED SOURCES OF INFORMATION

Give complete information for each source. When the author's name, the title of the article, or the date is not listed, write "none listed."

1. Author's name _____

Title of article _____

Book or magazine containing article _____

_____ Date of publication _____

Chapters and/or pages containing material _____

2. Author's name _____

Title of article _____

Book or magazine containing article _____

_____ Date of publication _____

3. Title of pamphlet or folder _____

Published by _____ Date of publication _____

Chapters and/or pages containing material _____

INTERVIEW SOURCES OF INFORMATION

1. Name of person interviewed _____ Date of interview _____

Title, position, and occupation _____

_____

Why is this person an authority on the subject? Be specific _____

_____

2. Name of person interviewed _____ Date of interview _____

Title, position, and occupation _____

_____

Why is this person an authority on the subject? Be specific _____

_____

_____

PERSONAL SOURCE OF INFORMATION

1. Personal source—your name _____

Why are you an authority on this subject? Include dates, places, and circumstances under which you became an authority. Be specific.

_____

_____

_____

Name _____ *Date* _____ *Type of Speech* _____

Time Limits:
Type of Outline:
Number of sources required:

TITLE _____

    I. INTRODUCTION

        A. Attention getter:

        B. Credibility:

        C. Arouse Interest:

    II. THESIS and PREVIEW:

    III. BODY (main points and supporting materials)

    IV. CONCLUSION (summary or other suitable conclusion)

PRINTED SOURCES OF INFORMATION

Give complete information for each source. When the author's name, the title of the article, or the date is not listed, write "none listed."

1. Author's name _____

    Title of article _____

    Book or magazine containing article _____

    _____ Date of publication _____

    Chapters and/or pages containing material _____

2. Author's name _____

    Title of article _____

    Book or magazine containing article _____

    _____ Date of publication _____

3. Title of pamphlet or folder _____

    Published by _____ Date of publication _____

    Chapters and/or pages containing material _____

INTERVIEW SOURCES OF INFORMATION

1. Name of person interviewed _____ Date of interview _____

    Title, position, and occupation _____

    _____

    Why is this person an authority on the subject? Be specific _____

    _____

2. Name of person interviewed _____ Date of interview _____

    Title, position, and occupation _____

    _____

    Why is this person an authority on the subject? Be specific _____

    _____

    _____

PERSONAL SOURCE OF INFORMATION

1. Personal source—your name _____

    Why are you an authority on this subject? Include dates, places, and circumstances under which you became an authority. Be specific.

    _____

    _____

    _____

Time Limits:
Type of Outline:
Number of sources required:

TITLE _____

    I. INTRODUCTION

        A. Attention getter:

        B. Credibility:

        C. Arouse Interest:

    II. THESIS and PREVIEW:

    III. BODY (main points and supporting materials)

    IV. CONCLUSION (summary or other suitable conclusion)

PRINTED SOURCES OF INFORMATION

Give complete information for each source. When the author's name, the title of the article, or the date is not listed, write "none listed."

1. Author's name _____
   Title of article _____
   Book or magazine containing article _____
   _____ Date of publication _____
   Chapters and/or pages containing material _____

2. Author's name _____
   Title of article _____
   Book or magazine containing article _____
   _____ Date of publication _____

3. Title of pamphlet or folder _____
   Published by _____ Date of publication _____
   Chapters and/or pages containing material _____

INTERVIEW SOURCES OF INFORMATION

1. Name of person interviewed _____ Date of interview _____
   Title, position, and occupation _____
   _____
   Why is this person an authority on the subject? Be specific _____
   _____

2. Name of person interviewed _____ Date of interview _____
   Title, position, and occupation _____
   _____
   Why is this person an authority on the subject? Be specific _____
   _____
   _____

PERSONAL SOURCE OF INFORMATION

1. Personal source—your name _____
   Why are you an authority on this subject? Include dates, places, and circumstances under which you became an authority. Be specific.
   _____
   _____
   _____

Name _____ Date _____ Type of Speech _____

Time Limits:

Type of Outline:

Number of sources required:

TITLE _____

    I. INTRODUCTION

        A. Attention getter:

        B. Credibility:

        C. Arouse Interest:

    II. THESIS and PREVIEW:

    III. BODY (main points and supporting materials)

    IV. CONCLUSION (summary or other suitable conclusion)

PRINTED SOURCES OF INFORMATION

Give complete information for each source. When the author's name, the title of the article, or the date is not listed, write "none listed."

1. Author's name _____

 Title of article _____

 Book or magazine containing article _____

 _____ Date of publication _____

 Chapters and/or pages containing material _____

2. Author's name _____

 Title of article _____

 Book or magazine containing article _____

 _____ Date of publication _____

3. Title of pamphlet or folder _____

 Published by _____ Date of publication _____

 Chapters and/or pages containing material _____

INTERVIEW SOURCES OF INFORMATION

1. Name of person interviewed _____ Date of interview _____

 Title, position, and occupation _____

 _____

 Why is this person an authority on the subject? Be specific _____

 _____

2. Name of person interviewed _____ Date of interview _____

 Title, position, and occupation _____

 _____

 Why is this person an authority on the subject? Be specific _____

 _____

 _____

PERSONAL SOURCE OF INFORMATION

1. Personal source—your name _____

 Why are you an authority on this subject? Include dates, places, and circumstances under which you became an authority. Be specific.

 _____

 _____

 _____

Name _____ Date _____ Type of Speech _____
Time Limits:
Type of Outline:
Number of sources required:

TITLE _____

    I. INTRODUCTION

        A. Attention getter:

        B. Credibility:

        C. Arouse Interest:

    II. THESIS and PREVIEW:

    III. BODY (main points and supporting materials)

    IV. CONCLUSION (summary or other suitable conclusion)

PRINTED SOURCES OF INFORMATION

Give complete information for each source. When the author's name, the title of the article, or the date is not listed, write "none listed."

1. Author's name _____

    Title of article _____

    Book or magazine containing article _____

    _____ Date of publication _____

    Chapters and/or pages containing material _____

2. Author's name _____

    Title of article _____

    Book or magazine containing article _____

    _____ Date of publication _____

3. Title of pamphlet or folder _____

    Published by _____ Date of publication _____

    Chapters and/or pages containing material _____

INTERVIEW SOURCES OF INFORMATION

1. Name of person interviewed _____ Date of interview _____

    Title, position, and occupation _____

    _____

    Why is this person an authority on the subject? Be specific _____

    _____

2. Name of person interviewed _____ Date of interview _____

    Title, position, and occupation _____

    _____

    Why is this person an authority on the subject? Be specific _____

    _____

    _____

PERSONAL SOURCE OF INFORMATION

1. Personal source—your name _____

    Why are you an authority on this subject? Include dates, places, and circumstances under which you became an authority. Be specific.

    _____

    _____

    _____

Name _____ Date _____ Type of Speech _____

Time Limits:

Type of Outline:

Number of sources required:

TITLE _____

    I. INTRODUCTION

        A. Attention getter:

        B. Credibility:

        C. Arouse Interest:

    II. THESIS and PREVIEW:

    III. BODY (main points and supporting materials)

    IV. CONCLUSION (summary or other suitable conclusion)

PRINTED SOURCES OF INFORMATION

Give complete information for each source. When the author's name, the title of the article, or the date is not listed, write "none listed."

1. Author's name _____
   Title of article _____
   Book or magazine containing article _____
   _____ Date of publication _____
   Chapters and/or pages containing material _____

2. Author's name _____
   Title of article _____
   Book or magazine containing article _____
   _____ Date of publication _____

3. Title of pamphlet or folder _____
   Published by _____ Date of publication _____
   Chapters and/or pages containing material _____

INTERVIEW SOURCES OF INFORMATION

1. Name of person interviewed _____ Date of interview _____
   Title, position, and occupation _____
   _____
   Why is this person an authority on the subject? Be specific _____
   _____
   _____

2. Name of person interviewed _____ Date of interview _____
   Title, position, and occupation _____
   _____
   Why is this person an authority on the subject? Be specific _____
   _____
   _____

PERSONAL SOURCE OF INFORMATION

1. Personal source—your name _____
   Why are you an authority on this subject? Include dates, places, and circumstances under which you became an authority. Be specific.
   _____
   _____
   _____

Time Limits:
Type of Outline:
Number of sources required:

TITLE _____

    I. INTRODUCTION

        A. Attention getter:

        B. Credibility:

        C. Arouse Interest:

    II. THESIS and PREVIEW:

    III. BODY (main points and supporting materials)

    IV. CONCLUSION (summary or other suitable conclusion)

PRINTED SOURCES OF INFORMATION

Give complete information for each source. When the author's name, the title of the article, or the date is not listed, write "none listed."

1. Author's name _____

   Title of article _____

   Book or magazine containing article _____

   _____ Date of publication _____

   Chapters and/or pages containing material _____

2. Author's name _____

   Title of article _____

   Book or magazine containing article _____

   _____ Date of publication _____

3. Title of pamphlet or folder _____

   Published by _____ Date of publication _____

   Chapters and/or pages containing material _____

INTERVIEW SOURCES OF INFORMATION

1. Name of person interviewed _____ Date of interview _____

   Title, position, and occupation _____

   _____

   Why is this person an authority on the subject? Be specific _____

   _____

2. Name of person interviewed _____ Date of interview _____

   Title, position, and occupation _____

   _____

   Why is this person an authority on the subject? Be specific _____

   _____

   _____

PERSONAL SOURCE OF INFORMATION

1. Personal source—your name _____

   Why are you an authority on this subject? Include dates, places, and circumstances under which you became an authority. Be specific.

   _____

   _____

   _____

Name _____ *Date* _____ *Type of Speech* _____

Time Limits:

Type of Outline:

Number of sources required:

TITLE _____

    I. INTRODUCTION

        A. Attention getter:

        B. Credibility:

        C. Arouse Interest:

    II. THESIS and PREVIEW:

    III. BODY (main points and supporting materials)

    IV. CONCLUSION (summary or other suitable conclusion)

PRINTED SOURCES OF INFORMATION

Give complete information for each source. When the author's name, the title of the article, or the date is not listed, write "none listed."

1. Author's name _____

Title of article _____

Book or magazine containing article _____

_____ Date of publication _____

Chapters and/or pages containing material _____

2. Author's name _____

Title of article _____

Book or magazine containing article _____

_____ Date of publication _____

3. Title of pamphlet or folder _____

Published by _____ Date of publication _____

Chapters and/or pages containing material _____

INTERVIEW SOURCES OF INFORMATION

1. Name of person interviewed _____ Date of interview _____

Title, position, and occupation _____

_____

Why is this person an authority on the subject? Be specific _____

_____

2. Name of person interviewed _____ Date of interview _____

Title, position, and occupation _____

_____

Why is this person an authority on the subject? Be specific _____

_____

_____

PERSONAL SOURCE OF INFORMATION

1. Personal source—your name _____

Why are you an authority on this subject? Include dates, places, and circumstances under which you became an authority. Be specific.

_____

_____

_____

Name _____ *Date* _____ *Type of Speech* _____

Time Limits:

Type of Outline:

Number of sources required:

TITLE _____

    I. INTRODUCTION

        A. Attention getter:

        B. Credibility:

        C. Arouse Interest:

    II. THESIS and PREVIEW:

    III. BODY (main points and supporting materials)

    IV. CONCLUSION (summary or other suitable conclusion)

PRINTED SOURCES OF INFORMATION

Give complete information for each source. When the author's name, the title of the article, or the date is not listed, write "none listed."

1. Author's name _____

Title of article _____

Book or magazine containing article _____

_____ Date of publication _____

Chapters and/or pages containing material _____

2. Author's name _____

Title of article _____

Book or magazine containing article _____

_____ Date of publication _____

3. Title of pamphlet or folder _____

Published by _____ Date of publication _____

Chapters and/or pages containing material _____

INTERVIEW SOURCES OF INFORMATION

1. Name of person interviewed _____ Date of interview _____

Title, position, and occupation _____

_____

Why is this person an authority on the subject? Be specific _____

_____

2. Name of person interviewed _____ Date of interview _____

Title, position, and occupation _____

_____

Why is this person an authority on the subject? Be specific _____

_____

_____

PERSONAL SOURCE OF INFORMATION

1. Personal source—your name _____

Why are you an authority on this subject? Include dates, places, and circumstances under which you became an authority. Be specific.

_____

_____

_____

Outline: **Prepare a 15–30 word complete sentence outline for three different introductions. Hand these to your instructor when you are asked to speak.**

Time Limit: **1–2 minutes for each introduction.**

Speaking notes: **None.**

First Introduction: What kind?

Second Introduction: What kind?

Third Introduction: What kind?

INSTRUCTOR'S COMMENTS:

Grade _____

Name _____ *Date* _____

Outline: Prepare a 15–30 word complete sentence outline for three different conclusions. Hand these to your instructor when you are asked to speak.

Time Limit: ½–2 minutes for each introduction.

Speaking notes: None.

First Conclusion: What kind?

Second Conclusion: What kind?

Third Conclusion: What kind?

INSTRUCTOR'S COMMENTS:

Grade _____

STUDENT SPEECH CRITICISMS

One part of a speech course provides a student with an opportunity to listen to a speech and evaluate it. It is especially helpful to criticize other speeches because it makes you a more careful listener.

In using the forms that follow, you should be fully aware that you are recording only your impressions of the speech. They will be governed by your physical comfort, attentiveness, and careful observations of all that you see and hear. To be most valuable, the impressions should be recorded with care and after some introspection into your own behaviors while you were observing the speaker. Careless observation of a speaker produces at best no more than half-valid criticism. In all fairness to the speaker you should listen carefully and observe closely the points you are going to rate and comment on when writing your impression. By doing this, you will increase the quality of your criticism and be of valuable help to the speaker.

SPEECH CRITICISM   DATE ....

Speaker ....   Subject ....

Critic ....

	Poor	Very weak	Weak	Fair	Adequate	Good	Very good	Excellent	Superior	
	1	2	3	4	5	6	7	8	9	Write Comments
1. Introduction										....
2. Clarity of purpose										....
3. Language										....
4. Body language										....
5. Eye contact										....
6. Use of voice										....
7. Enthusiasm, vigor										....
8. Confidence, self–control										....
9. Adaptation to audience										....
10. Organization of material										....
11. Conclusion										....

SPEECH CRITICISM   DATE ....

Speaker ....   Subject...............

Critic ....

	Poor	Very weak	Weak	Fair	Adequate	Good	Very good	Excellent	Superior	
	1	2	3	4	5	6	7	8	9	Write Comments
1. Introduction										....
2. Clarity of purpose										....
3. Language										....
4. Body language										....
5. Eye contact										....
6. Use of voice										....
7. Enthusiasm, vigor										....
8. Confidence, self-control										....
9. Adaptation to audience										....
10. Organization of material										....
11. Conclusion										....

— — — — — — — — — — — — — — — — — — — —

SPEECH CRITICISM   DATE ....

Speaker ....   Subject...............

Critic ....

	Poor	Very weak	Weak	Fair	Adequate	Good	Very good	Excellent	Superior	
	1	2	3	4	5	6	7	8	9	Write Comments
1. Introduction										....
2. Clarity of purpose										....
3. Language										....
4. Body language										....
5. Eye contact										....
6. Use of voice										....
7. Enthusiasm, vigor										....
8. Confidence, self-control										....
9. Adaptation to audience										....
10. Organization of material										....
11. Conclusion										....

SPEECH CRITICISM   DATE ....

Speaker ....

Critic ....

Subject ....

	Poor	Very weak	Weak	Fair	Adequate	Good	Very good	Excellent	Superior	
	1	2	3	4	5	6	7	8	9	Write Comments
1. Introduction										....
2. Clarity of purpose										....
3. Language										....
4. Body language										....
5. Eye contact										....
6. Use of voice										....
7. Enthusiasm, vigor										....
8. Confidence, self-control										....
9. Adaptation to audience										....
10. Organization of material										....
11. Conclusion										....

— —

SPEECH CRITICISM   DATE ....

Speaker ....

Critic ....

Subject ....

	Poor	Very weak	Weak	Fair	Adequate	Good	Very good	Excellent	Superior	
	1	2	3	4	5	6	7	8	9	Write Comments
1. Introduction										....
2. Clarity of purpose										....
3. Language										....
4. Body language										....
5. Eye contact										....
6. Use of voice										....
7. Enthusiasm, vigor										....
8. Confidence, self-control										....
9. Adaptation to audience										....
10. Organization of material										....
11. Conclusion										....

SPEECH CRITICISM   DATE ....

Speaker ....   Subject ....

Critic ....

	Poor	Very weak	Weak	Fair	Adequate	Good	Very good	Excellent	Superior	
	1	2	3	4	5	6	7	8	9	Write Comments
1. Introduction										....
2. Clarity of purpose										....
3. Language										....
4. Body language										....
5. Eye contact										....
6. Use of voice										....
7. Enthusiasm, vigor										....
8. Confidence, self-control										....
9. Adaptation to audience										....
10. Organization of material										....
11. Conclusion										....

— —

SPEECH CRITICISM   DATE ....

Speaker ....   Subject ....

Critic ....

	Poor	Very weak	Weak	Fair	Adequate	Good	Very good	Excellent	Superior	
	1	2	3	4	5	6	7	8	9	Write Comments
1. Introduction										....
2. Clarity of purpose										....
3. Language										....
4. Body language										....
5. Eye contact										....
6. Use of voice										....
7. Enthusiasm, vigor										....
8. Confidence, self-control										....
9. Adaptation to audience										....
10. Organization of material										....
11. Conclusion										....

SPEECH CRITICISM   DATE . . . .

Speaker . . . .   Subject . . . .

Critic . . . .

	Poor	Very weak	Weak	Fair	Adequate	Good	Very good	Excellent	Superior	
	1	2	3	4	5	6	7	8	9	Write Comments
1. Introduction										. . . .
2. Clarity of purpose										. . . .
3. Language										. . . .
4. Body language										. . . .
5. Eye contact										. . . .
6. Use of voice										. . . .
7. Enthusiasm, vigor										. . . .
8. Confidence, self-control										. . . .
9. Adaptation to audience										. . . .
10. Organization of material										. . . .
11. Conclusion										. . . .

- -

SPEECH CRITICISM   DATE . . . .

Speaker . . . .   Subject . . . .

Critic . . . .

	Poor	Very weak	Weak	Fair	Adequate	Good	Very good	Excellent	Superior	
	1	2	3	4	5	6	7	8	9	Write Comments
1. Introduction										. . . .
2. Clarity of purpose										. . . .
3. Language										. . . .
4. Body language										. . . .
5. Eye contact										. . . .
6. Use of voice										. . . .
7. Enthusiasm, vigor										. . . .
8. Confidence, self-control										. . . .
9. Adaptation to audience										. . . .
10. Organization of material										. . . .
11. Conclusion										. . . .

SPEECH CRITICISM   DATE ....

Speaker ....   Subject ....

Critic ....

	Poor	Very weak	Weak	Fair	Adequate	Good	Very good	Excellent	Superior	Write Comments
	1	2	3	4	5	6	7	8	9	
1. Introduction										....
2. Clarity of purpose										....
3. Language										....
4. Body language										....
5. Eye contact										....
6. Use of voice										....
7. Enthusiasm, vigor										....
8. Confidence, self-control										....
9. Adaptation to audience										....
10. Organization of material										....
11. Conclusion										....

- -

SPEECH CRITICISM   DATE ....

Speaker ....   Subject ....

Critic ....

	Poor	Very weak	Weak	Fair	Adequate	Good	Very good	Excellent	Superior	Write Comments
	1	2	3	4	5	6	7	8	9	
1. Introduction										....
2. Clarity of purpose										....
3. Language										....
4. Body language										....
5. Eye contact										....
6. Use of voice										....
7. Enthusiasm, vigor										....
8. Confidence, self-control										....
9. Adaptation to audience										....
10. Organization of material										....
11. Conclusion										....

Student's name _____ *Class and section* _____

1. Name, title, and position of speaker _____
_____
_____

2. Subject _____

3. Occasion _____

4. Place _____ Time _____ Date _____

5. Purpose of speech: ☐ To inform   ☐ To stimulate and arouse
☐ To convince   ☐ To get Action
☐ To entertain   ☐ Special Occasion

6. How long was the speech? _____
Was this too long? Too short, or about right? Explain. _____
_____

7. Was the speech appropriate for the speaker? Audience? Occasion? Explain.
_____
_____
_____
_____

8. Discuss the type of introduction and conclusion used. _____
_____
_____
_____
_____

9. What basic appeals did the speaker use? _____
_____
_____
_____

10. Was the proof logical? Emotional? Personal? Explain. _____
_____
_____
_____

11. Were sources of evidence stated accurately? Explain. _____

_____

_____

_____

12. Describe the speaker's platform behavior. (Include such details as posture, personal appearance, bodily movements, gestures, vocal characteristics, and eye contact) _____

_____

_____

_____

_____

_____

_____

13. Was the speaker's delivery effective or ineffective? Why? _____

_____

_____

_____

_____

14. Describe the speaker's use of language. (Include such details as word choice, articulation, pronunciation, clarity, vividness, and appropriateness.) _____

_____

_____

_____

_____

_____

_____

15. What was your overall reaction to the speech? _____

_____

_____

_____

_____

Student's name _____ Class and section _____

1. Name, title, and position of speaker _____
_____
_____

2. Subject _____
3. Occasion _____
4. Place _____ Time _____ Date _____
5. Purpose of speech:
   ☐ To inform   ☐ To stimulate and arouse
   ☐ To convince   ☐ To get Action
   ☐ To entertain   ☐ Special Occasion

6. How long was the speech? _____
   Was this too long? Too short, or about right? Explain. _____
   _____

7. Was the speech appropriate for the speaker? Audience? Occasion? Explain.
   _____
   _____
   _____
   _____

8. Discuss the type of introduction and conclusion used. _____
   _____
   _____
   _____
   _____

9. What basic appeals did the speaker use? _____
   _____
   _____
   _____
   _____

10. Was the proof logical? Emotional? Personal? Explain. _____
    _____
    _____
    _____

11. Were sources of evidence stated accurately? Explain. _____
_____
_____
_____
_____

12. Describe the speaker's platform behavior. (Include such details as posture, personal appearance, bodily movements, gestures, vocal characteristics, and eye contact) _____
_____
_____
_____
_____
_____
_____

13. Was the speaker's delivery effective or ineffective? Why? _____
_____
_____
_____
_____

14. Describe the speaker's use of language. (Include such details as word choice, articulation, pronunciation, clarity, vividness, and appropriateness.) _____
_____
_____
_____
_____
_____
_____

15. What was your overall reaction to the speech? _____
_____
_____
_____
_____

Student's name _____ *Class and section* _____

1. Name, title, and position of speaker _____

   _____

   _____

2. Subject _____

3. Occasion _____

4. Place _____ Time _____ Date _____

5. Purpose of speech: ☐ To inform ☐ To stimulate and arouse

   ☐ To convince ☐ To get Action

   ☐ To entertain ☐ Special Occasion

6. How long was the speech? _____

   Was this too long? Too short, or about right? Explain. _____

   _____

7. Was the speech appropriate for the speaker? Audience? Occasion? Explain.

   _____

   _____

   _____

   _____

8. Discuss the type of introduction and conclusion used. _____

   _____

   _____

   _____

   _____

9. What basic appeals did the speaker use? _____

   _____

   _____

   _____

   _____

10. Was the proof logical? Emotional? Personal? Explain. _____

    _____

    _____

    _____

11. Were sources of evidence stated accurately? Explain. _____

_____

_____

_____

_____

12. Describe the speaker's platform behavior. (Include such details as posture, personal appearance, bodily movements, gestures, vocal characteristics, and eye contact) _____

_____

_____

_____

_____

_____

_____

13. Was the speaker's delivery effective or ineffective? Why? _____

_____

_____

_____

_____

14. Describe the speaker's use of language. (Include such details as word choice, articulation, pronunciation, clarity, vividness, and appropriateness.) _____

_____

_____

_____

_____

_____

15. What was your overall reaction to the speech? _____

_____

_____

_____

_____

Student's name _____ *Class and section* _____

1. Name, title, and position of speaker _____
   _____
   _____

2. Subject _____

3. Occasion _____

4. Place _____ Time _____ Date _____

5. Purpose of speech: ☐ To inform   ☐ To stimulate and arouse
                       ☐ To convince   ☐ To get Action
                       ☐ To entertain   ☐ Special Occasion

6. How long was the speech? _____
   Was this too long? Too short, or about right? Explain. _____
   _____

7. Was the speech appropriate for the speaker? Audience? Occasion? Explain.
   _____
   _____
   _____
   _____

8. Discuss the type of introduction and conclusion used. _____
   _____
   _____
   _____
   _____

9. What basic appeals did the speaker use? _____
   _____
   _____
   _____
   _____

10. Was the proof logical? Emotional? Personal? Explain. _____
    _____
    _____
    _____

11. Were sources of evidence stated accurately? Explain. _____

_____

_____

_____

_____

12. Describe the speaker's platform behavior. (Include such details as posture, personal appearance, bodily movements, gestures, vocal characteristics, and eye contact) _____

_____

_____

_____

_____

_____

_____

13. Was the speaker's delivery effective or ineffective? Why? _____

_____

_____

_____

_____

14. Describe the speaker's use of language. (Include such details as word choice, articulation, pronunciation, clarity, vividness, and appropriateness.) _____

_____

_____

_____

_____

_____

_____

15. What was your overall reaction to the speech? _____

_____

_____

_____

_____

Student's name _____ *Class and section* _____

1. Name, title, and position of speaker _____
   _____
   _____

2. Subject _____

3. Occasion _____

4. Place _____ Time _____ Date _____

5. Purpose of speech: ☐ To inform   ☐ To stimulate and arouse
                        ☐ To convince   ☐ To get Action
                        ☐ To entertain   ☐ Special Occasion

6. How long was the speech? _____
   Was this too long? Too short, or about right? Explain. _____
   _____

7. Was the speech appropriate for the speaker? Audience? Occasion? Explain.
   _____
   _____
   _____
   _____

8. Discuss the type of introduction and conclusion used. _____
   _____
   _____
   _____
   _____

9. What basic appeals did the speaker use? _____
   _____
   _____
   _____
   _____

10. Was the proof logical? Emotional? Personal? Explain. _____
    _____
    _____
    _____

11. Were sources of evidence stated accurately? Explain. _____

_____

_____

_____

_____

12. Describe the speaker's platform behavior. (Include such details as posture, personal appearance, bodily movements, gestures, vocal characteristics, and eye contact) _____

_____

_____

_____

_____

_____

_____

13. Was the speaker's delivery effective or ineffective? Why? _____

_____

_____

_____

_____

14. Describe the speaker's use of language. (Include such details as word choice, articulation, pronunciation, clarity, vividness, and appropriateness.) _____

_____

_____

_____

_____

_____

_____

15. What was your overall reaction to the speech? _____

_____

_____

_____

_____

Student's name _____ *Class and section* _____

1. Name, title, and position of speaker _____
_____
_____

2. Subject _____

3. Occasion _____

4. Place _____ Time _____ Date _____

5. Purpose of speech: ☐ To inform ☐ To stimulate and arouse
☐ To convince ☐ To get Action
☐ To entertain ☐ Special Occasion

6. How long was the speech? _____
Was this too long? Too short, or about right? Explain. _____
_____

7. Was the speech appropriate for the speaker? Audience? Occasion? Explain.
_____
_____
_____
_____

8. Discuss the type of introduction and conclusion used. _____
_____
_____
_____

9. What basic appeals did the speaker use? _____
_____
_____
_____

10. Was the proof logical? Emotional? Personal? Explain. _____
_____
_____
_____

11. Were sources of evidence stated accurately? Explain. _____

_____

_____

_____

_____

12. Describe the speaker's platform behavior. (Include such details as posture, personal appearance, bodily movements, gestures, vocal characteristics, and eye contact) _____

_____

_____

_____

_____

_____

_____

13. Was the speaker's delivery effective or ineffective? Why? _____

_____

_____

_____

_____

14. Describe the speaker's use of language. (Include such details as word choice, articulation, pronunciation, clarity, vividness, and appropriateness.) _____

_____

_____

_____

_____

_____

_____

15. What was your overall reaction to the speech? _____

_____

_____

_____

_____

APPENDIX E

Sample Professional Speeches

Successful Schools
Good Teachers and Community Support

By Jack MacAllister

When I was invited here today, I accepted with mixed feelings. I liked the idea of spending time with business people who care enough about our children's education to involve themselves in the good work of the Colorado Alliance of Business.

But I was daunted by the prospect of talking about our educational system to people who are working at improving it as diligently as you are.

I remember the fellow Mark Twain told about who, when asked what to do about the menace of submarines, suggested they just boil the ocean. When asked how you go about boiling an ocean, the fellow replied, "Look, it's enough for me to come up with the solutions; it's up to you to boil the water."

Over the past several years, a flurry of reports, studies, and task forces has told us our children aren't learning enough. They've reported declining test scores, a weakening of our national purpose, and a diminishing ability to compete in world markets.

Our standards are too low, we are told, our teachers underpaid, our school day too short, and education too far down the list of our national priorities.

One team of researchers set out to determine what makes a school successful. After four years of studying more than a thousand high schools throughout the nation, do you know what they learned? Successful schools come from strong community support and good teachers.

Can there be a thinking person alive who is surprised by that? Still, it's a basic truth. Good schools *do* need *good teachers and strong community support.*

Some months ago we announced that U S West would build a major research center to explore and develop telecommunications services. We said the facility could eventually employ as many as 15-hundred scientists, engineers, and support staff.

We decided to build this center somewhere in the 14 Western states served by our three telephone companies. We told the states we were not interested in a "bidding war," not interested in giveaways at the taxpayer's expense.

What we *were* interested in was some 70 criteria, ranging from quality of life to business climate to good research facilities at major universities. And we wanted quality schools that would attract good employees.

Three of us from U S West visited all 14 states. We met with governors and senators and mayors and economic development people; with educators and business people and community leaders.

All pointed to the exceptional schools in their states. They took justifiable pride in the asset that is their school system. At times, I felt I had arrived in Lake Woebegon where all the women are strong, all the men good looking, and all the children above average.

I don't mean to make light of this. We truly were impressed by the renewed commitment to education throughout the West.

What troubled me, though, was that after each of these presentations, I asked, "Since your school system is so important to your state, can you tell us what resources you devote to it, what you pay your teachers, what commitment you've made to support their work?"

I must tell you that in far too many instances, there came at this moment what is known as "an awkward pause."

Later, educators told us that several politicians—some for the first time—asked what they needed to make their schools and teachers' salaries more competitive.

You probably know we decided to build our facility in Boulder, largely because of the impressive research being done at CU and CSU. But we decided something else too.

We decided we had to do more to solve, not just critique, problems facing our educators. So we have committed 20-million dollars over the next five years to support education at all levels in Colorado and the 13 other states we serve.

In a nutshell, here's what we'll do.

We'll support efforts to help our schools and colleges build on their strengths, to do better what they now do well. Our colleges cannot be all things to all people. They cannot excel in *all* fields. Nor should they try. But they *can* build their own identities.

They can build what Governor Romer has aptly called "pillars of excellence" that will keep Colorado and the West competitive.

But let me underscore another part of the U S West educational initiative; a fellowship to recognize and encourage elementary and high school teachers who bring excellence to their classrooms.

Each year three teachers—nominated by their colleagues, by parents, by students, and selected by a panel of parents, educators and community and business leaders—will receive a year's salary and expenses to take time off to further their professional development. Eleven other teachers will receive a $5,000 recognition award.

I am unaware of similar sabbatical for elementary and secondary school teachers in our region, but they represent the kind of opportunity we must provide if we are to recognize these men and women for what they are: not just public servants, but professionals to whom we entrust our future.

Each of us in this room can remember one or two or perhaps three teachers who had a lasting influence on our lives. You can't say exactly what made them exceptional. They had their own way of doing things. They could be tough and demanding and unconventional. But they were dedicated and caring, too, and they made education come to life. They made a difference in *your* life. Even today, you remember their names.

And aren't they the *heroes* of your life?

Why don't more of us recognize teachers for the heroes they are? Have we somehow lost the idea that the real heroes are those who have made the greatest contributions? I think not. But somehow our attention has been diverted. Perhaps the time has come to recognize today's teachers as the new heroes of the West. If we do not, surely we cannot expect our children to do so.

For me, one of those heroes was my father. He taught in the Iowa public schools for more than 40 years. I remember a time when he was ill, visiting him at the hospital. It was then that he told me how happy he was that I had chosen business for a career because, unlike teaching, it offered the hope of success and of status in the community.

I looked around at the overflow of flowers, and the baskets of cards. I thought about all the young people and those not-so-young who over the years came back to him time and again for advice, people whose lives had been changed by what he had instilled in them.

There are many measures of success, but none more meaningful than the wisdom and knowledge and understandings we have brought to others. "Teachers," a wise man said, "affect eternity; no one can tell where their influence stops."

Good teachers demand a lot from themselves. They seek opportunities to teach both within and outside the classroom. They are part of a noble profession, one that deserves our respect.

But we are foolish if we believe our schools can somehow do the job we want of them without resources and support.

And that support must come from all segments of our society. Our legislature must address such issues as educational opportunities for *all* students. It must concern itself with the disparity of opportunity that exists among school districts within our state.

Our educators must give special attention to the high drop-out rates of those who are economically disadvantaged.

And we in business must do more. That means devoting more funds and more people to the needs of our schools. It means providing employment opportunities that help needy youngsters stay in school. It means finding more ways to publicly recognize excellent teachers and outstanding educational programs.

By the mid-1990's we in Colorado potentially face a very real labor shortage, a shortage of qualified people for the increasingly complex jobs we must fill.

And our young people will face more competition, not only from within Colorado but from throughout the world.

Colorado, and all of America, has a choice. We will commit our energies to educating every young person in our cities and towns, or we will become a nation without skilled workers; a nation unable to compete in a global economy; a people whose progress is hampered by social inequity.

The need for more support of our schools and our teachers is one reason to admire the work of the Colorado Alliance of Business.

You're providing resources and training through your school-to-work program—SWAP, you call it—that helps teachers help youngsters who otherwise might not make it through school. These are kids who are behind in their studies, kids who miss class too often, kids who are considered "at risk" of dropping out.

For them, dropping out would mean entering society with few prospects and little hope. For us, it would mean a potential workforce that is unprepared, untrained, and unskilled.

That's why SWAP is so important. It provides teachers the time and the training to give these kids extra help in learning the basics, such as English and math, and in developing career skills.

And it's working. Young people tell us this program keeps them in school. One 15-year-old put it this way: "These teachers push us, they want us to do well, they *expect* us to graduate."

And the teachers? Well, they're being given the opportunity to do what they do best: attend to their students, motivate them, teach them what Socrates taught: that "the unexamined life is not worth living."

I want to propose today that we build on our partnership with these heroes of the West by expanding another of the Alliance's very successful programs: the summer job hunt that finds thousands of jobs for students throughout our state.

Could we offer a similar opportunity to our teachers? It would allow them to supplement their incomes and to learn more about the business world. It would allow *us* to learn from them and to benefit from their considerable talents.

Let me propose that the Alliance match the talents and interests of teachers available during summers or sabbaticals with the needs of business. U S West and other employers would benefit significantly from what is an underused resource in our community. I envision teachers holding temporary, responsible positions in companies throughout our state. It is an effort that U S West would be proud to support.

Early in this century the educator and statesman John Dewey said that "what the best and wisest parents want for their own children, that must the community want for *all* its children. Any other ideal for our schools," he said, "destroys our democracy."

If we want not to be the first generation of Americans to leave our schools poorer than we found them, we must do more than second guess, do more than wring our hands, do more than give advice.

It is *our* job to figure out how to boil the water.

Thank you.

The Enemies of Responsible Communication
The Voices, the Silences

By W. Charles Redding

Since, by definition, emeritus professors are hopelessly bogged down in the past, there should be no surprise if I ask you to go back 50 years to the year 1938. Life without television, without Dan Rather, without Johnny Carson, without Vanna White. But it was life full of radios, radios carrying news of war scares—especially in 1938, the year of Adolf Hitler in Vienna and Neville Chamberlain in Munich.

On Sunday evening, October 30, 1938, between the hours of eight and nine o'clock, any of us might easily have been tuned to the CBS radio network. If so, we would have heard an announcer's voice, breaking the music of an orchestra playing "La Cumparsita": "Ladies and gentlemen, we interrupt our program of dance music to bring you a special bulletin from the Intercontinental Radio News." Then, during the next hour, we would have been stunned to hear a series of increasingly hysterical voices, narrating an invasion of Martian monsters, landing first on a New Jersey farm, then unleashing poisonous gases over New York City.

The broken, anguished voice of an announcer: "Avoid bridges to Long Island—hopelessly jammed. All communication with Jersey shore closed . . . No more defenses. Our army wiped out . . . artillery, air force, everything wiped out. This may be the last broadcast."

Well, we would obviously have been listening to one of the most memorable events in broadcast history: the Orson Welles-Mercury Theatre production of *War of the Worlds.* It has been estimated that, of the six million people who heard the broadcast, no fewer than approximately one million, believing that they were listening to an authentic newscast, experienced serious levels of distress. Thousands were thrown into absolute panic.

In the furious controversy that followed the broadcast, the basic question was: "Were the writers and producers guilty of flagrant irresponsibility?" The issue is still debated.

We have nothing quite comparable in the 1980's. But we are living in the days of . . . shall we say *interesting* communication events. TV evangelists, speaking from humble but palatial headquarters, combine hellfire-and-brimstone denunciations of secular humanism with periods of rest and relaxation in motels. An administration lectures other governments on the evils of dealing with terrorists regimes, while, behind the scenes, its agents try to arrange bribes with hostage-takers and succeed in shipping weapons (enhanced by gifts of cakes and Bibles) to that bastion of "moderation," Iran.

These are the days we've also witnessed an American President traveling to Bitburg, making an appearance at a ceremony honoring Nazi war dead. And millions of people get most of their national and world news from TV newscasts in the form of brief, unrelated snippets, heavily interlarded with commercials for pain relievers and breakfast foods. As TV critic Tom Shales, recent Pulitzer Prize winner, has concluded: It is the rare writer or producer who "cares to be serious and relevant in prime time."

Media-bashing is, of course, a popular parlor game. But, as I'll be demonstrating shortly, human ingenuity has created an almost infinite number of ways to commit the crime of irresponsible communication. And many of these ways involve no verbal messages at all—they consist of silence.

My purpose this morning is a modest one: to suggest a point of view toward the problem of irresponsible communication, a point of view that may even modify, in some small measure, how we conceptualize "irresponsible communication" in both our teaching and our research.

Before we examine a few flesh-and-blood examples of "enemies of responsible communication," let me suggest three basic postulates.

The first postulate is that "responsible" is frequently used as a code-word for such attributes as "compliant," "safe," or "docile." I've heard corporate executives, for example, speak of "responsible" labor leaders, by which they mean docile union officials. Whenever we hear calls for "responsible criticism," we should look carefully for what may be lurking behind that God-term "responsible."

The second postulate reminds us that, just as "responsible" and "compliant" are not synonyms, so also "responsible" and "moral" (or ethical) are not true synonyms. To be sure, no immoral or unethical communicator could be at the same time a responsible communicator. In other words, morality is a necessary but not a sufficient predictor of responsibility. This means, we should note, that it is possible for an impeccably moral person to engage, on occasion, in irresponsible communication. For example, the faint-hearted moralist who shrinks from speaking out against blatant racism, or who sticks to safe, mealy-mouthed generalities.

Responsible communicators, in my judgment, must not only observe high moral and ethical standards; they must also freely acknowledge authorship of their communicative acts (whether utterances or silences). This means that they refrain from hiding behind "plausible deniability." And, lastly, responsible communicators make a serious effort to predict, within the limits of human capability, the *probable consequences* of their communication behavior. I would place this third requirement at the very apex of the essential attributes of responsible communicators. No matter how moral or well-intentioned a speaker may be, if he or she fails to demonstrate an active concern for predicting probable consequences of communicative acts, irresponsible communication is likely to occur. I would venture to suggest, for instance, that either President Reagan or his advisors—all individuals of moral integrity, we must assume—should have been able to predict the fall-out from the Bitburg visit.

There is no implication, of course, that predictions of communication outcomes can ever approach certainty. It was that eminent philosopher of Hollywood, Sam Goldwyn, who observed that predictions are risky—especially, he warned, those about the future. The criterion I'm talking about is *concern,* not 100 percent accuracy.

The third and final postulate has already been mentioned, but not formally articulated: Silence is frequently a communicative act, coequal in potential impact with voice. This means, therefore, that there is irresponsible Silence as well as irresponsible Voice. Let me suggest that there are, in fact, two identifiable forms of irresponsible silence. The first I have alluded to earlier: the faint-hearted failure to speak out when evil or injustice ought to be opposed. The second is what I call "illegitimate listening"—many forms of wire-tapping, of testing and surveillance of employees, and so on.

We are now in a position to visualize a simple two-part typology for categorizing the occasions in which "enemies of responsible communication" most often appear:

Type A—There is Voice where there ought to be Silence. (The silence could be either empathic listening or prudential restraint.)

Type B—There is Silence where there ought to be Voice.

These abstractions will, of course, be more meaningful as they are demonstrated in real-life episodes. Obviously, we could sit here the rest of the day, far into the night, recounting examples of irresponsible communication . . . (in fact . . . PRINTED PROGRAM—12:15 A.M.!!) The limitations of both time and organic-tissue fatigue compel mention of only a minuscule sample from an enormous universe.

Looking first at Type A cases (Voice where there should have been Silence), we could start with a famous example from American history. Many scholars tell us that the only reason our school children are not reading about President James G. Blaine is that the Reverend Samuel D. Burchard declared, at a meeting a few days before the Blaine-Cleveland election of 1884: "We don't propose to leave our party and identify ourselves with the party whose antecedents have been rum, Romanism and rebellion."

About a century later, in the Congressional election campaign of 1986, a midwestern congressman who had voted against aid to the Nicaraguan Contras found himself in an unsolicited starring role in the following TV ad: First we see soldiers running through the jungle, followed by views of southwestern U.S. landmarks. A man with a Spanish accent . . . provides the (voice over): 'One day we're going to take five to ten million Mexicans, and they're going to have one thing on their mind—cross over the border into Dallas, El Paso, Houston . . . San Diego, and each one has embedded in his mind the idea of killing ten million Americans.' This is followed by the congressman's picture on the screen, while a second voice intones, "Even so, Congressman (X) voted against . . . aid to the freedom fighters."

Of course, there's a long history of bloodthirsty rhetoric in American public life. Franklin D. Roosevelt, the only man ever to be elected four times to the Presidency, was a frequent target. For example, near the start of his second term, in 1937, a corporate executive was talking to a luncheon meeting about ways of getting rid of that "paranoiac in the White House." During the course of his analysis, he opined that "a couple of well-laced bullets would be the best thing for the country," adding that he was prepared to celebrate the occasion with a bottle of champagne."

If you regard this language as perhaps a bit on the intemperate side, be assured that there is at least one clergyman, speaking just a few days ago, whose zeal surpasses that of the 1937 executive. Last Sunday, in Indianapolis, there took place an event called the "Twelfth Annual Miss Gay USA Pageant." Not surprisingly, it drew a crowd of about 200 protesters, who were of course exercising their Constitutional rights of dissent. However, there was the clergyman who made an interesting pronouncement (duly publicized in the media):

If they try this another time, I'm telling you there's going to be bloodshed. . . . There are some red-blooded American men in Indianapolis, and we won't stand for this.

Messages like these, while perhaps difficult to explain in all their origins, are rather easy to recognize as "irresponsible." They clearly reflect violations of ethical or moral standards that would be espoused by most critics.

More problematic are those instances where either (a) the speaker's intent is other than what the words explicitly say (slips of the tongue, etc.) or (b) the speaker's words represent deeply embedded religious or cultural convictions, rather than any conscious desire to hurt anyone.

Consider: Evan Mecham, recently impeached governor of Arizona, made headlines when he defended the term "pickaninnies" as applied to black youngsters. And his educational adviser said that if a "student wants to say the world is flat, the teacher does not have the right to try to prove otherwise." Or we can recall that, about a month ago, a major-league baseball pitcher, objecting to the presence of a female umpire, told media reporters:

*I don't believe women should be in a leadership role. I don't think a woman should be
the president of the United States or a governor or mayor. . . .*

Understandably, this created an uproar, and the Houston Astros management hastened to issue an apology. The pitcher, in his defense, explained that he was simply giving voice to his sincere religious beliefs. Is this perhaps a case of a moral, well-intentioned speaker who made public remarks, considered by many to be irresponsible, because he failed to think through all the *probable consequences* of his words?

Of course, the problem with ill-informed or casual, off-hand remarks, uttered in public, is that we are living in an age of instant, world-wide transmission of messages. And, to make it worse, our age is also the first in history when human beings have it in their power to annihilate civilized life on this planet. The combination of these two facts lends special urgency to our discussions of "responsible communication" at this conference.

Important though the morality of a speaker's intent undoubtedly is, in this nuclear age when the world balances on the edge of the abyss, even "innocent" slips can trigger catastrophic consequences. The question of culpability must then be settled on the basis of a careful assessment of the speaker's ability, given all the circumstances, to predict the probable consequences. What, for example, are we to make of the innocent joke that Mr. Reagan made one Saturday morning, as he was speaking a few sentences into an "open" radio microphone—when he had assumed the mike was turned off? What he said was "My fellow Americans. I am pleased to tell you I just signed legislation which outlaws Russia forever. We begin bombing in five minutes." (Fortunately, alert technicians erased the sound track before it went out on the network.)

More reprehensible, because repeated in a number of campaign speeches, were the words of a congressional candidate in Indiana a few years ago. He insisted that America could survive a nuclear war so well that "Well over ninety percent of Americans would only read about it in the papers or hear about it on their radios or TVs." Then, to top the list is the comment of a candidate's campaign aide in 1984. Referring to one of the televised debates, he told reporters in a press conference: "You can say anything you want in a debate, and 80 million people hear it. If reporters then document that a candidate spoke untruthfully . . . so what? Maybe 200 people read it, or 2,000, or 20,000." No comment.

This depressing recital will be terminated by a horrendous example demonstrating that the consequences of irresponsible Silence can be every bit as devastating as those of irresponsible Voice. What must be the most catastrophic silence of all human history is the refusal of the Allied governments, during the years, roughly speaking, between 1933 and 1945, to raise a mighty uproar about the Nazi atrocities, especially those leading up to the Holocaust. Probably the most respected investigator of this tragedy is Walter Laqueur. His book *The Terrible Secret* (1980, 1982) summarizes the enormous body of authenticated documentary evidence that he amassed. There is time only for one of his most salient conclusions:

*Neither the United States Government, nor Britain, nor Stalin showed any pronounced
interest in the fate of the Jews. . . . In London and Washington the facts about "the final
solution" were known from an early date and reached the chiefs of intelligence, the
secretaries of foreign affairs and defense. But the facts were not considered to be of great
interest or importance. . . .*

For anyone who may entertain lingering doubts about the reality of "irresponsible Silence," Laqueur's writings will be educational.

Well, . . . what are we to conclude from all this? My over-riding desire is that we leave this conference "fired up" with a burning determination to make the concept of responsible communication a vivid part of our teaching, and at least an open mind toward the possibility of undertaking scholarly research on topics related to responsibility. If I may be permitted a bold, original metaphor, my remarks this morning have barely scratched the surface of the tip of the iceberg!

We all realize that ours is a field of study that, understandably and justifiably, has been preoccupied with discovering and transmitting methods of achieving various kinds of communication "effectiveness." Indeed, the highly moral individual who has a great deal to say for the improvement of the human condition is really being irresponsible when he or she scorns opportunities to improve communication effectiveness. But I urge that, in our public speaking assignments (to select just one of many possibilities) we devote every bit as much attention to raising questions about responsibility as we do about effectiveness. Rating charts, for example, can ask the student speaker: "What kinds of long-term effects, or spin-offs, involving what individuals or groups, do you believe might occur as a result of this talk?"

Secondly: For our profession as a whole (including CSSA specifically), I *strongly* urge us to undertake a special study, with the objective of generating proposals for our profession to do *something* that will help focus the consciousness of the general public upon issues of responsible communication in public discourse. I have in mind something roughly analogous to—but not duplicating—the accomplishments of our colleagues, the English teachers, with their well-advertised awards for "Doublespeak." Perhaps we could even encourage the establishment of "Special Offices of Responsible Communication" in such places as corporations, bar associations, medical societies, universities, and . . . yes, the White House!

Third: We must never forget that *morality by itself is not enough.* Responsible communication also requires: (a) *a serious concern for predictable consequences* (of both Voice and Silence); (b) *Acknowledgment of accountability for one's communication acts.* Two social psychologists—who, by the way, make prominent use of Aristotle's *Rhetoric*—have put the matter neatly. I am quoting Sabini and Silver, in their recent book *Moralities of Everyday Life* (1982), who declare: "We may *feel* responsible only for what we intend; we *are* responsible for all what we do (or say)."

This axiom would compel us, Sabini and Silver would probably say, to conclude that the Orson Welles *War of the Worlds* broadcast—given all the circumstances of October, 1938—was irresponsible communication.

A parting caveat is obligatory. On the basis of all that has been said, it would be easy to adopt the position that the one sure protection against irresponsible Voice would be to clamp down, either with externally applied pressure or with self-censorship. And of course, there are times when this is true. It is especially true in those rather infrequent instances where—to cite Mr. Justice Holmes in the famous *Schenk* case (1919)—"circumstances are of such a nature as to create *a clear and present danger*" if completely free speech were to take place. In an age where careless remarks could set in motion the chain of nuclear triggers, such danger is always with us. But the best remedy for irresponsible communication is to make sure that every instance of irresponsibility can be confronted with corrective, responsible speech. Suppression and censorship, except in emergency situations, are rarely the defense of choice against the enemies of responsible communication. In other words: *We must always remind ourselves that there are irresponsible responses to irresponsibility.*

Pax vobiscum.